Changing Federal Constitutions

TECHNISCHE
UNIVERSITÄT
DARMSTADT

Institute of Political Science

Forum of Federations

The Global Network on Federalism and Devolved Governance

Arthur Benz
Felix Knüpling (eds.)

Changing Federal Constitutions

Lessons from International Comparison

Barbara Budrich Publishers
Opladen • Berlin • Toronto 2012

A CIP catalogue record for this book is available from
Die Deutsche Bibliothek (The German Library)

ISBN 978-3- 8474-0000-4

Die Deutsche Bibliothek – CIP-Einheitsaufnahme
Ein Titeldatensatz für die Publikation ist bei Der Deutschen Bibliothek erhältlich.

Verlag Barbara Budrich Barbara Budrich Publishers
Stauffenbergstr. 7. D-51379 Leverkusen Opladen, Germany

86 Delma Drive. Toronto, ON M8W 4P6 Canada
www.barbara-budrich.net

Jacket illustration by Walburga Fichtner, Köln, Germany
Typesetting: Susanne Albrecht-Rosenkranz, Leverkusen, Germany
Printed in Europe on acid-free paper by
paper&tinta, Warsaw

Content

3. Constitutional Reform in Federal Systems with Divided Societies

4. Devolution and Regionalisation in Federalising States

5. Processes of Ratification

6. Evolution after a Constitutional Reform

Preface

The aim of this volume is to discuss constitutional reforms in federal and decentralising countries from a comparative perspective in order to identify structures, processes and strategies which have proven to be indispensable for successful constitutional amendment. Focusing on the modalities and procedures of various successful and failed constitutional reforms, the volume seeks to enable public officials, scholars, and students to learn from the constitutional reform experiences of other federal democracies by giving practical suggestions how future reforms could be designed.

The volume is based on a research project "Patterns of Federal Constitutional Reform" which was carried out at the Institute for European Constitutional Science, FernUniversität in Hagen and the Institute for Political Science, Technische Universität Darmstadt and funded by the German Research Foundation (DFG).

Experts from nine countries covered in this volume had the opportunity to participate in an international conference co-organised by the two institutes in Darmstadt and Hagen, the *Bundesrat*, and the Forum of Federations.

The *Bundesrat*, a constitutional body of the Federal Republic of Germany representing the *Länder* at the federal level, has taken a decisive role in the constitutional reforms of the German federation passed between 2006 and 2009. The Forum of Federations has been previously engaged in various comparative research projects concerning constitutional reforms in federal systems. The results of these projects have contributed to the conference and have informed this volume.

The conference "Changing Federal Constitutions – Lessons from International Comparison" took place at the premises of the *Bundesrat* in February 2011. The welcome address of the Secretary General of the *Bundesrat* and the opening speech of Minister Schwall-Düren standing in for the President of the *Bundesrat* are documented in this volume. The conference brought together high-level German and international participants to discuss the papers presented in this volume and to enrich the debate on constitutional change. Thus, authors received important feedback on their work. Through this international comparative approach, the conference enabled a wide-ranging exchange of experiences and helped generate models and ideas relating to constitutional change, as presented in this volume.

The event consisted of two days of panel discussion. This structure not only facilitated comparative discussions of substance matters, but also gave insights into the international diversity of federal systems and different challenges related to constitutional change. The volume follows the structure of the conference.

We would especially like to express our gratitude to Angelica Schwall-Düren, Minister for Federal Affairs, Europe and the Media and Plenipotentiary of the Federal State of North Rhine-Westphalia for taking part in the conference. To all those who presented papers and articles for discussion at the conference, and who made their manuscripts available for inclusion in this volume, we offer our sincere thanks for their contribution.

The concluding chapter enormously benefited from the participation of key-decision makers who themselves have been involved, in various capacities, with the nuts and bolts of constitutional negotiations and federal reforms. We therefore thank Peter Bußjäger, Peter Michael Huber, Arnold Koller, Volker Kröning and Georg Milbradt for sharing their first-hand experiences with us in a panel discussion during the conference on constitutional change in Austria, Germany and Switzerland.

We would also like to take this opportunity to thank Dirk Brouër, former Secretary-General of the *Bundesrat*, and Gerd Schmitt, Secretary-General of the *Bundesrat* for their support in organising the conference. Also, our thanks go to the moderators of the conference, Jonathan Bradbury, Nathalie Behnke, Markus Kaltenborn, Roman Pasquier and Richard Simeon, for the outstanding way in which they lead the discussions. Last but not least, thanks go to Iris Henke-Oelsner (Bundesrat) and Gabriele Goetz (FernUniversität in Hagen) for assisting us implementing the conference, Andreas Haaf, Andrea Fischer-Hotzel, Eike-Christian Hornig, Jörg Kemmerzell, Bettina Petersohn from the Technische Universität Darmstadt for their support during the conference and in editing this book, Linda Hilpold for her excellent translations, and Phillip Gonzalez at the Forum of Federations and Carl Stieren for editing the papers.

Darmstadt/Ottawa, October 2011 *Arthur Benz and Felix Knüpling*

Welcome Address of the Secretary General of the Bundesrat

Conference on "Changing Federal Constitutions – Lessons learnt from International Comparison", held on February 24th and 25th, 2011, in the Federal Council (*Bundesrat*)

There are many types of federal state structures, in which individual member states form one overall state. In Europe, these kinds of federal states arose through the joining of previously independent states, through the break-up of centralised states, or through the transition from monarchy to republic, and they include (because of global-political circumstances) those that saw this kind of state as the right solution in cases of conflict.

All these states have in common their citizens' desire that their various individual needs be provided for. At the same time, the federal state must outwardly act as one. This is why federalism will always be marked by the tension that exists between the federal state and its member states. Because of these tensions, there has always been, and will always be, a shift towards more centralisation or more decentralisation.

Germany can look back on a long history of federal structures as an essential part of the history of the German state. Federalism in its current form should first and foremost serve to make the State more responsive to the needs of its citizens and, at the same time, enable it to reliably and outwardly govern all the important issues relating to the survival and the dealings of the State. That the world does not come to a standstill in the course of this is neither new nor a secret. Therefore, it only stands to reason that the State – simply as a tool for living in this world – must also change, must also adapt.

Since 2006 in Germany alone, two joint federal-state commissions have studied reforming the federal state structure and the financial relationships between the federal government and the states. This has led to comprehensive amendments to the Basic Law. Of course, this evolution is not affecting Germany alone. In fact increasing globalisation forces all federal states to adapt to changing circumstances for the sake of their citizens.

The success of federalism always depends on whether the citizens of the country are committed to it. Looking over the fence to see what other countries are doing is an important step along this path. Therefore, it also makes sense that a research project by the FernUniversität in Hagen and the Technische Universität Darmstadt should study and compare the reforms of federal constitutions.

The *Bundesrat* is proud to host the academic forum on "Changing Federal Constitutions – Lessons learnt from International Comparison". Against the backdrop of its history the Prussian Upper Chamber as the seat of the *Bundesrat*, is predestined to serve as the setting for this event during which the constitutional reforms in countries such as Austria, Canada, Germany, Spain, and Switzerland were reported on.

The varied and interesting papers presented at this event can be found in this publication.

Gerd Schmitt

Introduction

Arthur Benz and Felix Knüpling

1. Federal constitutions

During the past three decades, two simultaneous processes have been taking place in nearly every country in the world: globalisation and regionalisation. These two processes have called for a reform of the territorial organisation of many countries. Consequently, constitutional reforms have begun in a number of countries and some of these reforms have successfully made it through the ratification process. Discussions about constitutional change are ongoing, and further reforms will be necessary.

This volume is about constitutional change in federal countries and countries that are federalising or decentralising. Constitutions are at the core of the organisation of a state. Or, as Alan Tarr writes, "a constitution embodies a society's fundamental choices about government" (Tarr, 2005: 8). The constitution provides the basic framework and states the principles of a country. A constitution can be symbolically important in fostering unity or conflict within the country. In federations, written constitutions are essential to establish the framework within which each order of government operates.

Thus, it is the constitution that defines the authority of each of the orders of government – the federal, the regional and sometimes the municipal governments – so that each order is somewhat protected from the other. No single level is constitutionally subordinate to the other. Thus, federal constitutions have guaranteed the territorial integrity of the constituent units of the federation – such as provinces, states, cantons or *Länder* – against unilateral alteration by the federal government.

Federal systems require a constitution providing for a stable and reliable division of power. It might not suffice to guarantee stability of a federal system (Riker, 1964; Filippov, Ordeshook and Shvetsova 2004), but it is certainly a necessary condition. At a minimum, the constitution must establish certain key institutions and allocations of responsibility within the federal system (Majeed, 2006). In allocating powers, a constitution determines which powers are the exclusive prerogative of each order of government and which powers are shared or concurrent. It assigns power to the various offices and indicates the aims for which political power is to be exercised. In most countries it also establishes limits on the exercise of governmental power, most obviously by elaborating rights that are to be secured against violation by governments.

The constitution of a federal country also determines what the constituent units of the federal system are. It may establish two orders of government with local governments created by and controlled by the constituent governments. Or it may institute a three-order federal system giving constitutional status to local governments and guaranteeing them certain powers. Or it may design an even more complex variation, as in Belgium's double federation of overlapping language communities and regions.

The federal constitution also decides what role the constituent units will play in the structure and operation of the federal government. In most federal systems, the constituent units participate, in one way or another in the process of constitutional amendment. Many federal systems also ensure a further role for the constituent units by creating a bicameral federal legislature, with the upper (federal) chamber representing – and often elected by – the constituent units of the federation.

In addition to the division of powers and guarantees of autonomy for the various orders of government, there is a need for rules and mechanisms to facilitate the co-operation and coordination of governments in the overall governance and management of a federation. Most federal constitutions say little about institutions or processes of intergovernmental relations beyond the role of the judiciary in resolving intergovernmental legal disputes. There are institutions and processes intended to foster intergovernmental co-operation and coordination in most federations; some are constitutional, but most are not.

2. Varieties of federalism and their constitutions

Federations differ greatly in their social and economic composition and their institutions. They include very large and very small countries, rich and poor countries, those with homogenous and those with diverse populations. Some federations are long-standing democracies, while others have more recent and troubled histories of their practice of democracy. Some federations are "coming together" federations (Stepan, 1999) of formerly separated entities. Some federations evolved from formerly unitary states. Federations can also be viewed along the centralisation-decentralisation continuum. While some are highly centralised, in other federations constituent units enjoy a larger degree of autonomy (Griffiths, 2005).

As federations vary in many aspects, so is every country's constitution somewhat distinctive, a reflection of the history, culture, and character of its population. This applies to both federal and unitary countries. Not surprisingly, constitutions vary greatly in their length, specificity and accessibility.

For example, the older federations usually have much shorter constitutions than those created since the middle of the 20th century. Those constitutions written before modern governments are often silent on current major governmental responsibilities, such as environmental issues. Moreover, their allocation of powers can rely heavily on a few basic principles (for example, residual powers, national interest, trade and commerce) whose interpretation may have evolved very differently from the original intentions of the constitution's authors (Kincaid, 2004). Shorter constitutions tend to be more flexible than those with very detailed lists of powers for the different orders of government.

There is a large measure of choice as to what is put into a constitution or left to ordinary laws. This can lead to major debates because advocates can seek to constitutionalise provisions to give them symbolic recognition or the extra protection of the constitution or both. Constitutional provisions around the definition of the country, the recognition of minority nationalities, language rights, and religion can be very important in dividing or uniting a population. In more recent constitutions, there are often long sections on social and economic rights. Ideally, there should be broad consensus around constitutional provisions because it is the "basic law." This is the reason for special thresholds required for approval of a constitutional amendment (for example, a two-thirds majority vote in the federal legislature) (Watts, 2008).

3. Relevance and difficulty of constitutional change

Constitutions must be flexible and allow adaptation to changes in society or political context. Several broad factors have contributed – and will continue to contribute – to changes in federal constitutions and the federal systems they govern, producing either new constitutions or changes within existing arrangements. For example, processes of democratisation have provided an impetus for new or revived federations in Africa, in the former Soviet bloc, and in Latin America and therefore triggered constitutional negotiations. Other important developments have been economic, as federal constitutions have sought to accommodate and manage the shift from localised to national economies and, more recently, the shift to globalisation.

International political developments have also had a significant impact. The development of the European Union has dramatically affected European federations. In a similar way, the creation of NAFTA had an impact on the three North American federations: Canada, Mexico and the United States.

Finally, some developed federal democracies have had to confront new challenges to their constitutional orders. Unification in Germany has led to calls for re-examining the federal structure and particularly the system of fiscal equalisation. In Canada, the rise of separatist sentiments in Quebec led in the 1980s and 1990s to "mega-constitutional" politics in which Canadians debated a series of proposals to radically restructure their constitution. The resurgence of ethnic, linguistic, and religious loyalties and regional economies ("new regionalism"; Keating, 1998) has created challenges for virtually all federal systems, as they seek to combine unity and diversity.

However, federal constitutions are considered to be difficult to change. When a country adopts a federal system, it necessarily embraces complexity in government, and the tasks of the federal constitution are correspondingly multiplied. The complexity of federal constitutions is enforced through the fact that they need to balance rigidity with flexibility. Rigidity is needed to ensure that minorities and regional identities are being protected because otherwise federal cohesion might be undermined, in the extreme case through secessionist movements. However, flexibility is needed to adapt to domestic political or social changes as well as to international developments that produce the need for constitutional change.

Thus, federal constitutions have special procedures and majorities for their amendment, often requiring some measure of consent by the legislatures or populations of constituent units. This is particularly true in federations, where constituent units are granted a role in constitutional amendment, especially in coming-together federations as opposed to formerly unitary federations. Federal countries often give constituent units an absolute veto over certain matters affecting them directly, notably changes in their boundaries or merger with another unit. Federations vary greatly in how much consent is necessary to change the powers of all constituent units: this can range from not much more than a majority to virtual unanimity.

Finally, consent for constitutional amendments usually involves legislatures and executives, but there can also be a requirement for a majority or special majority in a referendum vote. As well, constituent units may have a smaller role or no role at all in relation to amendments that do not affect them directly. Constituent units are usually free to amend their own constitutions, when changes are within the permitted bounds of the federal constitution.

Amendment rules have often made constitutions difficult to change and the politics of constitutional amendment can prove very divisive (Kincaid, 2004). As a consequence, federations frequently look for alternatives to constitutional amendment, as is shown in this volume.

4. Cases covered in this volume and contributions

This volume seeks to contribute to informed deliberation on constitutional matters by presenting overviews of more or less recent constitutional changes in six countries that we consider to be federal (Austria, Belgium, Canada, Germany, Switzerland and Spain), and three countries that are in a process of either federalisation (Italy), devolution (UK) or decentralisation/regionalisation (France). We found it particularly interesting to compare the challenges of constitutional change in federal countries with those in unitary (albeit decentralising) countries. Such a comparison is also useful in testing the hypothesis that federal constitutions are more difficult to amend than unitary constitutions.

The topic is introduced in part 1 by a political statement on constitutional negotiations in Germany and a comparative and historically inspired overview on constitutional reform in federal countries. The next three chapters of the volume are structured around the nine "country studies." They are grouped in three chapters, one dealing with constitutional change in co-operative federalism, one with federal countries that have divided societies and the last with formerly unitary states that are decentralising or federalising. Two thematic chapters follow. One deals with processes of ratification and the other with constitutional evolution after a constitutional reform has either failed or succeeded. Again, the two thematic chapters largely focus on the nine countries or case studies selected among the countries covered in the volume.

Informing the analyses of constitutionalism within the twelve chapters is a series of questions that are basic to understanding constitutional arrangements in any federal system:

- In which forums or institutions are constitutional reforms elaborated? Who is involved and which procedures apply?
- Are certain procedures more suitable than others for federal reforms?
- How does the institutional framework of a political system influence the processes of reform and their outcomes?
- What are the roles of parties and the impact of party systems? To what extent do interests of the civil society affect reform negotiations?
- Which procedures could be applied to ratifying future constitutional reforms and which conditions influence the chances of successful ratification?
- How do constitutional reform processes affect constitutional evolution?
- How do countries cope with the failure of federal reforms? Does failure end in an impasse or can it be compensated by constitutional evolution?
- To what extent can an international comparison give us new ideas about how to design constitutional reforms (especially in Germany)?

The first part is introduced by Angelica Schwall-Düren, who gives a historical appraisal of constitutional negotiations in Germany with a focus on the two recently concluded federalism reforms. She argues that federal countries need to achieve the right mix of unity and diversity, allowing for differences without letting these distinctions detract from the community as a whole.

Thus, according to her, federalism must make contradictions compatible, which underlines how politically challenging constitutional changes are.

John Kincaid leads us into the variety of federalism, elaborating on the relevance of constitutional reform in federal systems as seen from a comparative and global perspective. Beyond shedding light on stability and change of federal constitutions, by emphasising the normalcy of constitutional change and development and by explaining causes of change, the author reviews common concepts used in debates and research on constitutional politics. By putting the cases covered in this volume into a broader comparative perspective, Kincaid also admonishes us to be careful with generalisations.

Part 2 discusses constitutional changes in "co-operative" federalism. Dieter Freiburghaus and Gérard Wettstein analyse from different angles – Wettstein as a former civil servant participating in the reform; Freiburghaus as a political scientist – the negotiations leading to a new fiscal equalisation scheme in Switzerland. Freiburghaus describes in detail the process leading to the referendum on the reform and presents ten interrelated factors leading not only to a successful negotiation, but also a successful referendum. Foremost, so Freiburghaus argues, it was the "intelligent design" of the process that helped in convincing the Swiss people to vote in favour of the reform. Focusing on the process of negotiations, Wettstein extracts conditions leading to an agreement on the reform by the involved parties before it was put to referendum.

In contrast to the Swiss case, the convention process in Austria did not lead to a successful reform of the constitution, at least not as set out at the beginning of the process. Peter Bußjäger explains why the convention failed – seeing the lack of political leadership and political consensus for a reform as the main obstacle – and gives an outlook as to what the future might hold in terms of a reform of Austria's federalism and the constitution.

The third case study in the category of co-operative federalism is Germany. Anton Hofmann's contribution centres on the two recent stages of federalism reform in Germany, "Federalism Reform 1", concluded in 2006, and the 2009 "Federalism Reform 2". He describes the background and the process, and based on an analysis of the outcomes of the two reform steps, he argues that the reforms can be considered a success that was ultimately achieved through political leadership and a broad consensus by both orders of government that a reform was necessary.

Part 3 deals with constitutional negotiations in federal systems with divided societies. In his chapter on constitutional negotiations in Belgium, Dave Sinardet stresses the complexity of Belgian federalism and the conflicts to be coped with. His case study on the fifth state reform passed in 2001 shows how party interests dominated the decision-making process on constitutional change. Sinardet describes how compromises could be found, in particular due to the common interest and determination of the parties forming the federal majority.

Nadia Verrelli looks at how the so-called Charlottetown Accord was being negotiated, the fifth round of "mega-constitutional politics" in Canada, at whose core were discussions about Canada's identity as a federal country, and in particular the role of the province of Quebec, but also of Aboriginal peoples. She describes not only how an agreement was found, but why it was subsequently voted down in a federal referendum.

In their contribution, César Colino and José Olmeda discuss bilateral constitutional negotiations on statutes of autonomy for Spain's constituent units, the 17 autonomous communities. By focusing on the recent reforms in Catalonia and Andalusia, they show the limits of such an approach of federal constitutional change that, in the particular case, was not supported by an agreement at the central level and was partially rejected by the Spanish Constitutional Court.

The focus of part 4 is on formerly unitary states and provides an analysis of constitutional issues of devolution and regionalisation in unitary states. James Mitchell discusses the process of negotiating devolution in the UK, arguing that devolution has been successful as a response to particular problems of legitimacy in components, or "constituent units," of the UK. However, he warns that the unintended consequences and spillover effects of devolution were paid little attention. He argues that devolution only displaced the problem of legitimacy rather than resolving the problem within the asymmetrical system that exists in the UK.

Italy is a country that has undergone a longer process towards federalisation, starting in the late 1970s, as Franco Bassanini reminds us in his article on Italian constitutional negotiations. This process, moving back and forth, has not come to an end yet and is far from complete, as the author writes, and has to balance the interests of different regions in economically difficult times.

One might be surprised to find France being covered as a case study in this volume. However, as Patrick Le Lidec in his contribution on decentralisation in France describes, the French government is in fact more constrained by regional and local governments than commonly imagined. Also, his analysis challenges the assumption that unitary states have a more flexible constitution that adapts more easily to change. France, he writes, is confronted with constitutional blockages (not necessarily perceived or debated as such) that seriously handicap the reform of the territorial organisation of the state and the vertical sharing of responsibilities.

Part 5 covers the first of two general topics, looking at processes of ratification. Markus Kaltenborn provides a comparative overview of amendment rules and ratification processes, also including cases that are not part of the nine case studies in this volume. He shows that the amendment rules vary across the board of federal as well as unitary countries. No systematic differences exist between federal and unitary states with respect to the formal and material rules that govern constitutional amendments, according to the author.

In his contribution on ratification by legislatures in EU member states, Carlos Closa, like Kaltenborn, challenges the relevance of the federal-unitary distinction regarding rules and their effects. He tests the hypothesis that constitutional rigidity, usually found in federal systems, implies a lower amendment rate while constitutional flexibility permits a higher amendment rate. His preliminary conclusion is that in many cases variables other than rigidity or flexibility of the constitution have to be factored in to explain change or failure of change, for example, the role of political actors and the relations among the political parties involved in the process. This view is echoed by many authors in this volume.

The role of regional actors in the ratification process is the subject of Jörg Kemmerzell and Bettina Petersohn's article. Reforms usually affect the power distribution between all orders of government, so the authors maintain, and therefore involvement of regional actors in processes of constitutional reform is essential. Applying a veto player framework and covering the nine countries under scrutiny in this volume, they conclude that with some exceptions federal reforms are mostly dominated by the federal level and reproduce existing conflicts of day-to-day politics.

Part 6 deals with evolution after the reform of constitutions, be they successful or not. In his article on Austria, Christoph Konrad starts where Peter Bußjäger has left off. Based on an overview of the broader history of constitutional reform in Austria, Konrad provides a survey of the developments parallel to and since the convention and a concluding attempt to evaluate the state of Austrian federalism today.

Constitutional change in Canada after Charlottetown is the subject of Marc-Antoine Adam and Martin Fournier's contribution. Their article discusses the institutional changes that occurred in Canada after the failure of the "mega-constitutional" reform, as described by Nadia Verelli in her case study in this volume. After reviewing the key factors influencing the country's institutional and constitutional environment, they examine the changes that have taken place since 1992, arguing that these changes, achieved through a non-constitutional route, pose significant challenges to certain fundamental principles underlying the Canadian Constitution. They touch on federalism, the rule of law, and the protection of minorities.

This volume started off with a political assessment of federalism reform in Germany. It concludes with an outlook on the state of federalism in Germany and potential effects of recent reforms. Describing the previous constitutional amendments of federalism in Germany since unification in 1990, Wolfgang Renzsch provides a preliminary assessment of their impact on federal and *Länder* governance, in particular considering the two major reforms concluded in 2006 and 2009. The glass is half full, rather than half empty, as he argues, but he also sees some major challenges for federalism in Germany lying ahead, touching on intergovernmental relations, the reform of the equalisation mechanism and the administrative nature of German federalism.

In the concluding part, we summarise the patterns of constitutional change we find in the case studies. We also suggest a number of lessons that can be learned from comparing different cases of constitutional change. This conclusion raises the general question of whether so different cases can be compared in a meaningful way and whether can we learn from international comparison. For reasons explained in the following section we do think that comparative research on constitutional change in federal systems has scientific and practical values.

5. Comparing incomparable cases?

Processes of constitutional reform can vary widely from one federal or decentralised country to another, as this volume demonstrates. This variation can be traced by to a number of differences between the cases included in this volume:

The first difference can be seen in the type of political system. These political systems range from former unitary states entering a process of decentralisation, such as France, to those devolving power to particular regions, such as the United Kingdom, to countries in the midst of federalisation, such as Italy or Spain and finally to well-established federal systems, such as Germany or Canada. Patterns of democracy and party systems vary accordingly in these states.

The second difference is how countries respond to particular problems, such as the following:

- lack of efficiency in over-centralised states or log-jammed intergovernmental relations of countries with co-operative federalism,
- poor integration of regionally concentrated groups demanding to be acknowledged as distinct nations,
- questions of legitimacy caused by the complexity of multilevel governance.

The difference presumably affecting constitutional reform is that agendas of reform policies and reform processes reveal different patterns of conflict. The types of conflict differ between federations with symmetrical and those with asymmetrical relations linking the federal government to the constituent units. Some conflicts are based on demands for autonomy and others are based on demands for a redistribution of power and resources.

The fourth difference concerns the international context. Member states of the European Union differ from non-member countries such as Switzerland and Canada.

Finally, there are different ways of constitutional change – by amendment according to formal rules, by judicial decisions or by interpretation in legislative and executive decisions in "normal" policy-making.

This variety raises the question of comparability. As social scientists have discussed at length, a small number of cases including many variables causes methodological problems. They should prevent us from drawing general conclusions on a correlation between causes and effects. Therefore, case studies as presented in this volume do not allow us to test hypotheses or elaborate theories explaining the causes and consequences of federal constitutional reform. Instead, we can find patterns of conditions, including driving forces and constraining factors which, in a particular state at a particular time, contribute to make constitutional reforms a success story or a case of failure.

However, variety and complexity of cases do not rule out learning from comparison.

First of all, the country reports tell us that constitutional reform can be designed in quite different ways. Irrespective of the formal rules for amendments, consultation and negotiation on constitutional issues can be organised in many ways. Thus governments initiating a reform have to make a choice among different options. Structure and procedures which really matter are rarely entrenched in constitutional law; they at best are indirectly influenced, but never determined by the rules for constitutional amendment. Traditions in political systems or existing structures of government and democracy need to be taken into account, but they do not prevent governments from also introducing innovative organisations and procedures.

Second, challenges of reform are not as different as they may appear at a glance (Benz and Colino, 2011: 379-383). It goes without saying that centralised, unitary states are confronted by different problems compared than those of decentralised or federal states. Multinational states face other challenges compared to mono-national states. In addition, federal systems with severe economic disparities are under higher pressure and constraints than economically balanced states. Nonetheless, territorial structures of Western democratic states have been affected by similar dynamics during the late 1970s. Due to the rise of the welfare state, the invention of new technologies and the internationalisation of politics and policy-making, they all saw a trend towards centralisation of powers. Centralisation occurred either by a shift in fiscal resources to the centre or by "authority migration", i.e. an incremental drift of powers to central legislatures, governments or administrations. Against this trend, pressures towards regionalisation emerged, driven by economic developments, regional movements and parties or by existing regional and local governments' efforts to regain power (Marks et al., 2010). Moreover, since states can no longer rely on growing revenues, they have to consolidate their budgets with consequences that differ from region to region. Regional parties and movements often arise when particular regions suffer from economic disadvantages or when a well developed region is assumed to or expected to contribute to transfer of resources to other regions.

Finally, both decentralised unitary and federal systems have to cope with the challenge of multilevel governance. The increasing interdependence of policies made at the different levels has to be managed in coordination across territorial boundaries and levels of government. The more a constitution tries to separate competences, the greater the need to find appropriate modes of coordination to avoid the negative effects of competition or cancelling out each other's actions. However, multilevel governance can end in a tangle of responsibilities or in ineffective joint decision-making.

When meeting the challenges of these contradictory developments and pressures, all countries included in our case studies had to change federal or regional aspects of their constitution. Regardless of the formal rules for amendments and the types of changes, powerful actors with competing interests dominate processes of politics, either formally or informally. In unitary states as in federal countries, central governments and parliaments have to consider such regional actors as governments, parliaments, parties or organised civil society. In constitutional policy affecting the territorial organisation of a state, joint decision-making is the rule rather than the exception regardless of how multilevel governments work in other policy fields (Benz, 2011).

Case studies can bring to light how the challenges caused by the dynamics of a multilevel government are met in different countries. They can also show which types of constitutional change governments have invented and applied and under which conditions particular types of policy-making succeed or fail. For these reasons, we can lean from international comparison. It is the aim of this volume to contribute to a fruitful exchange in an important topic in studies on federalism and in governing federal systems.

References

Benz, Arthur (2011): Escaping Joint-Decision Traps: National and Supranational Experiences Compared. In: Falkner, G. (ed.): The EU's Decision Traps: Comparing Policies. Oxford: Oxford University Press, 199-216.

Benz, Arthur/Colino, César (2011): Constitutional Change in Federations – A Framework for Analysis. In: Regional and Federal Studies 21, (4), 377-402.

Filippov, Mikhail/Ordeshook, Peter C./Shvetsova, Olga (2004): Designing Federalism: A Theory of Self-sustainable Federal Institutions. New York: Cambridge University Press.

Griffiths, Ann L. (2005): Handbook of Federal Countries. Montreal: McGill-Queen's University Press.

Keating, Michael (1998): The new regionalism in Western Europe: territorial restructuring and political change. Cheltenham, UK/Northampton, Mass.: Edward Elgar.

Kincaid, John (2004): Comparative Observations. In: Kincaid, J./Tarr, A. (eds.): Constitutional Origins, Structure, and Change in Federal Countries. Montreal: McGill-Queen's University Press, 409-448.

Marks, Gary/Hooghe, Liesbet/Schakel, Arian H. (2010): The Rise of Regional Authority: A Comparative Study of 42 Democracies. New York: Routledge Chapman & Hall.

Majeed, Akhtar (2006): Introduction. In: Majeed, A./Watts, R./Brown, D. (eds.): Distribution of Powers and Responsibilities in Federal Countries. Montreal: McGill-Queen's University Press: 3-7.

Riker, William H. (1964): Federalism. Origins, Operation, Significance. Boston/Toronto: Little Brown & Co.

Stepan, Alfred (1999): Federalism and Democracy: Beyond the U.S. Model. In: Journal of Democracy 10, (4), 19-34.

Tarr, Alan (2004): Introduction. In: Kincaid, J./Tarr, A. (eds.): Constitutional Origins, Structure, and Change in Federal Countries. Montreal: McGill-Queen's University Press, 8-11.

Watts, Ronald L. (2008): Comparing Federal Systems. Montreal: McGill-Queen's University Press, (3rd ed.).

1. The Relevance of Constitutional Change

Unity versus Diversity. Federalism as an Ever Evolving System*

Angelica Schwall-Düren

The former *Preußisches Herrenhaus*, the upper chamber of the Prussian parliament, representing the German principalities, now houses the *Bundesrat*. This building, which might be seen as an architectural symbol of German federalism, is certainly an appropriate venue a conference on changing federal constitutions. Federal structures are an integral component in the history of the German state. The federal roots of our state can be traced back through many centuries and have assumed a plethora of different forms during this time.

Yet what purpose does the federal system serve? What kind of justification can be given today for the considerable effort it entails, the constant threat of falling into the trap of complex political entanglements, the lengthy process of negotiating agreements between the Federation and the federal states? There is a clear historical explanation for the origin of this system: the multiplicity of diverse states in Germany could not be overcome by concentrating power in the hands of one central ruler. The vanity of regional princes may also have played a role. Even if some still accuse politicians in the federal states of being in love with power, the reasons substantiating the federal system extend far beyond this consideration. It is always important to recall that after the Second World War the Western Allies established the German federal states with a view to putting an end once and for all to the horrors experienced during the sole phase of a centralised German state as manifested in the power-grasping era of *Gleichschaltung* in the Third Reich.

Federalism – as Dieter Grimm once stated during his time as a judge at the Constitutional Court – has a remit to enable a system that is the precise opposite of a centralised, uniform and autocratic political structure:

- a political system that takes account of regional particularities;
- a political system in which *no* political camp can set the tone in isolation whilst excluding all others from political responsibility; and

---

* This article is based on the opening address of Minister Angelica Schwall-Düren at the conference „Changing Federal Constitutions“ in the *Bundesrat*, Berlin. Minister Schwall-Düren spoke for the incumbent president of the *Bundesrat*

- a political system that must face up to the challenge of a comparative critique, for it does not hold all the reins of power.

This enumeration evokes the most important reasons for organising the state along federal lines: proximity to the citizens, division of power and competition to find the best ways of resolving problems.

Federal structures also reflect historical continuities and the specific modes in which states have developed. They ensure that regional particularities are reflected and can be preserved. Federal structures can therefore help to channel tensions between individual components of a nation state and the central government. This applies in particular in multi-ethnic or multi-lingual states.

One thing holds true for all federal states: the balance between the two tiers of the system – the central state and the regional level – is complex and delicate. As a consequence, a need for reforms does arise over and over again in response to internal or external triggers.

Constitutional reforms, or, to be more precise, reforms of the federal system, have repeatedly been on the agenda in the Federal Republic of Germany ever since the founding of the state: These have ranged from the reform of the financial regulations in the late 1960s, the Committee of Enquiry on Constitutional Reform in the 1970s, the "minor" constitutional reform in the early 1990s right up to the most recent reform of the federal system during the last decade.

Over the years the relationship between the Federation and the federal states has been re-adjusted and fine-tuned over and over again. I do not wish here to pre-empt Mr Hofmann's presentation, in which he offers an introduction to the complex structures of the German federal system. I would, however, like to note one key point, taking Germany as an example: *one* constant feature in federal structures is perpetual change and the ever-present need for adjustments.

Looking to the countries neighbouring Germany, Belgium is one topical example of this phenomenon. The country currently finds itself in a situation that is anything but straightforward! Struggling to strike the right balance in Belgium's federal system is putting the state's capacity to act to the test and is gnawing away at the very substance of the country's existence as a state – as has repeatedly been the case in the past, too.

The decisive question is whether a renewed reform of federal structures will, at some point, produce a durable and stable outcome or whether this once again is only one phase in an ongoing process. Will decentralisation at some point attain some kind of natural equilibrium or is this a process that will gradually lead to disintegration of the state?

The example of Belgium can certainly not be transposed directly to other contexts. However the same questions arise in many other cases in which state structures are reorganised or decentralised.

Belgium is a multilingual federation. That means the underlying situation is particularly riddled with tensions. Yet at the same time, this multilingualism can also constitute an opportunity, as the example of South Tyrol demonstrates. Over the last few years, South Tyrol has tapped into the competitive advantages offered by its bilingual status. The region is booming and is now a stable and integral part of Italy within the context of ever-closer ties across Europe.

These examples raise a host of far-reaching questions:

- Does federalism strengthen or weaken regional "nationalisms"? Or do these kinds of nationalism per se form a continuum with certain strands in history that pre-date the federal state, for example in Spain? What does this signify for the reform of federal constitutions?
- Is it possible to formulate general goals, design principles or strategies for reforming federal systems? Or does this notion fail simply because it is not possible to genuinely compare the various systems and cultures involved?

All federal systems share the notion of focussing attention on the citizen; the aims of these systems always include taking at least part of the decisions as close as possible to the man or woman in the street. Ultimately the success of federalism is rooted in its ability to garner support from citizens for the ideas and goals of this type of state structure. This of course also holds true when reforming federal structures.

However in this context there may at times be contradictions between proximity to citizens and the expectations of citizens. Surveys for example reveal that the German public would like to see uniform provisions throughout the country for matters such as the school system or protection of non-smokers. In these policy areas however the German federal system protects the sovereignty of the federal states and their right to take their own decisions. In certain areas the most recent reforms have even extended the scope of the federal states' sovereignty. This contradiction may constitute the most significant challenge for reforms of federalism. Ultimately the system cannot function unless it takes both local and regional particularities into account whilst also securing public acceptance.

The world of politics must therefore promote acceptance of federal structures and explain the need for constant adjustments. At the end of the day this vital component of our constitution must be comprehensible to our citizens and enjoy their support.

Perhaps there is a need for an entirely new understanding of federalism in the light of globalisation and the growing significance of the European level. Yet the importance of the regions is in no way diminished in the context of these phenomena! Quite the contrary! It would be truer to state that the multi-tiered federal system in Europe renders debate more lively. I am referring here to striking the right balance between Brussels, the nation states *and* the regions.

In certain spheres globalisation makes it essential to focus on a more united European approach. Within the tiers of the power structure underpinning the European level however there is scope for regionalisation to become an increasingly dynamic force.

Structural policy offers one example of this. In Europe cohesion is envisaged in terms of regions. That is why cohesion policy is dealt with under the aegis of regional policy. The regional dimension is also gaining importance in the context of cross-border cooperation.

Yet once again it is a question of ensuring the general public is on board too as we travel towards this European future. Surveys however reveal with shocking clarity the rapid pace at which interest in European integration is dwindling.

Here again we have to ask the thorny question: how is it possible to combine decentralisation, proximity to citizens and public assent? I am convinced that regions play a more important role than ever in this context; they give people a sense of belonging in a particular place, shape their identities, offer people a sense of being at home and thus provide security and roots in the rapid transformation processes triggered by globalisation.

The edifice of federalism will probably never be entirely completed, irrespective of whether we think of the "old house" of the nation-state or the somewhat "newer high-rise" of the EU. Our constitutions and the EU Treaty are the blueprints yet this framework affords room for manoeuvre for the clients constructing the building. And at times there will be a need for an extension or a redevelopment project.

It is important that a house like the *Bundesrat* is not merely a building, but a home, so that people can feel a sense of attachment to it and can develop their potential within it. Federalism must serve people and should not constrain them. Federal systems need to achieve the right mix of unity and diversity, allowing for differences without letting these distinctions detract from the community as a whole. In other words: federalism must make contradictions compatible.

That is not an easy task. I am speaking here from my own experience as a former member of the Commission on Federalism and having been actively involved in the difficult journey from the Nice Treaty to the Lisbon Treaty.

Constitutional Change in Federal Countries: Comparative Considerations

John Kincaid

Modern federalism and constitutionalism coincide because a federation is based on a voluntary covenant or compact. A federation that unifies independent political communities has no inherent powers because it comes into being through constitutional action. A federation established by devolution retains inherent powers, while its constituent political communities exercise powers granted to them. Either way, "a federation is a subject of *constitutional* law because it is the agent of its own constitutional authority *vis-à-vis* its member states; relations between the federation and its member states are constitutional," not international (Schmitt, 1992: 40). A federation is intended to be perpetual, but perpetuation requires, among other things, a constitution subject to adaptation, amendment, and perhaps replacement over time.

The first proto-federal constitution was the Fundamental Orders of Connecticut of 1639, which united "the Inhabitants and Residents of Windsor, Harteford and Wethersfield" into one polity. The United States is the home of the two oldest written constitutions still governing today: the Massachusetts Constitution of 1780 and the federal Constitution of 1788. The Massachusetts document has been amended 120 times; the U.S. Constitution has been amended only twenty-seven times.

Not all U.S. constitutions have displayed such endurance. The first U.S. constitution, the Articles of Confederation, lasted only eight years (1781-89). Louisiana has had eleven constitutions since it joined the union in 1812. Georgia, one of the original thirteen states, has had ten constitutions. Nonetheless, among national constitutions, the U.S. Constitution is exceptionally old, as are some state constitutions (e.g. the Maine Constitution of 1819).

By contrast, the French Constitution of 1791 lasted only two years. It succumbed to the reign of terror, which produced another two-year constitution, followed by a four-year constitution and a three-year constitution, and then ten more constitutions until France adopted its fifteenth and last constitution in 1958. The Netherlands Constitution of 1795 lasted only three years; the Swiss Constitution of 1798 lasted four years. Thus, three of the four national constitutions of the eighteenth century, the world's first modern written constitutions, lasted for only two to four years. The world's first modern federal constitution has survived for 224 years, although, ironically, the very endurance of the U.S. Constitution has made it "increasingly atypical by global standards" (Law and Versteeg, 2012: 74) and less of a model for other countries, especially since the end of the Cold War. These founding examples, however, should put the lie to notions that federal constitutions are necessarily more transitory than unitary constitutions.

1. Constitutional change: normal, not exceptional

Given that all federations and most non-federal countries have written constitutions, I define "constitutional change" as encompassing replacement or amendment. A polity changes its constitution via amendment or via replacement – although the definitional line between these mechanisms is fuzzy because, in some cases, amendments can be so thorough as to produce *de facto* replacement. The Swiss, for example, have constitutional traditions of total and partial revision (Arts. 193 and 194 of the 1999 Constitution). Total revision entails amending all or most parts of the existing constitution. This last occurred in 1874. Some U.S. states use a similar amendment procedure. Utah even has a permanent Constitutional Revision Commission. If a revision is "total", however, it is tantamount to replacement, and the product is usually treated as a new constitution, as was the Swiss Constitution of 1874.

Amendment and replacement can be interrelated; that is, amendments might ensure the stability and, thereby, longevity of a constitution, while replacement might ensure the stability and longevity of a polity. The first modern federal example of the latter was the replacement of the Articles of Confederation by the U.S. Constitution in 1789, which ensured endurance of the "perpetual union" created by the Articles. Whether amendment is preferred over replacement and vice versa depends on political circumstances that are more contingent than predictable (Reynolds, 2002). There is too little research to determine when and why circumstances generate one or the other process, although it should be noted that constitutions "contemplate their amendment but almost never their replacement" (Landau, 2012: 6). There is, however, research showing that even though amendment is the most common of the two methods of change, replacement is remarkably frequent.

Indeed, the fates of the three short-lived constitutions of the late 1700s are more typical than is the endurance of the U.S. Constitution. A study of all the world's constitutions from 1788 to the present found that the median life-span of national constitutions is only nineteen years (Elkins et al., 2009: 129) – exactly the number of years that Thomas Jefferson declared in 1789 to be a constitution's ideal life-span. The "dead should not govern the living," he contended; therefore, a constitution should be replaced after nineteen years of service. James Madison replied that such cycles would generate "pernicious factions" that would paralyse government. Jefferson himself developed a greater appreciation of constitutional longevity after becoming president of the United States in 1801, but worldwide, constitutional replacement of considerable frequency has been the norm, not constitutional longevity. For example, between 1990 and 2009, at least 110 countries wrote or reformed constitutions (Williams, 2009: 1).

The authors of the global empirical study did not analyse federal constitutions separately, but my analysis of the constitutions of the twenty-five extant federal countries yielded interesting patterns. Since adopting their first federal constitution, these twenty-five countries have had eighty-three constitutions having a median age of only eleven years (with an average age of 25 years). This short life-span suggests that federal constitutions, overall, experience considerably more constitutional change or instability than the global median of nineteen years. However, if one considers only the current constitutions of these federal countries, the median age leaps ahead to 30 years, suggesting more stability. The average age of these current constitutions is 48 years. By contrast, the median age of all current national constitutions is 25 years, with an average age of 35 years. Fully 46% of all constitutions are only 1 to 20 years old, while 11% are 21 to 29 years of age, 18% are 30 to 39 years old, 7% are 40 to 49 years old, and 18% are 50 or more years of age.

Among the eight advanced Western federations – Australia, Austria, Belgium, Canada, Germany, Spain, Switzerland, and the United States – the median age of all fifteen of their constitutions is 33 years (with an average age of 63 years). The median age of their current eight constitutions is 64 years (with an average age of 86 years). This latter age would be older were it not for the new Swiss Constitution of 1999, which is only thirteen years old but replaced a constitution that had lasted for 125 years.

Thirteen of the extant federal countries have had only one constitution, amounting to a median age of 30 years (with an average age of 46 years). Eighteen of the federations have had two or three constitutions. Their median age is 22 years (with an average age of 46 years). Five of the federal polities have had four or more constitutions whose median age is 7.5 years (with an average age of 12 years). These last five federations, however, account for 64 percent of all the federal constitutions since 1788.

Constitutional stability and longevity, therefore, are comparatively robust in federal countries as indicated by the facts that 52% of federal countries have had only one constitution with a median age of 30 years, while 28% – Argentina, Austria, Comoros, Germany, Pakistan, Switzerland, and the United States (counting the Articles of Confederation as the first U.S. constitution) – have had only two or three constitutions with a median age of 22 years. Only 20% of federal countries – Brazil, Mexico, Nigeria, Russia (including USSR), and Venezuela – have had more than three constitutions with a median age of 7.5 years. Thus, only one-fifth of federal countries today display a history of constitutional instability.

The authors of the global study found "a decline in constitutional life spans after World War II" (Elkins et al., 2009: 131). They attributed the decline to changes in the global environment that have made it easier for groups that aspire to statehood to dissolve constitutional bargains. The opposite is true for federal constitutions. The median age of pre-World War II federal constitutions was 8.5 years; their post-war median age increased to 16 years, suggesting that framers of federal constitutions improved their performance. Part of this progress is due to the post-war emergence or re-emergence of federal systems in such politically stable European countries as Austria, Belgium, Germany, and Spain. However, India and Malaysia are notable examples of non-Western post-war federal constitutional longevity in contrast to Pakistan, which has had six constitutions, and Nigeria, which has had seven constitutions.

These findings, coupled with the frequency of amendment actions in most countries, suggest that constitutional change is the normal, not exceptional, mode of constitutional existence. The findings also suggest that federal constitution-makers have gotten better at persuading constituent groups to adhere to their constitutional bargains and to value constitutional endurance. The findings further suggest a certain maturation in federal constitutionalism that contributes to durability, although in some cases, durability might reflect rigidity or paralysis more than maturity.

2. Factors associated with constitutional longevity

The comparative study of "constitutions" is some 2,300 years old; yet the field remains under-theorised, and we know little about what makes constitutions work and endure over time. Given the short life-span of most constitutions, constitutional endurance seems to need explanation more than constitutional change. It is useful to look at factors that seem to be associated with constitutional longevity in order to place constitutional change in a better perspective.

Interestingly, the authors of the global empirical study (Elkins et al., 2009) found constitutional design factors to be associated more often with constitutional longevity than many external environmental factors. Traumatic events, such as defeat in war or an economic crisis such as the Great Depression, do not jeopardise the lives of constitutions, nor is the level of national economic development a predictor of constitutional change. Regime change, however, does stimulate constitutional change, and democracy makes a difference. Constitutions last longer (about 21 years) in democracies than in authoritarian regimes (about 15 years).

Path dependence appears to contribute to constitutional endurance. Countries having traditions of constitutional longevity are more likely to have more enduring constitutions. Citizens become habituated to constitutional practices, experienced at managing conflict within constitutional parameters, and willing to defend constitutional values. Constitutionalism itself is likely to become rooted in the polity's political culture in a manner thought necessary by Rousseau and Hegel, for example (Ritchie, 2005). As Aristotle put it more than two millennia ago, the most important means "for ensuring the stability of constitutions" is to educate the "citizens in the spirit of their constitution" (Barker, 1962: 233). Some scholars have termed this "constitutional identity," namely, the notion that "a constitution acquires an identity through experience" (Jacobsohn, 2010: 7) and develops "dialogically." Such habituation also is likely to ensure significant institutional continuities across replacements of constitutions over time.

Constitutions that are written in an inclusive manner and contain inclusive provisions have more endurance than constitutions promulgated by exclusive groups or elites. This type of process was advocated by John Adams:

> We must invite the People, to erect the whole Building with their own hands … this could be done only by Conventions of Representatives chosen by the People in the several Colonies, in the most exact proportions … Congress ought now to recommend to the People of every Colony to call such Conventions immediately and set up Governments of their own … for the People were the Source of all Authority and Original of all Power (Adams, 1775).

Recent federal and quasi-federal examples of such inclusion are the 1988 Constitution of Brazil and the 1996 Constitution of South Africa. Brazil's constitutional process was an open, participatory one in which 12 million voters signed petitions proposing 122 provisions and individuals sent 72,719 suggestions to the assembly that wrote the constitution. The document also, for example, combats prejudice and discrimination explicitly (Souza, 2005: 81). Likewise, the process in South Africa sought to achieve democratic legitimacy and "popular ownership" of the document through "sufficient consensus" and to ensure safe harbours for the country's various racial and ethnic groups (Steytler, 2005: 317). This process "has been hailed as a key part of the successful transition from the oppression of apartheid to a democratic society" (Hart, 2003: 7).

However, an important factor in South Africa's success, which is usually overlooked, is the dog that did not bark, namely, Nelson Mandela's refusal to build a cult of personality and use his charisma to engineer a popularly supported constitution allowing him to be president for life. Similarly inclusive constitution-making was pursued in Eritrea (1994-97), Russia (1993), and Zimbabwe (1999-2000), but manipulation by powerful leaders produced unhappy results. In Eritrea, the People's Front for Democracy and Justice has never implemented the 1997 constitution. In Russia, the people approved a constitution engineered by Boris Yeltsin to concentrate powers in the presidency. In Zimbabwe, the people rejected the proposed 2000 constitution, believing that it reflected President Robert Mugabe's wishes more than their own. Sometimes, therefore, "direct popular participation through constitutional politics have … emerged as tools for undermining constitutionalism and have helped charismatic presidents claim popular mandates and establish authoritarian constitutions" (Partlett, 2011: 3) as also happened in Belarus in 1995-96 and Kazakhstan, a nominally federal country, in 1995.

Constitutions that have amending processes that are neither too easy nor too difficult also survive longer. Elkins et al. suggest that the amending process in India's 62-year-old federal constitution strikes a balance between flexibility and rigidity that is "just right" (Elkins et al., 2009: 140). India has a three-tier hierarchy of amendment procedures by which some provisions are easier to amend than others. Certain provisions, including state names and boundaries, can be amended by a simple majority vote of the national parliament. Other provisions can be amended only "by a majority of the total membership of each house and by a majority of not less than two-thirds of the members present and voting" plus approval of the president (Majeed, 2005: 190). Other provisions, especially the "federal" provisions, can be amended only by the above parliamentary procedure as well as the consent of at least one-half of the state legislatures followed by the president's assent. The endurance of India's constitution is rather remarkable, given its "militant" character and "transformative" purposes (Jacobsohn, 2010). Its principal author, B. R. Ambedkar, an untouchable by birth, aimed the constitution at the caste system, oppressive elements of family structures, and reactionary features of Hinduism.

South Africa's constitution also has a hierarchy of amending procedures. Section 74 allows most amendments to be passed by an affirmative vote of two-thirds of the members of the National Assembly. However, if an amendment affects provincial powers or boundaries, or alters the Bill of Rights, at least six of the nine provinces in the National Council of Provinces also must approve it. Amending Section 1, which establishes South Africa as a sovereign, democratic state and sets forth the country's founding values, requires approval of three-quarters of the members of the National Assembly. The Constitution has been amended sixteen times since 1996 – an average of one amendment per year. The Constitution and the country have been stable, although the stability might be due as much to the dominance of the African National Congress (ANC) as to the quality of the Constitution.

Specificity in both scope and detail also contributes to constitutional survival, in part because specificity usually reflects "careful bargaining at the time of constitutional design" (Elkins et al., 2009: 103) over issues of importance to participants in the drafting process. If the process is openly inclusive, it is likely to reveal matters of importance and lead to accepted outcomes that give most political groups a vested interest in defending the constitution. More specificity often requires more time to draft the constitution, and that specificity may be more conducive to later amendment rather replacement of a constitution.

Of course, a constitution can have too much as well as too little specificity. Like flexibility, how much scope and detail to enshrine in a constitution is a matter of balance, context, and political imperatives. Since 1788, the average constitution has had 14,000 words. Brazil's 1988 document contained some 65,000 words at birth. India's constitution has "swelled to over 140,000 words" (Elkins, 2009: 105). By contrast, the U.S. Constitution, even with its twenty-seven amendments, contains only 7,762 words.

Social heterogeneity, such as racial, ethnic, linguistic, and religious diversity, tends to militate against constitutional durability. Elkins et al. calculate that constitutional life expectancy "in maximally heterogeneous states is thirteen [years] versus twenty-three … in maximally homogeneous states" (2009: 138). Given that most federal polities are more culturally diverse than non-federal polities, heterogeneity accounts partly for the instability of some federal constitutions. Population and territorial size also generate heterogeneities. The average population of federal countries is 355% larger than that of non-federal polities. Additionally, seven of the world's eight territorially largest nations – Argentina, Australia, Brazil, Canada, India, Russia, and the United States – are formally federal (Kincaid, 2010).

Designers of most federal constitutions, therefore, face exceptional challenges of heterogeneity not faced by designers of most non-federal constitutions. Nonetheless, heterogeneity combined with stabilising design features such as inclusion, specificity, and flexibility appear to contribute to constitutional longevity, perhaps because an inclusive process and sufficiently specified design can mobilise acceptance of the constitution while flexibility can assure all groups of the possibility of change in the future. James Madison's notion of the extended republic set forth in *Federalist* 10 in 1787 might apply here as well. A diversity of competing groups operating in a democratic environment across a large territory might prevent any one group from subverting the constitution.

In summary, the factors associated with constitutional endurance appear to be mostly internal to a polity and its constitution. The evidence also suggests that one factor in the endurance or stability of a constitution is the ability to change it via amendments, though not too easily. The ability to amend rather than replace a constitution, moreover, suggests a certain level of constitutional identity and political satisfaction that short circuits pressures for constitutional replacement.

3. Issues of explicit versus implicit change

Some scholars distinguish between explicit and implicit constitutional change (Voigt, 1999). Explicit constitutional change is said to encompass textual change – presumably both amendment and replacement, while implicit constitutional change is said to comprise all "changes that do not affect the written text" (Behnke and Benz, 2009: 217). This distinction has some utility, but it can be problematic and obscure more than it reveals, especially with regard to written federal constitutions.

Explicit constitutional change certainly includes amendments. They change the text. Replacing one constitution with another constitutes explicit change, too. Replacement and amendment are usually very different processses of constitutional change, even though the outcomes from each process are not always dramatically different. For example, Mexico's 1917 constitution has been amended so frequently and substantially "that only about 75 percent of its structure remains intact" (Elkins et al., 2009: 180); yet, the 1917 Constitution is deemed to be still in place (see also González, 2005). It might be argued that these amendments amounted to implicit change because they comprised a *de facto* replacement of the old constitution by a dominant authoritarian party (i.e. the PRI) acting under the guise of constitutional continuity, but this would distort the notion of implicit change, which assumes no textual change. Furthermore, the amendment process may have been crucial to maintaining constitutional stability and regime legitimacy. Replacements, moreover, sometimes involve dramatic, transformative changes of considerable historical moment, such as replacing an authoritarian constitution with a democratic one, a unitary constitution with a federal one, or a parliamentary system with a presidential system.

The notion of implicit constitutional change assumes the existence of an unambiguous original explicit position from which one can detect an implicit change. This is an enterprise fraught with difficulties. From the outset, a written constitution is subject to multiple interpretations. Who is to say which interpretation is an implicit change, especially if advocates of each interpretation claim fidelity to the constitutional text? Even if interpretation A, let's say, prevails during the first decades of a constitution's life but is later overturned judicially or legislatively by interpretation B, it would be incorrect to label interpretation B but not interpretation A as an implicit change. Both are interpretations of the text. In turn, if a government clearly ignores or contravenes provisions of the constitution, are these actions merely implicit changes as opposed to violations of the constitution?

A danger in the concept of implicit change is that it elevates to constitutional status institutions and policies established by non-constitutional means, including means that diminish or exclude the people compared to their roles in constitutional amendment or replacement. In the United States, for example, advocates of the national institutions and policies produced during New Deal era of the 1930s have sought to legitimise the New Deal as a "constitutional revolution" even though there was no constitutional change to that effect (e.g. Ackerman, 1991). In turn, critics of U.S. Supreme Court interpretations of the federal Constitution sometimes accuse the court of improperly promulgating judge-made amendments to the Constitution (e.g. Krock, 1964), while supporters cheer the decisions. It also is important that citizens remain cognizant of the fact that the text of their constitution has not changed even if the political use of the constitution appears to have changed it or is legitimised by leaders as a "constitutional" change.

The concept of implicit change also is vague, and "implicit" itself means something that is suggested, implied, or not clearly expressed; yet, a clearly expressed interpretation of a constitution by a supreme or constitutional court is hardly implicit. Likewise, a written statute can have constitutional impact or achieve constitutional status.

This is not to say that change of constitutional magnitude and import is confined only to amendment and replacement. Some analysts (e.g. Hart, 2003; Jacobsohn, 2010) suggest that a constitution should not be viewed as an act of completion but as an invitation for conversation to foster the dialogical development of the document. In heterogeneous polities, especially, an incrementalist approach to constitution-making, the use of ambiguous language, the avoidance of clear decisions, and the inclusion of contrasting provisions can facilitate peaceful constitutional development (Lerner, 2011).

Such development can take the forms of interpretation, supplementation, and infidelity. A written constitution is invariably subject to interpretation over time. Interpretation can be embodied in legislation, executive action, judicial rulings, and political behaviour. In the contemporary era, courts have come to play the pre-eminent interpretative role in democratic polities, but the courts are usually responding to the actions of the national legislature or executive or of the constituent governments. In a federal system, interpretation is likely to be influenced by intergovernmental processes. Interpretation also is deployed in order to adapt the constitution to changing social, economic, and technological facts.

Supplementation refers to political institutions and practices that emerge to effectuate a constitution and fill its voids. Two major examples from the United States are political parties and judicial review, neither of which is mentioned in the federal Constitution. Many of the Constitution's framers opposed political parties; yet parties emerged very quickly to effectuate Jefferson's 1800 election to the presidency only twelve years after ratification of the Constitution. The parties soon pushed the Constitution in a direction generally agreed to be more democratic than envisioned by its framers, but thereby helped to perpetuate the Constitution and foster affection for it. Judicial review (i.e. the authority of the U.S. Supreme Court to declare a law enacted by Congress or an action of the president to be unconstitutional), which is not mentioned in the Constitution, was first asserted by the Supreme Court in 1803 (*Marbury* v. *Madison*. 1803. 5 U.S. [1Cranch]: 137). This was a huge change of constitutional import. Most of the framers expected the President, not the Court, to decide the constitutionality of federal laws (Amar, 2005: 179). In light of the American experience, many federal constitutions now address political parties and judicial review.

Infidelity refers to constitutionally important change that occurs when political elites or others act in disregard or defiance of specific provisions of a constitution or the entire constitution without abrogating the document. A major example of infidelity in the United States was the refusal of the Congress, Supreme Court, and presidents to enforce for eighty-six years the Fourteenth Amendment, which was added to the federal Constitution in 1868 explicitly to protect black Americans freed from slavery. A dramatic example was massive public defiance of the Eighteenth Amendment (1919) that prohibited the manufacture, sale, or transportation of alcoholic beverages. That amendment was repealed in 1933 (Amendment XXI). Research would probably uncover examples of infidelity to certain provisions of every federal constitution. In Canada, the constitution invests the federal government with powers of reservation and disallowance over provincial laws; yet, political forces soon rendered those powers "dead letters" (Knopf and Sayers, 2005: 110), thereby facilitating the development of a federal system that is considerably more non-centralised than envisioned by the constitution. In some Latin American federations and currently developing federations, infidelity has often been the normal rather than exceptional mode of constitutionally significant development.

In summary, constitutional change can be said to occur through replacement and amendment, while constitutional development occurs through interpretation, supplementation, and infidelity. Although bright lines cannot be drawn between these modes of change, they are distinct and different as to actors and behaviour, if not always in outcomes.

4. Dynamics of constitutional replacement and amendment

Before turning to the dynamics of constitutional replacement and amendment, which are important foci for this volume, several caveats are in order.

For one, the volume's focus is on developed countries, mostly Western European nation-states. Less research has been conducted on constitutional change in non-Western and developing countries, which, generally, have experienced the most constitutional change in recent decades.

Second, an important complication in examining constitutional change and development in Western European countries is the existence of the European Union, which, itself, imposes changes on member states and also imposes boundaries on the scope and nature of constitutional change and development within the member states (e.g. Kokott, 2010; Tomuschat, 2010). Generalisations cannot be made, therefore, from only Western European cases.

Third, it is important to eschew normative terms such as "reform" and "evolution." These terms entail value judgments. Advocates of constitutional change commonly use the term "reform," but what some groups regard as "reform" might be viewed by other groups as reaction, deprivation, or assault. The term "evolution" implies progress and development, but constitutional change can result in devolution rather than evolution. Contemporary Venezuela is one example of a federal constitution devolving into authoritarian unitarism (Brewer-Carias, 2010).

Another common distinction is between "constitutional politics" and so-called "normal politics". "Nearly all normative and positive work on constitutions proceeds from the assumption that constitutional politics are fundamentally different in character from ordinary politics" (Ginsburg et al., 2009: 210). In this view, for example, a constitution should be drafted by a constituent assembly whose delegates deliberate based on long-term interests and cannot run for office immediately after serving in the assembly (Elster, 1995). This assumption has been called into question (e.g. Elkins et al., 2009), in part because in some countries, such as post-communist Eastern European countries, constitutional change has been "so closely associated with political change" as to make constitutional politics hardly "distinguishable from ordinary politics" (Teitel, 1997: 2069). Furthermore, "normal" parliamentary politics can sometimes effectively produce stable, popularly accepted constitutional change. Parliaments, moreover, are normally empowered to propose and sometimes also enact amendments.

This distinction may have value in some cases of constitutional replacement, but has less value in cases of constitutional amendment, except perhaps when amendment involves a major constitutional change. The distinction has little value in cases of constitutional development that involve interpretation, supplementation, and infidelity. These latter processes may sometimes involve politics that is not "normal" but not overtly constitutional either. In the end, the idea of "normal politics" is vague puzzle because "normal" is not subject to definitive definition.

Furthermore, given the frequency of constitutional replacement and amendment worldwide, constitutional change is best viewed as a key subject of so-called "normal" politics. What is ordinarily different about constitutional replacement and amendment is that the decision rules are usually more stringent than the decision rules applicable to "normal" political decision-making. Otherwise, though, politics usually proceeds quite normally through processes of constitutional replacement and amendment. In addition, in some federations, such as Austria, Belgium, Brazil, and India, constitutional amendments requiring low voting thresholds as well as constitutional statutes, para-constitutional laws, and special laws requiring simple-majority or reduced super-majority legislative voting all bring constitutional amendments well within the purview of "normal" politics.

Constitutional change since World War II has been associated, in part, with four waves of change that have swept the post-war world.

One wave might be called the liberation wave, which began with the liberation of colonies from their imperial masters. Comoros (five constitutions), India (1949), Malaysia (1957), Nigeria (seven constitutions), Pakistan (six constitutions), St. Kitts and Nevis (1983), and the United Arab Emirates (1971) are the seven post-colonial federations. Most of these countries have experienced considerable constitutional change since independence. Three have had five or more constitutions as they have attempted to establish stable governments. Three of these countries have made constitutional changes through amendments. Malaysia has had about 650 amendments that have diluted the original constitution to the point of *de facto* replacement (Faruqi, 2008). Because India's constitution contains details that are often treated by statute in other countries, the Constitution has been amended ninety-four times, almost twice a year, and has otherwise been changed significantly by interpretation and supplementation since the fall of the monopolistic Congress Party in the late 1980s. The UAE significantly amended its 1971 interim constitution and established it as a permanent constitution in 1996. Only St. Kitts and Nevis has had a stable constitution, although some political leaders are calling for substantial amendment. The deputy prime minister, a leader of the Labour Party, is a major advocate for change, in part because the Labour Party did not sign the 1982 constitution agreement.

A second liberation wave came with the collapse of the USSR. This wave produced three troubled federal arrangements: Russia (1993), Bosnia and Herzegovina (1995), and Serbia and Montenegro (2003). The Russian Constitution is difficult to amend, but amendments made in 2008 significantly altered the political system to enhance the centralisation of power under Vladimir Putin and his United Russia Party. Interpretation, supplementation, and infidelity also have changed the constitution substantially. The Constitution of Bosnia and Herzegovina frames a very unstable and virtually paralysed polity. Significant amendments proposed in 2006 failed to achieve the needed approval of two-thirds of the House of Representatives. Serbia and Montenegro lasted only for 3.5 years.

The second post-war wave might be called the democratisation and redemocratisation wave that produced federal and quasi-federal democracies based on post-war constitutions in Argentina (1956), Austria (1945), Belgium (1993), Brazil (1988), Ethiopia (1994), Germany (1949), Iraq (2005), South

Africa (1996), and Spain (1978). Mexico re-democratised under its 1917 federal constitution. In Latin America, democratisation generated constitutional replacement in Brazil and constitutional change in Argentina and Mexico through amendment, supplementation, and interpretation. Replacement in Brazil, however, did not quiet amendment agitation. Brazil's 1988 constitution has been amended fifty-seven times, for an average of 2.5 amendments per year.

The constitutions of Ethiopia, Iraq, South Africa, and Spain reflect the overthrow of authoritarian regimes. Ethiopia's constitution has been durable, but its longevity is probably due to the monopolistic position of the Ethiopian People's Revolutionary Democratic Front (EPRDF), which has excluded opposition parties from governing at the centre and in the states. As noted above, South Africa's constitution has already been amended sixteen times in a political environment in which one party, the ANC, dominates the political system. Spain's Constitution has been amended less frequently, partly because it allows autonomous communities to negotiate autonomy statutes with the national government; nevertheless, the constitution remains highly contested, and various political forces advocate change.

The constitutions of Austria, Belgium, and Germany reflect restorations of democracy. Austria restored its 1920 constitution, and because the Constitution can be changed through simple constitution acts, it has undergone hundreds of major and minor revisions while the major parties in the political system have been unable to agree on a replacement or substantial amendment of the Constitution. Belgium restored its 1831 constitution after the war and has engaged in continual constitutional change for sixty-six years, the most radical change occurring in 1993 when the new Article 1 declared Belgium to be a federal system. The Constitution has been amended twenty-three times since the coordinated text of 17 February 1994 was published in the Belgium's Official Journal. Germany's Basic Law has been changed some sixty times (almost once a year since 1949).

A third wave combines elements of the liberation and democratisation waves in what might be called a wave of communal freedom in which national, ethnic, racial, linguistic, and religious communities asserted autonomy and equality claims, especially in Belgium, Bosnia and Herzegovina, Canada, Comoros, Ethiopia, India, Italy, Malaysia, Nigeria, Pakistan, Russia, South Africa, Spain, the United Kingdom, and the United States. This wave also generated the dissolution of four federal systems: Czechoslovakia, USSR, West Indies, and Yugoslavia.

Most of these extant federal countries have been engaged in either continuous or episodic constitutional change involving replacement and amendment as well as interpretation, supplementation, and infidelity. The heterogeneity of these countries, and especially the demands for self-government made by territorially based communal groups in many of these countries, require continual adjustments and refinements of a constitutional nature. In some of these countries, constitutional politics is "normal" politics because communal self-government claims involve distributions of policy-making and fiscal powers as well as resources and revenues that often require constitutional settlements.

Some of these countries, such as Belgium, India, Malaysia, and South Africa, have relied on amendment change. Belgium, for example, experienced episodes of major amendment change in 1970, 1980, 1988, 1993, and 2002 (Deschouwer, 2005). Other countries, such as Nigeria and Pakistan, have experienced frequent replacements. By contrast, Canada, where Quebec's "Quiet Revolution" of the 1960s has been an important model in this communal-freedom wave of constitutional change, failed to achieve a *de jure* settlement of its most fundamental cultural cleavage via constitutional replacement or amendment. However, the Constitution was patriated and amended by the Constitution Act 1982, which was approved by every province except Quebec. Subsequent efforts (Meech Lake in 1990 and Charlottetown in 1992) to achieve constitutional settlements with Quebec failed, and Canadians, suffering from "constitutional fatigue," turned instead to constitutional supplementation, interpretation, and infidelity to hold the country together.

The Canadian case suggests that constitutional replacement or amendment is not always necessary to maintain a federation. Six of Switzerland's twenty-six cantons have never ratified any of Switzerland's three modern constitutions (Kincaid, 2005: 416); yet, Switzerland endures. Indeed, given that Quebec nationalists have a fundamentally different view of the Canadian Constitution and confederation than do most other Canadians (e.g. Gagnon and Iacovino, 2007), a settlement via constitutional replacement or amendment is unlikely. However, many French Quebecers and some English Canadians do not regard their country's current constitutional *modus vivendi* as fully legitimate. Compared to Americans, for example, Canadians' have less trust and confidence in all their governments and more often believe their province is not treated with the respect it deserves in the federal system (Kincaid and Cole, 2011). In more fragile federal environments, a Canadian-type solution might not be feasible.

Although the United States has not experienced demands for self-government by any territorially based communal groups (except Indians), the black civil-rights movement that emerged during the late 1950s made claims for autonomy and equality that generated three amendments (i.e. XXIII, XXIV, and XXVI) to the U.S. Constitution and a much more important reinterpretation of the Fourteenth Amendment that significantly centralised U.S. federalism in contrast to the mostly decentralising consequences of communal movements in most of the other heterogeneous countries. Regarding Indian claims for territorial autonomy, the federal government, which has plenary authority for Indian affairs, has moved in opposite directions. Congress, as well as presidents from Richard M. Nixon (1968-74) to Barack Obama have generally strengthened Indian self-government while the Supreme Court has weakened it (Wilkins and Richotte, 2003).

A fourth wave contributing to constitutional change has been the rise of the European Union. The coming of the Maastricht Treaty (1993), in particular, motivated constitutional amendments, interpretations, and supplementations in the member federations intended to protect constituent political communities from excessive power losses to the EU, establish mechanisms to give constituent political communities a larger voice in national negotiations with the EU, and allow constituent political communities to conclude treaties or other legal agreements with foreign governments. Although Switzerland is not an EU member, it is surrounded by the EU and coordinates its laws and practices with the EU through bilateral agreements. Formation of its 1999 constitution reflected, in part, the need to adapt to the EU and respond to increased assertions of cantonal rights, as in the founding of the Conference of Cantonal Governments in 1993 (Schmitt, 2005: 353). The process that produced the 1999 constitution had started in 1966 but did not achieve momentum until the 1990s, at which point it crossed a threshold enabling a broader constitutional change.

The EU has played an important role also in providing the single market and the peace and security that have enabled communal, national, and regional entities in Belgium, France, Italy, Spain, and the United Kingdom to assert autonomy claims and demand devolution in ways that were deemed destabilising, subversive, and dangerous in the past. In light of the EU's member-state decision-making structure and democratic deficit, moreover, some of these entities could develop aspirations for their own membership in the EU.

The one federal country not mentioned thus far is Australia because it was not significantly affected by any of the above waves of change. Australia's constitution of 1901 has not been replaced, nor has it been amended frequently. The Commonwealth Parliament has put forty-four amendment proposals to the people; only eight have been approved during the Constitution's 110-year history. This record of infrequent amendment cannot be attributed to Australia's double-majority ratification process because a similar process exists in Switzerland where amendments have been very frequent and where twenty-six heterogeneous cantons, compared to Australia's six, more homogeneous states, would seem to render amendment much more difficult than in Australia. The only Australian amendment remotely related to the above waves is a 1967 amendment counting Aborigines for constitutional purposes and allowing the federal government, in addition to the state governments, to make laws for them.

In summary, social and political movements appear to play a significant role in constitutional change, especially through replacement and amendment. Some of these movements are of external origin, but all changes depend on internal, domestic circumstances. However, in a globalising world with emerging transnational constitutional norms, growing international-domestic interactions will increasingly affect domestic constitutional change.

Internally, political parties seem to be important. A single monopolistic or otherwise powerful party or a strong coalition of parties can effectuate constitutional replacement and amendment. Where parties are weak and coalitions are divided internally, interpretation, supplementation, and infidelity are likely to predominate, unless the parties can be forced into replacement or amendment by social movements. These latter modes of change also appear to be more feasible when parties, interest groups, and charismatic leaders mobilise citizens to support change. Constitutional change through elite negotiations can succeed if the elites represent powerful parties or a coalition, but where voters are accustomed to having a voice in important political matters, elite negotiations might not be ratified by voters. Elite negotiations run the risks of (1) paralysis because they have more vested interests than the general citizenry and (2) deviation from the preferences of the average voter because they hold more extreme views than most citizens. In heterogeneous societies with deep cultural cleavages, however, it may be difficult or impossible to mobilise parties or citizens for constitutional replacement or amendment.

Other internal factors affecting change seem to include tradition. Some countries have a tradition of constitutional replacement and amendment; others do not. Although Australia and Switzerland have similar amendment procedures, Australians rely much more on supplementation through political action and conventions, along with judicial interpretation, than on amendments, which have averaged about one every fourteen years (Saunders, 2005). The Swiss indulge in amendomania. Although the constitution of 1848 was amended only once (in 1866), it was replaced through total revision by the constitution of 1874, which was amended 155 times (an average of 1.2 amendments per year). The 1999 constitution has already been amended about seventeen times (an average of 1.4 amendments per year). Similarly, Article 3 of the Swiss Constitution is similar to the Tenth Amendment to the U.S. Constitution; yet, change with respect to the balance of state-federal power in the United States has occurred much more through interpretation than in Switzerland where amendments have been needed to invest the federation even with minor powers such as subsidies for hiking trails (Linder, 2010: 48).

These examples suggest, as well, that common-law federations rely less on constitutional replacement and amendment than do civil-law federations. Constitutional change seems to be contingent also on the extent to which the constitution is treated as a sacred text to be changed only under extraordinary circumstances, the extent to which the constitution is a framework for governance that relies more on interpretation and supplementation than on amendment or replacement, the extent to which the constitution is a central rather than peripheral governance document, and the extent to which patterns of intergovernmental relations are conducive to change and innovation. Interestingly, however, economic and technological change seem not to be major drivers of constitutional change.

All constitutional provisions are not equal, however. Some components of constitutions seem to be more difficult than others to change by replacement or amendment, although this facet of change needs more research. In federal countries, especially stable, developed ones, the difficult-to-change components are likely to include the distribution of powers between the federation and its constituent governments, the representation of the constituent political communities in the federation government, the structure and power of the judiciary, the boundaries of the constituent jurisdictions, and key fiscal arrangements such as revenue sharing and equalisation. Most federal countries engage in some type of fiscal equalisation, for example, but these policies frequently evoke controversy and resentment among constituent jurisdictions. Yet, it is difficult to change these arrangements, in part because no jurisdiction wishes to be a net loser. The Swiss did manage to amend their fiscal equalisation scheme as part of the 1999 constitutional replacement process but only after many years of debate and negotiation, a credible threat by the Socialist Party to impose a tax harmonisation scheme that would have been costly to the wealthy cantons, and a promise by the Federal Ministry of Finance to subsidise the change (Behnke and Benz, 2009: 222-23). Otherwise, however, almost all of the core features and institutions of the previous Swiss constitution were carried over into the new one, as is common across constitutional replacements in some federations.

Finally, some constitutions reflect a hierarchy of values in which some core, fundamental provisions are immune to amendment, such as the "eternity clause" in Germany's Basic Law (Art. 79[3]), while other provisions can be amended only with difficulty and still other provisions can be amended rather easily. Hence, even within a single federation, constitutional change by amendment can be variable.

5. Conclusion

This analysis suggests that constitutional change via replacement and amendment, as well as development through interpretation, supplementation, and infidelity are normal, not exceptional politics in federal polities. The normalcy of constitutional change is probably due to the very negotiated nature of federal polities and by the powers of self-government possessed by the constituent political communities that produce intergovernmental relations requiring continual adjustment. In some cases, constituent political communities also possess a credible exit option that can be used as leverage to obtain change and accommodation. At the same time, though, federal constitutions are not less stable than unitary constitutions. On the contrary, the very negotiated nature of federal constitutions seems to enhance endurance even while facilitating peaceful change over time.

References

Ackerman, Bruce (1991): We the People: Foundations. Cambridge, MA: The Belknap Press.

Adams, John (1775): Autobiography, part 1, "John Adams," through 1776, sheet 28 of 53 [electronic edition]. Adams Family Papers: An Electronic Archive. Massachusetts Historical Society. http://www.masshist.org/digitaladams/

Amar, Akhil Reed (2005): America's Constitution: A Biography. New York: Random House.

Barker, Ernest (ed.) (1962): The Politics of Aristotle. New York: Oxford University Press.

Behnke, Nathalie/Benz, Arthur (2009): The Politics of Constitutional Change between Reform and Evolution. In: Publius: The Journal of Federalism 39, (2), 213-240.

Brewer-Carias, Allan R (2010): Dismantling Democracy in Venezuela: The Chávez Authoritarian Experiment. Cambridge: Cambridge University Press.

Deschouwer, Kris (2005): Kingdom of Belgium. In: Kincaid, J./Tarr, A. (eds.): Constitutional Origins, Structure, and Change in Federal Countries. Montreal/Kingston: McGill-Queen's University Press, 48-75.

Elkins, Zachary/Ginsburg, Tom/Melton, James (2009): The Endurance of National Constitutions. New York: Cambridge University Press.

Elster, Jon (1995): Forces and Mechanisms in the Constitution-Making Process. In: Duke Law Journal 45, (2), 364-396.

Faruqi, Shad Saleem (2008): Document of Destiny – The Constitution of the Federation of Malaysia. Shah Alam: Star Publications.

Gagnon, Alain-G./Iacovino, Raffaele (2007): Federalism, Citizenship, and Quebec: Debating Multinationalism. Toronto: University of Toronto Press.

Ginsburg, Tom/Elkins, Zachary/Blount, Justin (2009): Does the Process of Constitution-Making Matter?. In: Annual Review of Law and Social Science 5, 201-223.

González, Juan Marcos Gutiérrez (2005): United Mexican States. In: Kincaid, J./Tarr, A. (eds.): Constitutional Origins, Structure, and Change in Federal Countries. Montreal/Kingston: McGill-Queen's University Press, 206-38.

Hart, Vivian (2003): Democratic Constitution Making. Special Report 107. Washington DC: United States Institute of Peace.

Jacobsohn, Gary Jeffrey (2010): Constitutional Identity. Cambridge MA: Harvard University Press.

Kincaid, John (2005): Comparative Observations. In: Kincaid, J./Tarr, A. (eds.): Constitutional Origins, Structure, and Change in Federal Countries. Montreal/Kingston: McGill-Queen's University Press, 409-448.

Kincaid, John (2010): Federalism and democracy: Comparative empirical and theoretical perspectives. In: Burgess, M./Gagnon, A.-G. (eds.): Federal Democracies. London: Routledge, 299-324.

Kincaid, John/Cole, Richard L. (2011): Citizen Attitudes Toward Issues of Federalism in Canada, Mexico, and the United States. In: Publius: The Journal of Federalism 41, (4), 53-75.

Knopf, Rainer/Sayers, Anthony (2005): Canada. In: Kincaid, J./Tarr, A. (eds.): Constitutional Origins, Structure, and Change in Federal Countries. Montreal/Kingston: McGill-Queen's University Press, 103-142.

Kokott, Juliane (2010): The Basic Law at 60 – From 1949 to 2009: The Basic Law and Supranational Integration. In: German Law Journal 11, (1), 99-114.

Krock, Arthur (1964): In the Nation: Judge-Made Amendments to the Constitution. In: The New York Times (16 June), 5A.

Landau, David (2012): The Importance of Constitution-Making. In: Denver University Law Review 89, (2), forthcoming. http://papers.ssrn.com/sol3/papers.cfm?abstract_id=1950405 [last access: 25 December 2011]

Law, David S./Versteeg, Mila (2012): The Declining Influence of the United States Constitution. In: New York University Law Review 87, forthcoming. http://papers.ssrn.com/sol3/papers.cfm?abstract_id=1923556 [last access: 25 December 2011]

Lerner, Hanna (2011): Making Constitutions in Deeply Divided Societies. Cambridge: Cambridge University Press.

Linder, Wolf (2010): Swiss Democracy: Possible Solutions to Conflict in Multicultural Societies. London: Palgrave Macmillan.

Majeed, Akhtar (2005): Republic of India. In: Kincaid, J./Tarr, A. (eds.): Constitutional Origins, Structure, and Change in Federal Countries. Montreal/Kingston: McGill-Queen's University Press, 179-207.

Partlett, William (2011): Making Constitutions Matter: The Dangers of Constitutional Politics in Current Post-Authoritarian Constitution Making. Social Science Research Network. http://papers.ssrn.com/sol3/papers.cfm?abstract_id=1924958 [last access: 25 December 2011]

Reynolds, Andrew (ed.) (2002): The Architecture of Democracy: Constitutional Design, Conflict Management, and Democracy. Oxford: Oxford University Press.

Ritchie, David T. (2005): Organic Constitutionalism: Rousseau, Hegel, and the Constitution of Society. In: Wayne State University Journal of Law in Society 6, 36-81.

Saunders, Cheryl (2005): Commonwealth of Australia. In: Kincaid, J./Tarr, A. (eds.): Constitutional Origins, Structure, and Change in Federal Countries. Montreal/Kingston: McGill-Queen's University Press, 12-47.

Schmitt, Carl (1992): The Constitutional Theory of Federation (1928). Telos 91 (Spring), 26-56.

Schmitt, Nicolas (2005): Swiss Confederation. In: Kincaid, J./Tarr, A. (eds.): Constitutional Origins, Structure, and Change in Federal Countries. Montreal/Kingston: McGill-Queen's University Press, 348-380.

Souza, Celina (2005): Federal Republic of Brazil. In: Kincaid, J./Tarr, A. (eds.): Constitutional Origins, Structure, and Change in Federal Countries. Montreal/Kingston: McGill-Queen's University Press, 76-102.

Steytler, Nico (2005): Republic of South Africa. In: Kincaid, J./Tarr, A. (eds.): Constitutional Origins, Structure, and Change in Federal Countries. Montreal/Kingston: McGill-Queen's University Press, 312-346.

Teitel, Ruti (1997): Transnational Jurisprudence: The Role of Law in Political Transformation. In: Yale Law Journal 106, (7), 2009-2080.

Tomuschat, Christian (2010): The Effects of the Judgments of the European Court of Human Rights According to the German Constitutional Court. In: German Law Journal 11, (5), 513-526.

Voigt, Stefan (1999): Explaining Constitutional Change: A Positive Economics Approach. Cheltenham: Edward Elgar.

Wilkins, David E./Richotte, Keith (2003): The Rehnquist Court and Indigenous Rights: The Expedited Diminution of Native Powers of Governance. In: Publius: The Journal of Federalism 33, (3), 83-110.

Williams, Susan H. (ed.) (2009): Constituting Equality: Gender Equality and Comparative Constitutional Law. New York: Cambridge.

2. Constitutional Reform in „Co-operative“ Federalism

Swiss Federalism, Fiscal Equalisation Reform and the Reallocation of Tasks

Dieter Freiburghaus

1. Introduction

The reform of the fiscal equalisation scheme and of the allocation of tasks between the federal government and the cantons (NFA – *Neugestaltung des Finanzausgleichs und der Aufgabenverteilung zwischen Bund und Kantonen*) was one of the longest and most difficult constitutional reform processes ever undertaken in Switzerland. Since 27 articles were either amended or newly incorporated into the constitution, the project was to be ratified in a mandatory referendum requiring a double majority of votes: in Switzerland and in a majority of the cantons. The people went to the polls on 28 November 2004. 64% of the Swiss voters and a majority of 23 of the 26 cantons voted "yes".

This clear endorsement may be surprising because of the complexity of the bill dealing with the essence of Swiss federalism and the highly contested reallocation of resources. It was particularly surprising because two similar constitutional reforms in Switzerland had previously more or less failed. As early as in the 1970s, an attempt had been made to reallocate the powers of the federal government and the cantons. However, apart from some minor adjustments, the reform failed. After that, a fundamental reform of the Federal Constitution (*Bundesverfassung*) was on the political agenda for decades. Initially, there were grand plans for a whole new constitution. In the end, the nature of the reform was to be somewhat more modest and went into the direction of "updating". In 1999, the voters and the cantons half-heartedly approved it. Now, in the case of the NFA, there was a clear "yes" to such a fundamental reform. How can this be explained? Drawing general conclusions from these three cases of constitutional reform in Switzerland or in other federal states would certainly overrate the explanatory power of political science. Yet, as is generally known, if we really want to, we can learn from every example.

In the following sections, the process leading to a reform of the Swiss financial equalisation scheme will be analysed, with a focus on the amendment of the constitution. Before discussing the structure, process and results of the reform, we first need to place it in the general context the Swiss federalism and debate on the constitution of the past 40 years.[1]

---

1 To understand the financial and economic aspects of the project, it is important to know that in Switzerland, all three levels of government collect their own taxes for which they

2. The federalism debate in Switzerland

Economic growth and modernisation after World War II had created insecurity within Swiss society. People spoke of a "Helvetic malaise" (Imboden, 1964). The impression was widely held that the existing institutions were no longer able to deal with the new challenges. This resulted, on the one hand, in initiatives to completely revise the federal constitution and, on the other hand, in efforts to reallocate powers between the central state and the cantons. However, these two deeply entwined reform movements only led to effective results at the turn of the century.

The reallocation of power between the federal government and the cantons has been one of the most controversial issues in the debate of the Swiss federal state since it was founded in 1848 (Freiburghaus and Buchli, 2003). During the 20th century, tasks of the state grew exponentially. Many newly emerging competences were directly assigned to the federal level (national highways, nuclear power plants, environmental protection, etc.) and policy-making of both levels of government became increasingly interlocked, leading to what has been termed "cooperative federalism" and "executive federalism" (Bussman, 1986). In the 1960s, this was perceived to be a weakness of federalism, and various proposals to solve this problem were put forward.

In 1972, the first real push towards reform was given by a parliamentary initiative ("Motion Binder") commissioning the Federal Council to review the vertical division of competences. A study group, followed by a study commission, was set up to prepare proposals. In 1981, the Federal Council tabled the first package of measures regarding the reallocation of tasks, which comprised a smorgasbord of rather modest amendments. The project was met with harsh criticism because the cantons feared that the whole project was intended to solve the budget problems of the federal government at their expense. The package was undone and divided into smaller units. In the end, only a couple of proposals were implemented. A second package introduced in 1988 contained from the outset only minor corrections in the allocation of tasks. This long and laborious process by and large missed its goals (Klöti and Nüssli, 1987).

Spurred on by the "Helvetic malaise", discussions also turned to a comprehensive revision of the Federal Constitution in the 1960s. Due to a number of partial revisions from 1874 onwards, the *Grundgesetz* had become confusing, and in many ways it no longer reflected the constitution as it was actually lived.[2] Since 1967, various groups of experts worked on a fundamental

can partly set the tax rate. Of the total tax revenue collected today, approx. 45% goes to the federal government, 33% to the cantons and 22% to the municipalities.

2 The Constitution of modern Switzerland dates back to 1848. A first total revision occurred in 1874.

formal and substantive revision, which induced a broad public discussion. During the economically turbulent 1970s, however, enthusiasm decreased. Most of the substantive proposals were rejected by hostile coalitions of interest groups, and the project seemed to be running out of steam.

In 1985, the Federal Council once again put the topic on the agenda and decided to initiate a formal review of the constitution and an "update" of the text ("Toilettage"). Other desirable substantive reforms should follow through subsequent partial revisions (including the Federal Fiscal Equalisation scheme and the distribution of competences between the federal government and the cantons). This idea took hold. In 1998, Parliament adopted the Federal Council's respective reform proposal. One year later, the people and the cantons approved of the new constitution following a lacklustre referendum campaign. The amendments came into effect on 1 January 2000. In the course of the process, the federalism articles of the Constitution, too, were amended in a modest way (Freiburghaus, 2001).

The reform of the fiscal equalisation scheme under scrutiny here is the result of this intertwined, long-term reform process. Nonetheless, it can be considered a distinct project because it had a confined scope – the review of the fiscal equalisation scheme – and it was discussed within distinct forums.

Fiscal equalisation is a relatively recent federal responsibility that was first enshrined in the constitution in 1959. Previously, the federal government had, however, supported the Alpine cantons in particular by subsidising road construction and agriculture. In addition, the highly progressive direct federal income tax had – and still has – an indirectly equalising effect: cantons with a larger share of affluent citizens contribute more to the financing of the state than others. According to the revised version of 1959, the amount of transfers between the federal government and the cantons (subsidies, cantonal share of federal taxes) was calculated according to the fiscal capacity of the latter. This vertical equalisation with horizontal effects never produced satisfactory results and was increasingly criticised in the 1980s. The most important arguments were:

- Three functions were to be fulfilled using one instrument: fiscal equalisation in terms of supporting the poorer cantons, providing incentives to pursue federal goals, and subsidising special burdens (in particular, those of the Alpine cantons). This made it impossible to construct a rational scheme of fiscal equalisation.
- Criteria such as the economic wellbeing of the cantons as well as their expenditures were included in the decisive indicator, the index of fiscal capacity. Accordingly, the effects of equalisation could be partly manipulated, since a higher amount of public spending could lead to an increase in federal support.
- Since many federal grants were tied to co-financing of the cantons, the rich cantons were in a much better position to take advantage of such ar-

rangements than the poorer cantons. As a result, fiscal equalisation sometimes went into the wrong direction.

- The special burdens of the Alpine regions were compensated for, but not those of the central and urban regions.
- With this system, the cantons became increasingly dependent on the federal government (Eidgenössische Finanzverwaltung, 1991).

The reform of the fiscal equalisation scheme was thus excluded from the comprehensive revision of the federal constitution. In the two cases of reform mentioned above (reallocation of power, comprehensive revision of the federal constitution), all relevant political actors were involved from the outset, which made political guidance and control largely impossible. In contrast, the negotiation of the NFA was restricted to a few financial experts. Only when the proposal was watertight, so to speak, did it set sail upon the stormy political seas – and survived. All in all, this NFA process took almost twenty years to the day and was extremely complex.

3. A "constitutional moment"

One of the reasons why earlier plans to comprehensively reform the Swiss federal system never succeeded were the financial details: The cantons argued that the federal government only intended to balance its budget at their expense. From their point of view, any reform of the allocation of power could only succeed if the financial question was solved. Therefore, the reform task at hand was redefined and the agenda was rearranged: While previously the reallocation of tasks was the principal aim and the actors involved had then realised that this would have major financial implications, it was now decided that the question of finances should be resolved. However, in order to do this, disentangling competences became unavoidable.

It was the heavy criticism levelled at the Federal Fiscal Equalisation scheme mentioned above that worked as a catalyst for reform. It became increasingly obvious that the respective instruments fell short to achieve their goals. Therefore, both the federal government and the cantons were basically in favour of completely reviewing the fiscal equalisation system. This willingness developed continuously, but the year 1988 was decisive. At that time, the Financial Directors' Conference (*Finanzdirektorenkonferenz* – FDK)[3] asked the Swiss Finance Administration (*Eidgenössische Finanzverwaltung* – EFV) to prepare a "fiscal equalisation balance sheet" documenting the various financial flows between the federal government and the cantons and assessing their effectiveness.

3 This is the conference of cantonal finance ministers that meets regularly.

The overall project was divided into sub-projects. Each one had its own agenda and its own procedures of negotiating, decision-making and ratification. Each sub-project was evaluated in one way or another, and only if it was perceived to be on solid ground, the reform process continued. These particular features made up a significant condition for success.

4. Setting the agenda: defining the constitutional problem

Setting a political agenda is most often based on negotiations. The way in which the problem is defined narrows down the solutions available and, therefore, is an eminently political act. This is why the line between the phases of agenda setting and negotiation is blurred. It can be drawn at that moment when the Federal Council decided to initiate the review of the fiscal equalisation scheme and set up a respective project team. However, the team took shape during the agenda-setting phase and had some influence on the definition of the problem.

The decisive actors during the entire process were the EVA and the FDK. Later on, the Cantonal Government Conference (*Konferenz der Kantonsregierungen* – KdK) also played an important role. The FDK discussed all issues of state finances and occasionally made recommendations. It represented the interests of the cantons vis-à-vis the federal government. It maintained various working groups. In the case of the NFA the working group on fiscal equalisation was particularly active. One of its sub-groups dealt with the politically and technically crucial key factors of fiscal equalisation. This means, in Swiss terms, that approximately ten people (cantonal ministers and senior civil servants) belonged to the innermost circle that dealt with this problem. All persons involved knew each other well and had worked together for many years.

In 1988, the FDK – or rather, its working group "key factors to distribute fiscal resources (*Finanzausgleichsschlüssel*)" – asked the Swiss Finance Administration to prepare a "fiscal equalisation balance sheet". Various parties were interested in this clarification: the poorer cantons wanted more money, the wealthier ones did not want to pay more; the cantons wanted more federal money but less federal influence, the federal government wanted the opposite; the cantonal finance ministers wanted general grants to be channelled through their treasuries, while colleagues in other departments preferred special grants. However, no one could successfully deny the necessity to first shed some light on finances. At the outset, the result of this review was not clear. Therefore, Rawls's "veil of ignorance", formulated as a theoretical concept, was applied as a practical tool to establish "fairness".

In the following years, the specialists from the Swiss Finance Administration analysed financial flows between the federal government and the cantons. In 1991, they presented their report, "A Fiscal Equalisation Balance Sheet" (Eidgenössische Finanzverwaltung, 1991). The document contained 36 pages of text and various tables in the appendix. This balance sheet confirmed everybody's worries: lack of transparency, wrong incentives, inadequate evaluation tools, few or no equalising effects, and even a reallocation in favour of the affluent cantons. Thus, there was an urgent need for action.

Now it was again up to the FDK to take action. It commissioned its working group, which was working on key factors to distribute fiscal resources, to elaborate ideas for a comprehensive review of the fiscal equalisation scheme. The group followed the recognised principles of fiscal federalism: disentangling and simplification of financial flows (and thus disentangling of powers), separation of incentives and redistributive instruments, a more objective basis for calculating financial capacities, separate equalisation of burdens and revenues, introduction of a horizontal equalisation scheme and political control of the impact of equalisation. In 1992, the working group presented its so-called "*Orientierungsrahmen*" (framework of guidelines), which addressed the criticism of the existing fiscal equalisation scheme and formulated proposals for its reform (Finanzdirektorenkonferenz, 1992).

This framework of guidelines served as a point of reference for the entire project. The basic elements of reform developed there were indeed implemented in the actual reform. This success was partly achieved due to the existence of initially formulated principles which were undisputed among financial experts – and were therefore accepted by all ministers of finance. Thus, there was a shared world view of the small circle of people involved. Other interested parties were kept at a distance up to that point because of the highly technical nature of the matter.

In October 1992, the FDK wrote a letter to the head of the Federal Minister of Finance, in which it outlined the guidelines of a new system and asked the national government to initiate a respective reform process. "It proposes that the Swiss Minister of Finance establishes a commission of experts and readily agrees to collaborate with equal representation." (FDK, 1992: 14). Obviously those taking part in this kind of commission would largely be the same experts that had drawn up the guiding framework.

The Federal Council basically agreed with this kind of approach. It was, however, aware that there would be political problems later on, when the winners and losers became visible. With the envisaged goal of a very solid foundation in mind, the Federal Council and the Ministers of Finance jointly commissioned four of the most eminent scholars of public finance to provide expertise on this reform. They presented their reports in March 1994 confirming the criticism of the existing fiscal equalisation scheme and approved of the proposals of the "*Orientierungsrahmen*" (Frey et al., 1994). In this way it was made sure that, at least from an academic viewpoint, this project would not encounter fundamental opposition. This was a kind of "functionalist" approach: delegating policy-making to experts partly led to de-politisation.

Therefore, the "*Orientierungsrahmen*" and the expert reports defined the problem quite precisely, yet still in financial and fairly abstract terms: it was about disentangling financial flows, assigning different instruments to different functions, reinforcing the equalising effect and making it politically manageable. Following from this was the necessity to separate competences, due to two reasons: Firstly, it constituted a precondition to disentangle financial flows; secondly, it was necessary to increase efficiency in order to gain resources required to fund greater financial equalisation without disproportionately burden the financially strong cantons. At the same time, the cantons would gain additional autonomy, which, at least regarding the acceptance of the reform, was an argument in favour of the reform – in reality it often seems that the cantons do not really want more autonomy. It was evident that such a reform would require a new constitutional foundation; it was less clear, however, which amendments exactly were necessary. The experts of constitutional law were still being kept at a distance. Moreover, the abstract nature of the existing provisions still left a lot of discretion for negotiated solutions on particular issues.

As mentioned earlier, parallel to the NFA project the comprehensive revision of the Federal constitution was underway. If there had been a desire to amend other aspects of federalism, then these would have had to be dealt with in this second process, thus preventing the agenda from being overloaded. The NFA project had the aim of reorganising fiscal equalisation. However, one requirement for this was, as shown, a clearer division of competences between the federal government and the cantons – although not in terms of a fundamental reallocation of power, but rather in terms of disentanglement and increased efficiency. With this, disentanglement had a clear aim beyond ideological battles about the principle of subsidiarity. The basic principles of Swiss federalism were not at stake, or only insofar as federalism was to be strengthened. In any event, no one called this goal into question, at least as long as it was expressed in abstract terms.

With regard to the general context, the project was undertaken at a time of a strained budget. Therefore, no additional money would be available at all; tax increases were completely ruled out; and a fundamental reform of the tax system was out of the question, too. In short, the reform was not supposed to involve any costs for either the federal government or the cantons. With this argument it was possible to ward off any respective demands at an early stage. Referenda are often lost in Switzerland – and it was clear that a referendum would be inevitable – because too much is packed into a bill, which makes it rather expensive. The tendency to do so is embedded in consociational democracy as the Parliament must take into account as many interests as possible. However, in the case of a referendum, this can lead to an accumulation of opponents. Since the planned reform of federalism would significantly affect economic interests, it was important not to add other issues.

5. Negotiations

The negotiating process consisted of three phases that were distinct both in terms of the institutional structure and the task at hand. The first phase extended from the decision by the Federal Council to initiate the reform (1994), to the project team's report "Guidelines" and the respective consultation procedure (1996).[4] The second phase began with a new project team (1997) and ended when the team presented a comprehensive "Final Report", which was once again sent out for consultation, with the results published in March 2000. Next came the third phase during which the constitutional and legal documents were prepared. These were introduced in Parliament in November 2001; the referendum was held in 2004.

The aim of the first phase was to translate the framework of guidelines of the FDK into a definite project to reform the fiscal equalisation scheme and to ensure the necessary support. As the name suggests, the guidelines were only the basic ideas of what was still an abstract project, and the difficulties, as we know, are in the details not yet elaborated. Therefore, there was still a "veil of ignorance", albeit a thinner one.

The second phase was all about fleshing out the abstract principles. Now the distribution of competences and the financial flows had to be clarified. This was certainly the trickiest part of the project, since all the important interested organisations now got involved. The question was whether they could be satisfied with modest adjustments, or whether the very essence of the project would be jeopardised. The consultation process for this specified proposal clearly revealed some objections, which were largely offset by further modifications made during the third phase.

The institutional stakeholders, the FDK and the Swiss Finance Administration ("*Eidgenössischen Finanzverwaltung*" EFV), who had already set the agenda continued to lead negotiations. Both were able to provide for man-

4 Consultations are a regular part of the Swiss legislative process. Draft legislation, usually with explanations, is distributed among interested organisations (cantons, parties, civil society organisations) in order to gather evidence. Other interest groups and organisations can also participate as the process is very open. The evidence is analysed by the administration and usually summarised in a report. The result is not binding for the government; however, it often leads to amendments of the proposal. In the subsequent Message to Parliament of the government the most important results of the consultation are presented. They serve to highlight and take into account all potential criticism and objections so that the proposal will succeed both in Parliament and in the referendum. This instrument is typical of a political system based on consensus and consociationalism.

power from the secretariat of the FDK and staff from the EFV. Over time, other stakeholders got involved.

Meetings of the committees mentioned earlier were not open to the public, although, in Switzerland, it is generally not difficult to get information. The small size of the country means that "people know each other"; confidentiality is often not that important. On the other hand, there is a certain trust among insiders, which, admittedly, has suffered over the last few years. It should also be emphasised that for a long time the public showed little interest in this reform project.

Parliament, party members or interest-group representatives did not have any formal rights during the negotiations, but such processes are weakly formalised in Switzerland. Aside from the finance ministers, the senior civil servants of the departments of finance also played an important role. Financial experts were invited to provide expertise at different points. It was only with the consultation on the "guidelines" at the end of the first phase that broader public was formally given the opportunity to present their opinion. This is the usual practice in Switzerland.

5.1 Phase 1 (1994-1996): Preparing the "guidelines"

As mentioned above, the first phase extended from the decision by the government to initiate a review to the consultation procedure on the guidelines. The term "negotiations" cannot be understood literally here because this process was designed to reach a solution in an expert committee rather than through the usual political quarrels. The small circle of specialists described above set out to prepare a rough outline of the reform, by considering criticism of the existing fiscal equalisation scheme and the financial directors' "*Orientierungsrahmen*". However, the technical aspect of the process cannot clearly be separated from the political one: political interests left their marks on every stage of the process, and each participant was aware of them. The political system possesses a remarkable ability to modify a specific task according to the context. Here, the (cantonal) finance ministers initially did not get involved as representatives of cantonal interests but rather as experts on public finance (Freiburghaus, 1989). This allowed them to distance themselves from the demands of their colleagues in the other departments and then to present their solution as the only technically feasible one.

The EFV and the FDK readily agreed to establish a project team that included an executive committee and five working groups. The executive committee consisted of four EFV representatives and four cantonal finance ministers who had already been heavily involved in the project before. Parity was important. It was chaired by Ulrich Gygi, director of the EFV, who reported directly to the minister of finance. The project groups were to deal with the following topics:

- disentanglement of competences and financial flows between the federal government and the cantons;
- inter-cantonal collaboration and equalisation of burdens;
- clarification of the roles of and new funding mechanisms between the federal government and the cantons;
- strengthening of the self-financing capacity of the cantons;
- a new national equalisation scheme.

These issues were defined in the agenda-setting phase, the "*Orientierungsrahmen*" and the reports of the financial experts. They were, as it were, institutionalised by the working groups. In the course of the negotiating process, these issues were transformed only by expressing them in more specific terms (particular elements will be discussed below). These groups consisted of three to five senior federal and cantonal civil servants who were either financial experts or who were dealing with policies heavily affected by the reform, e.g. when a jointly exercised power was to be separated. Occasionally, academic experts would also take part. A project management team of three people – seconded by the SFA – oversaw the practical work.

The negotiations within the project team were characterised by Switzerland's "culture of consociationalism", which plays a central role in such committees. Since, in the end, there had to be a compromise acceptable to (almost) everyone, and since there was a whole host of veto points, it made little sense to go into the negotiations assuming an extreme and inflexible stance. Relying on this culture, negotiators signalled early where compromises seemed possible.

The potential lines of conflict were clear-cut and were largely centred on the issue of fiscal equalisation. On the one side, there were the representatives of the federal government who had to make sure that the project would not cause additional burdens for the Federal Treasury and that Parliament would continue to be able to control financial flows. The federal government was interested in horizontal equalisation among the cantons. On the other side, the cantons, in turn, were less enthusiastic. It would have been possible to leave horizontal financial equalisation within the financial flows between the federal government and the cantons, but then the important aim of simplification and transparency would not have been achieved. The cantons thus had the common goals of a continuing responsibility of the federal government for the fiscal equalisation scheme and of obtaining as much money as possible from it. Another cleavage manifested itself between the financially strong and financially weak cantons: the former wanted as little equalisation as possible, as this would be at their expense in one way or another, while the latter wanted substantial redistribution. However, the abstract nature of the discussion during this phase made it possible to confine these conflicts. Each party was always careful to keep or introduce instruments that could come in useful later on.

Yet, the new fiscal equalisation scheme was also dependent on the disentanglement of powers, as mentioned earlier. As long as this was discussed in abstract terms ("clarity", "simplicity", "stronger federalism", etc.), everyone agreed. That the actual implementation of this aim would be difficult was well known from past experience. What turned out to be a particularly tricky problem were externalities of services provided by the larger, central cantons, from which the smaller and peripheral cantons often benefited. The central cantons insisted on a stronger and legally binding financial participation of all beneficiaries. Another conflict arose between the central and the Alpine cantons, with both claiming special burdens. While the Alpine cantons had ample experience in jointly pushing their demands, the central cantons were not yet used to act accordingly. Also, the role of the cities in this process was still unclear, although they were particularly relevant in the more populated cantons.

The formal result was the report entitled "*Grundzüge*" (Guidelines), dated 1 February 1996 (Grundzüge, 1996). The document included 66 pages of text and a few appendices. The main results may be summarised as follows:

- The report emphasised the comprehensive nature of the planned reforms: federalism was to be strengthened and revitalised by means of a clear separation of powers according to the principle of subsidiarity and a fiscal equalisation determined to strengthen the financially weak cantons and compensate individual cantons for special burdens.
- All in all, the "self-financing capacity" of the cantons was to be strengthened. They should be enabled to finance more responsibilities from their "own" funds, i.e. their own revenue as well as general grants.
- The separation of powers was supposed to increase efficiency thus releasing additional funds at the same time that would be available for fiscal equalisation. The potential savings were estimated to be 3 billion Swiss francs. This estimate had no reliable basis; however, it provided the means – at least in the minds of the actors involved – for compensating the "losers", thus turning a zero sum game into a positive sum game.
- Fifty areas of joint policy-making were to be scrutinised more closely. Of these, 21 were to fall exclusively within the jurisdiction of the cantons and 8 within that of the federal government. In these areas, the existing earmarked transfers were to be discontinued. When complete disentanglement of powers was not possible, a functional division would take place. This meant that the federal government was to limit itself to framework legislation in that field. Furthermore, instruments of New Public Management were to be implemented (contract management, global budgets, etc.).
- In the past, the differences in financial strength and burdens of the cantons were equalised by the same instruments. They were now to be separated.

- The economic strength of the cantons varied considerably and so did, as a result, the potential tax revenue. By means of "resource equalisation", a politically defined harmonisation and a minimum level of resources was to be achieved. A "financial capacity index" that could not be manipulated was to form the fundament of calculation, based on the potential tax revenue determined according to standardised criteria.
- The equalisation of resources, on the other hand, was to be achieved through two instruments: the financial capacity of the cantons was to be harmonised through transfers from the wealthier to the poorer cantons. If this did not amount to a previously defined minimum level of resources, the federal government was to fund the rest. The main parameters had not yet been determined at this point; however, the models calculated in the "Guidelines" assumed a minimal fiscal base for each canton of 87% of the average level.
- The cantons bearing a particular burden, such as road construction in the Alpine cantons, were to be supported through grants by the federal government.
- Specific burdens were also borne by the densely-populated central cantons. They provided services, like universities, hospitals, or public transport, which were used by people from neighbouring cantons. Such tasks were to be fulfilled in inter-cantonal collaboration with burden sharing. All cantons were to be compelled to do this (obligatory contracting).

At this stage of the process the result was not particularly controversial within the project team. Each representative saw its interests temporarily protected. Usually, only quite detailed constitutional or legislative projects are subjected to consultation. In this case this procedure was already used for the "Guidelines". In this way, the project was put to its first political test so that the actors involved could more easily anticipate potential objections. Over 50 groups – cantonal governments, political parties and civil society organisations – were invited to participate, while another 70 interested organisations or groups presented opinions on their own initiative, which were also taken into account in the analysis. Comprising only 40 pages of text, the report on the results of the consultation procedure (Eidgenössisches Finanzdepartement, 1996) was comparatively brief. Those consulted largely approved of the concept. Only the federalism sceptics of the Social Democratic Party were unhappy with the way things were going: they wanted as many powers as possible to be transferred to the federal government and they argued against higher general grants as they mistrusted the cantons. Others primarily presented arguments that served to protect their vested interests. With regard to the separation of specific powers, those actors raised their voice that had hitherto been rather influential in a policy field and now feared to loose influence, such as lobbying organisations on the federal level. It was already evident that the greatest resistance would come from this side.

Inter-cantonal collaboration with sharing of burdens was approved. However, the high degree of complexity of such arrangements was criticised. The peripheral cantons emphasised their services for the central ones (like recreation). As could be expected, obligatory contracting was disputed by the smaller cantons. The equalisation of resources was in principle met with approval, although the affluent cantons warned against too high burdens. Various sides criticised the proposed index of resources: the poorer cantons argued that the envisaged equalising effect would be too weak. The agglomerations underlined the special burdens they had to bear (such as coping with problematic groups of society). All in all, no one was surprised by the results of the consultation procedure, and those engaged in the project could live with them. Yet, it was now important to get on board those forces that would be pivotal in the referendum.

5.2 Phase 2 (1997-2000): Fleshing out the "guidelines" and the final report of the project team

In 1996, the insider group of financial experts could, by and large, agree on a revised fiscal equalisation scheme and the redistribution of powers. However, during the consultation procedure it had become obvious that the "Guidelines" could not simply be translated into legislation because too many objections had been raised. In addition, the "Guidelines" had deliberately left open a number of details so that later a broader consensus could be reached through concessions. Overall, it was obvious that this project would lead to far-reaching constitutional amendments that would have to be approved of by voters and cantons in the obligatory referendum. Therefore, at least half of the cantons had to be won over. In consequence, a greater variety of stakeholders had to be involved in the imminent phase of specification. It was only in this phase that bargaining became dominant and the project inevitably ran the risk of losing its clear-cut profile.

This phase was very much organised like the previous one. First a reorganised project team fleshed out the "Guidelines". On 31 March 1999, this team presented a 250-page "Final Report" to the Federal Council. Next, the government initiated another consultation procedure, this time, with more than 150 participants. The opinions presented were analyzed and summarised by the Finance Administration, resulting in probably the most comprehensive consultation report ever: published on 31 March 2000, it comprised more than 250 pages.

The new project team invited a greater number of stakeholders to take part, especially experts from the policy fields affected by the separation of powers. However, the basic structure remained the same: At the top was a political steering committee made up of three representatives each from the federal government and the cantons. On the federal side, these were the Minster of Finance, the Minister of the Interior and the Minister of Foreign Affairs. On the side of the cantons, the president of the FDK, the president of the KdK and another representative took part. This steering committee supervised the project, assigned tasks to the working groups, assessed interim results, provided new momentum and finally summarised the results for the Federal Council. It also decided on issues the working groups could not agree on.

The practical work in the project was supervised by a executive committee, the membership structure of which, too, was based on parity. It was chaired by the director of the FDK, while six more federal representatives came from the departments and ministries affected. The cantons delegated three FDK representatives and four more representatives from other ministries. In addition, there were also five representatives with observer status (the Federal Chancellery, the municipalities, the KdK, among others). Management on a day-to-day basis lay in the hands of a project management team consisting of four individuals – three from the EFV and one from one of the cantons. Work in detail was assigned to eight project groups with equal numbers of federal and cantonal representatives, respectively. These were mostly higher-ranking civil servants from the departments affectted. Three groups dealt with cross-cutting issues (subsidiarity and new forms of funding between the federal government and the cantons, inter-cantonal collaboration, financial equalisation in a narrow sense) and five dealt with specific policies (social welfare/social policy, transportation and energy, education, the environment/forestry/agriculture/housing, justice, and security). Later on, another working group responsible for the overall balance of fiscal equalisation was set up. These (small) working groups collaborated with federal and cantonal departments, called in outside experts and consulted with interested parties.

The basic aim was to transform the reform as defined by the "Guidelines" into draft legislation. This had various implications: First, a large number of parameters could now be adjusted. Moreover, it was now time for calculating the (financial) impact of different configurations on various budgets (federal government and 26 cantons) and policies. At the same time, it was clear that the result had to be widely acceptable even if this would include compromises regarding some of the principles. The work of those groups dealing with the disentanglement of powers was particularly difficult because it often entailed a fundamental reform of the existing structure of jurisdiction. This would meet with opposition from the affected stakeholders. Finally, legal experts had to transform the whole project into constitutional and legislative amendments. Surprisingly, all this was accomplished within two years.

Since the minutes are not publicly available, it is not possible to trace the behaviour of actors and the dynamics of the process in detail. In general, the same lines of conflict existed as during the initial phase, except that discussions no longer focused on principles, but rather on specific changes in terms of competences and financial flows – and that negotiations no longer just included financial experts, but a large number of stakeholders, now that a wide range of policies was under consideration. As a consequence, the FDK as main representative of cantonal interests somewhat lost influence with the "Cantonal Government Conference" (the KdK) becoming a new important stakeholder and coordinator. Below are a few of the most important conflicts documented by the changes in the project.

- Separation of powers proved to be extremely difficult, since affected actors who opposed a fundamental change had formed networks based on the existing interlocked structures. They included lobby groups operating at the federal level, and the cantonal authorities that wanted to continue to be funded directly by the federal government.
- In particular policy fields, lobby groups claimed that it would be intolerable if standards would vary from canton to canton, with different services provided (such as those for the disabled). They felt that the cantons wanted to save money at the expense of vulnerable groups. The spectre of "1000 wheelchair users on the *Bundesplatz*" was conjured up. This argument also corresponded to the general position of the Social Democrats and gave it additional weight.
- Up to this point, the plan had been to compensate the special burdens of the Alpine regions. In the meantime, however, the urban areas had successfully claimed that they, too, had special burdens to bear, in particular with respect to particular population groups concentrated in urban areas (the unemployed, asylum seekers, alcoholics, etc.). These burdens also had to be compensated for.

The formal and substantial result of these negotiations was the 1999 document titled „*Der Neue Finanzausgleich zwischen Bund und Kantonen*" (The New Fiscal Equalisation Scheme between the Federal Government and the Cantons). The most important substantial proposals, especially those that deviate from the "*Grundzüge*" are outlined below:

- Now, 15 competences were to be assigned to the cantons and six to the federal government, while 17 areas were to be partially disentangled. For the reasons outlined above, the disentanglement was not as far-reaching as originally planned.
- Sixteen competences were to remain shared; however, new forms of intergovernmental coordination and compensation were to be tested (such as New Public Management, contracts, general grants, etc.).
- Nine competences were to be exercised through inter-cantonal collaboration with sharing of burdens. The federal government would be able to declare such agreements as generally binding, i.e. it should be able to force the cantons into compliance (obligatory contracting). The respective pro-

cedural hurdles, however, were set quite high. Furthermore, it was suggested that this kind of inter-cantonal law should override cantonal law.
- The fiscal equalisation scheme was largely designed as outlined in the "Guidelines". Nine hundred million Swiss francs were to be redistributed among the cantons; the cornerstones for the equalisation mechanism, however, were to be determined by Parliament.
- Alpine cantons as well as urban cantons were to benefit from the compensation of burdens. The former fall under "geographic-topographic" scheme, while the latter fall under" social-demographic" scheme.

The entire package was expected to increase efficiency worth 2 – 2.5 billion Swiss francs without cutting public services. The document also contained tables with calculations demonstrating what each Canton could expect in terms of finances. Only five cantons would see increasing burdens (net contributors). The increase varied from 11 francs per capita in the canton of Waadt to 172 francs per capita in the canton of Basel-City.

The appendix included a legislative proposal for the amendment of the constitution (eight new or substantially amended articles and a few other modifications regarding the fiscal equalisation scheme in a narrower sense, 22 new or amended constitutional articles relating to reallocation of tasks). In addition, the appendix included a first proposal for federal legislation on fiscal equalisation as well as a template for an inter-cantonal framework agreement on collaboration and the respective burden sharing.

This much more detailed project was now again be subjected to a comprehensive consultation procedure. This time, 58 "official participants" were contacted and another approximately 160 interested parties presented opinions on their own initiative. In principal, the project was still largely approved. With a few exceptions, there was no criticism on the basic elements. Disputes continued along the lines that had already become evident in the consultation procedures on the "Guidelines". However, some additional significant objections were raised:

- The social welfare organisations were firmly opposed to giving more power to the cantons in the field of social policy.
- Fundamental political criticism focused on inter-cantonal collaboration. It was argued that this would lead to cumbersome, complicated, potentially undemocratic governance at the expense of the parliaments. Moreover, the federal government was denied the right to force the cantons into joint decision-making.
- The left-wing parties and organisations preferred tax harmonisation over the envisaged equalisation of resources.
- The financial and statistical bases of the "resources index" were also criticised. For some, the impact of equalisation was too high, for others, too low.

- The symmetrical design of burden equalisation (for Alpine and urban cantons) proved to be clever, as most of the cantons could now expect subsidies under one or the other heading. Of course, criticism was levelled at the indicators to be used, with each canton trying to pull the blanket over to its side.

In summary, the consultation procedure proved that the project was still on the right track and that major amendments would not be necessary. It also revealed the core elements that would potentially meet with serious opposition. Yet, in this phase of adjusting and fine-tuning, the initial abstract principles remained valid and they now indicated where modifications could easily be made and where they would threaten the substance. Furthermore, it was useful that the various elements were closely linked and almost impossible to separate, so that individual parts could not be broken off from the whole.

5.3 Phase 3 (2000-2001): Preparing the legislative proposals and the message to Parliament

All in all, the final report by the project team of the second phase served as the basis for the final proposals. It was worthwhile, however, to take into account the important objections raised by the participants during the consultation procedure and the reflections of the financial experts. Still, the number of actors involved was limited. Yet, the various positions were now known, and an attempt had to be made both to save the essence of the project and to make concessions to "dangerous" interest groups. The executive committee proved to be too cumbersome and was now replaced by a "*Petit Comité*" which also included the increasingly important cities. In Switzerland, "*Petit Comité*" generally means that key decision makers resolve controversial points behind closed doors. The existing working groups were reorganised and focused on the remaining controversial points. In addition, ten more expert reports on various sensitive issues were commissioned (see the lists in Bundesrat, 2001: 2550-2551).

The formal result was the „*Botschaft zur Neugestaltung des Finanzausgleichs und der Aufgaben zwischen Bund und Kantonen (NFA)*“ (Message to Parliament on the Reform of the Fiscal Equalisation Scheme and the Allocation of Tasks between the Federal Government and the Cantons) from 14 November 2001 (Bundesrat, 2001). This 270-page document not only retraced the entire process to date, but also explained the basic principles as well as the details of the reform right up to the individual constitutional and legislative articles complete with tables and calculations.

These results need not be presented in detail, as they correspond to a large extent to the "Final Report". Here are a few of the most important developments:

- The index of resources, essential for equalisation, was revised once again and improved. Quantitatively, only estimates were possible, since not all basic statistical elements were available at the time to carry out the calculation. The complexity of this formula was now so high that every canton could find a little screw to turn in its favour.
- The equalisation of fiscal resources ("*Ressourcenausgleich*") continued to consist of a horizontal component (between cantons) and a vertical component (between the federal government and the cantons). While until then both sides had contributed an equal share, the federal government was now to bear the heavier burden. The main parameters were to be set and modified by parliament. Thus, it was not yet clear which canton would finally win or loose. So there was still a "veil of ignorance" that would later be lifted by the parliament. With this, the MPs gained an essential power, which certainly helped to win them over to the project.
- The indexes for compensation of burdens ("*Lastenausgleich*") of the Alpine and urban cantons were comprehensively revised to respond to various objections. Here, too, there were many screws that could be turned.
- As regards the separation of competences and criticism relating to it, only one example of a compromise shall be given: while individual payments for the disabled were to fall to the federal government (Disability Insurance), the residences and facilities (collective services) would be transferred to the cantons. To prevent them from "saving money off the backs of the disabled", the federal government was to determine detailed objectives for such facilities. In doing so, the democratically constituted cantons were denied the ability to continue to implement these policies independently. However, against the powerful lobby groups for the disabled insiting on a clearer division of competences was hardly possible.
- Despite the criticism of the participants of the consultation procedure, the Message insisted that the federal government should be able to impose horizontal collaboration and sharing of expenditures on defiant cantons. The federal government had to take into account the requests from the central cantons, which complained about the free-riding tactics of the others. But the hurdles for this kind of federal coercion were now very high and opponents could hope that it would never be applied – which is the case until today.
- A new instrument was the compensation of special hardship ("*Härteausgleich*") of poorer cantons, which, despite all modifications, would receive less under the new system – indeed, because they had profited from the old system. Now, 430 million Swiss francs a year were provided, with two-thirds funded by the federal government and one-third by the cantons. This was to be for a limited time only, and parliament would periodically decide how to go on.

As a consequence of these modifications, not much remained of the increased efficiency envisaged earlier. Had it actually ever existed, it was now used up and spent to buy consent.

6. Ratification

The NFA was approved of in two steps: first, both houses of parliament had to vote in favour of it. Then the (mandatory) vote by the people and the cantons followed.

6.1 Parliamentary decision

The *„Bundesbeschluss zur Neugestaltung des Finanzausgleichs und der Aufgaben zwischen Bund und Kantonen“* (Federal Decision on Financial Equalisation Reform and the Reallocation of Tasks) of November 2001, which was sent to the parliament with the "Message" mentioned earlier, and the fiscal equalisation bill were dealt with and passed by the Council of States in 2002 and the National Council in 2003. The bill led to intense debate in both houses of parliament – initially within the respective committees, then in the plenums. The overall project was mostly deemed positive, both its attempt to strengthen federalism and the designated instruments. After various disagreements between the chambers were resolved, the final vote was held on 3 October 2003: the National Council voted 126 to 54 in favour, while the Council of States voted 38 to 2 in favour. The nays came from the Left-wing/Green camp and from the cantons that would become net contributors. In the National Council, the leftists moved for having the entire field of social policy excluded from the bill but without success. On the issue of horizontal financial equalisation, the frontline ran right through the conservative camp: parts of the People's Party and the Liberals found that the burden placed on the financially strong cantons was too high.

Both chambers discussed various changes and some were adopted. After the disagreements between the chambers were resolved, two substantial amendments remained:

- The conditions under which an accord between cantons can be declared universally binding were made more restrictive: the areas in which this was to be possible were listed, and parliament retained the right to decide, which in the original government bill would have been the responsibility of the Federal Council.
- The protection of the financially strong cantons against "plundering" was reinforced by the argument of the importance of inter-cantonal tax com-

petition. The bill had provided for the payments of the net-contributor cantons into the equalisation scheme to be approximately as high as those of the federal government. The former were now limited to 80% of the latter.

In the end, the separation of powers turned out to be much less extreme than it had been hoped for at the beginning; it was, as shown, smoothed in the course of the process. Of the previously shared competences, six were assigned to the federal government and ten to the cantons; nine competences were to be exercised through inter-cantonal cooperation. Moreover, there are 17 competences that are exercised jointly by the federal government and the cantons.

The long negotiations involving all the important interest groups bore fruit: no one was able to form a majority or a strong minority in parliament that could fundamentally fight the reform. But then came the decisive step: the referendum.

6.2 The referendum

In the introduction, the question was raised why such a complex draft finally overcame the hurdle of the referendum so elegantly. The process as such provides some aspects of the answer: the patient search for acceptable compromise. Before taking a closer look at the referendum, some general information on direct democracy in Switzerland seems to be necessary.

6.2.1 The instruments of direct democracy in Switzerland

The referendum is the most important right of political self-determination of the people of Switzerland. Fifty thousand eligible voters can initiate a referendum on a bill passed by parliament. If the referendum takes places, only a simple majority of yes votes is sufficient to pass a law. To amend the federal constitution, a referendum is mandatory. In this case a double majority of cantons and voters is required. A canton vote is the majority of popular votes in the respective canton. This means, among other things, that a majority of smaller cantons with a minority of the population can reject an amendment bill, even if the majority of the population throughout the country approves of it. This way, minorities are protected in Swiss federalism.

Direct democracy has been practiced for a long time. The mandatory constitutional referendum has existed since the founding of the federal state in 1848, while the optional legislative referendum was introduced in 1874. At the time, 30,000 eligible voters could resort to a referendum; today there have to be 50,000. Since then, however, the population has more than doubled, and in 1971 women, too, got the right to vote. Therefore, it has become easier to resort to a referendum. The number of optional referendums has increased significantly; nowadays, there are between two and three every year at the federal level. Over time, the popular rights have continuously been expanded, such as the right to initiate a partial revision of the constitution of 1891 or the referendum on international treaties of 1921.

These instruments of direct democracy have reshaped the political system of Switzerland. All legislative procedures and constitutional reforms take place, so to speak, in the shadow of the referendum. Therefore, the whole legislative process – from the first administrative review to the readings in parliament – is always not only about the goals of a bill and how to achieve them but also about whether or not there will be a referendum later on and what its chances of passing would be. The most important effect of the popular rights lies in their indirect effect on the process of constitutional negotiation.

Referendum democracy in particular has three effects: Firstly, high-flying, far-reaching, reform bills full of abstract ideas and ideals will have few chances to be accepted in a referendum. Pragmatism, small steps and the art of the possible characterise the political process. The system of permanent all-party government reinforces this trend towards incrementalism. Secondly, all interest groups that potentially are capable to resort to a referendum and to win a campaign are included in the political processes at an early stage. They take part in expert groups and are invited to provide input into the consultations. Thirdly, these interests do not only take part in negotiations, their interests are to be considered substantially. If any groups, even small ones, feel disadvantaged, the bill is likely to fail. People feel some kind of solidarity with minorities that are fighting for their rights. This is why it is often necessary to bring those groups over to the winning side through concessions. As a consequence, lawmaking in Switzerland requires the art of reaching compromises in protracted negotiating processes.

Yet, does this not lead to seemingly endless processes? Are reforms not forever procrastinated? As a matter of fact, the processes are indeed very long. The NFA reform took almost twenty years. However, moving slowly does have its advantages, since it gives civil society the time to solve problems in autonomy, thus reducing state intervention. In addition, moving slowly in politics has advantages for the economy, since investors know what to expect. If, therefore, liberalism and conservatism enjoy a stronger position in Switzerland than elsewhere, it is because there is an institutional bias in their favour.

But does the need to include all interest groups not inevitably inflate the state sector and public spending? Apparently not, as is revealed by a comparison of Switzerland's public expenditure quota with that of other countries. All Swiss stakeholders know that if something costs Swiss taxpayers a lot more in the end, the project will fail at the referendum stage. This instils a strong sense of discipline. The Swiss do not like paying taxes and that is why they have included tax rates in the constitution: increases are only possible with a double majority of the people and the cantons.

Yet, do not many constitutional initiatives destabilise the political system? Absolutely not, since usually the people agree to proposals made by parliament and the government – exactly because both try to anticipate what the people want. In order to avoid a referendum, during the preparation of bills and the readings in parliamentary committees compromises are made until roughly 80% of the MPs feel they can support the bill. Since 1848, there have been 175 popular initiatives for constitutional amendments. These were rejected in 90% of the cases. During the same period, there were 379 mandatory and optional referendums. In two-thirds of all cases, the parliamentary proposal was approved of. The popular trust in the authorities is therefore intact.

Just as everywhere else, people do not govern themselves in Switzerland; they leave the real work to the political elite. However, the people retain an almost unrestricted right to object; they are the final authority, the sovereign. And, as mentioned earlier, this right has serious implications even if it is not used. The *vox populi* does not make it easy for decision-makers but it is very useful for the system: direct democracy hardly alienates those governed from those governing. It creates a kind of pre-stabilised legitimacy.

6.2.2 The NFA referendum

All of this was evident during the referendum on the NFA. The federal decision had to be submitted to the people and the cantons since they included constitutional amendments. People went to the polls on 28 November 2004. After an overwhelming majority in the two houses of parliament had approved of the bill, and only the canton of Zug was officially against it, it appeared that its adoption was guaranteed. However, there were two complications: On 16 May 2004, the people had rejected a complex financial package, on which – for the first time in history – the cantons had successfully resorted to a referendum. This was taken to be a bad omen for the NFA bill. The Federal Minister of Finance appointed thus a distinguished expert and federalist as a "delegate for cantonal financial matters" to the Finance Administration to provide the cantons with an additional voice. The Social Democrats spoke out against the proposal but hardly cared to organise a convincing no-campaign. Heavy opposition arose only from associations of disabled and social welfare organisations, who raised the spectre of social exclusion.

As usual, the bill was presented to the Swiss in the so-called "*Bundesbüchlein*" ("federal booklet"), a brochure summarising the bill, the government's position and that of parliament, as well as the most important arguments against it as presented by the opponents. Only seven pages long, it introduced this comprehensive package to the people. The 27 constitutional amendments were attached. The referendum campaign was lacklustre; the turnout at 35.5% was low. This, however, meant that it was mostly politically informed and interested voters convinced by the arguments provided who went to the polls. The reform benefited from this. The bill was approved of with over 64% of the votes. Only three of the six cantons burdened as net contributors in fiscal equalisation voted against it (Schwyz, Zug and Nidwalden).

An analysis of the vote showed that a majority of people casting a vote had confidence in the bill as it had been prepared by parliament and the government. Even a majority of generally left-wing voters voted "yes". Age, education, gender, language and residence (urban/rural) hardly played any role, which was a great success. The no-votes were higher in the net contributor cantons and by people who followed the arguments of the associations of the disabled. The amendments to the federal structure (strengthening horizontal collaboration) had hardly any impact, neither positive nor negative. The principle of a stronger equalisation between "rich" and "poor" was mostly approved.

7. Evolution after the referendum

The reform led to changes to many federal laws and regulations. Hardly any policy was left untouched. This, of course, also applied to the cantons. If the amendments to federal laws had been lumped together with the constitutional amendments to form a single package, this would have demanded too much from citizens, which often leads to rejection. Yet, if it had not been done, people would have run the risk of selling a "pig in a poke", i.e. of leaving the people in the dark. This could also have lead to failure.

How to deal with this dilemma? First, only the constitutional amendments and the new fiscal equalisation scheme were subjected to the referendum, but at the same time, future legislative reforms were outlined. This was a tightrope walk, but a successful one: two years later no referendum was called against the implementation legislation. Another year later the third legislative package came along dealing with the detailed terms of resource and burden equalisation. Up to this point the definite numbers were not yet fixed, but now it came down to francs and centimes each canton would receive and pay. Yet, even then, there was no call for a referendum; the political caravan had already moved on. On 1 January 2008, the reform came into effect. There are, in fact, ongoing disputes, especially from the net contributors and the urban centres, but for the time being it can be warded off with the argument that it is still too early to assess the results. In addition, it is argued that there are some parameters that could be adjusted by political decision. However, no fundamental challenge to the new system has yet been made.

8. Reasons for the successful implementation of the NFA

How can the clear majority of the people and the cantons in favour of this very ambitious federalism reform be explained? Was there a positive climate for a reform in 2004? Was the state coffer overflowing? Did the people dare a giant leap forward? Did Switzerland even have a charismatic finance minister? None of these reasons apply. The conditions for success are to be found in the practice of everyday politics and in the characteristics of the political institutions in Switzerland. Much has already been said, therefore, the explanation will be summarised in ten points:

1. From past experiences, Swiss politicians had learned the lesson that federalism reforms trying to avoid financial issues are doomed to fail. Therefore, this time the bull was grabbed by the horns and money became the central issue. The redistribution of competences was no longer the point of the exercise but rather a necessary prerequisite for a new form of fiscal equalisation. In this way, a fundamental discussion about which level was responsible for what could be avoided and, at the same time, the agenda was simplified. Other and more comprehensive issues of federalism were referred to the total revision of the federal constitution. What was new and unfamiliar, was the power of the federal level to coerce cantons into cooperation with horizontal burden sharing; although high hurdles ensured that this instrument was not taken too seriously.
2. The need and urgency to completely revise the existing fiscal equalisation scheme were undisputed because its weaknesses were obvious. The federal government and the cantons were caught up in a tangle of fees, allotments and subsidies. The lines between incentives and redistribution were blurred. In the end, it was hard to determine who exactly was benefiting, and sometimes it even appeared to be the financially strong cantons. The cantons could manipulate the mechanism through their own financial policies. In addition, the disparity between the cantons had increased over the years. The tax burden in the financially weak cantons continued to increase, the affluent cantons lowered their tax rates, and therefore, the call for substantial tax harmonisation became increasingly louder. The liberal and conservative parties did all to avoid this solution. Therefore, there was no opposition to reform as such from either the Left or the Right, as each side could hope for some advantage.
3. The debate focussed on a few central ideas on the reform of fiscal equalisation: clarity and simplicity, separation of powers and financial flows,

objective determination of fiscal capacity, separation of general equalisation and compensation for special burdens as well as more autonomy for both levels of government. These principles were supported both by experts and federal and cantonal finance ministers. Or more precisely: the finance ministers agreed on these principles and allowed eminent professors of economy to confirm that they were the right. Therefore, who could object?

4. Rawls's "veil of ignorance" was used to ensure fairness. The above-mentioned principles were agreed upon early in the process, when no one could yet know the impact they would have on the individual actors. An additional safeguard was applied: to allay fears and to ward off any envy, the new fiscal equalisation was to be cost-neutral on the one hand for the federal government and, on the other hand, for all the cantons together. This way, the killer argument of tax increases lost its credibility and died down.
5. Translating these central ideas into actual policy occurred in four phases and, as in mountain climbing, step after step, with fixation of intermediary result. Each of these steps took one or two years, and each time, the project team and thus the number of participants grew in size. In the final phase, over 100 specialists took part in the effort. Many consultations were held with roughly 200 contributions each. They indicated general approval but also made clear where serious resistance would possibly arise. This could then be taken into account when the central ideas were fleshed out.
6. How was it possible to bring the central ideas, the inner logic, through this political process largely unscathed? This required institutional protection. From the beginning, there was a core group consisting of the Federal Minister of Finance and some of his senior civil servants on the one side and the finance ministers of the influential cantons on the other. This "Council of Elders" with equal representation played a decisive role in the ever-growing project team and served as a political steering committee. As experts in state finances, its members constituted an "epistemic community" against which financial laypersons would have had difficulty arguing. In addition, the cantonal finance ministers had their own vested interest in reform: more unconditional funding from the federal government meant that it was to be included in their budgets.
7. Nonetheless, there were losers or groups that presented themselves as such. In order to get a majority, some of them had to be brought on board. Three examples shall be given: 1) the disabled were accommodated in that the federal government continued to determine minimum requirements for facilities; 2) Alpine regions were no longer the only ones compensated for special burdens, but also the urban centres; 3) hardship compensation ensured approval of those cantons who found

themselves in a worse situation under the new formula. In all three instances, the resistance of powerful opponents was reduced or broken.

8. Most of these concessions cost money, although cost-neutrality had been promised. So where to get the money from? The clearer separation of powers would make public services more efficient and thereby less expensive. According to estimates, between two and three billion Swiss francs could be saved. This (fictitious) money could then be used to buy off potential opponents. The plan worked out, and cost-neutrality could by and large be achieved.
9. When this carefully composed package was introduced in parliament, it had to be protected from being undone. To do this, members of parliament had to be given the opportunity to decide on a few crucial parameters, like the level of equalisation among the cantons, the contribution of the federal government in order to guarantee a minimum budget for the poorer cantons, or the size of the special funds. Since these issues were, and would be decided in the future by parliament, it was satisfied and approved.
10. Since tax-payers had not been burdened, since ten cantons became net contributors and 16 net recipients, since the three major middle-class parties as well as the federal business association "Économie Suisse" agreed, the negotiation process was followed by a low-key referendum campaign resulting in a low turnout and a clear positive vote. Only the net contributors Zug, Schwyz and Nidwalden said "No". Sympathy for these "rich" cantons was limited.

So how can the project's success be explained? There are, as shown, many reasons. However, what was crucial was a long, carefully planned process in which, on the one hand, the fundamental principles could be maintained while, on the other hand, a majority could be won through concessions. The design of this process seemed to be "intelligent", but no one designed or directed it. A small group of members of government, civil servants and experts simultaneously played the roles of father, midwife and godfather, and accompanied the child until it had grown up. These people had known each other for a long time, had often worked together before and shared similar views on the state, society and finances. They had political experience at all levels of government and knew the peculiarities and moods of the people. Keeping this kind of committee small enough to be able to work informally and still make it more or less representative belongs to the highest art of Swiss consociational democracy: the Social Democrat from French Switzerland must be part of the group just like the Catholic from Central Switzerland and the Liberal from Thurgau. Therefore, few *viri probati* are chosen who each wear several hats at once, so that everyone feels represented. It may be a privilege of a small country to entrust some of its problems to committees that operate like a class reunion.

References

Bundesrat (2001): Botschaft zur Neugestaltung des Finanzausgleichs und der Aufgaben zwischen Bund und Kantonen (NFA) vom 14. November 2001.

Bussmann, Werner (1986): Mythos und Wirklichkeit der Zusammenarbeit im Bundesstaat. Patentrezepte oder Sackgasse? Res publica helvetica. Bd. 19. Bern: Haupt.

Eidgenössisches Finanzdepartement (1996): Der neue Finanzausgleich zwischen Bund und Kantonen. Grundzüge. Bericht über die Vernehmlassungsergebnisse. Bern, 23 October 1996.

Eidgenössische Finanzverwaltung (1991): Finanzausgleichsbilanz. Bilanz des bundesstaatlichen Finanzausgleichs. Bern, Mai 1991.

Finanzdirektorenkonferenz (1992): Finanzausgleichsbilanz und Orientierungsrahmen für die künftige Ausgestaltung des bundesstaatlichen Finanzausgleichs. Brief an den Vorsteher des Eidgenössischen Finanzdepartements vom 25. Oktober 1992.

Freiburghaus, Dieter (1989): Interfaces zwischen Wissenschaft und Politik. In: Schweizerisches Jahrbuch für Politische Wissenschaft 29. Bern: Haupt, 267-277.

Freiburghaus, Dieter (2001): Die Schweiz Der Föderalismus nach der neuen Bundesverfassung und die Mitwirkung der Kantone an der Außenpolitik. In: Europäisches Zentrum für Föderalismusforschung Tübingen (ed.): Jahrbuch des Föderalismus 2001. Baden-Baden: Nomos Verlagsgesellschaft, 296-305.

Freiburghaus, Dieter (2005): Bedingungen für eine gelingende Föderalismusreform: Die Neugestaltung des Finanzausgleichs und der Aufgabenteilung zwischen Bund und Kantonen in der Schweiz. In: Europäisches Zentrum für Föderalismusforschung Tübingen (ed.): Jahrbuch des Föderalismus 2005. Baden-Baden: Nomos Verlagsgesellschaft, 506-515.

Freiburghaus, Dieter/Buchli, Felix (2003): Die Entwicklung des Föderalismus und der Föderalismusdiskussion in der Schweiz von 1874 bis 1964. In: Swiss Political Science Review 9, (1), 29-56.

Freiburghaus, Dieter/Zehnder, Vital (2003): Horizontale Kooperation zwischen den Kantonen und die „systematisch-pragmatische Zusammenarbeit" in der Zentralschweiz. In: Europäisches Zentrum für Föderalismusforschung Tübingen (ed.): Jahrbuch des Föderalismus 2003. Baden-Baden: Nomos Verlagsgesellschaft, 270-283.

Frey, René L. et al. (1994): La péréquation financière entre la Confédération et les cantons. Expertise rélative aux aides financières et indemnités de la Confédération en faveur des cantons mandatés par l'Administration fédérale des finances et la Conférence des directeurs cantonaux des finances. Berne: EDMZ.

Frey, René L. (2001): Ziel und Wirkungsanalyse des Neuen Finanzausgleichs. Bericht zu Händen der EFV und der KdK. Basel, 14 May 2001.

Grundzüge (1996): Der neue Finanzausgleich zwischen Bund und Kantonen, Grundzüge. Bericht der vom Eidg. Finanzdepartement und der Konferenz der kantonalen Finanzdirektoren gemeinsam getragenen Projektorganisation. Bern und Luzern, 1 February 1996.

Imboden, Max (1964): Helvetisches Malaise. In: Polis, Evangelische Zeitbuchreihe 20.

Klöti, Ulrich/Nüssli, Kurt (1987): Die Neuverteilung der Aufgaben zwischen Bund und Kantonen. Ein Reformversuch zwischen staatspolitischen Idealen und finanziellen Interessen. Zürich: Forschungsstelle Politikwissenschaft der Universität Zürich.

Why Federal Reform Succeeded in Switzerland*

Gérard Wettstein

1. Introduction

The Reform of Swiss federalism began in 1991 with the initial analyses on the effectiveness of fiscal equalisation within a federal state prepared by the Swiss Finance Administration (*Eidgenössische Finanzverwaltung* – EFV).[1] The results of this inquiry were sobering and led to additional analyses and follow-up work at both the political and the expert level. The Financial Directors Conference (*Finanzdirektoren-Konferenz*; FDK)[2], in turn, prepared its own report to confirm the results concerning fiscal equalisation, the so-called "*Orientierungsrahmen 1992*" (framework of guidelines; FDK, 1994). Subsequently, the EFV and FDK jointly commissioned a report to be prepared by experts to shed a critical light on fiscal equalisation at that time and to submit reform proposals (see Frey et al., 1994).[3] In this way, the essential preliminary work was done. In 1994, the Federal Council (federal government) launched the first project team to reform the federal fiscal equalisation scheme.

The reform contained four mutually dependent and complementary areas:

1. the division of powers and finances between the federation and the cantons;
2. the institutionalized cooperation between the cantons, including rules for sharing the burdens of expenditures;
3. new ways of cooperating and sharing financial responsibilities between the Federal Government and the cantons;

* This article is an updated version of an earlier publication which appeared in „leges – Mitteilungsblatt der Schweizerischen Gesellschaft für Gesetzgebung und der Schweizerischen Evaluationsgesellschaft", 2002 (2), 35-54.

1 The EFV is an office within the Swiss Department of Finance.

2 Members of the FDK are all the cantonal financial directors (cantonal "ministers"). The directors' conferences help with the lateral coordination of each political portfolio (social, environment, education, justice, etc.). Moreover, an important goal is to speak as one, thus carrying more weight at the federal level.

3 Regarding the preparation of the NFA submission: Botschaft des Bundesrates vom 14. November 2001 zur Neugestaltung des Finanzausgleichs und der Aufgaben (NFA), Bundesblatt 2002, 2314ff.

4. a newly designed fiscal equalisation scheme aimed at eliminating the disparities that exist between the cantons (equalisation of resources) and compensating for the excessive special burdens the cantons are confronted with (equalisation of geographic and socio-demographic burdens).

The first three areas, in particular, involved policies relevant for the territorial organisation of the state and went beyond a reform merely motivated by financial policy.

2. The reform process

In 1994, the EFV, represented by its Directorate, and the cantonal politicians, represented by the FDK, were faced with the question of what form financial equalisation should take and which course of action should be envisioned.

Regarding the first question, both bodies quickly agreed that a comprehensive reform of federalism should be elaborated. It should also tackle in a comprehensive way, the problems resulting from entangled powers and responsibilities of the federal and the cantonal governments, the disparities that exist between the financially strong and weak cantons, the inadequate cooperation between the cantons, and so on. A "mini-reform", for example, of only the fiscal equalisation scheme in the narrowest sense, was not considered to be appropriate.

When in 1994 the reform actually began, the problems of how to structure the project, or rather, how to proceed, and whether to include experts or not, were of particular importance. The following questions arose: Should a small working group composed solely of "experts" be set up that would proceed in a purely technocratic manner and, in the end, submit scientifically substantiated conclusions to the politicians? Or, on the contrary, should the politicians draw up the guidelines for the experts and, during the entire process, remain involved in order to avoid "technocratic" influence right from the start and to ensure that the proposals are "politically realistic" and acceptable? Or, could a combination of both models be found in order to advance the project in a creative and pragmatic process?[4]

These questions were not explicitly asked. However, participants were right from the beginning well aware that a solution designed and drafted by "technocrats" was doomed to fail in the process of political decision-making. People were overwhelmingly convinced that political approval of such a far-reaching reform proposal could only be achieved if the federal and the can-

4 Following Habermas's "pragmatic model" (Habermas, 1968).

tonal governments were included from the beginning both at the technical and the political level with neither side being given any exclusive rights or privileges.

Thus, it was determined to follow a pragmatic course: At the end of 1994, the Federal Council set up a project team with delegates from the federal (EFV) and the cantonal (FDK) governments represented on equal terms. During the initial phase, the team would develop the basic concept to remedy the flaws of fiscal equalisation.[5] Early in the process, expert reports were commissioned to assess the deficits found by the EFV and the FDK. In 1996, the report on the main features of the NFA based on this preliminary work was presented and sent for consultation (EDF, FDK, 1996).

In 1997, based on the largely positive results of the consultation held on the main features of the NFA, the Federal Council commissioned the project team composed of equal numbers of representatives of the Federal government and the cantons to translate the concept into reality. In the process, the project team had to take into account the essential guidelines prepared by the Federal Council after the consultation and adopted in its resolution of 23 October 1996. This resolution served as the basis for the mandates of the project groups as it defined the principles to be elaborated in greater detail.

In the process, the following observations are notable:

1. It was necessary to expand the project team to include three levels, since the political dimension of the project now became to the fore. At this point, the Cantonal Government Conference (*Konferenz der Kantonsregierungen* – KdK) replaced the FDK as the partner of the federal government.
2. The project team included a political steering committee under the direction of the minister (*Direktor*) of the Swiss Department of Finance. This first strategic level of the project organisation had to assess the milestones from a political standpoint. It was composed of three representatives of the Federal Council and three representatives of the cantons. In addition, the cities and the municipalities sent one representative into the committee. This steering committee met regularly and became increasingly important as the project progressed. Its meetings could last several hours, and supposedly "technical" issues often turned into political discussions on fundamental issues.
3. The pre-consultation body was the so-called "guiding committee", which formed the second strategic level. It included seven delegates of the can-

5 Often, it is the administration that "picks up" the decisions of the Federal Council. The responsible minister forwards the submission prepared by the administration, often without making any revisions, to the entire Federal Council, including the corresponding draft of the resolution, which de facto determines the resolution passed by the Federal Council prior to the meeting. During the meeting itself, the undisputed issues are generally passed with no discussion in an administrative sense.

tons[6] and seven of the federal government, as well as one joint representative of the cities and municipalities nominated by the Swiss Association of Cities and Municipalities. The committee was chaired by the EFV director. In this way, the composition of the committees expanded considerably compared with the initial project team:

- At the federal level, the affected ministries and the Federal Chancellery were included.
- The cantons were no longer represented by the FDK on the guiding committee, but rather by the KdK, which included special departments that were affected.
- For the first time, cities had a seat in the project team, whereby a core desire of the third level of government could be fulfilled.

4. At the operating (third) level of the project organisation, a management team was responsible for the proper handling of the reform. Its members coordinated the work, supervised the project groups, which were also equally composed of representatives of the federal and cantonal governments, and which carried out their own in-depth work. It fell to this management team to integrate the complex work in details and to ensure that the designated working groups complied with the essential guidelines provided by the political steering committee.
5. The KdK, with one civil servant represented in the operational management team, handled the political coordination of the cantons. The coordination effort was considerable, in part because the KdK had to have a majority of at least 18 cantons to pass a binding opinion. On the other hand, this implied corresponding cantonal government resolutions – a cascade, which required time.
6. When it came to the financial policy section of the NFA, the KdK was joined by the FDK, which in these matters, actually took control of the cantonal side and coordinated efforts with the ministers of finance. Its secretariat was included on an ad hoc basis at the operating level, as were the group for financial affairs of the cantons which served as a link to the cantons.
7. After the successful referendum had been held in November 2004, the structure of the political steering committee was simplified. Now a Federal Council delegation was waived. Still the steering committee was chaired by the director of the Swiss Department of Finance, as well as by the finance minister. Senior civil servants from the finance and justice departments remained to represent the federal government. In contrast, the cantonal representation did not change, nor did that of the cities and municipalities.

---

6 Cantonal representation had to meet various criteria. It had to include the resource-rich as well as resource-poor cantons and, due to the specific, technical issues, the affected cantonal directors' conferences.

Despite the indisputable, occasional sluggishness of the consensus-oriented process, another, presumably "more efficient" procedure would have been doomed to fail. As experience gained in particular during the 1970s reveal, a technocratic approach to define and solve problems was never crowned by success. Such an approach corresponds to a way of thinking that was defeated in the failed "comprehensive planning concepts" in transportation, media or energy policy. It would have also run aground in the case of the reform of the financial equalisation programme. To draft a proposal "at the green table", which probably would have been consistent in theory, implied risking that such a draft would be withdrawn due to the political reality. Comprehensive issues must be dealt with in a way adapted to the political culture of Switzerland. The inherent basic conditions[7] demanded an opposite, pragmatic process, which, in fact, requires perseverance but is not tainted with the stigma of elitism and exclusion by the relevant stakeholders, notably, the cantons.[8]

The project structure outlined above continued to exist when the three motions to parliament were drafted. However, the steering team was subsequently dispensed with, since the essential elements of the report were already available and including special department appeared to be unnecessary. In its place, a smaller group, the so-called "petit comité" (small committee), was formed, in which the cantons[9], the municipal association, as well as the EFV were represented. Accordingly, fewer stakeholders were directly involved, which facilitated negotiations and decision-making and allowed to speed up the project as demanded by politicians. This way, the constitutional dimension of the project was not appropriately taken into account, at least not to the desired extent. Discussions on constitutional issues were somewhat too short, or, in retrospect, could only be held "between" meetings of the project team.[10]

---

7 Neidhart (2002) assumes three interconnected basic conditions shaping Swiss politics: the "small size of the state", "plurality" and "historicity".

8 This desired inclusion led to a successful "preventive balance of interests" in the federation, with the result that conflicts of interest do not immediately impact on parliamentary processes and party politics (Neidhart, 2002: 270). In fact, the level of conflicts between the federal and the cantonal governments and among the cantons could be reduced during the negotiations on the project and during the parliamentary phase. Thus the "preventive balance of interests" could be achieved.

9 The presidents of the KdK, FDK and the Western Switzerland Governors Conference.

10 The Federal Department of Justice was not represented in the "petit comité", which, in light of what happened, is to be criticised. This shortcoming was compensated for after the work on the constitutional amendments was finished. Then the Federal Department of Justice was, in fact, included in the steering committee, however only by specialized civil servants.

3. Evaluation

3.1 High demands on coordination

A critical evaluation of the project work comes to mind in view of the complexity of the draft[11], the number of stakeholders involved (all departments, the Federal Chancellery, all cantons, the association of cities and municipalities, each one on a political and administrative level, as well as, at some points, organisations that were directly affected), the time dimension (start of the actual reform efforts in the early 1990s, with increasing political pressure to present the package to parliament at the end).

Over 100 people were involved in the project team. This breadth and variety (number and origins of the stakeholders) may be surprising. But, in view of the problem and the policies affected, it was necessary. Inevitably, serious coordination problems arose. The management team in particular had to continuously communicate the overarching goals of the reform to the individual project groups in order to prevent the work from reaching a dead end. Furthermore, it had to integrate the often diverging proposals and to present them to the higher level project committees for a decision.

Following Fritz W. Scharpf (1973), we can distinguish basically two ways to coordinate complex projects. In the case of negative coordination, decision alternatives expressly opposed by individual departments are usually eliminated (Scharpf, 1973: 88). The departments or the actors involved will focus their attention in reviewing proposal on possible negative impacts on their particular jurisdiction and veto those that may involve negative effects (Scharpf, 1973: 87f.). In other words, the departments are not primarily interested in innovative decisions but rather to defend their own status quo and to maintain their policy domain over which they have decision-making powers.

In contrast, positive coordination is characterised by the simultaneous discussion of all connected decision-making areas and possible alternatives relating to the issue (Scharpf, 1973: 91). This kind of coordination allows for decisions by mutual supported and complementary contributions of the involved departments. What is crucial is that all alternatives by all affected actors are simultaneously set on the agenda. In this way, a policy can be drafted that complies with the real extent of interrelated problems regarding their degree of innovation and their scope. Scharpf's reflections (1973: 90ff.) have shown that positive coordination quickly comes to limits due to the constrained ability to process information, while decision-making is much easier

11 A total of 26 constitutional provisions had to be revised. The implementation affected at the federal level 33 laws. Moreover, cantonal legislation also had to be revised, mainly as a result of the reallocation of powers.

in the case of negative coordination between the participating departments.[12] Even if all the members of the project team are, in principle, willing to make innovative decisions, a positive coordination would be difficult to execute and would necessarily end in frustration due to a complete standstill (Scharpf, 1973: 93).

In essence, a project team that encompasses more than 100 people, some of whom represent diverging positions, can only be led applying negative coordination. In negotiations or consultations on the manifold problems, those actors were presented, that felt their jurisdiction to be immediately affected. The dialogue beyond the limits of the particular sectors was rather modest. One should not forget that in the case of the NFA, different policy areas were affected, to varying degrees. Yet proposals to reform public transportation were hardly discussed by delegates representing the social security system – and vice versa. As Scharpf illustrated from an administrative studies perspective, process permeating different jurisdictions and policy domains would hardly be manageable (or even feasible). From the point of view of the project management, it can be concluded with some satisfaction that negative coordination worked fairly well – which was not self-evident considering the stakeholders involved.

---

12 As mentioned above, only one area of decision-making or proposal is simultaneously dealt with in the case of negative coordination. Therefore, all that is checked is whether a proposed decision (or, at the most, its updating) could have a *negative* impact on the respective status quo and in which way this occurs. On the other hand, in the case of positive coordination, the relationship between each alternative and the departments is considered. Scharpf determined the following law: in the case of negative coordination, the number of the resulting relationships is limited to $R_n = (n\text{-}1)\ x\ a$, in which a is the number of alternative decisions at the disposal of each decision-making jurisdiction and n is the number of participating departments. In the case of positive coordination, the number of departments to coordinate as well as the alternatives offered is squared, i.e.: $R_p = n\ (n\text{-}1)\ x\ a^2$. With respect to the NFA project team (number of participating departments or actors), for the sake of simplicity, *11* were calculated over the entire project: 7 departments, the Federal Chancellery, as well as the KdK, FDK and the Association of Cities and Municipalities. These three organisations, for their part, coordinated the interests of the cantons and the cities, respectively, which logically means that they too pursued correspondingly coordinated efforts. If we assume *three different* models to be discussed relating to the federal compensation of socio-demographic burdens, in negative coordination the relationships that must be checked by the project team are 30, i.e. a still manageable number. In the case of positive coordination, that number rises to 990 relationships that would need to be considered during the decision-making process. Of course, not all organisations or interests represented on a project team would be involved in the efforts of positive or negative coordination. It always depends on whether the actors see themselves affected by a decision. Yet, the model clearly illustrates the limits of positive coordination, in particular, when dealing with more complex, innovative projects.

3.2 Opportunities for innovation and their limits

However, negative coordination does not inevitably mean that the mechanisms restricting innovation have to dominate. In fact, participants consistently searched for innovative solutions their particular areas, and they were successful.[13] Insight and the real pressure[14] to actively cooperate instead of passively resist prevailed. In the end, it fell to the project management team to consolidate and collect the somewhat fragmented pieces of the individual sectors to a package.

It has to be added that within the framework of such a reform, it would have been an illusion to comprehensively revise individual policy sector as well. The federal system had been overloaded and coordination had inevitably failed due to the reasons mentioned above. Complexity also sets limits, yet, it does not make it impossible to find opportunities for innovation.

3.3 Comprehensive and discursive decision-making

The established project team was able to early and quickly recognise politically awkward situations and to initiate the appropriate discussions between the stakeholders. Diverging opinions were always on the table, so that work on the project basically did not grind to a halt. The federal government, the cantons and the cities held a productive dialogue, which was at times quite controversial and sometimes almost led to political disaster. However, as the discourse was institutionalised and as the project management team could fall back on a variety of functioning networks, unfavourable constellations could be avoided. In the case of looming problems, ad hoc groups were called upon to quickly provide feasible solutions. Members of these groups sometimes accepted to work during unusual hours.

The criteria applied to include the cantons were contrived in that the financially weak, average and powerful cantons were represented equally. This key of distributing positions was applied in all bodies down to the individual project groups. Furthermore, the group of the central cantons of the *Ro-*

13 Thus, the work on the fiscal equalisation programme proved to be the actual engine driving the reform of the forest policy.

14 The working groups could not act in a "politically vacuum". Rather they were bound by their mandates which were approved by the political steering committee. Due to the balance of power between federal and cantonal representatives, sometimes a kind of "pillerisation" could be observed in certain policy fields. This emerging pattern could not be entirely broken up. It fell to the project management team and, in particular, the working group leaders (generally, a member of a cantonal executive branch, or the directorate of a federal department), not to lose sight of the overarching goals of financial equalisation, to do its own preparatory work and to "coerce" those directly affected into actively taking part instead of passively resisting.

mandie and the *Deutschschweiz* were represented, as well as the alpine cantons. In addition, not only the financial and political perspectives had to be taken into account, but also the constitutional ones. The KdK took care of this and coordinated the interests of the conferences of ministers. This proved to be a difficult task. The conferences of ministers assumed a right to comment on the NFA from their particular point of view.[15] Not surprisingly, these comments did not always conform to the proposals of the KdK, or the joint proposals of the project team. It is difficult to say how intensely the KdK representatives discussed this with the ministers and how often they took part in the respective board meetings and annual conferences.

Of course, there were always attempts to slow down the reform process, if not completely stop it. Well-organised interest groups approached the media, individual members of the project team, members of parliament or even individual members of the Federal Council to defend the particular interests of their group and to wield their influence. The critique that the pre-parliamentary decision-making process worked to balance particular and short-term interests, while the general and long-term interests were neither supported nor appreciated (according to Linder, 1987: 202f.), did not apply to the negotiations on financial equalisation reform.

This finding cannot be explained with the structure of the project team alone. Other conditions had been crucial for achieving a comprehensive reform aimed at the public welfare, like, for instance, the resoluteness and stability of the political project committees, open communication of civil servants with politicians, the disclosure of a concealed obstruction (see Huber, 2000: 203ff.). What mattered was to resist public "attacks" of lobby groups.[16]

However, this requirement was not met consistently. At the beginning of the project, requests from organisations for (public) podium discussions as part of annual conferences, press conferences or other public events were answered hesitantly and in some instances also negatively. It was the project management team, which stepped into the breach, although it was only responsible for operational functions. This way, it assumed a role for which it was not initially conceived and which it, strictly speaking, would not have been politically

15 See for example, the 8 November 1999 edition of the *Neue Zürcher Zeitung* (NZZ): "Social Directors (SODC) Sceptical of the New Financial Equalisation Program" (p. 13). The SODC, however, was not opposed to the proposals as such with respect to social services. Rather, it requested supporting measures. This demand was taken into account in the first Federal Council report (Federal Gazette 2002, p. 2440ff.).

16 According to knowledge gained from economics, four ideal types of groups can be identified in processes of innovation: the opponents, the sceptics, the followers, and the pioneers. As it turned out during negotiations on the NFA project, sceptics had not been given sufficient voice, at least in the early stages of the project, although this particular group can provide a significant impetus and, with its critical attitude, finally help to achieve the decisive breakthrough the process. Often, there is a risk that critical voices will be disregarded while fundamental opponents prevail.

authorised to fulfil. However, this did not interrupt the political discourse. What was important was that the project management team closely followed the political guidelines of the reform package. Thus it avoided the risk of being forced or of slipping into a role to which it was not entitled.

3.4 The NFA: A balanced, win-win solution

In negotiating, redistributive conflicts have to be solved that can be rather complicated. In principle, they are characterized by two asymmetries:[17] Firstly, the existing resources are unevenly distributed. As a result, a change in these creates winners and losers. Secondly, those stakeholders that control the resources to be reallocated are aware of their stronger veto power and can benefit from any dissent, i.e. in the event the negotiations fail. This means that negotiators must have an interest in the collective advantages. In any case, the sum of the advantages and disadvantages of all those participating must be positive.[18] This basic prerequisite was a decisive factor in the success of the NFA project.

When the overall balance was calculated, which listed the (purely) quantitative financial changes compared to the actual state of each individual canton, negotiations run the risk that public discussion would turn into a confrontation of "winners" and "loser" and that this perception would become the dominant factor. Indeed, the collective advantage of fiscal equalisation reform temporarily moved to the background, with debates focused instead on the distributive issues of the resource balance. The arguments partly based on extrapolation and, for this reason, simply indicating an approximate trend. In other words, the discourse was at risk of dealing with an issue that was of virtual nature. The narrow "optics of calculation" seemed to prevail.

In this situation, a report prepared by experts helped to refocus the discussion on the system and the "mechanics" of a new order (Frey, 2001: 19). Thus the danger of narrowing the negotiations to a purely pecuniary conflict instead of dealing with new instruments and their relevance for the political system was banned in due time. However, to this end those politically responsible on the project team had to seize their leadership role and counter any individual interests that could have threatened the collective goal set for the project. After they hesitated to adopt this role at the beginning of the project between 1997 and 1998, eventually the changed strategy gave way to active political negotiating.

17 For more details, see Benz, Arthur, "Umverteilung durch Verhandlungen? Kooperative Staatspraxis bei Verhandlungskonflikten"; *Staatswissenschaften und Staatspraxis* 1991, pp. 46-75, quotation: Brunner, 2000: 91.

18 Scharpf, in Benz, Scharpf and Zintl, "Horizontale *Politikverflechtung*. Zur Theorie von Verhandlungssystemen, Frankfurt, 1996, p. 14ff., quotation: Brunner, 2000: 91.

Another factor that could have threatened the reform was an imbalance of power. This could not take hold because the NFA instruments included the possibility of mutual compensation[19]: Overall, the rich cantons would bear an even greater burden after the reform than before. However, their expenditures for services with external effects would be compensated for by an inter-cantonal burden sharing. In addition, there are the following institutional "profits" for all the cantons:

- constitutional entrenchment of cantonal autonomy in fulfilling their responsibilities;
- constitutional entrenchment of the principle of subsidiarity;
- constitutional entrenchment of the criteria for allocating powers;
- constitutional entrenchment of inter-cantonal cooperation and the sharing of burdens;
- constitutional entrenchment of the new forms of cooperation and financial equalisation between the federal government and the cantons to strengthen their partnerships.

This showed that the NFA package reflected the famous "win-win situation": supposed "losers", who, in fact, must pay more in future, could also become winners based on the "NFA mechanism" (not least based on the bundling of different issues in a coherent package deal). This was in particular felt in the small or smallest cantons. Initially, they feared the "paternalism" of the larger cantons due to a substantial expansion of inter-cantonal collaboration and due to the need to participate in burden sharing. However in the course of negotiations they acknowledged that, without the modernisation of the financial equalisation program and federal structures, their very existence would be called into question in the mid- to long-term. As they noticed, in a small federal state only sovereignty shared with other cantons can mean true sovereignty.

4. Key factors of success

Reforms that follow a comprehensive approach and affect alleged "vested rights" of individual groups and bureaucratic structures are, by their very nature, difficult to achieve. The danger of a "cumulative veto" due to the creation of (opposing, that is, "unholy") alliances is high. Therefore the crucial question is how such reforms are to be approached so that they have a chance to succeed. In hindsight, the case of the NFA process reveals the factors for success:

---

19 As defined by Scharpf, *Politikverflechtung*, p. 81f., quotation: Brunner, 2000: 91.

1. From the start, the project team established by the Federal Council equally represented the relevant interests, at the political as well as the administrative level. Political leaders and civil servants were involved in a constant dialogue among equals. This process made it possible for appropriate solutions, which were neither "technocratically cumbersome" nor politically "illusory". The principle of equality was maintained throughout the entire project, also during the drafting of the three reports of the Federal Council.
2. In light of the scope of the amendments (constitutional and ordinary law), dividing the process into several steps was essential:
   - First, the main features of the reform were worked out and sent for consultation (1996). In this way, an early political feedback could be received, the political conflicts could be checked out and corrections made in due time. The report on the principles of the reform was extremely important. It allowed moderating the resulting individual interests that arose from time to time at the political and technical levels, by referring to a basic agreement.
   - The report on implementation of the project was based on the results of the initial consultation (1998). It contained the wording of the constitutional amendments and first suggestion to the ensuing legislation implementing these amendments.
   - Based on the results of the second consultation, the first report to the Federal Council could finally be drafted (2001).
   - After the constitutional reform, the laws implementing the federal constitution had to be revised (second report, 2006), while the fiscal issues of the reform were adjusted following the third and final report.

   A one-step legislative process, as applied for the attempt of a reallocation of powers during the 1980s, was explicitly abandoned. Such a process would have been impossible in view of the complexity of the reform. It was the declared intention of the federal and cantonal governments that the constitutional fundament should be amended before they take on the many cross-sectional and specific laws.
3. The important steps in the project's progression were supported by experts. Expertise was used not to make pre-parliamentary decision-making a "scientific" task, but rather to continuously control the path already cleared. The aim was to avoid the reproach of a superficial work. Of course, some of the expert reports commissioned by the project team were accused if not of being partisan then at least expressing a one-sided opinion. In this situation, it was not surprising that "opposing expert reports" – even if they were not called this – were prepared.[20]

---

20 For example, on the question as to whether a stronger horizontal fiscal equalisation could promote the emigration of mobile lawyers, two reports came to different, at some points di-

4. The success of the reform project not only resulted from a joint effort of the federal government and the cantons. It was also supported by interdepartmental collaboration at the federal level[21], which so far was not achieved on this scale and this intensity. The cooperation between the finance administration, as the lead ministry, and the federal justice ministry can be described as successful, even exemplary, especially regarding the drafting of legal norms of the constitution and of fiscal equalisation laws.
5. The KdK and the FDK deserve credit, for each one undertook the indispensable (political) work to coordinate the cantons. It is true that this required a lot of political and administrative effort, which took time. Without a doubt, the project would not have reached the parliamentary stage if this main pillar of cantonal political and administrative coordination had not existed.
6. The Federal Council never substantially commented on the contents of the submission during the entire duration of the project. In fact, two Federal Council resolutions were adopted which outlined the essential guidelines for the working groups elaborating the project. Regarding the reports on the public consultation, it maintained its political distance and only took notice of the reports. In this way, the Federal Council kept all options open until its decision was adopted.
7. Although still in the draft phase, individual proposals were submitted in parliament that sought to influence particular aspects independent of the overall context of the ongoing work. In other words: attempts were made in parliament to shape amendments before the draft of the executive was tabled in the legislature.[22] In these situations, the Federal Council always followed its motto: Parliament will get a look once the Federal Council has adopted its report to the two houses. Thus the coherence of the entire draft could be maintained and, to a large extend, watered-down or contradictory decisions could be avoided.[23]

---

ametrically opposed conclusions. One was commissioned by the project team from Dr. Kirchgässner of the University of St. Gallen, and the other presented by the "directly affected" canton of Zug and prepared by "Economics Consultants B.S.A.", Basel.

21 Horizontal cooperation between the affected ministries.

22 For example, Thomas Onken's premise, "*Wahrung der übergeordneten Interessen- und Koordinationsaufgaben beim Fuss- und Wanderwegnetz",* transferred by Parliament on 15 December 1998.

23 Lobby groups tried to influence proposals even before they were adopted by the Federal Council. These attempts caused the problem that one particular viewpoint was emphasised according to the motto: "The overall concept is right, but just in the policy field affecting us". In such situations, it was worthwhile to remember the overall perspective, i.e. the "general mechanics" of the reform, and to demonstrate that an isolated perspective on a particular policy field, even if it may be justified, did not meet the intentions of the reform. If one had followed the logic of special interests, the draft would have quickly lost its conceptual, federalist, political and financial balance.

8. As part of an ongoing information policy, the media were informed about "milestones" of the project in order to inform about any progress made.[24] This strategy prevented any indiscretions that could have (intentionally) led to confusion and false information. Instead, the state of affairs was openly communicated.[25] This proactive information policy certainly proved to support the project.
9. As story of the NFA project (including the reports) proves, "speed" in an economic sense alone is not a useful standard to evaluate federal reform. Integration, coherence and a politically clever strategy agreed to by the stakeholders involved pay off. Over the years, with a modest operational structure, it became possible to advance a proposal for reform and come to a successful result and complete enactment (2008), admittedly at the cost of a workload that, from time to time, stressed the participants to the limits of their capacities.

The entire reform was presented as a package negotiated and agreed between the federal government and the cantons. Not least due to its complexity and the interdependence of its parts, it was approved under the label "The Revitalisation of Federalism" by parliament and the people.

References

Brunner, Stephan C. (2000): Möglichkeiten und Grenzen regionaler interkantonaler Zusammenarbeit. Zürich: Schulthess Juristische Medien.

Bundesrat (2001): Botschaft des Bundesrates vom 14. November 2001 zur Neugestaltung des Finanzausgleichs und der Aufgaben (NFA). Bundesblatt 2002: 2314ff.

EFD (Eidgenössisches Finanzdepartment) und FDK (Finanzdirektorenkonferenz) (1996): Der Neue Finanzausgleich zwischen Bund und Kantonen. Grundzüge. Bericht der vom Eidgenössischen Finanzdepartement und der Konferenz der kantonalen Finanzdirektoren gemeinsam getragenen Projektorganisation. Bern und Luzern.

FDK (Finanzdirektorenkonferenz) (1992): Finanzausgleichsbilanz und Orientierungsrahmen für die künftige Ausgestaltung des bundesstaatlichen Finanzausgleichs. Luzern.

Frey, René L. (2001): Ziel- und Wirkungsanalyse des NFA. Universität Basel 2001. http://www.efd.admin.ch/dokumentation/zahlen/00578/00860/index.html?lang=de [accessed: 13 July 2011]

Frey, René L./Spillmann, Andreas/Dafflon, Bernard/Jeanrenaud, Claude/Meier, Alfred (1994): Der Finanzausgleich zwischen Bund und Kantonen. Expertise zu den

24 No fewer than 16 media releases were released upon the publication of the report on the implementation of the NFA (1998).

25 See for example, the media release of 9 November 2000, in which reasons for the delay were extensively and openly discussed.

Finanzhilfen und Abgeltungen des Bundes an die Kantone im Auftrag der Eidgenössischen Finanzverwaltung und der Konferenz der kantonalen Finanzdirektoren. Bern: EFV/FDK.

Habermas, Jürgen (1968): Technik und Wissenschaft als Ideologie. Frankfurt am Main: Suhrkamp Verlag.

Huber, Paul (2000): Keine Reformstrategie ohne politischen Mut, Entschiedenheit und Teamgeist. In: Emery, Y. (ed.): Grossbaustelle Verwaltung – Bilanzen und Ausblicke. Lausanne: Presses Polytechnique et Universitaire Romandes, 203-216.

Linder, Wolf (Principal) (1987): Politische Entscheidung und Gesetzesvollzug in der Schweiz. Schlussbericht des Nationalen Forschungsprogramms Nr. 6. Bern: Haupt.

Neidhart, Leonhard (2002): Die politische Schweiz. Zürich: NZZ-Verlag.

Scharpf, Fritz (1973): Planung als politischer Prozess. Aufsätze zur Theorie der planenden Demokratie. Frankfurt am Main: Suhrkamp Verlag.

The "Austrian Convention": The Failure of an Ambitious Reform

Peter Bußjäger

1. Introduction

The Austrian Constitution (*Bundesverfassung*) came into being in 1920 as result of a constitutional compromise between two ideologically divided political camps. During the debates aimed at constitution-making in 1920, the positions of the Christian Social Party promoting a strong federal system based on the Swiss model, clashed with those of the opposed Social Democratic Party favouring a unitary state. As a result, a political system was created that appeared to have all the characteristics of a federal state but worked in an extremely centralised way. These centralising tendencies have not been reduced over time but increased even more until today (Pernthaler, 1989: 356). The need to reform this constitution is one of the recurring topics of constitutional discussions in Austria. The debates surrounding fundamental state reform have been intensified over the last few years, especially after more or less radical proposals had been launched demanding the abolition of the *Länder*[1] or, at least, their amalgamation into larger regions. After various attempts to reform the federal system, and especially following the failure of federal state reforms between 1989 and 1994, the public became increasingly unhappy with the existing system. Completely new ground was broken in 2003 with the creation of the so-called "Austrian Convention" aimed at a fundamental renewal of the *Bundesverfassung* by 2005. The introduction of this type of convention, clearly modelled after the EU Constitutional Convention, was explicitly envisioned in the 2002 agenda of the new Federal Government under Chancellor Schüssel.

Following an invitation by the Chancellor, a founding committee of the Austrian Convention was struck on 2 May 2003, comprised of, among others, the Chancellor and the Vice-Chancellor, the three Presidents of the National Council, the President of the Federal Council, the chair of the Conference of

1 Constituent units of the Austrian federation are called *Bundesländer* or *Länder*; heads of the *Länder* governents are the "*Landeshauptmann*" or "*Landeshauptfrau*". The Conference of the *Landeshauptleute* is an informal institution established in the 1960s in order to coordinate the positions of the *Länder* before entering intergovernmental negotiations on the federal level. Decisions within the Conference fall under the unanimity rule, but due to the informal character of the Conference they are not legally binding.

the *Landeshauptleute* and the chair of the Conference of Presidents of *Länder* Legislatures (*Landtagspräsidentenkonferenz*). The founding committee installed the convention with the task of preparing proposals for fundamental state and constitutional reforms that would also set the preconditions for efficient administration. The future constitution, so the basic idea, would allow for a modern, cost-efficient, transparent and citizen-oriented way of governing and delivering of public services (Khol, 2003: 36-37).

This broad mandate coincided with the task of a total revision of the constitution. The project of a total revision was surprisingly initiated with an enormous time pressure although the political system was in no apparent political crisis at that time. The shortcomings of the federal system had long been known, above all the federal allocation of powers and competences and the collaboration of the *Länder* in federal lawmaking (Federal Chancellery, 1991). But the need for reform was also widely acknowledged with respect to democratic provisions (instruments of direct democracy, democratic control mechanisms vis-à-vis the executive) and to the state of law, e.g. the extent of legislative ties for the administration or the codification of the fragmented catalogue of fundamental rights. Finally, the torso-like character of the actual constitutional document, the Federal Constitutional Law (FCL) had been – and is still – an entire reform project as such. Either hollowed out or supplemented by innumerable constitutional laws and individual constitutional clauses the Federal Constitutional Law had turned into one document among many that altogether formed the Austrian Constitutional Law (Wiederin, 2008: 45-49).

2. Institutions of the Austrian Convention

2.1 Plenum

According to the intentions of the founding committee, the plenum of the Convention was supposed to be a forum for discussing the committees' results similar to the European Convention. And, technically, it fulfilled this role: in the plenum, each chair presented individual committee reports, which were then followed by a general discussion. However, the statements presented were largely fruitless and often repeated or reinforced the views that had already been expressed by the involved parties or groups. Thus, participants did not enter into deliberations or livelier discussions which could have led to any substantial progress on the reform topics. The plenum never gained momentum. As a result, the discussions were consistently short, most of them not lasting longer than two hours, although the sessions were scheduled for the whole day.

The debates in the plenum were preceded by preliminary discussions within the political parties. Since the experts delegated to the plenum by each party also participated in these meetings, the political camps were reproduced within the Convention (see paragraphs below 4.a). Therefore, it comes as no surprise that the plenum became a stage for party politics exposing their differences instead of trying to overcome them (Bußjäger, 2005: 5).

Furthermore, due to the restrictive time limits placed on the contributors to the debate in the Convention[2] a discussion similar to a parliamentary debate could never unfold. When the time limit was finally lifted in the fall of 2004, the effect of this measure fell flat and a final attempt to revive the plenum had failed.

In retrospect, the plenum fulfilled the following functions:

- The reports by the committee chairs raised the level of information of the participants, provided they were interested.
- To a certain degree, impressions of the mood could be gained from the statements made by the members of the Convention, which helped to assess the chances for a consensus.
- The plenum held a total of three hearings with interest groups. These were one of the few opportunities for civil society to actively take part in the discussions, aside from submitting statements that were forwarded to the different committees (Hämmerle, 2005: 367-370).

Since the plenum formed one of the Conventions' three leading institutions the assessment of its work has to be particularly critical: all in all, it was not exceedingly effective.

2.2 Steering committee

The standing orders[3] of the Austrian Convention not only provided for the steering committee to be the administrative body, but also equipped it with considerable power. In accordance with § 37 of the standing orders, the steering committee prepared a final report on the discussions of the Convention on which it had to agree in consensus (§ 19). In those instances in which there was no consensus the different points of view were to be documented (§ 37).

Consequently, the path was cleared for important decisions to be made ultimately by this committee, in which all the leading political powers of the time – government and opposition – were united.[4] When the Convention ended in January 2005, its members were:

2 In general, the time set aside for speeches was reduced to five minutes. The committee chairs were each granted 15 minutes to present their reports.

3 For more information, visit www.konvent.gv.at/.

4 Beginning in 2002, the federal government was a coalition composed of the ÖVP and the FPÖ, while the SPÖ and the Greens were in opposition.

- Franz Fiedler, Convention Chair (President of the Austrian Court of Audit until June 2004)
- Andreas Khol, National Council President (ÖVP)
- Peter Kostelka, Ombudsman (beginning with 21 May 2004 successor of Heinz Fischer who had retired from the Convention and was eventually elected Federal President) (SPÖ)
- Claudia Kahr, Constitutional Court Judge (affiliated with the SPÖ)
- Herbert Scheibner, FPÖ parliamentary party whip (succeeded retired Justice Minister Dieter Böhmdorfer on 22 July 2004)
- Eva Glawischnig, Member of the National Council (Greens)
- Angela Orthner, President of the legislature of Upper Austria (ÖVP)

Overall, the steering committee failed in meeting important aspects of its mission. It was unable to overcome the sometimes deeply divergent positions and to use its smaller circle of members to generate new ideas or pave the way for consensus in the Convention. The steering committee hardly succeeded in moving beyond party conflicts and ideological boundaries. Even the chair, Franz Fiedler, was unable to act as a unifying figure to bridge the divergent opinions within the committee (Bußjäger, 2005: 3-5).

The steering committee was unable to fulfil its function according to the intentions of the founding committee and the standing orders, namely, to be a management body. Deeply rooted disagreements were more common within the steering committee itself in which the fault lines ran along the political camps, dividing the governing parties ÖVP and FPÖ from the opposition, SPÖ and Greens, on most issues. Examples regarded fundamental rights, mechanisms of parliamentary oversight, direct democracy or state responsibilities and goals. However, with respect to the extremely controversial issue of reforming the federal state, the fault line divided parts of the ÖVP from the majority of the members of the steering committee.[5] Federalism was, therefore, also a matter of controversial debates within the steering committee.

2.3 Committees

As early as 2003, a total of ten committees had been established with mandates assigned by the steering committee of the Austrian Convention. Originally, the committees were supposed to deliver decisive proposals for the new constitution by consensus. However, it quickly became clear that the required consensus would not be reached. Consequently, the steering committee had to be content with alternatives presented by the committees

5 It was somewhat different in the case of Committee 5 in which representatives of the *Länder* governed by the SPÖ (Vienna, Burgenland, Salzburg) also took up decidedly federalist positions.

(Bußjäger, 2004: 260-262). During the first half of 2004, the committees prepared their reports, which explained in great detail the respective areas affected but contained relatively little agreement on the difficult issues of the allocation of powers and financial resources, the reform of the administrative structure, and fundamental rights (Konrath, 2005: 358-360).

It must have become quite clear no later than in the spring of 2004 that the Austrian Convention would face serious time pressure in preparing a draft for the new constitution. The ensuing challenge for the political leaders was also clear: political guidelines had to be set in order to prevent the teams of experts within the committees from simply going around in circles when drafting proposals (Bußjäger, 2005: 2).

In fact, the steering committee assigned new, complementary mandates to each committee – but rarely with the concrete framework or guidelines that would have been necessary to find a way out of the impasse. In this way, the committees were meaningfully employed and the steering committee was temporarily relieved of the pressure to make decisions. However, the moment of political decision-making was merely postponed with the time left to find a consensus vanishing. But the committees themselves were not responsible for this situation: they were not concerned with politics but established to provide expert knowledge and information on potential solutions. They were unable to gain any momentum that would have helped to overcome the fault lines within the Convention concerning the truly crucial questions (Bußjäger, 2005: 2).

2.4 Specific requirements for Convention discussions

2.4.1 The absence of designated political representatives and the formation of political camps

The political parties dominated the Convention. In principle, a strong partisan commitment in constitutional policies and basic rights of a state is not wrong in itself. In the case of the Austrian Convention, however, the commitment of the politicians was reduced to freezing the camps so that the discussions hardly went beyond existing ideologies and positions of the respective political camps. Since the actual decision-makers were largely absent, the discussions were led by their deputies who considered it as their duty not to relent too early. In consequence, discussions in the Convention in 2004 were stirred into a deadlock situation, in which every camp defended its positions against the other.

Apart from the reproduction of political camps in the discussions, meetings of the committee and the plenum were often held without the designated political actors. While the representatives of the federal government, the

Landeshauptleute, and the special-interest groups used the opportunities granted to them by the standing orders and sent deputies to the meetings, the representatives of legislative bodies and members of the National Council, the Federal Council or the *Länder* legislatures did not appear at all in many instances. Committee meeting protocols clearly document the high number of politicians being absent or deputised. This absence could, on the one hand, be explained partly by the complexity of the material to be dealt with and the need to draw on expert knowledge for the discussions. On the other hand, it may have offered the opportunity of weighing alternatives based on expert knowledge within the committees, thus letting them fill out the role they were originally intended for. In this way, the political decisions made later in the process would have gained greater legitimacy, first and foremost those made by the steering committee. The political representatives could not and did not assume the role of the experts and discussions in the committees remained within the frame of ideological positions and confrontations without bridging any conflicts. As mentioned earlier, the steering committee, in particular, was unable to come to any significant political decisions on the difficult questions of reforming the federal system (Bußjäger, 2005: 6-7).

2.4.2 The role of the experts

In addition to politicians and their deputies, a number of well-known experts in the areas of constitutional law and administrative law were also members of the Convention. Since these experts were lawyers in all cases, one could speak of a lawyers' monopoly within the Convention.

Besides the "*Virilisten*"[6], the group of experts also included representatives of the highest courts[7] as well as others who were delegated by political bodies, but who were not actually designated political representatives.[8]

The discussions that were held revealed quickly that even the experts in the negotiations largely brought along their own preconceptions. First and foremost, various distinctive features of the Austrian Constitutional Law Doctrine predominated, such as a strong positivist bias. The fact that the experts were considered part of the political camps was particularly striking: they took part in the meetings of "their" parties prior to the discussions as was expected of them.

---

6 They were a group of experts that performed no political duties and who were, therefore, described as "*Virilisten*" See also the decision made by the Founding Committee on 2 May 2003 (www.konvent.gv.at), which refers to nine "*Virilisten*" that are to be assigned from a certain pool of experts.

7 The Presidents of the Constitutional Court, the Administrative Court and the Supreme Court also participated as members of the Convention.

8 For example, Bernhard Raschauer, a professor at the University of Vienna and a renowned expert in the field of administrative law and state responsibilities, was nominated as the representative of the Chamber of the Liberal Professions.

In short, the experts could not play an independent role and became, in principal, political representatives themselves. In the end, since the politicians were in retreat, the experts also argued very defensively on many issues. It can therefore be doubted that including independent experts in the Convention – an idea that had been promoted occasionally – would have made much difference. They too would have brought their preconceptions with them and, sooner or later, would have slipped into the role of political representatives (Bußjäger, 2005: 7-8).

2.4.3 Media coverage

Reporting by the media on the Convention was very intense during the entire session of the Convention. Considering the political capital and expertise invested in the Convention this kind of coverage could have been expected. In addition, the protagonists of the Convention knew how to stage the project for the media right from the start. Media interest became even more intense in the fall of 2004 as the Convention faced increasing time pressure. As it became obvious that huge disagreements could not be resolved, press commentaries became more critical. On different occasions it was possible to see that various Convention members were withdrawing from the project, which was accordingly spread and commented throughout the media.

All in all, the media coverage of the project was appropriate in accordance with its importance. It was substantially more intensive than the reports prepared by the same media on the European Convention (Bußjäger, 2005: 8).

3. Results

3.1 The report of the steering committee

The steering committee of the Convention submitted its report in January 2005. It was adopted on 28 January 2005, during the last meeting of the plenum as the final report of the Convention. The comprehensive volume summarised agreements and disagreements and included furthermore those draft texts which were presented to the committees. Not included were the numerous draft texts which were introduced to the Convention from outside – reasonably – because these drafts were generally not reviewed in detail during any discussions and were available as documents on the Convention's home page.

The report on the results of the deliberations were compiled on the basis of the committee reports by the chair, Franz Fiedler, but contained no assessments on most of the items. Part of the report also formed the draft constitution that Franz Fiedler presented on 12 January 2005. In Fiedler's own words, the draft was to "move alongside the consensus", but in the areas where no agreement had been found it went beyond and broke the mould – which will be discussed later in this chapter.

3.2 The scope of the consensus reached by the Convention

The Convention was able to reach a consensus in those areas that were comparatively neutral in terms of (power) politics:

3.2.1 Simplification and incorporation of the constitutional documents

Initially, the goal was to achieve a unified constitutional document incorporating all those constitutional laws that had turned the Austrian Constitution into an extremely fragmented and confusing collection of laws. It was more or less part of the undisputed common sense of the Convention that this task was of political importance and formed one of the priorities of the Convention. Committee 2, which was responsible for this task, had prepared various proposals that would have led to the incorporation and streamlining of the constitutional text. Uncontested was the introduction of an incorporation law similar to the German Basic Law that was to prevent the fragmentation of constitutional law in the future. Insofar as the constitutional clauses could not be abrogated, they were also to be absorbed as constitutional implementation laws and interim laws.

In this way, by using a few tricks, the conditions would have been met to prepare a somewhat cohesive constitutional document, however not entirely free of casuistic details.

3.2.2 Maintaining the status quo in the main features of the state structure

When it came down to the main features of the state structure and institutional organisation, the Convention agreed to maintain the status quo. Aside from the facts that a vague commitment to maintain the principle of the federal state had been already included in the mandate of the founding committee and that there was never a serious alternative to a republican and constitutional democracy, the Convention agreed on maintaining the status quo in various institutions exceeding these basic principles:

- A two-chamber system should be kept. The number of members of the National Council was to remain unchanged at 183. The number of members of the Federal Council was also to remain unchanged at 62.
- The electoral procedure was left unchanged. Accordingly, the National Council will be elected by the population according to the principles of

proportional representation. Federal counsellors continued to be delegated by the *Länder* legislatures.

- The institution of a head of state with comparatively limited powers elected by the population was to be maintained.
- The territorial structure and number of *Länder* as sub-state entities remained largely unchanged. The principle of responsible government was also kept with the *Länder* governments to be elected by the corresponding *Länder* legislatures.
- Federal and regional administrative authorities were to maintain their current structures.
- The existing constitutional structure of municipal governments was to remain unchanged. It was even considered to reinforce the guaranteed existence of small municipalities.

3.2.3 Legal protection

Committee 9 of the Convention had agreed on the introduction of a regional administrative jurisdiction. As a basic principle, the law requires that each case must be moved to an administrative court after initially being brought before the authorities. In the *Länder*, this function was supposed to be fulfilled by the administrative courts of the *Länder*. In the case of legal protection against federal authorities, the Federal Administrative Courts were also to be taken into account. Despite the consensus on the introduction of a regional administrative jurisdiction, there were still some ambiguities concerning, for example, the number of federal administrative courts that should be established for which types of administrative cases.

4. The conflict over federalism in the Austrian Convention

Reforming the Austrian federalism represented probably the most controversial topic in the Convention. In the end, the federal state had proven once more that it cannot be reformed.[9]

At the same time, it was part of the shared understanding of the Austrian constitutional law doctrine that the allocation of powers and resources between the federal level and the *Länder* needed to be reformed (Weber, 2003: 46). The necessities for reform clustered around several characteristics of the current allocation of powers and resources which

9 According to the Convention member Ewald Wiederin, a university professor specialising in constitutional and administrative law during the last meeting of the Convention on 28 January 2005 (www.konvent.gv.at).

- is marked by a particularly high degree of fragmentation and false reasoning,
- raises difficult problems regarding demarcation[10], also with respect to economically and socially important issues,
- hinders, at times, appropriate solutions,[11]
- causes, as is generally believed, Austria's federal system to exhibit all in all a high degree of centralisation, and
- reduces the jurisdictions of the *Länder* in practice to "residual competences"[12] (Pernthaler, 2004: 315).

However, there is no shared understanding with regard to the possible solutions of these problems especially whether the direction of reform ought to be a strengthening or a weakening of the federal structure.[13] Considering this deeply entrenched political as well as academic disagreement on the effectiveness of federal structures, it comes as no surprise that the Austrian Convention could not make any substantial progress concerning federal reforms.

4.1 Previous reform attempts and the paradigm shift of the Austrian Convention

The first demands by the *Länder* for the reform of the federal system were already uttered in the 1950s. The most important comprehensive reform programs were part of the government agendas of 1964 and 1976 (Berchtold, 1989: 15-21 and 50-53), of which only a small portion was achieved. The biggest reform project to date has been initiated in 1989 with the appointment of a structural reform commission, which prepared its report in 1991 (Bundes-

10 Take for example the controversial matter of jurisdiction with respect to the measures restricting personal freedom in nursing homes. They were judged divergently by the Austrian Administrative Court (VfGH 28.06.2003, G 208/02) according to various points of view thus creating new demarcation problems.

11 A typical example is the implementation of the EU Data Protection Directive (95/46/EG) into the Austrian legal system: since the federal government is only responsible for regulating automated data communications, the content of the regulations contained in the data protection guideline, which relates to manually created data files, had to be divided according to the appendix principle between the federal level and the *Länder*, which resulted in an unreasonable fragmentation of the data protection law.

12 This holds true despite the fact that the general clause of Article 15 § 1 FCL is regarded, in theory, to be a primary and comprehensive source of residual power for the *Länder* that is supposed to be interpreted in a dynamic and encompassing way. The problem lies in the fact that not only has this general residual power been hollowed out by many jurisdictional exceptions in favour of the federal government (Art. 10, 11, 12), but the prevailing understanding of the concept of residual power has also leaned towards a negative connotation (Pernthaler, 2004: 316).

13 Overall, the majority of the Austrian constitutional law doctrine is supposed to hold a critical position with regard to the principle of the federal state.

kanzleramt, 1991). This report then induced negotiations between the Federal Government and the *Länder* governments on the structural reform of the federal state. In 1992, the negotiations were terminated but only with a political agreement on the restructuring of the federal state signed by the federal Chancellor at that time, Franz Vranitzky, as well as by the chair of the Conference of the *Landeshauptleute* at the time, Lower Austria's governor, Siegfried Ludwig (Institute for Federalism, 1998: 1; Institute for Federalism, 1993: 22-23 and A/4). This agreement was not legally binding; it was simply a "gentlemen's agreement" which was translated into a government bill clearly watered-down by the Federal Government. After the provisions for federal reform within the government bill were weakened further during parliamentary discussions, the members of the Conference of the *Landeshauptleute* opposed the bill unanimously. In consequence, the National Council did not enact it but later attempts to restart the reform process also failed (Bußjäger, 1996: 8-17).

The reasons for the eventual failure of the "federal state reform" of 1994 can be found not only in the lack of a common position amongst the *Länder* or in their lack of readiness to assume federal responsibilities, but also in the fact that the impetus for federal reform in Austria had already faded away at that time. Under these circumstances, status-quo oriented powers within the ministerial bureaucracy as well as the *Länder* bureaucracies could easily oppose any reform.

The Austrian Convention, in comparison, started under completely different circumstances. At the eve of the Convention, discussions surrounding federalism focused on reducing or pushing back federal powers (Bußjäger, 2004: 253-256). This striking paradigm shift was also noticeable in the discussions of the Convention as well as during its hearings with special interest groups.[14]

The framework of the European Union served furthermore as an argument supporting anti-federalist positions: given Austria's integration into the European multi-level system, the subdivision of Austria is mostly seen as redundant and cost-intensive. This argument relates to another internal aspect of the Austrian federal state. While the subdivision of the federal state into nine *Länder* forms an integral part of the Austrian identity, the related consequences, namely diversification and differentiation, do not (Wiederin, 2004: 58).

4.2 The attempt to throw a great pitch: the "Fiedler Draft"

On 12 January, 2005 the chair of the Austrian Convention Franz Fiedler presented his long announced draft for a new federal constitution to the steering

14 See the hearings of 22 November 2003, 15 December 2003 and 26 January 2004 at www.konvent.gv.at.

committee of the Convention. The draft represented Fiedler's personal efforts and was not based on the consensus of the steering committee.[15]

The public eagerly waited to see whether Fiedler's work would entail a way out of the impasse. But it must have been clear to the members of the Convention that it was very unlikely. In the past Fiedler had taken a centralist position in the controversial matter of federal reform, which limited expectations that he would propose a middle ground easing the way to find a consensus.

Fiedler presented a so-called "Three-Pillar Model", with one pillar representing the exclusive legislative jurisdiction of the federal government, the second representing the exclusive jurisdiction of the *Länder* and a third pillar of so-called shared jurisdictions jointly exercised by the federal and the *Länder* governments. Under the first pillar, all important policies would be assigned to the federal government. "Health", "Schools and education", and the "Economy" were declared to be exclusively federal responsibilities (Art. 91). As the responsibility for executing the laws in these instances were supposed to lie with the same level passing the law (Art. 94 of the draft), this would leave the *Länder* with no significant opportunity to collaborate in any of these areas. They would become implementers on behalf of the federal government. Furthermore, Fiedler's idea to side responsibility for executing laws with that of lawmaking[16] would have caused additional problems, as the execution of federal laws by independent *Länder* administrations would have been eliminated. In consequence, the power of central agencies would have been increased but overall bureaucracy unduly expanded.

In Article 91 and 92, the Fiedler Draft devised approximately 50 new competences instead of the current, casuistic list of competences. This revision would have been impressive enough, but the relation of the existing powers to the newly transferred ones was in many ways extremely unclear. For example, the draft did not mention which legal entity would be responsible for the important policies of rescue services or disaster relief. Ultimately, the Constitutional Court might have been asked to determine the limits of jurisdictions in a flood of proceedings.

Apart from the lack of clarity in the allocation of powers, the Fiedler Draft did not offer any solution for reforming the Federal Council and missed to provide for a comprehensive reform of federal and *Länder* administrations. The Federal Council had been debated controversially but the draft contained only little changes. In certain cases, the Federal Council was enabled to enter into a conciliation procedure with the National Council.

But it would not have had any leverage to effectively appeal the decisions of the National Council since no absolute veto was granted. With regard to administrative reforms, the draft was especially spiritless and unclear.

15 Report of the Convention, Part 4B, Draft Federal Constitution.

16 Art. 94 of the Draft.

For example, with respect to education, it remained open as to whether the school councils of the *Länder* should continue to exist or not. The same thing applied to police services in the *Länder*. The large number of federal authorities operating directly within the Länder (workplace inspectors, torrent and avalanche obstruction specialists, federal social welfare agents, etc.) would not have been reduced and the administrative landscape would have remained fragmented.[17]

In retrospect, one of the few rays of hope was the proposed reform of the administrative courts of the *Länder* (Article 220 and following) on which a consensus had existed in the Convention. However, even this solution proved to be ambivalent because it would have empowered the federal government to establish as many of its own administrative courts as it deemed necessary in its areas of jurisdiction. Those seeking legal protection would have been confronted with a confusing number of administrative courts and intransparent jurisdictions.

Regarding the financial relationships, the draft would not have strengthened the *Länder* and municipalities or changed their subordinate position within the fiscal equalisation scheme. On the contrary, the Federal Government could have unilaterally altered the so far jointly negotiated Stability Pact (Art. 26), thus, interfering extensively in the ultimate decision-making authority of the *Länder* and the municipalities.

At first glance, it must surprise that the Fiedler Draft often seizes on those proposals which had found the least support during committee discussions. In this way, it could not lend itself to contributing to any kind of consensus after the deliberations had come to an end. On the contrary: it encouraged the *Landeshauptleute* to submit a counter-proposal (see para. 4 below.). However, interpreted in light of historic practices and developed administrative culture, the proposals become more comprehensible. The idea of state reform in Austria has long been viewed from a "josephinistic" standpoint. This means that administrative reform is understood to be executed in a top down fashion with the central authorities as main actors, whereas the idea of a regionally diverse and independent evolution holds little attraction. In particular, the state and administrative reforms over the last few years were imbued with a "neo-josephinism" (Bußjäger, 2002a: 232-234). According to this, reform is not understood to be carried out jointly by all levels of government but rather as an action decreed and executed from above in an educational manner. Based on this understanding the promoters of reform are supposed to be federal stakeholders[18] who generally demonstrate a high degree of resistance to innovation (Bußjäger, 2002b: 159-160).

17 The revision of these confusing landscapes would have been an important part of the administrative modernisation of Austria. The Fiedler Draft avoided discussing this topic.

18 According to the author's opinion, several supporters of the strongly "josephinistically" inspired administrative reform in Austria were members of the Austrian Convention. Aside

4.3 The position of the Landeshauptleute

When it became clear that a reform draft with centralising directions was going to be released by the chairmen of the Convention, the heads of the *Länder* created a working group gathering representatives from the *Länder* Burgenland, Lower Austria, Carinthia and Vorarlberg (Konrath, 2005: 361). Established late in the deliberation process, this working group was supposed to assemble the position of the *Länder* that were afterwards discussed and agreed upon by all of them. Presumably, it was the tabling of the Fiedler Draft that gave impetus to the coordinated efforts of the *Länder* and led to an agreement. On 19 January 2005, exactly one week after the presentation of the Fiedler Draft, the chair of the Conference of the *Landeshauptleute* and governor of Burgenland Hans Niessl presented the position of the *Länder*. Finding a consensus, the working group could rely on a series of earlier discussions held by the *Landeshauptleute*, in which the basic positions were already outlined or expressed in reference to individual cases. For the first time a comprehensive position paper on the allocation of powers had been prepared for a federal reform process.

Similar to the Fiedler-Draft, the paper prepared by the heads of the *Länder* also presented a three-pillar model with exclusive jurisdictions for each level and a third pillar of shared responsibilities. The allocation of powers differed of course from what was proposed by the Convention's chair, but did not contain big surprises as well: construction laws, regional planning and nature conservation were all seen as falling under exclusive jurisdiction of the *Länder*. For mandatory schools, the draft offered two alternatives either that they are legislated exclusively by the *Länder* or subsumed under the third pillar of shared jurisdictions. Hospitals, power stations and environmental protection were provided for under the third pillar. Overall, the allocation of powers had to be described as completely balanced and resembled in important aspects the positions of the chair of Committee 5, Peter Bußjäger, who had in fact introduced those months earlier.[19]

In the discussions held in the media, the *Landeshauptleute* ran into criticism for the "double majority" model they proposed as decision-making rule for all policies under the third pillar as well as for the financial equalisation laws and all laws that would increase the financial burdens of the *Länder*. This double majority model was based on the idea that the laws enacted by the National Council should receive the approval of the majority in the Fed-

---

from the Convention's chair, Fiedler, Bernhard Raschauer is worth mentioning, who was the chairman in 2000/2001 of then vice-chancellor Susanne Riess-Passer's Responsibilities Reform Commission, which prepared its own sensational report in March 2001 (see Bußjäger, 2002a: 227).

19 All documents are available as part of the steering committee's report dated 20 January 2005 (www.konvent.gv.at).

eral Council as well as the approval of seven of the nine *Länder*. This model was not entirely new: the requirement of a double majority was also included in the proposal of committee chair Bußjäger, but there, a simple majority of the *Länder* was regarded necessary. Since cooperation of the *Länder* in financial matters was made a requirement, criticism focused on the opportunities of blocking legislation that were opened up for each level. Although several arguments could be made in favour of joint legislation regarding the provisions of fiscal federalism, the proponents could not easily fend off the uttered criticism.

Against the backdrop that the Convention could not present a suitable and comprehensive proposal for reforming federal institutions including the transformation of the Federal Council into an effective second chamber representing the interests of the *Länder*, proponents of true federalist reforms were left with nothing else than focusing on opportunities of direct collaboration of the *Länder* by intergovernmental mechanisms. Since the elimination of the Federal Council itself was never part of the discussions, the proposals would have entailed the institutionalisation of the Conference of the *Landeshauptleute* that had already a long tradition in the federal state of Austria as a complementary body.

The participation of the Federal Council and the *Länder* in federal legislation was also intended to maintain some meaningful leeway for the *Länder* when implementing the policies subsumed under the third pillar. In practice, the strengthened position of the *Länder* might have led to bargaining processes, in which the stakeholders representing the federal and *Länder* bureaucracies were enabled to define the limits of the regulatory power of the federal government for the policies in that pillar. Principally, this form of slowing down the federal legislative process corresponded well with the enshrined tradition of a cooperative federal state in Austria and might also have had a positive effect on the quality of the laws enacted (Bußjäger, 2005: 27).

5. Other areas of conflict

5.1 Administrative reform caught between the resistance to innovation and the wrong track

The Austrian Constitution contains many detailed requirements on the shaping of administrative structures. For the implementation of federal laws, there is the so-called indirect federal administration model. The laws of the federal government are implemented by the heads of the *Länder* and their authorities in accordance with Art. 102 and 103 of the FCL, while a substantial part of the laws remain reserved for the federal government to be executed by its own federal authorities (see the catalogue of Art. 102 Para. 2 FCL). Contrary to Germany and Switzerland, federal laws are rarely implemented autonomously by the *Länder* administrations (Art. 11 FCL). The administration of schools and police services, for example, is largely assigned to the Austrian federal government. Furthermore, the Constitution also sets out in relative detail not only the structure of these federal authorities[20], but also the structure of *Länder* administrations.[21]

A fundamental revision of these structures has been a part of the canon of administrative reforms discussed for decades but never been realised (Bußjäger, 1999: 339). The resistance to innovation among the Austrian bureaucracy has always been too strong. In the past decade, there was a greater awareness that effective administrative reform could also be achieved by means of simple laws. One result was the administrative reform law of 2001, which re-assessed county administrations.

As has been mentioned above, the Convention discussed the issue of administrative reform once again at the constitutional level: surprisingly, indirect federal administration emerged unchanged from the discussions and a general consensus prevailed on keeping constitutional ties of the *Länder* bureaucracies. Representatives of the *Länder* bureaucracies believed they possessed greater legal validity than the *Länder* parliaments since their structure was set in stone by the Federal Constitutional Law (for example, see Steiermark's top civil servant at the time, the director of the *Länder* offices, Gerhart Wielinger, in the Austrian Lawyers Commission, 2004: 121-122).

Regarding the maintenance of the indirect federal administration of laws, several factors were decisive: on the one hand, the federal government was hardly prepared to give up controlling the implementation of federal laws and limit itself to vastly reduced federal oversight. On the other hand, indirect federal administration provided the *Landeshauptmann/Landeshauptfrau* with a prominent position in the Austrian constitutional system. The abolition of indirect federal administration in favour of the *Länder* implementing laws autonomously would have empowered the *Länder* governments while the position of the *Landeshauptmann/Landeshauptfrau* would have been weakened. To understand this complex relation fully one has to take into account that a politically powerful head of one *Land* could successfully fight against federal constraints in implementing laws and fend off too much federal control. Whether the *Länder* executive would be in a similar powerful position was however less predictable. That's why the heads of the *Länder* put more emphasis on preserving their powers than on attempting to reduce federal control on implementing laws. In consequence, the interest of the major stake-

20 Art. 81a and 81b of the Federal Constitution with respect to schools, Art. 78a to 78d with respect to policing.

21 For example, in the Federal Constitutional Law on the offices of the *Länder* governments.

holders on both the federal and the *Länder* level supported maintaining the status quo.

During the deliberations in the Convention this status quo oriented faction was challenged mainly by representatives of the SPÖ or organisations dominated by the Social Democrats, such as the Austrian Federation of Municipalities. They submitted proposals that would have clearly altered the existing structure of the general state administration but generated no consensus.

It was proposed for example to transfer responsibilities of the county administrations which are maintained by the *Länder* to a new to be created (municipal) administrative level. The larger cities that are mostly dominated by the SPÖ (this is mostly true of cities with a statute)[22] were supposed to be at the core of this new administrative level. However, these types of "regions with their own statute" did not form a basis for consensus. Representatives of the smaller municipalities fought strenuously against the possible absorption of municipal autonomy by such a new administrative entity equipped with a separate statute.

Similarly the proposals of the representatives of the SPÖ to reform the administration of schools and police services were not able to reach a consensus in the discussions. Again, a new type of region located between the *Länder* and the conventional county administrations was to be created with the intention to weaken the mostly conservative *Länder* and their counties. With regard to the administration of schools and the police additional proposals were made by the representatives of the ÖVP. The goal was wrapping the status quo in new, constitutional clothes that would be acceptable to ministerial bureaucrats and their political higher-ups. The members of the Convention could also not agree on this proposal.

Consequently, the discussions on the reform of the administrative structure fell victim to party politics and rivalries across all administrative levels, which made it practically impossible to reach an agreement (Bußjäger, 2005: 30).

5.2 Finances

Committee 10 of the Convention was responsible for dealing with the issue of the fiscal federalism and pursued the ambitious goal of making proposals regarding the "consolidation of the responsibilities for revenues and expenditures". It actually held this discussion but did not achieve any significant consensus.

Besides the many conflict issues, an "artificial disagreement" dominated the discussion on fiscal federalism: the *Bundesverfassung* is highly central-

22 See the Convention's report, Part 3, Committee 3, Point XIII.3.

ised with respect to the financial constitution. Surprisingly, the demand for autonomous fiscal power was not part of the list of demands of the Austrian *Länder*. However, under the heading of a "consolidation of the responsibilities for revenues and expenditures" this question was to be dealt with by Committee 10. Representatives of the *Länder* declined any interest in strengthening their own fiscal powers, for which they were greatly criticised in the media. In doing so, they provided the Federal Government representatives, who outwardly demonstrated their openness to fiscal federalism, with good ammunition to argue that the *Länder* were obviously interested in gaining more power but not more responsibility.

In reality there was no disagreement because also the representatives of the federal government were not really interested in enlarging the fiscal autonomy of the *Länder*. The federal government's residual power to determine which level should be allowed to levy taxes was never seriously questioned.[23] Basically, the discussion simply revolved around the willingness of the federal government to transfer some taxes to the *Länder* but only those bringing in relatively little revenue and having little potential for expansion, like property taxes on which the arguments focused primarily. However, the transfer of singular taxes into *Länder* jurisdiction could have been declined with better arguments than those brought forward by them.[24]

5.3 Fundamental Rights

The socio-politically highly significant discussion of the re-creation of the Austrian Catalogue of Fundamental Rights relates only marginally to federal issues and shall, for that reason, be only briefly discussed here. In many respects the Austrian Catalogue of Fundamental Rights dates back to 1867[25] and has been expanded many times over the last few decades. In particular the European Human Rights Convention has enjoyed constitutional status in Austria since 1964. Nevertheless, so far these rights are concerned with traditional, liberal fundamental rights that are understood as individual rights vis-à-vis the state. Fundamental social rights that allow for claims for entitlements from the state are not part of the Austrian Catalogue of Fundamental Rights.

---

23 See the Convention's report, Part 3, Committee 10, Point III.4.

24 For example, it was argued that various tax rates in the *Länder* and consequently in the smallest regions, contradicted the efforts of the EU to harmonise taxes. In addition, in times of rolling back public administrations, they would burden tax payers with the creation of parallel administrations and the necessary but bureaucratic partition of tax revenue. Furthermore, the economically weak regions would be disadvantaged in this competitive tax situation and, as a result, a first step would be made towards the end of solidarity (Report of the Convention, Part 3, Committee 10, Point III.4.).

25 The State Basic Law of 21 December 1867, on the general rights of state citizens for those in kingdoms and states represented in the imperial council, RGBl. No. 142 i.d.F. BGBl. No. 684/1988.

A very intense discussion was held in the Convention about fundamental social rights, whose introduction was strenuous demanded by representatives of the SPÖ and the Greens and declined by the conservative side with reference to the threat of the state being overwhelmed by entitlements. Committee 4, which was responsible for this question, offered no solution. In the steering committee and in the negotiations between representatives of the business sector and unions, a consensus was reached on the wording of various fundamental rights. The Catalogue of Fundamental Rights contained in the Fiedler Draft however did not win the approval of the SPÖ and the Greens because of their concerns with the legal provisions for implementation which they considered as insufficient. Remarkably, from a federal standpoint, a consensus on the basic wording was obviously fairly easy to reach on such fundamental social rights for which the *Länder* and the municipalities would ultimately have to bear the costs.[26]

6. Summary and future outlook

Several reasons account for the failure of the Convention: on the one hand, the lack of determination on the part of the leading political elites to propose clear guidelines and, in conjunction with this, the non-attendance of politicians in the committees of the Convention. On the other hand, the steering committee failed to reach a consensus on the decisive issues and the chair of the Convention did not prove to be the mediator that the steering committee and the Convention would have needed. Based on the reactions to the "Fiedler Draft", it was obvious that this paper would not help building a consensus. At the same time, the opportunity was lost to adopt a completely new constitution during the 2006 parliamentary session of the National Council, let alone hold a referendum.

The current Federal Government, in office since 2008, no longer pursues the project of a total revision of the *Bundesverfassung* in its agenda. Therefore the alternatives remain to completely abandon the project, to quietly pursue the discussions for constitutional reforms and if necessary implement changes under potentially different political circumstances during the next parliamentary session or to gradually implement those aspects that could be agreed upon as partial achievements in an incremental manner.

Judging from current reactions, the discussions regarding a completely new constitution might be continued. However, it is difficult to assess what the results of these debates might be in the end. From the point of view of

26 See Art. 62 (Right to Services of General Interest) and Art. 64 (Right to a Place to Live) of the Fiedler Draft.

Austrian federalism, the *Länder* survived the Convention relatively unscathed, which was not guaranteed at the beginning of the discussions in the Austrian Convention. This does not mean that Austrian federalism will find its way out of its defence. On the contrary: the pressure on the *Länder* will not decline and they will have to develop a new awareness of a modern, sustainable federalism in order to legitimise their continued existence.

On the federal government side, only limited federalist innovations can be expected: "neo-josephinism" and the resistance to innovation will continue to be the primary characteristics of the "sclerotic federal state". Therefore, it will be the responsibility of the *Länder* to prove that a federal distribution of power is not only democratically more effective, but also more efficient. They will have to demonstrate their readiness to bear federal responsibility. This kind of assertive, not defensive, federalism will also have to prove itself within the financial relationships between administrative units and determine, for example, whether and where fiscal federalism makes sense or not. Even more important will be to raise the awareness of the meaningfulness of legal differentiation and political pluralism within the Austrian society against the backdrop of the European multi-level system (Bußjäger, 2005: 33).

References

Berchtold, Klaus (1989): Die Verhandlungen zum Forderungsprogramm der Bundesländer seit 1956. Wien: Braumüller.

Bundeskanzleramt (ed.) (1991): Neuordnung der Kompetenzverteilung in Österreich. Wien: Bundeskanzleramt.

Bußjäger, Peter (1996): Ist der Bundesstaat noch reformierbar? In: Journal für Rechtspolitik (JRP) 4, (1), 8–17.

Bußjäger, Peter (1999): Die Organisationshoheit und Modernisierung der Landesverwaltungen. Wien: Braumüller.

Bußjäger, Peter (2002a): Zwischen Modernisierung und neojosephinistischen Holzwegen. In: Die Verwaltung 35, (2), 223-237.

Bußjäger, Peter (2002b): Der sklerotische Bundesstaat – Modernisierungsprobleme im österreichischen föderalen System. In: Zeitschrift für Politik 49, (2), 149-170.

Bußjäger, Peter (2004): Der Österreich-Konvent als Chance oder Inszenierung? – Der Bundesstaat Österreich vor einem neuen Anlauf der Verfassungsreform. In: Europäisches Zentrum für Föderalismusforschung (ed.): Jahrbuch des Föderalismus 2004. Baden-Baden: Nomos, 251-263.

Bußjäger, Peter (2005): Klippen einer Föderalismusreform. Innsbruck: Institut für Föderalismus.

Hämmerle, Kathrin (2005): „Niemand soll sagen können, er wäre nicht gehört worden…". Betrachtungen zum Österreich-Konvent aus Sicht der Zivilgesellschaft. In: Österreichische Zeitschrift für Politikwissenschaft 34, (4), 367-380.

Institut für Föderalismus (ed.) (1998): Materialien zur Bundesstaatsreform. Innsbruck: Institut für Föderalismus.

Institut für Föderalismus (ed.) (1993): 17. Bericht über die Lage des Föderalismus in Österreich (1992). Wien: Braumüller.

Khol, Andreas (2003): Der Österreich-Konvent: Auf dem Weg zu einer neuen Verfassung. In: Forum Parlament 1, (2), 34-38.

Konrath, Christoph (2005): Dann bleibt es eben so: Föderalismus und Kompetenzverteilung als Themen des Österreich-Konvents. In: Österreichische Zeitschrift für Politikwissenschaft 34, (4), 351-365.

Österreichische Juristenkommission (eds.) (2004): Der Österreich-Konvent – Zwischenbilanz und Perspektiven. Wien/Graz: Neuer Wissenschaftlicher Verlag.

Pernthaler, Peter (1989): Föderalismus und Verantwortung nach der österreichischen Bundesverfassung. In: Haller, W. (ed.): Festschrift für Ulrich Häfelin zum 65. Geburtstag. Zürich: Schulthess Juristische Medien, 351-369.

Pernthaler, Peter (2004): Österreichisches Bundesstaatsrecht. Wien: Verlag Österreich.

Weber, Karl (2003): Möglichkeiten der Verfassungsreform. In: Forum Parlament 1, (2), 44-48.

Wiederin, Ewald (2004): Bundesstaat neu. In: Österreichische Juristenkommission (eds.): Der Österreich-Konvent – Zwischenbilanz und Perspektiven. Wien/Graz: Neuer Wissenschaftlicher Verlag, 49-78.

Wiederin, Ewald (2008): Verfassungsbereinigung. In: Lienbacher, G./Wielinger, E. (eds.): Öffentliches Recht. Jahrbuch 2008. Wien/Graz: Neuer Wissenschaftlicher Verlag, 45-66.

Constitutional Negotiations in Cooperative Federalism – The Case of Germany

Anton Hofmann

In Germany, two reforms of federalism, adopted in 2006 and 2009, enabled the legislative jurisdictions between the federal government and the *Länder* to be more clearly separated and the financial constitution to guarantee a more equitable distribution between generations. In both the so-called Federalism Reform I and Federalism Reform II, it took a long time to prepare a final draft bill, and in both cases, failure could not be ruled out. In the end, favourable general conditions in each case led to the success of the reforms.

1. The initial context

Towards the end of the 1990s, the need to reform the German federal state became obvious in many instances. Already in the 1960s and 1970s, legislative responsibilities were transferred to the federal government through numerous amendments of the Basic Law (the German Constitution).[1] In addition, the federal government had made extensive use of its power in the areas of concurrent as well as framework legislation, leaving the *Länder* with only a few legislative and mainly organisational responsibilities. There was talk of purely "cooperative federalism" instead of "*Gestaltungsföderalismus*", i.e. a federalism where governments compete for best solutions when making policies.

While the *Länder* had lost ground, even at the federal level the negative consequences were felt to an increasing extent. Over the years, the number of federal laws requiring the approval of the *Bundesrat* had grown to approxi-

1 Examples: Art. 74 a BL (1971): Introduction of concurrent federal legislation concerning the remuneration and care of state civil servants; Art. 74 Para. 1 N. 24 BL (1972): Introduction of concurrent legislation concerning waste disposal, clean air and noise control; Art. 75 Para. 1 No. 1 a BL (1969): Introduction of framework legislation concerning the principles of the university system.

mately 60 % of the federal legislation.[2] The reasons for this development were the multifaceted regulations contained in federal laws concerning the administrative organisation and procedures of the states, combined with the so-called "uniform theory" developed by the Federal Constitutional Court. Accordingly, a law always required approval of the *Bundesrat* representing the *Länder* governments, even if it affected the *Länder* only by one procedural provision.[3] This gave the *Bundesrat*, first and foremost, the chance to block legislation that had been passed by the *Bundestag*. Federal legislation was in particular threatened by blockades during the last few years of the Kohl government and then later under the Schröder government, when opposing political parties controlled majorities in the *Bundestag* and the *Bundesrat*.

Furthermore, the distribution of power and responsibilities between the federal government and the *Länder* as enshrined in the Basic Law was criticised as not being suitably "europeanised". This, in particular, became clearer through the steadily increasing importance of the laws put forward by Brussels. For example, the federal government always had to translate European directives in the very broad area of environmental law into framework legislation. Subsequently, all 16 *Länder* had to work out detailed laws in this field. This legislative process carried out over three levels was found to be lengthy and very cumbersome.

The need for reform was also felt in the financial relationship between the federal and the *Länder* governments which had to be reviewed in detail not only because of the constantly rising level of public debt. It was obvious that the provisions of the Basic Law regarding a debt limit had proved as ineffective and that more restrictive tools were required. The need for reform also existed in those areas in which joint federal-*Länder* financing had been set up according to the provisions passed during the first Grand Coalition in the 1960s.[4] In these policy areas that fell under jurisdiction of the *Länder* and were originally their autonomous responsibility, the federal government had gained more and more political influence in exchange for making money available for the *Länder* thereby establishing a quasi "golden leash".

---

2 The proportion of laws requiring approval rose from 41.8% in the 1st legislative period (1949-1953) to 49.4% in the 5th legislative period (1965-1969), to 60% in the 10th (1983-1987) and 59.5% in the 13th legislative period (1994-1998).

3 Decision on Elder Care Case of 24.10.2002 (2 BvF 1/01) as well as the decisions on Assistant Professors of 27.07.2004 (2 BvF 2/02) and Student Tuition Fees of 26.01.2005 (2 BvF 1/03).

4 Financial Reform Act of 1969.

2. The process of constitutional reform

At the end of the 1990s, the factors mentioned led to a widespread readiness at the federal and the *Länder* level and in all the parties to start a process of reforming German federalism. The goal was, first and foremost, to make the allocation of legislative, financial and administrative powers between the federal government and the *Länder* more discernable and, in doing so, to strengthen the decision-making powers of the *Bundestag* and the *Länder* legislatures. The issue had been on the agenda of the Premiers' Conference since 1998. At the end of 1999, the governments of Bavaria and Bremen were put in charge of federalism reform on behalf of the *Länder*. Early on, the federal government also saw the need for reform. It was made official in late 2001 through a joint resolution by the heads of the federal and *Länder* governments declaring the need to review the structure of the federal state.

During these early discussions, it quickly became clear that a comprehensive review of the federal-state financial relationship, in particular, the provision for an effective debt threshold for public finances, would exceed the scope of a single federalism reform, in particular since financial equalisation between the *Länder* had to be adjusted due to a decision of the Federal Constitutional Court of 11 November 1999.[5] Therefore, it was decided to divide the reform efforts into two steps. The separation of the legislative powers as well as a reduction in the number of the tools for joint financing was supposed to be at the heart of the first Federalism Reform. Only then would a comprehensive review of the financial relationship between the two levels be tackled within the framework of Federalism Reform II. The adjustment of financial equalisation between the *Länder* would be negotiated in a separate process that had to meet the deadline of 31 December 2002, set by the Federal Constitutional Court.

As the commissions on reforming federalism were established, the decision was made in both cases to consciously avoid the model of the constitutional convention, i.e. an expert commission that was to represent society as much as possible. Since the areas that were to be included in the reform were obvious, all actors involved agreed from the start that the problems to be solved did not require expert knowledge but rather political decisions. Therefore, the commissions were to be composed of political decision-makers only, aside from a few experts.

5 Decision of 11 November 1999, File No. 2 BvF 2/98, 2 BvF 3/98, 2 BvF 1/99 and 2 BvF 2/99.

2.1 Federalism Reform I

On 16 and 17 October 2003, the *Bundestag* and the *Bundesrat* decided to establish a joint commission on modernising the structure of the federal state.[6] The *Bundestag* and the *Bundesrat* each sent 16 members to the commission. The 16 minister presidents participated as delegated members on behalf of the *Bundesrat*. Edmund Stoiber, the Bavarian Premier at that time, and Franz Müntefering, federal parliament party whip for the SPD at that time, were elected as chairs of the commission. A two thirds majority of commission members was required for decisions on amendment proposals. However, in fact no official votes on individual topics discussed were held, as it soon became clear that an agreement would only be possible as part of an overall package deal.

In eleven meetings of the commission, each one prepared in great detail by both chairs, the delegates worked step by step towards this comprehensive package deal. Yet, no agreement could be reached among the members of the commission on the reform concept[7] presented by the two chairs at the final meeting of the commission in December 2004. However, the discussions continued beyond this date. The discussions primarily centred around the allocation of powers between the federal and the *Länder* governments in the areas of education/universities, environmental legislation[8], internal security[9], the involvement of the *Länder* governments in European matters, as well as the division of liability between the federal and *Länder* government in case that a supranational commitment is broken (in particular, the European Stability Pact). By May 2005, the chairs had succeeded in bringing about an agreement on these important issues that had remained unresolved.

Reform efforts were interrupted by events after the SPD lost the state elections in North Rhine-Westphalia on 22 May 2005, which led to the early dissolution of the *Bundestag* and, as a result, momentarily stopped the elaboration of the reform of federalism. After the 2005 federal election, the newly formed Grand Coalition government took up the reform proposal that had come close to form the negotiation result. During the coalition negotiations, agreement was found especially with regard to a particularly sensitive subject: The right of the *Länder* to enact laws that deviate from existing federal legislation. Moreover, the paper prepared by the former chairpersons of the reform commission based on the achievements of the negotiations was attached as an appendix to the coalition agreement without significant changes.[10]

---

6 *Bundestag* Printed Matter 15/1685; *Bundesrat* Printed Matter 750/03.

7 Procedural Document 104 – new – of 13 December 2004.

8 In particular hunting, conservation, land use, land distribution, regional planning, and water supply.

9 In particular measures against terrorism, disaster management and civil defense.

10 Coalition agreement between the CDU, the CSU and the SPD of 11 November 2005, Appendix 2.

After this reform concept was revised during an editing conference and another political round in February 2006, the prepared draft bills were presented to the *Bundestag* and the *Bundesrat* in March 2006.[11] During the legislative process, these bills were changed only in a few aspects that were essentially editorial in nature. Thus the completed reform proposal presented by the chairs of the commission and revised in cooperation with representatives of the federal government in May 2005, passed the legislative process. The reform came into effect on 1 September 2006[12].

2.2 Federalism Reform II

Apart from including the reform of legislative jurisdictions in the coalition agreement of 11 November 2005, concluded between the CDU, the CSU and the SPD, the reform of constitutional rules concerning financial relations was formulated as another goal of the Grand Coalition. With its resolution of 15 December 2006[13], the *Bundestag* and the *Bundesrat* established the "Joint Commission on the Modernisation of Federal-State Financial Relationships" to be chaired by Günther H. Oettinger, the Premier of Baden-Württemberg at that time, and Peter Struck, the SPD parliamentary whip at that time. The composition of the commission and the decision-making arrangements remained mainly the same as those for Federalism Reform I. The commission was designed to comprehensively review the federal-*Länder* financial relations, as well as rules on public administration at all levels. An "open list of issues" attached to the resolution defining the agenda of the commission included, among others, "the development of substantive criteria for an acceptable indebtedness (introduction of debt limits and a "debt brake"), "measures against bureaucratisation and to increase efficiency in administration", as well as "strengthening the autonomy of governments at all levels".

On 8 March 2007, the members of the second reform commission held their constituent meeting. During subsequent commission meetings, the discussions focused, first and foremost, on the particular rules of limiting and reducing public debts, as well as on financial assistance for the poorer *Länder*. A debt relief fund paid by the federal and the *Länder* governments according to specific shares and determined to cancel all existing debts, which initially was introduced into the discussions by one of the chairmen, Günther Oettinger, was unsuccessful in gaining the required majority. Further

11 Draft bill to amend the Basic Law, *Bundestag* Printed Matter 16/813 and *Bundesrat* Printed Matter 178/06; Draft of federalism reform ancillary law, *Bundestag* Printed Matter 16/814 and *Bundesrat* Printed Matter 179/06.

12 Federal Law Gazette 2006 I Pg. 2034.

13 *Bundestag* Plenary Protocol 16/074; *Bundestag* Printed Matter 16/3885; *Bundesrat* Printed Matter 913/06.

negotiations proved to be difficult, notwithstanding the fact that the members of the commission were trying to finalise the reform project during the 16th legislative period. At its last meeting on 5 March 2009, the commission eventually succeeded in agreeing on a model for the debt brake, as well as on the level of assistance for a defined group of financially weaker *Länder*.[14] The proposals elaborated by the commission subsequently passed the legislative process with clear majorities in both houses.[15] The amendments to the Basic Law came into effect on 1 August 2009. Due to the many interim provisions, the rules governing the debt brake will come into effect no sooner than 2016 for the federal government and 2020 for the *Länder* governments.

3. Important results of the reforms

3.1 Federalism Reform I

The Federalism Commission I agreed on a number of significant amendments to the Basic Law including the rules defining when a federal legislation requires the assent of the *Bundesrat*, the separation of legislative powers of the federal level and the *Länder*, partly through increasing exclusive responsibilities, partly through the transfer of many legislative issues to a newly created type of concurrent jurisdiction allowing the *Länder* parliaments to deviate from federal law, and a reduction in the number of cumbersome tools of joint financing.

3.1.1 Changes concerning the assent of the *Bundesrat* in federal legislation

After the constitutional amendment, the assent of the *Bundesrat* in federal legislation will no longer be required in order to control the provisions of the federal government concerning the organisation and procedures of *Länder* administration (Art. 84 BL, old version), but rather depend on financial consequences of federal laws for *Länder* budgets (Art. 104a Para. 4 BL, new version). Through this change, the proportion of laws subject to the veto of a majority in the *Bundesrat* will be greatly reduced.

---

14 Resolutions of the *Bundestag* and *Bundesrat* Commission on the Modernisation of the Federal-State Financial Relationships, Commission Printed Matter 174.

15 Draft bill on the amendment of the Basic Law (Articles 91c, 91d, 104b, 109, 109a, 115, 143d), *Bundestag* Printed Matter 16/12410, *Bundesrat* Printed Matter 262/09; Draft of ancillary law on Federalism Reform 2, *Bundestag* Printed Matter 16/12400, *Bundesrat* Printed Matter 263/09.

3.1.2 Separation of legislative powers between the federal and the *Länder* level

Since the reduction in the proportion of laws requiring approval of the *Bundesrat* primarily benefits the federal government, it was important that the changes made in the separation of powers support the interests of the *Länder* for more leeway and room to manoeuvre as well and in doing so enhance the meaning of "effective federalism". In fact, the *Länder* legislatures received a significant range of legislative powers in different policy areas.

The differentiation of concurrent legislation mentioned above is an important tool in this regard. In those areas that the Basic Law places under this type of legislative power, the *Länder* parliaments have the fundamental right to pass laws, as long as the federal government does not exercise its legislative jurisdiction. Should the federal government choose to exercise its power, each individual *Land* parliament can pass a law deviating from the federal law. In the relationship between federal and *Länder* law, the law prevails which was passed later. To avoid a ping-pong effect, i.e. a competition with the federal government and the *Länder* alternately making changes to the law within a short period of time, there is a time limit for legislation. Furthermore, in some narrowly defined areas the Basic Law stipulates areas not subject to "deviating legislation". To facilitate federal lawmaking in the areas falling under the new type of concurrent legislation, the federal government is freed from the necessary clause, Art. 72 Para. 2 BL, thus terminating the necessity to give reasons for the need of federal legislation that had existed before. With the introduction of the right for the *Länder* to deviate, the former framework legislation no longer applies. This clearly simplifies the very cumbersome legislative process in cases transposing European regulations into national law.

In particular, the autonomy of the *Länder* was strengthened in administration and in matters of their civil service. They received the exclusive legislative responsibility for their civil servants and judges, including remuneration and care. Other transfers of powers to the *Länder* can be found in the areas of the penal system, the right to assemble in public, the support of social housing, the regulation of noise due to behaviour, the nursing home care, and commercial law with primarily regional relevance (e.g. laws governing store hours and restaurants).

Following the reform, federal legislation concerning the admission to universities and academic degrees and relating to environmental affairs like hunting, nature conservation, land distribution, land use, regional planning, and water supply are subject to the deviation provisions. Even if the federal government sets the rules on the organisation and procedures of *Länder* administration implementing federal laws, Art. 84 Para. 1 BL now gives the *Länder* the fundamental right to deviate – with the consequence that the *Länder* cannot veto such a law in the *Bundesrat*.

3.1.3 Reduced number of instruments for joint financing

At the heart of this change lies the elimination of the spending power of the federal government in the area of education, one of the core areas of *Länder* jurisdiction. It implemented the aim of separating powers and of reinforcing the autonomy of the *Länder*. Now, the federal and *Länder* governments co-operate only to determine the effectiveness of the education system based on international comparative evaluations and, in this regard, jointly prepare reports and recommendations. All in all, financial assistance from the federal government will no longer be available in areas of exclusive legislative jurisdiction of the *Länder*. Furthermore, all financial assistance provided for the "Promotion of Residential Construction" and for "Improvement of Municipal Transportation" – were eliminated while simultaneously agreeing on a settlement to compensate the *Länder* financially.

3.2 Federalism Reform II

At the heart of Federalism Reform II was the entrenchment of a debt brake for the federal government and the *Länder* governments into the constitution. In addition, it was agreed upon an adjustment of the federal-*Länder* relationship in some administrative matters.

3.2.1 Financial issues

The rule constraining public debt included in Art. 109 and 115 BL consists essentially of three components. Between 2011 and 2016, the new structural deficit of the federal budget has to be gradually reduced in equal increments until it is not higher than 0.35% of the gross national product (GNP). Beginning in 2020, the *Länder* governments will no longer be allowed to incur deficits. Economic fluctuations can, however, be taken into account. By derogation from this rule, annual debt can be increased in times of recession, provided that governments accept a commitment to pay back the debt in better economic times (a so-called "flexible budget"). For the federal government, the debt settlement process was constructed in accordance with the European Stability and Growth Pact, to ensure that the debt incurred during a recession will be repaid in prosperous times. Furthermore, there are exceptions to the ban on making debts for specific, extraordinary emergency situations (for example, natural disasters) that are beyond the control of the State but heavily impact the State's financial situation. However, the federal and the *Länder* governments have to repay the debts they incurred under this provision.

An early warning system and a stability council that report to the federal as well as the *Länder* finance ministers and the federal minister for Economic Affairs were established to control and monitor the debt brake. If a looming budgetary emergency situation is perceived, a five-year financial restructuring program must be agreed to by the respective *Land* or the federal government. No majority was reached with respect to the suggestion made during discussions that infringements of the debt brake by the federal or the *Länder* government should automatically be subject to sanctions (e.g. surtaxes on income taxes).

To help them stay within the debt limit, the financially weak states of Bremen, Saarland, Schleswig-Holstein, Berlin and Saxony-Anhalt will receive 800 million euros in total funding between 2011 and 2020, one half to be financed by the federal government and the other half by the *Länder* governments. However, to receive the support, these *Länder* must follow a strict funding regulation.

3.2.2 Administrative issues

The negotiating parties also agreed upon a closer cooperation between the federal and the *Länder* governments in the near future with regard to the planning, installation and operation of their IT systems. The cooperation was constitutionally enshrined in a new Art. 91c BL and developed in greater detail in a separate treaty signed by the federal and the *Länder* governments. In addition, the commitment by the governments to a voluntary benchmarking of administrative performance – according to the model of the PISA arrangement – was constitutionally enshrined in a new Art. 91d BL. Moreover, the ban against financial support provided by the federal government to *Länder* in the areas where the federal government has no legislative powers was relaxed in accordance with Art. 104b BL: the possibility of the federal government guaranteeing financial assistance in the event of a natural disaster and extraordinary emergency situations was expanded. A few administrative details were also clarified.

4. Assessment of the results

4.1 Federalism Reform I

Most importantly, the aim of "a separation of powers between the Federal Government and the *Länder*" that was set at the beginning of the process was actually achieved. Of course, *Länder* such as Bavaria, which are economically and administratively strong, would have appreciated gaining more powers and responsibilities, whether in the area of exclusive legislative jurisdiction or by enhanced opportunities for deviations from federal law. Since, however, during the reform process, the principle of symmetric federalism in which all states enjoy the same powers and obligations was never questioned by anyone, a compromise had to be found that took into account the capacities of the economically weaker states.

This principal aim of separating powers was achieved most effectively by reducing the number of laws requiring approval of the *Bundesrat*. Indeed, between September 2006 and February 2009, the share of these federal laws was at approx. 39% and thus substantially lower than before the reform came into effect (approx. 60%).[16]

During the discussions, the federal government repeatedly expressed its fear that *Länder* legislators would behave irresponsibly given their newly won legislative powers. In the area of the penal system, there was talk of an anticipated "meanness competition". These fears proved to be unfounded. Meanwhile, it is generally recognised that the *Länder* laws based on decentralised powers have succeeded. This is also true with respect to the penal system, which provides a good example of *Länder* legislators being able to deal with difficult legislative issues just like federal legislators.

The newly created provision for deviating legislation was – and continues to be – sharply criticised by the informed public. However, at present it can be seen that it has proved to provide an effective tool to disentangle legislative responsibilities. The argument, deviating legislation would lead to a fragmentation of laws and sectionalism, misjudged the fundamental concerns of Federalism Reform I, i.e. a reinforcement of effective and competitive federalism. This goal cannot be achieved without the constitutional rights of the individual *Länder* to pass laws implementing different regulatory concepts. The criticism also disregarded the prevailing consensus reached at the end of the 1990s across the entire political spectrum that centralist and unitary efforts must be countered to strengthen the federal system and democracy.

The new deviating legislation benefits all participants. On the one hand, the federal government can implement its own concept, which was not possible by the former framework legislation or by concurrent legislation subject to the necessity clause. On the other hand, deviating legislation gives the *Länder* the opportunity to adopt this federal concept or to pursue their own ideas. The resulting competitive relationship between the federal and the *Länder* governments as well as between the *Länder* themselves, generally revitalises the legislative process and improves the quality of the laws at the federal as well as the *Länder* level.

Technically, the separation of powers could have also been achieved through a dual federalism model in which clear, exclusive federal and regional jurisdictions are established. The reform debate, however, quickly demonstrated that agreement on such a clear separation could not be achieved. Through deviating legislation, a way was found that would not

16 See the expert report by Scientific Services of the *Bundestag* on the Impact of Federalism Reform of 27 August 2009 (3 – 321/09).

completely put the burden on one side or the other and that, at the same time, makes the federal constitution of the Basic Law better adjusted to European integration.

Parliamentarians of *Länder* legislations need time, of course, to make use of their newly created room to manoeuvre which partly was opened only recently due to intermediary provisions. In some areas, greater activity on the part of *Länder* legislators in some areas would have been highly desirable. Sometimes, it is not easy to gain the necessary majority in a *Länder* parliament to pass a law deviating from federal law. However, the fact that up to now many *Länder* have only reluctantly made use of deviating legislation is in no event an appropriate argument against the basically correctness of this tool. In any case, not even the critics have been able to propose a better idea so far.

4.2 Federalism Reform II

Even if the full impact of the rules regarding the debt brake, which were at the heart of Federalism Reform II, will not be felt for a couple of years, there are some indications as to the possible consequences. For example, federal and *Länder* finance ministers are already using the powerful argument of the new constitutional provision as a protection against the desire of departments for increasing expenditures. Admittedly, this situation has not prevented Germany from terminating the year 2010 with an exceptionally high new indebtedness. The reason for this was the economic and banking crisis, which reached a historic scale. Despite these difficult basic conditions, the federal Minister of Finance had to take into account the rules that would in future limit borrowing. Considering the ineffectiveness of the current rule entrenched in articles 109 and 115 BL, the introduction of a strict debt limit in the spirit of fairness between generations has to be regarded as a considerable success. Even if the rule governing borrowing under extraordinary circumstances could have been stricter, it is clear from the new requirements that public debt will no longer be the rule, but rather the exception.

The combination of strict debt limits on the one hand and funding for financially weak *Länder* on the other represents an overall compromise. Without the guarantee of compensation, the governments of these *Länder* would not have agreed to a constitutionally defined limit on new debts. Inversely, governments of the financially strong *Länder* and the federal government could only be persuaded to make this fund available in case the governments profiting from the grant accepted strong controls of their budget. This agreement is supposed to ensure that the funding will not pour into a bottomless pit.

From Bavaria's point of view, the *Land* with the lowest debt per capita, another positive result is that the idea of a fund to repay pre-existing debt was not implemented. This kind of fund would have gone against the principle of the political and budgetary responsibility of individual *Länder* and local governments and would not have been affordable for the financially strong states. First of all, it would have burdened the *Länder* with small debt rates which, in the past, had demanded sacrifices on the part of their citizens in the interest of more solid *Länder* finances. Paying into a fund to repay existing debts would have led to an unacceptable bias in the federal structure. The Federal Constitutional Court had already determined that, as a rule, every *Länder* government has to bear the financial burdens and is responsible for the consequences of its own financial and political decisions[17]. Of course, a provision would have been desirable that would have imposed the repayment of pre-existing debt by the federal and the *Länder* governments. However, no majority emerged regarding this kind of solution.

Within the framework of Federalism Reform II administrative issues took a back seat compared to financial issues. Nonetheless, it is noteworthy that the reform succeeded by avoiding any contradictions to Federalism Reform I. Any transfer of powers to the federal government in this field or the approval or expansion of joint administration would have been inconsistent with the goal of Federalism Reform I to separate powers between the federal and the *Länder* governments.

5. Conclusion

Both reforms of federalism proved the ability of German federalism to be modernised. The results revealed not only cosmetic changes of the Basic Law, but rather implemented reasonable, substantial changes to the federal-*Länder* relations. The significant efforts of participants in the process to ensure success show that an important and necessary constitutional change of German federalism is a difficult but not a hopeless endeavour.

The experiences made during the discussions could be helpful for any future attempts at reform. The following insights seem to be especially important:

- Comprehensive reforms of federalism aiming at significant adjustments of federal-*Länder* relations can only succeed if some basic conditions coexist. First and foremost, a fundamental condition to start a reform is a broad consensus inside the federal government and among the *Länder* governments on the need for reform. The negotiation process always has to be oriented towards the relevant issues and, as far as possible, free from tactical party politics. This primarily requires that, during the re-

17 Decision of the Federal Constitutional Court of 19 October 2006, File No. 2 BvF 3/03.

form process, no political events will act against the goal of the reform or make it look unachievable. Furthermore, the success of the reform presumes a political situation with clear majorities within the negotiating committees and finally also in the legislative process. Last but not least, it always comes down to individual persons who have a vision and who shape and guide the reform process using their powers of persuasion.

All these factors existed for both federalism reforms. In the case of Federalism Reform I, it was, among other things, frustration about governability triggered by the *Bundesrat*'s opportunity to block legislation which struck all political powers equally and led to a broad consensus on the need for reform aiming at disentangling powers and relations between the federal and the *Länder* governments. With Federalism Reform II, it was the steadily rising public debt which placed a great burden on fairness between generations and which made the need for reform apparent. Furthermore, in the case of both reforms, the discussions were not disturbed by major political events that could have justified abandoning the envisaged goal. If, for example, the global economic and financial crisis in 2009 requiring large-scale financial and political measures had occurred six months earlier, the introduction of a debt brake would have hardly been possible.

- The Grand Coalition of the CDU, the CSU and the SPD formed the political framework for both reforms and contributed to its success. It allowed the federal government, the majority parties in the *Bundestag* and all leaders of *Länder* governments to be bound together in the reform efforts without requiring to leap over any major party or political trenches. The discussions leading to the Federalism Reform I, took place, in large part, during the Red-Green coalition, but eventually succeeded after the reform proposals were included in the CDU/CSU-SPD coalition agreement. With both reforms, it was the main stakeholders, in particular the chairs, who were convinced that the envisaged goals could be attained, who always kept the reform process moving forward and, therefore, contributed immensely to its success.

  The window of opportunity in which all the necessary basic conditions are available rarely opens and only for a short period of time. The right timing and a keen political sense to recognise it are certainly important factors in the success of federalism reforms.
- In federalism reforms, the cleavages do not inevitably divide the federal government and the *Länder* governments, and they also are not necessarily defined by party politics. Conflicts of interest to be dealt with in negotiations depend much more on the purpose of the reform. This can imply that in a package deal the roles of different participants can vary from issue to issue. It is particularly important to understand this aspect in order to assess the chances of success, for usually all the issues relating to

reform will be connected (as was the case in Federalism Reform I and II). If the lines of conflict are too complex, they can make the drafting of an overall compromise difficult. Therefore, it is of utmost importance that powerful stakeholders in a reform commission can sound out chances for compromise despite a complex jumble of interests.

- When selecting the issues that will become the object of reform, a middle ground has to be found. Should the reform process consider too few issues, it quickly runs into a yes/no situation with respect to the central issue, leaving little room for compromise. If the number of issues is too great, the complexity makes it difficult to arrive at an overall solution.
  This can be easily demonstrated at both federalism reforms. For example, the central financial issues of Federalism Reform I had to be set aside until a later date to allow sufficient time for solving the difficult problems of reallocating legislative powers. In the case of both reforms, the basic conflicts had been moderated through a mutual give and take on other, less salient issues that directly related to the central issues. In any case, both reforms were so broadly laid out that, in the end, all sides could see something in it for them. This also is proof of the quality of both federalism reforms, for a reform which, in the end, only recognises clear winners and clear losers is certainly not a good reform.

3. Constitutional Reform in Federal Systems with Divided Societies

Federal Reform and Party Politics. The Case of the Fifth Belgian State Reform

Dave Sinardet

1. Introduction

Constitutional reform processes in federal political systems are often analysed through a focus on the different identities and interests of the constituent entities. Regions, communities, *Länder*, provinces, cantons or other federated institutions tend to be regarded as unitary actors, much like states in international relations theory. Certainly in so-called "multinational" federations, the collectives that these institutions represent are also considered this way ("the Flemish", "the Walloons", "the Québécois", "the Catalans"). This is very often the case in domestic political and media discourse, but also occurs in international academic work.

While specific interests of sub-state institutions and collectives can of course be a crucial factor to understand decision-making processes that lead to federal reform, largely or entirely conducting analysis through this lens can lead to forms of methodological nationalism: not so much because these collectives would explicitly be considered as natural realities, but because they do tend to be looked at as undifferentiated and homogeneous entities with single collective rational interests, such as is mostly the case in discourse of sub-state nationalist parties.

Such one-dimensional analysis also runs the risk of underestimating and obscuring other crucial dynamics at play, such as that of party politics: the reasons, motivations and interests individual parties can have in engaging (or not) in federal reform. Parties may even try to exploit regional or cultural identities and interests, in the pursuit of other partisan goals, in which case analysing federal reform solely or mainly in terms of those interests can play into those partisan strategies.

While party politics is undoubtedly a relevant lens to analyse constitutional reform in federations in general, this is particularly true for the case of Belgium, which has often been characterised as a "partitocracy". Moreover, Belgium is also a consociational federation, which again implies a very important role for political parties and their elites. In Belgium, analysing the role of political parties is thus essential to understand political and societal evolutions and therefore also to understand federal reform. They are an often underestimated factor in historical accounts of evolution towards federalisation of the country, but also remain crucial to explain specific institutional reforms at later stages up until today. We will show this through an analysis of the decision making procedures that led to the 2001 *Lambermont* reform, the fifth reform of the Belgian state since 1970, negotiated by the liberal, socialist and green government parties, with key roles for Flemish nationalists and French-speaking Christian Democrats. But first, we will develop some more general considerations on the role of political parties in federal reform.

2. Federalism and party politics

Recently, the literature on federalism has started to show attention for the role of political parties in federalisation processes and more particularly for the interests and rationales behind parties' positions on federal reform. Indeed, these are not necessarily solely or primarily driven by deep convictions on nation and identity or by the will to reflect or construct socio-cultural realities, as is often assumed. While these may largely be the motivations of substate nationalist parties, traditional parties have often been known to adapt their positions on decentralisation as a strategy to react to electoral threats of sub-state nationalist parties. This is more often the case for typical governing parties, who have a general tendency to adapt their positions to electoral evolutions, as well as for parties which have most to fear from the success of sub-state nationalist parties in elections and are ideologically closer to them (particularly on the left-right axis). For instance, the success of the right wing Lega Nord in 1990's Italy mostly lead centre right parties to become more strongly in favour of decentralisation, while the success of the left wing Scottish National Party in the UK had a similar effect on the positions of the Labour Party, at first mostly in Scotland but increasingly also on the national level (Mazzoleni, 2009: 212-213; Mitchell, 1998).

There is however another, less analysed strategic reasoning that can determine parties' positions on federal reform. As argued by O'Neill (2003), for parties whose electoral support at sub-state levels appears more secure than their prospects in national elections, decentralisation can represent a desirable strategy, as it maximises electoral possibilities. This is mostly the case for parties with strong support in specific regions, low expectations to control power at the centre and stable support over time. O'Neill (2003) showed the importance of such partisan political calculations as explanation for decentralisation for Latin American democracies, but similar dynamics can be observed in Western European federations. At different times and in different contexts, national left wing opposition parties have favoured decentralisation so as to create new political institutions in which they would have more chance to be in power. This was for instance the case in Italy of the 1960s, France of the 1970s and to a lesser extent also in Spain. In 1990s' Italy however, with the Lega Nord being very strong in the north, left wing parties opposed decentralisation (Mazzoleni, 2009; Sorens, 2009). The nationalist turn of Labour in Scotland during the Thatcher years can also be explained by the fact that Labour's electoral situation in England – and thus in the UK – was very unpromising while they kept on being the strongest party in Scotland (Mitchell, 1998).

Particularly the examples of Italy and the UK show that these two types of party political strategies to favour decentralisation – response to electoral threats and opportunity for political power at new levels – are often linked. Indeed, parties who are ideologically closest to sub-state nationalist parties will have most to fear on the electoral level, but will often also be the ones profiting from decentralisation to specific regions. This is because sub-state nationalist parties generally tend to adopt the dominant ideological position in their region. This can in turn be explained by the fact that these parties will of course always be able to exert more political power on the regional than on the national level as their electoral base is generally entirely regional. Also, staying in tune with the dominant ideological current in the region can reinforce their claim to represent the whole region and permit to attack the legitimacy of the national level, in which this position is generally less strongly represented. While dominant parties in a specific region thus have a double electoral interest in favouring decentralisation, sub-state nationalist parties have a double interest to be ideologically close to the dominant political current in their region.

This double dynamic can be seen at work in Belgium, where Flemish sub-state nationalism has always been dominantly right wing and associated with Flemish Catholicism while its Walloon counterpart was always more left wing, close to the Walloon labour movement, as well as secular. Simultaneously, the catholic party and socialist party were always the leading political forces in respectively the Flemish and Walloon region, which often contributed to their stances being associated with those of Flanders and Wallonia as a whole. Consequently, in the north of Belgium, the Flemish catholic party and to a lesser extent also other right wing parties have gone furthest in adopting positions in favour of regional autonomy, with the Flemish Socialists and Greens generally being more reluctant. The south shows a mirror image, with federal reform mostly being advocated by the French-speaking Socialists – certainly in the 1970s and 1980s – and the French-speaking catholics being most reluctant. Not only did the Flemish Socialists and the French-speaking Christian Democrats have less to fear from the competition of sub-state nationalist parties as they were not fishing in the same ideological pond, they also had no interest in more decentralisation, as they were not electorally strong enough in their region to reap the benefits.

Regionalism and federalism in Belgium have always been linked to the socio-economical left-right divide and to a lesser extent also to the philosophical divide between Catholics and Liberals. As Huyse (1981: 124) explains, the gain of importance of the community issue from the 1960s onwards can in part be explained by how pacification of the two main divisions in Belgian political life, which had occurred in the years after the war through consociational pact-making, was not as complete as it might have seemed. As well in the north as in the south of the country, strong factions within both majority groups (Catholics in Flanders, Socialists in Wallonia) opposed the status quo, that had taken form in pacts and found in regional and cultural ideas "new, more compelling instruments for the diffusion of their clerical/anticlerical or socioeconomic blueprints", leading Huyse (1981: 124) to conclude that "the federalist idea became more attractive to more people in the 1970s not strictly for linguistic or cultural or ethnic reasons, but because it bears the promise of the ultimate achievement of socialism in Wallonia and of a sort of Catholic model of societal harmony in Flanders". This dynamic contributed to the split of political parties, leaving Belgium without any national party of importance since 1978.

The difference between the Belgian case and those of the aforementioned federations is that in Belgium both parties that were strong in their region were not in opposition on the national level. Quite to the contrary, the Flemish Christian Democrats and French-speaking Socialists were very often also in power on the national level. However, it is probably not a coincidence that they mostly became strong defenders of regionalisation when their hopes to gain an overall majority on the national level became quite unrealistic and they realised they would always have to share power on the national level with one another. Also, the consociational mould in which federalisation in Belgium was carried through, strengthened the logic that the regional balance of power would generally also be respected in national coalition-making, turning a coalition of Christian Democrats and Socialists into the most evident coalition for a very long time (see Swenden, 2002).

This consociational logic also reinforced the dominance of party politics (Sinardet, 2010). In a consociational system, parties are the prime actors who mobilise the different societal or cultural groups, aggregate their interests and recruit their elites. It is between these elites that the overarching consensus has to be found. In other words, parties notably "provide the two-way linking mechanism between the mass and the elite of the encapsulated sub-cultures" (Luther, 1999: 5). Belgium can consequently be considered as a "partitocracy", implying amongst other things that government is dominated by the political parties of the majority (De Winter, 1998).

Taking into account party politics in the analysis of federal reform of course does not mean one should put aside regional interests altogether. Specific interests of regions can obviously also play a part, as well for positions of political parties active in these regions, as for federal reform as such. For instance, the fact that the French-speaking socialist party in Belgium has since the state reform of 1993 become much more hesitant in advocating federal reform and later downright hostile to further large scale decentralisation, followed in this stance to more or less extent by all French-speaking parties, can be attributed to the fact that the socio-economical and financial situation of the Walloon region was such that it was not perceived in its interest to regionalise many more competences. Nevertheless, party politics remains a crucial but underestimated lens through which to analyse federal reform in Belgium up to this date, as we will show by analysing the 2001 *Lambermont* reform.

3. The fifth Belgian state reform

Before getting into the details of the decision-making process, it is important to sketch the framework within which the *Lambermont* reform took place.

First of all, it should be noted that *Lambermont* can actually not be labelled as a constitutional reform *strictu sensu*. It was the first of the Belgian state reforms which did not include any revision of the constitution. In Belgium the constitutional revision procedure entails that only articles listed for revision and approved by Parliament before elections (then called pre-constituent assembly) can be revised by the newly elected parliament after elections (then called constituent assembly). In the case of *Lambermont*, the federal coalition was bound by a very limited declaration of revision of the Constitution voted by the previous majority. This was however not a fundamental problem as many crucial aspects of state reform, such as competence transfers and financing, are not contained in the Belgian constitution, but in special laws, which can be changed without prior declaration of revision. They do however require a simple majority in both language groups on top of the overall two thirds majority also needed for constitutional revision.[1]

Next, to understand why this fifth Belgian state reform came onto the political agenda, it is necessary to point to different elements in the political context before, during and after the government formation of 1999.

The most important catalyst was undoubtedly the problematic financial situation of the French-speaking community. This was regulated by the Special Finance Law (SFL), which determines the financing of the regions and communities and was originally voted in 1989, to be amended in the previous state reform of 1993. The original SFL of 1989 had foreseen a transitory period of ten years for the formula used to count the number of school children

1 Still, for some reforms on the agenda the absence of constitutional reform was controversial. According to a critical advice of the legislation section of the Council of State, the regionalisation of the communal and provincial law would have to be voted through a revision of article 162 of the Constitution, which had not been declared open for revision. However, the parties decided to not take into account this advice and were later confirmed in their position by the Constitutional Court, which ruled that a revision of article 162 was indeed not necessary. For more details on this constitutional debate, see Pas, 2002.

per community, which was at the basis of the system to determine the criteria of division between the communities of the part of the VAT they receive from the federal level. In 1999 a new system therefore had to be found, implying that at least this rather small technical discussion would have to be dealt with (Pagano, 2002).

But this was not as essential as the structural underfunding of the French-speaking community and specifically of its education system, which takes up the large share of the budget. Dealing with this was a priority for at least some of the French-speaking parties. One of their core demands was that the financial means transferred from the federal VAT revenues, which largely served to finance the communities, would evolve with economic growth (as was already the case for the means of the income tax that largely served to finance the regions). That this hadn't been the case from the start was considered as a fundamental mistake of the francophone negotiators of 1989.

There were also incentives for institutional reform on the Brussels level. First of all, again related to the SFL, the French-speaking Community Commission (COCOF) was also in need of financial means. Next to this, institutional measures had to be taken to avoid a potential blockage of the Brussels regional institutions: there was fear that the Flemish extreme right party Vlaams Blok might get an absolute majority within the Dutch-speaking language group through which it would be able to block the Brussels government formation, for which a majority in both language groups is needed.

Another element was the demand for further autonomy by Flemish parties. This had surfaced in the years preceding the federal election of 1999, and regional fiscal autonomy was one of the most prominent issues. More specifically, the resolutions of the Flemish parliament of March 1999 were generally considered as an important trigger. These quite radical resolutions, most notably demanding regionalisation of a large number of federal competences, were perceived by some as the official demand platform of the Flemish region and therefore also of the Flemish parties. Because a number of politicians, journalists and political commentators gave quite some importance to them, they reached a symbolical status (even when the next state reform of 2007 was on the agenda, references to these resolutions were still made). However, in reality, they cannot really be considered as the unanimous position of the Flemish parties. Although this was often represented differently, parliamentary support for the resolutions was far from unanimous, as they were only voted entirely by MPs of three Flemish parties (the Christian-democratic CVP, the liberal VLD and the Flemish-nationalist Volksunie). Considering the resolutions too radical, the socialist SP had abstained on all or part of three out of five resolutions while the Greens of Agalev abstained on all five and the one French-speaking representative of the UF voted against. Considering the resolutions not radical enough, the extreme right Vlaams Blok had left the parliament before the vote (Reynebeau, 2009: 193).

Also, during the 1999 federal election campaign, the issue of state reform had been pushed to the background by the "dioxin crisis", after revelations that dioxin-like toxins were detected in animal food products and that the then government would have covered this up. Following the elections, the new majority of Liberals, Socialists and Greens, often referred to as purple-green government (in Flanders) or rainbow government (in French-speaking Belgium) wanted to make a clean break with the previous coalition of Christian Democrats and Socialists on different levels, including the creation of a more peaceful climate between the communities (in the previous years relations between the leaders of the Flemish and Walloon governments had been rather tensed). The 1999 federal government agreement read: "The Belgian federal state has to be improved so that the community tensions can be definitively resolved and harmonious relations between our regions and communities can be ensured." Putting much emphasis on resolutions that were considered very controversial by French-speaking parties did not fit into this picture.

But more fundamentally, the Flemish parties in the new federal majority of 1999 did not consider the resolutions as the ultimate guide to a new state reform. The VLD, while in opposition, had been quite radical on the state reform issue, but this was also to put pressure on the then Flemish majority. The party did still advocate more regional autonomy, mostly on the fiscal level as this would permit the Flemish government to attribute tax cuts. Yet autonomy as an end in itself was not a priority. Moreover, while the unanimity and radicalism of Flemish parties on autonomy demands is often overestimated, it is forgotten that among the francophone parties some – mostly the regionalist wing within the French-speaking socialist party PS – were also in favour of a number of competence transfers.

Another catalyst for state reform was the key position of the Flemish-nationalist Volksunie (VU) in the Flemish government. The parties of the purple-green coalition had decided to govern together on the federal as well as on the regional levels. This was in line with the tradition to form congruent government coalitions, which makes cooperation between governments easier. But is also another element which strengthens the power of party headquarters as they can control the different governments (Swenden, 2002). However, on the Flemish regional level, Liberals, Socialists and Greens did not have a sufficient majority and had to include the VU in the coalition[2]. For this party, more autonomy for the federated entities was obviously an important priority. Because of this, the reform was also important for the survival of the Flemish coalition. Moreover, as the federal majority only had 94 out of

2 Total congruence was also not achieved at the Brussels level, where the Flemish Christian Democrats were necessary to reach a majority in the Dutch-speaking language group of the Brussels parliament (given the high score of the Flemish extreme right party Vlaams Blok that nobody wanted to govern with), while the French-speaking Greens of Ecolo decided not to participate in the Brussels coalition as they were not necessary for a majority.

150 seats, the VU was also necessary to reach the necessary two-thirds majority for institutional reform on the federal level. However the party was dealing with serious internal conflicts on the party line that had to be followed, divided as it was between a softer progressive wing and a radical nationalist and conservative wing. The internal divisions that would occur on the evaluation of the *Lambermont* reform eventually split the party.

What can also be considered as an additional incentive for the reform to take place, was the will and ambition of the new prime minister, the Flemish liberal Guy Verhofstadt, to show that Belgium could be governed in a different way, without the Christian Democrats who had been in power continuously since 1958. Such an ambition was also strongly present among the French-speaking Liberals of the PRL-FDF-MCC, led by vice prime minister and minister of foreign affairs Louis Michel, and more generally animated the entire new coalition. One aspect of Verhofstadt's ambition was to show that he could also negotiate a state reform, without the Flemish Christian-democratic party, which been at the heart of the four previous state reforms (1970, 1980, 1988 and 1993).

In what follows, we will review the crucial phases of the decision making process as well as the conflict lines which appeared in the negotiations, showing how these were often dominated by party politics. The analysis is amongst other things based on in depth interviews conducted with politicians and collaborators that played a prominent role in the *Lambermont* process.

4. The negotiation procedures

4.1 The Conference of State Reforms (COSTA/COREE)

In a first stage, discussion and negotiation on state reform in Belgium tends to be attributed to a commission, working group or forum. This will often explicitly include politicians with different functions and from different levels, such as MPs, regional government ministers, etc. Such was also the case at the start of the *Lambermont* process. However, *Lambermont* also showed that the members of these bodies should in the first place be considered as party representatives.

In 1999, in line with the government agreement of the new federal coalition of Liberals, Socialists and Greens, a commission was created to discuss institutional matters, officially called "Intergovernmental and Interparliamentary Conference for Institutional Renewal"[3], but quickly re-baptised by (part

3 "Intergouvernementele en Interparlementaire Conferentie voor Institutionele Vernieuwing" (IICIV)/"Conférence Intergouvernementale et Interparlementaire du Renouveau Institutionnel" (CIIRI)

of) the press in "Conference for State Reform" (COSTA/COREE)[4]. As its name suggests, it was composed of government members and parliamentarians of the different entities, by the number of 31. It was chaired by Philippe Moureaux, vice-president of the PS and president of its Brussels section and Patrik Vankrunkelsven, president of the VU. Simultaneously, on the level of the Brussels region a "Brussels COSTA/COREE", also called "mini-COSTA/mini-COREE", was installed. It was composed of Brussels political representatives and presided by the mayor of the city of Brussels François-Xavier De Donnéa (PRL).

However, members of the COSTA and Brussels COSTA were not chosen by these governments or parliaments, but by the political parties. It was decided that all parties, besides the extreme right, were invited to participate, including the Christian-democratic opposition (the Flemish Christian Democrats were however present in the Brussels government, as they were necessary to form a majority within the Dutch-speaking language group).

It is also as party representatives that the COSTA members should be seen. Members of parliament did not specifically represent viewpoints or interests of their parliament but rather those of their parties. Balances within parties, such as between different currents (left vs. right, regionalist vs. federalist), were more important to determine who would be part of the COSTA. The commission also contained the typical institutional experts of the parties, regardless of which political mandate they held at that moment. For instance, Marcel Cheron was an obvious choice to represent the French-speaking Greens of Ecolo, not so much because he was a member of the parliaments of the Walloon region and the French-speaking community as well as of the Senate (as a community senator), but rather because he was considered as one of the main institutional specialists of Ecolo and had already participated in the state reform process of 1993. Another example is Philippe Moureaux, senator, but also one of the main institutional specialists of the party, having played an important role in the negotiation of the two previous state reforms (and thus also the original SFL).

The *Lambermont* negotiations do not only illustrate the dominance of parties, but also that of the party leaderships and therefore also the limited political relevance of commissions containing many representatives. In this case, the COSTA merely started up the reform process. It was installed on 20 October 1999. Two working groups were created, one on the division of competences, the other on the financing of regions and communities. However, given the presence of the Christian-democratic opposition, it was quite clear that the main decisions would not be taken there. The second working group already ended its activities in December 1999, the first in March 2000. The COSTA's general activities were postponed in May 2000.

4 "Conferentie voor de Staatshervorming" (COSTA) / "Conféréncе pour la réforme de l'Etat" (COREE)

They were not very important, even though in the margin of the official meetings some ground was prepared, mostly by its two presidents. As the different crucial stages of the *Lambermont* process show, the main decisions were taken by a restricted number of top-politicians from the seven parties necessary to vote the agreements: the Dutch-speaking and French-speaking liberal, socialist and green parties as well as the Flemish-nationalists of the VU.

4.2 The Hermes and Lambermont Agreements

The first general decisions on state reform had been taken during the 1999 federal government negotiations between the main party presidents, including the decision to install the COSTA but also to revise the SFL, even if the latter agreement had remained unofficial.

During the period of activity of the COSTA and mini-COSTA, the only important decision on institutional matters was not taken by these commissions, but within the federal government, assisted by the minister-presidents of the federated entities. This led to the nightly Saint-Elois agreement of December 1999, which put an end to the transitory period for the financing of the communities (for more details, see Delwit and Hellings, 2002: 100).

The first main political agreement was reached in April 2000, following pressure from the VU which threatened to leave the Flemish government if no advance was made on federal reform. The COSTA negotiations were simply taken over by Prime Minister Verhofstadt and conducted by the "*Kernkabinet*" or "*Kern*", composed of the top ministers of the federal government. Certainly Guy Verhofstadt and Louis Michel were clearly the actual leaders of their parties, even though they did not preside them at that moment. After eight months of official activity in the COSTA, the core of the federal government reached an agreement in five days. Again held partially during the night, these negotiations resulted in the *Hermes* Agreement on 15 April. This mainly consisted of the regionalisation of agriculture and sea fishery as well as foreign trade. In the following months, technical negotiations were organised to translate the agreement in law texts, which turned out as rather complicated. This was finished in July, but an agreement on the financial consequences of these regionalisations was still lacking, as this had not yet really been debated. It was clear that an agreement on the SFL was necessary before the transfers of competences could be definitely executed.

The essence of the fifth state reform was again negotiated by the core of the federal government, in October 2000. Once more, five days of negotiation resulted in a nightly agreement on 16 October, generally called the *Lambermont* Agreement, referring to the name of the official residence of the prime minister where the agreement was negotiated[5]. Representatives of the governments of the federated entities were also present during these negotiations, which was actually unusual and which would not be the case again during the important stages of the negotiation of the sixth state reform in 2011. This made it easier to include the VU in the negotiations, which was not part of the federal majority, while the fact that all the other federal majority parties were also represented in the regional governments did not create further complications. It was also a way to involve regional representatives as well as different factions of the parties in the negotiation and to make sure they would be bound by the result (for instance, the regionalist wing of the PS was mostly represented in the Walloon government, through its minister-president Jean-Claude Van Cauwenberghe). Nevertheless, when some crucial decisions were taken, this often happened in more limited company, although negotiators still held contact with other party representatives. The *Lambermont* Agreement included the most important demands of the parties: a gradual increase of financial transfers from the federal level to the communities, regional fiscal autonomy in the form of regionalisation of a number of taxes (such as recording fees, television and radio tax) as well as the right for the regions to attribute cuts, increases or deductions to the federal income tax within determined margins[6], the regionalisation of communal and provincial law, the attribution of the competence of development cooperation to regions and communities for those aspects relating to their existing competences and from 2004 onwards, de-federalisation of control on parties' election expenses. The execution of the *Hermes* Agreement was also part of the deal.

Afterwards, the *Lambermont* Agreement had to be translated into law texts, which was done under the responsibility of the two COSTA-presidents and the two federal ministers of institutional reform, Johan Vande Lanotte (SP) and Louis Michel (PRL-FDF-MCC), but in practice mostly through negotiations among technicians of the seven concerned parties. However, as the initial agreement consisted of only a few pages, it was on a number of points rather vague, which resulted in about 40 elements that were too political to be resolved on a merely technical level and had to be dealt with by the top-politicians again. This happened in January 2001. Half of these elements were dealt with during three nightly meetings, leaving the most difficult ones for another nightly negotiation round. It resulted in an agreement in the morning of 23 January, still referred to as *Lambermont(-bis)* or, by the French-speaking press as *Saint-Polycarpe* Agreement. It consisted in a con-

5 The name *Lambermont* Agreement was first used by part of the Flemish press. The francophone press continued its tradition to give the agreement the name of the Saint of the day, but was initially divided between *Sainte-Thérèse* and *Sainte-Perlette*. Part of the Flemish press at first referred to the agreement of *Sint-Hedwig*.

6 It was decided that these margins would be – 3,25% to + 3,25% of the total receipts for the years 2001 to 2003 and would be raised to – 6,75 to + 6,75 from 2004 onwards.

sensus on two draft proposals of law, which foresaw amongst other things more exceptions to the regionalisation of communal and provincial law, a limitation to 91% of the coupling to economic growth of the financial transfer to the communities for education and the requirement of inter-governmental cooperation agreements in ten matters.

While it seemed that the political agreement on the *Lambermont* reform was definitely finalised, the announcement of four out of eight federal VU-MP's – including the then president of the party Geert Bourgeois – that they would not vote the agreements quickly made clear that this was not the case. The announcement signalled a deep division within the VU, as the majority of the party council did give its support to the agreement, which had largely been negotiated by former party and COSTA-president Vankrunkelsven and to a lesser extent by Flemish minister Bert Anciaux, both part of the moderate wing of the party. Around the same time, the FDF – which hadn't had its own representative participating in the negotiations – also announced that it would not vote the special law, containing the regionalisation of the communal and provincial law because this implied that the Flemish government gains legislative authority over the facility communes around Brussels (communes in the Dutch-speaking language region with administrative and other facilities for francophones). As the FDF only had two MPs in the Chamber, efforts were first concentrated on convincing the dissident VU-MPs.

This resulted in some new talks between Bourgeois and the other Flemish negotiators, led by VLD-president Karel De Gucht. Because of the ongoing VU-demands, these negotiations, largely held in February and March 2001, were again highly political.

The VLD could obviously not fundamentally renegotiate the agreement, as the other partners – mostly the francophone parties – did not want to come back on the delicate balance contained in the agreement. This is why the new agreements with the dissident VU-MP's mainly concerned the planned cooperation agreements, as well as the addition of a new one, and the negotiation of a Brussels reform. Another element which politicised negotiations again were the attempts to resolve the problems raised in the meantime by the advice of the Council of State on the draft proposals of law. These were also used by the VU to demand adjustments in their direction. The final negotiations on these matters were again held during a nightly meeting, this time pressured by a deadline of 22 March, when the cooperation agreements and the revised proposals of law had to be validated by the Committee of Concertation and the federal Council of Ministers.

4.3 The Lombard and Saint-Boniface Agreements

The dominance of the party dynamic can also be seen at work on the level of the Brussels COSTA, which was restarted on 12 February 2001, also as part of attempts to convince the dissident VU-MPs to agree to *Lambermont*. These had let their support for the whole reform depend in large part on the Brussels result, which had until then been of quite marginal importance. Therefore, the agenda for these Brussels negotiations was somewhat altered, with demands for an increased representation of Dutch-speakers on the Brussels regional and communal level becoming quite crucial. This time, the Brussels COSTA was led by Daniel Ducarme, the president of the PRL-FDF-MCC, which was the largest party in Brussels. De Donnéa had become minister-president of the Brussels region in the meantime and did not find the functions compatible. As talks went difficultly, by the end of April, negotiations were limited to the majority parties and the VU (thus excluding CVP and PSC) and increasingly dominated by Verhofstadt and the party leaders, certainly on the Flemish side (on the francophone side, negotiators were already higher in the party hierarchy, such as Moureaux and Ducarme). Again, a nightly negotiation (smeared by additional federal financial transfers for Brussels) led to the *Lombard* Agreement in the morning of 29 April, which was consequently signed by the Brussels negotiators.

The *Lombard* Agreement included an increase in the number of regional parliament members up to 17 for the Dutch language group and 72 for the French language group as well as an additional five mandates, on top of these 17, for the Flemish Community Commission. On the local level, a system was introduced that obliges municipalities where at least one municipal councillor of both language groups signed the act of presentation of the mayor to also have an alderman of both language groups. A guaranteed representation of Dutch-speakers in the police councils was also foreseen. The community commissions were refinanced, with half of the means coming from the region and half from the federal level. To prevent a blockage of the Brussels institutions it was decided that if a majority within a language group is not achieved for a parliamentary vote, it can be repeated a month later and will then only need a support of one third of the votes within that language group (but obviously still an overall majority) (for more details, see Nassaux, 2001).

The *Lombard* Agreement however did not convince the dissident VU-MP's. Their support becoming ever more uncertain and the survival of the federal government becoming increasingly unsure if this crucial reform would not be voted, eyes turned towards the French-speaking Christian Democrats of the PSC for support, or rather for abstention as this was sufficient to get the special laws through parliament. Although the PSC was in the opposition, it was difficult for them to refuse cooperating as they would be accused by the other francophone parties of blocking refinancing of the French-speaking education system, which would certainly be difficult to explain to their "natural" rank and file of the catholic education world. Collaborating was also a way for the PSC to become politically relevant again.

Therefore, in May 2001, a new type of negotiation started, this time only between the French-speaking parties: the three government parties and the PSC-opposition, mostly represented by their presidents. These negotiations concerned the use that would be made of the new financial means for the French-speaking community, including the share that would go to non-official (catholic) schools. They ended in an agreement in the morning of 5 June, referred to as the Agreement of *Saint-Boniface* (for more details, see Delwit and Hellings, 2002: 103-104).

However, because the PSC also had to abstain on the vote of the special law on competence transfers, there were again discrete talks between them and all of the majority parties. The PSC had demanded "a gesture", as they could not vote the law without any modifications. On 28 June, again, a nightly meeting brought a solution, this time in a different formula: Dutch-speaking and French-speaking parties were at different places, but remained in contact. It is only in the middle of the night that a delegation of the French-speaking parties joined the Flemish politicians at Verhofstadt's cabinet, after which an agreement was found in the morning. The most important element was that the federal government would sign the treaty of the Council of Europe on the protection of national minorities, a typical francophone demand. This was however largely symbolical, as it would also have to be signed by the regional parliaments.

4.4 The parliamentary debates and votes

Party discipline in Belgium is very strong. Therefore parliamentary debates and votes are generally subordinated to the result of negotiations between the majority parties, or in the case of state reforms, between parties holding a two thirds majority in parliament. The success of ratification in parliament largely depends on the success of these negotiations. This renders discussions in parliament at best interesting, but often not very politically or constitutionally relevant (see also Alen, 2002: 9-10). There were, however, some notable exceptions in the past, when parliamentary dissidence endangered state reform processes. This was also the case for *Lambermont*, where four of the VU-MPs voted against the entire reform and the two FDF-MPs abstained on half of the reform. However, this should not be interpreted as an indication of the power of parliament, but rather as that of the existence of problematic internal party divisions. Indeed, the discord within the VU came to the surface long before the debates in parliament started and the fact that the VU did not survive these votes, shows how unusual and challenging it is when such divisions occur. In case of the FDF, a split from the French-speaking liberal party did not happen in 2001, but finally proved unavoidable ten years later, when a similar conflict with the rest of the party came to the surface during the next state reform process.

In fact, while party dominance over parliament is a general characteristic of Belgian politics, the ratification procedure of the *Lambermont* Agreement made this very explicit. While law texts are normally introduced and debated in parliament when a parliamentary majority is guaranteed, in this case negotiations between party leaders to find a two thirds majority were still going on. This was because the majority had to deal with the defection of part of the VU and of the FDF, but nevertheless wanted to go very fast (which can of course be considered as a strategy to secure a majority in its own right). This is also why the *Lambermont* Agreement had been divided up into two proposals of law: the one on the SFL was introduced in the Chamber, the one on competence transfers in the Senate. This permitted a quicker parliamentary treatment as the Chamber and the Senate could work simultaneously on their half of the agreement[7]. The vote in the Senate did not constitute a problem, as two out of three VU-senators voted the agreements. But the necessary two-thirds majority in the Chamber remained uncertain until the very end.

When the government had already introduced its proposals of special law, the Brussels COSTA was still negotiating. The *Lombard* Agreement reached one month later, was added to the deposed law texts in the form of amendments by MPs of the majority. Discussions in the commissions were still going on in May 2001, when discrete contacts were made with the PSC. On 30 May, during plenary discussions in the Chamber, it became definitely clear that the four VU-MPs would not vote the special law on the financing of regions and communities. In the meantime, negotiations were going on between the "*Kern*", the PSC and the moderate VU-wing. Five technical amendments of the PSC were introduced, which delayed the vote for a week and gave time to the French-speaking majority parties to negotiate with the PSC. They reached the *Saint-Boniface* Agreement the day before the successful vote of 6 June in the Chamber, on which the PSC eventually abstained[8].

A similar scenario developed for the vote of the special law on the transfer of competences. In the morning of the day that the law had to be voted in the Chamber, negotiations between the majority parties, the moderate wing of the VU and the PSC, led to an agreement. As debates took a little longer than

7 Another way the federal government speeded up the procedure was by giving the legislation section of the council of state only one month to produce an advice on the two law texts.

8 The MPs of the six majority parties (VLD, PRL-FDF-MCC, SP, PS, Ecolo, Agalev) and four out of eight VU-MPs voted in favour, the MPs of CVP, Vlaams Blok, and four VU MPs voted against and the MPs of PSC and FN abstained.

foreseen, the special law was voted around 1 p.m. on 29 June[9]. The *Lambermont* reform had now definitely passed.

5. Conflict lines

Media coverage of the conflict lines in the state reform process largely focused on the division between the communities. This is not surprising as Dutch-speaking and French-speaking media – there are no national media in Belgium – generally tend to frame information from the perspective of the community divide (Sinardet, 2011, 2012). The main conflict line was therefore considered to be that between political elites of the two communities, if not between the two communities as a whole. This also concurred with much of the political discourse surrounding the reform. The strong tendency, certainly in public declarations but sometimes also in negotiations, to not let differences amongst Flemish and amongst Francophone parties show too much, contributed to reinforce this representation.

Of course, the conflict line between Dutch-speaking and French-speaking parties was important, as the reform concerned distribution of powers and financial means between the different regions and communities. There was a trade off between a demand shared by the French-speaking parties (refinancing the French-speaking community) and a demand shared by the Dutch-speaking parties (more autonomy in fiscal and other matters). Nevertheless, analysing in terms of party interests again permits to distinguish other relevant conflict lines that hide between the community divide.

5.1 Majority vs. opposition

The most important conflict line in terms of party interests and strategy was that between majority and opposition, even if this was not entirely stable over in the course of the process. The main goal of the federal majority parties (and of at least part of the VU, which participated in the Flemish regional government) was to reach a compromise and carry through a reform they considered necessary. Therefore, they wanted to avoid as much as possible that conflicts between them would arise. The opposition, and particularly the Flemish Christian Democrats of CVP, did obviously not want the reform to succeed. Even though CVP was not overtly against the regionalisation of ag-

9 The MPs of the six majority parties (VLD, PRL-FDF-MCC, SP, PS, Ecolo, Agalev), voted in favour, with the exclusion of the 2 FDF-MPs, as well as four VU-MPs. The MPs of CVP, Vlaams Blok, FN and four VU-MPs voted against. The MPs of PSC and FDF abstained.

riculture and development cooperation, it mobilised farmers unions and NGOs close to it, to oppose them.

That the conflict line between majority and opposition was at least for some parties more important than that between the language groups can be seen from the intense contacts and cooperation between the two liberal parties, VLD and PRL-FDF-MCC, and mostly between prime minister Guy Verhofstadt and vice-prime minister and minister of foreign affairs Louis Michel, who had a common interest and a strong ambition to succeed. Rather than as opponents, they saw each other as partners in the pursuit of a political agreement. They would regularly sit together to discuss what would be an acceptable compromise for the different parties. More generally, in that period, top-politicians of the two liberal parties had regular informal meetings to discuss important political matters and synchronise positions. There were however also moments of tension between Michel and Verhofstadt, mostly caused by the difficulties with the VU. Verhofstadt had convinced Michel to go along with some additional elements of the reform because this would secure the votes of the dissident VU-MPs, but in the end this turned out not to be the case. The tensions mostly occurred on the question of the increased representation of Dutch-speakers in Brussels, contained in the *Lombard* Agreement as the FDF was strongly opposed to this, causing divisions within Michel's own party (see below).

A strong collaboration also existed between the two green parties, not only on a strategic but also on a more ideological level. The Greens had always been the Belgian party family with the closest ties between the Dutch-speaking and French-speaking party and formed a common parliamentary group in the Chamber (see Heylen, 2006). This did not mean they went to the negotiations with a common demand platform (although on some issues, such as the regionalisation of development cooperation they did defend common positions). Rather they concerted and agreed to not hinder each other on issues that were a priority for one of both parties. These structurally close ties were less present among the Socialists, although they obviously also had contacts, amongst other things through cabinet personnel (for instance the PS-specialist on the SFL worked in the cabinet of vice-prime minister and budget minister Johan Vande Lanotte of the SP).

Trust and collaboration within the federal coalition was however not limited to the party families, but also crossed other party borders, certainly within the "Kern". For instance, on constitutional matters, there was a large trust in Johan Vande Lanotte (also professor of Constitutional Law at the University of Ghent).

The conflict line between majority and opposition was however not stable over the entire period of the reform. This was mostly due to the two parties for whom the linguistic divide is their core-business and who hold the most radical positions on the issue. During the course of process, the VU got strongly internally divided and half of its MPs in the Chamber finally decided to position themselves on the other side of the conflict line (eventually leading to the split of the party). This was also the case for the FDF, which decided to only vote in favour of one of the two special laws containing the reform.

As a consequence, the French-speaking Christian Democrats of PSC made an inverse movement and, although in opposition, got involved in negotiations and finally decided to support the reform by abstaining rather than voting against in parliament. Just like for the reforms of 1970 and 1993, *Lambermont* passed with the help of votes from opposition parties.

5.2 Divisions between majority parties

The common will to succeed obviously did not stop the majority parties from diverging on the content of the reform and sometimes made negotiations difficult. But again, these different positions cannot simply be brought back to a division between Dutch-speaking and French-speaking parties. Often other, more concealed, interests also played a part and created diverging and often complex conflict lines, differing from issue to issue.

On the regionalisation of foreign trade, the VU and the PRL had the most opposite views. The demand came from the VU, for which it was a symbolically important tool to reinforce the international image of Flanders. The regionalist wing of the PS also pushed for regionalisation, even though the party as a whole did not have a pronounced preference. The PRL, and most notably minister of foreign affairs Louis Michel, on the contrary, wanted to limit regionalisation as much as possible. They had close ties with stakeholders, who were generally opposed to regionalisation, such as the corporate world (and more specifically the national federation of employers VBO/FEB[10]) as well as the Royal Palace[11]. Even the liberal ministers in the Walloon and Brussels government who would gain this competence, were opposed to a far reaching regionalisation: they would have to invest additional financial means, as those transferred would be insufficient. The operation had to be budgetary neutral for the federal state, but services (such as the law service, country databanks, etc.) would be divided into three, creating extra costs. Prime Minister Verhofstadt was also pressured by the Royal Palace and business circles, but realised that an agreement would not be possible without this regionalisation. He therefore convinced Louis Michel to go along and find a way to "limit the damages". Most other parties were also not

10 Verbond van Belgische Ondernemingen / Fédération des Entreprises de Belgique.

11 The existing official vehicle for foreign trade, BDBH/OBCE (Belgische Dienst voor Buitenlandse Handel / Office Belge du Commerce Exterieur) was governed in parity by the government and the business world while the Prince accompanies foreign trade missions.

really enthusiast but accepted that keeping the VU on board would come at the price of a loss of efficiency and of credit in business circles. The issue was therefore to retain a minimum of coherence and unity. This would be secured through the creation of an intergovernmental "Foreign Trade Agency", organising joint missions of the regions. This agency could still be accompanied by the Prince (as he is able to open doors to important political and other contacts, he was considered an asset for such missions). Most tensions occurred on the cooperation agreement between the regions which was necessary to implement this and which became one of the objects of negotiation in the attempts to convince the dissident VU-MPs. The latter, led by Geert Bourgeois, could not accept that the federal level would also organise missions by itself or with only one of the regions, without needing the agreement of all regions, as they were suspicious about the role of the palace and absolutely wanted the federal level to be subordinated to the regions by granting them a veto right. However, the French-speaking Liberals (but also other parties) considered such veto rights would lead to a loss of efficacy.

The demand to regionalise agriculture was strongly advocated by regionalists within the PS and particularly by José Happart, who was already minister of agriculture in the Walloon government (smaller competences related to agriculture had already been transferred in 1980 and 1993) and would see his competence and budget be forcefully increased. Traditionally, agriculture had always been considered the domain of the Christian Democrats, until the Walloon-regionalist Happart – himself a fruit farmer – joined the PS in the 1980s. On this matter, Happart obviously had a strong ally in the VU, although in the later phase of negotiations it was mostly him who wanted to push regionalisation as far as possible. The rest of the PS and most other parties did not consider regionalising agriculture strictly necessary but did not mind, neither. For PRL-FDF-MCC, SP and Ecolo agriculture was at the time far from their core-business. However, the Flemish Liberals were close to the smaller farmers union ABS (Algemeen Boeren Syndicaat), which was in favour of regionalisation as it saw this as a way to gain more influence compared to the very powerful Boerenbond, closely associated with the Christian Democrats. In this sense, it was not a surprise that agriculture was regionalised under a coalition with Liberals and without Christian Democrats. For the Greens, it was a lesser harm: if some competences had to be regionalised, it would better be agriculture (and foreign trade) than aspects of social security. However, Agalev absolutely wanted some elements to stay federal. During government negotiations, and after a campaign strongly dominated by the dioxin crisis, the Greens had obtained the creation of a "Federal Agency for the Safety of the Food Chain", which would take over important parts of the administration of agriculture (mainly inspection services). Magda Aelvoet, who was minister of Public Health, wanted the new agency, which fell under her competence, to be able to fully function. This is why she saw to it that norms and control concerning vegetable and animal products (corresponding to two departments of the agriculture administration) would explicitly be excepted from regionalisation. Later, during the translation of the agreement she also resisted demands to entirely transfer animal welfare.

The conflict line on the regionalisation of development cooperation was mostly between VU and (part of the) PS on the one hand and the Greens on the other. The matter came onto the table quite surprisingly during the negotiation marathon of mid-October 2000, as a consequence of an alliance between VU and PS-regionalists, this time mostly Van Cauwenberghe who wanted to link development cooperation to the Walloon business world. PRL-FDF-MCC was also in favour, according to some because Louis Michel was not able to get a grip on the budget of the secretary of state for development cooperation, Eddy Boutmans (Agalev), with whom relations were tensed.

The Greens had first reluctantly let the regionalisation pass, but became increasingly opposed after pressure from the strongly displeased NGO-world, traditionally close to the Greens, and strong mobilisation from within both parties. Some green MPs even threatened to not vote part of the reform. Other parties were not necessarily convinced that regionalising development cooperation was a good idea (and sometimes also had in their midst, as would become clear later, outright opponents to the plan), but considered this as a necessary element to round up the general state reform deal.

Development cooperation would stay controversial during the consequent negotiations on the translation of the decisions into law texts, as it was an issue on which the VU wanted to go further, while the green parties tried to turn the clock back. Verhofstadt pressured the Greens to give up their opposition, as this could convince VU-dissidents to vote the reform. The fact that the party was starting to fall apart and that the Liberals wanted to attract some of the VU-personnel to their party also played a part. The compromise between the VU's demand of formal guarantees that the agreement would actually be executed and the Greens attempts to make sure that execution could be avoided was a constitutional absurdity: the special law stipulated that a working group would be created which by the end of December 2002 would have to advise on which aspects of development cooperation would be regionalised. The Greens were quite certain that this working group would not reach a consensus and in any case, a new special law would have to be voted to execute the reform[12] (for more details, see Boutmans, 2008).

Concerning the SFL, the division was largely between Dutch-speaking and French-speaking parties. However, even on this issue, some nuances have to be made. It is generally assumed that for all Francophone parties refi-

12 The reform would indeed not be carried through, due to a lack of consensus in the Commission. In a report on state reform to the King of January 2008, Guy Verhofstadt proposed to abolish the passage in the special law and thus to "re-federalise" development cooperation.

nancing the French-speaking community and thus French-speaking education, was the main priority. However, the demand first came from Ecolo, which was considered as a rupture of the initial pact between francophone parties to refuse further advances in state reform. Ecolo was however quite quickly joined by the PS. Both parties realised there was an acute problem with the financing of French-speaking education, but also had strategic reasons for their position. Not only were they both close to the non-profit sector in general, they also wanted to attract (electoral) support from (the trade unions of) catholic education, traditionally attached to the Christian Democrats of the PSC, then in the opposition. In circles of catholic education, Ecolo had already become a serious competitor for the PSC.

Although they could not openly oppose the demand, the French-speaking Liberals were initially reluctant, which can be explained by four factors. First of all, there is an ideological debate hiding behind that on the SFL. The question is not only whether more financial means should be transferred to the communities, consequently leaving less available for the federal level, it is also whether more money should be transferred to education – traditionally a more left wing demand – for which the communities are competent, consequently leaving less available for tax reductions – one of the main priorities of the Liberals – for which the federal level is largely competent. Some experts warned that combining a large transfer and a tax reduction would lead to structural budgetary problems at the federal level. Second, while in those days the Liberals also tried to recuperate voters and/or political personnel of the ailing PSC, the wing situated in the trade unions, the non-profit sector and the catholic education system was politically and sociologically not their natural public. Third, there was the realisation that francophone demands on financing would imply also opening the door to Flemish linguistic demands on Brussels and its periphery, such as an increased representation of Dutch-speakers in the Brussels region and communes and the regionalisation of the local and provincial law. The FDF fiercely opposed these demands, which made the PRL-FDF-MCC leadership fear that this might create tensions in its alliance with FDF, which is indeed what happened (see above). Fourth, as the French-speaking Liberals had been in opposition for many years, they did not have a clear long term view on the exact state of the finances of regions and communities. However, gradually they realised that the financial situation was indeed very problematic. In January 2000, Pierre Hazette, minister of secondary education in the French community government, declared in a notorious interview in *Le Soir* that he was very worried because the ignorance of the financial needs would "one day explode".

Dutch-speaking parties did not demand a refinancing of the communities, but were not opposed, as obviously also the Flemish community which they also governed would receive extra means, even if it didn't really need or ask them. Certainly ministers in the regional government did not mind seeing their budgets increase. There was more reticence among the SP, as budget minister Vande Lanotte was worried about the budgetary consequences for the federal level. Agalev shared this preoccupation, but also had to take into account that refinancing was a priority for its "sister party" Ecolo, which made it take an intermediary position.

The SFL-demands of the francophone parties were in the negotiation strongly linked to Dutch-speaking demands on fiscal autonomy. However, here also party ideologies and interests made positions on the heart of the matter somewhat diverge.

While on the regionalisation of some federal taxes, an agreement was easily found, the possibility for the regional governments to attribute cuts or increases on income tax almost blocked the reform. Dutch-speaking parties had agreed that this would be a common demand. It was a priority for VU and VLD (as this made it possible to give tax cuts at the Flemish level), SP and to a lesser degree Agalev supported it, but were not strongly in favour as they feared that this would permit a more liberal policy of tax cuts on the Flemish level, where the majority is traditionally more to the right. SP and Agalev, together with PS and Ecolo, also insisted that fiscal autonomy should not endanger the progressive nature of the tax system. Most French-speaking parties – and specifically Ecolo and PS – were very reluctant on this issue, as they feared this could create fiscal competition between the regions to the profit of the richer Flemish region, thus endangering national solidarity. Because the Flemish region would see its financial means increase due to the refinancing of the communities (even if this was mostly a francophone demand), it would be able to strongly reduce taxes, with the Walloon region not being able to follow, leading to fiscal competition and a shift of activity from the Walloon to the Flemish region. It is only in the end of the negotiation, when they realised that the reform would not succeed if fiscal autonomy was not granted, that the French-speaking parties agreed, be it after negotiating a number of exceptions.

On the linguistic issues concerning Brussels and its periphery, positions on the heart of the matter were largely determined by whether a party was Dutch-speaking or French-speaking. However, the essence of the conflict was between the VU and the FDF, who held quite radical and diametrically opposed positions, with other parties situated in between these two extremes on the continuum, not always considering these issues as the first and foremost priority. The difference in priority clearly showed in the intra-francophone division that occurred between PS and FDF. While the PS was also rather opposed to the Flemish demands, it did consider that a deal could be made, in return for a strong increase of financial means for Brussels. This was clearly externalised in one of the deals that was made which implied that Brussels communes who had a Dutch-speaking alderman in their college would receive extra means from the federal level. The division also existed within

PRL-FDF-MCC, as the liberal wing did agree to *Lombard* even though the FDF had meanwhile left the negotiation table. In the end, as well on the regionalisation of communal and provincial law, as on the increased political representation of Dutch-speakers in Brussels (contained in the *Lombard* Agreement) a compromise between VU and FDF proved impossible to find, leading both parties to at least partially defect. The FDF abstained on one of the two special laws, while half of the VU-MPs voted against the reform as a whole.

5.3 Divisions within parties

While party discipline is a trademark of the Belgian political system, the *Lambermont* reform nevertheless also reinforced some internal party conflict lines, in some cases leading to strong divisions and in one case even to the demise of a party.

This was of course the case with the VU, where the *Lambermont* process aggravated the already strong division between a more radical and moderate wing, finally leading to the split of the party in October 2001. The tensions within the VU would dominate the state reform process for months, as they made the necessary parliamentary support uncertain and ongoing negotiations necessary.

Within PRL-FDF-MCC, there was also a conflict line between a more moderate and more radical wing on linguistic issues, which largely coincided with respectively the PRL-MCC and the FDF-component in the party. While Louis Michel's priority was that the reform would succeed, the FDF did not want to accept too many concessions on their core-business. Although this created numerous tensions, their consequences could in the end be limited to the FDF not voting part of the reform. However, in the next state reform, the same conflict line re-appeared, and eventually led to the FDF splitting off in September 2011.

Much less fundamental conflict lines sometimes occurred within other parties, such as that between regional and federal ministers or MPs. This was somewhat the case for the VLD. Although Verhofstadt was the uncontested leader, there were limits to what he could get away with as he did still have to take into account the interests and position of Patrick Dewael, who was minister-president of the Flemish Region. While Dewael had taken a much less regionalist profile than his predecessor Luc Van den Brande (CVP), he nevertheless could not distance himself from the resolutions voted by a majority of the Flemish parliament (including his own party) in 1999, to which the opposition often referred. Even though state reform is voted exclusively in the federal parliament, he also had to defend the agreement against the opposition in Flemish parliament, which evaluated whether it sufficiently met Flemish demands. The regional-federal tension was less strong within SP and Agalev, as it was VLD that led the Flemish government, automatically making Dewael into a symbol of Flemish interests. Since the VLD had defended very "Flemish" positions when it was in opposition in the previous legislature and specifically at the time of the debates on the resolutions its action was now scrutinised carefully.

Within the PS, the differences between federal and regional ministers more strongly coincided with ideological differences, as the most important representatives of the regionalist wing within the party, Van Cauwenberghe and Happart, were active on the regional level. Although the regionalist wing had lost a great deal of influence compared to one or two decades earlier, it still had to be taken into account, which sometimes created tensions, such as on the regionalisation of agriculture. When the COSTA was created, Happart (supported by Van Cauwenberghe) strongly pressured its co-president Philippe Moureaux, also of the PS, who he considered to be too strongly centred on Brussels interests and too incomprehensive towards "Walloon" and rural sensitivities such as agriculture. In the later phase of negotiations Happart wanted to push regionalisation further than experts of the PS thought it sensible to go, given the financial impact this would have on the Walloon region. During negotiations on the Brussels Lombard-agreement, a conflict of interest also arose between the Brussels PS, which strongly wanted to refinance the Brussels region and the COCOF and political personnel active at the federal level, who were concerned of the repercussions this could have on the federal budget.

There were also some division within other parties on the financial issue. Within the PRL-FDF-MCC, regional ministers tended to go along with the demand of refinancing of the communities, while on the federal level (and certainly the cabinet of the minister of finance Didier Reynders), there was fear that this would cause federal budgetary problems and endanger the federal fiscal reform and tax cuts program dear to the Liberals.

6. Conclusion

We have argued that party politics is an important, but often underestimated lens through which to analyse federal reform, certainly in Belgium. As our analysis of the *Lambermont* reform of 2001 showed, political parties dominated the negotiation process, also at times when commissions or the parliament were officially dealing with the reform. For a profound understanding of the content of the reform, the interests of each of the parties are again a crucial variable which cannot be entirely brought back to that of their region or language community.

The importance of the parties would become even more explicit during the negotiation of the next Belgian state reform, which was responsible for the longest government formation process in the world. While the *Lambermont* negotiations left an important place to the top ministers in the federal government and sometimes even to those of the regional governments (the former however being among the top decision-makers of their parties, if they were not the de facto leaders), the next state reform process would be largely dominated by the party presidents, mostly due to the fact that it coincided with the government formation. Also, strategic party interests can account for much of the blockages and the length of the process from 2007 onwards. While party dynamics – and certainly the strong will to succeed of the governmental majority parties and of the prime minister – can help to explain the success of the *Lambermont* reform, some years later it will be part of the explanation for the longest political crisis in Belgian history.

References

Alen, André (2002): Algemene beschouwingen bij de vijfde staatshervorming van 2001. In Alen, A. (ed.): De vijfde staatshervorming van 2001. Brugge: Die Keure, 1-24.

Boutmans, Eddy (2008): Internationale solidariteit, staatshervorming en goed bestuur. In: Sinardet, D. (ed.): Dossier staatshervorming: de rationele benadering. Gent: stichting Gerrit Kreveld, 34-42.

De Winter, Lieven (1998): Parliament and Government in Belgium: Prisoners of Partitocracy. In: Norton, P. (ed.): Parliaments and Executives in Western Europe. London: Frank Cass, 97-122.

Delwit, Pascal/Hellings, Benoit (2002): La nouvelle réforme de l'Etat: processus, contenu, method. In: Administration publique. Revue du droit public et des sciences administratives 26, (2-3-4), 99-106.

Heylen, Kathleen (2006): Duet met communautaire noten. De evolutie van de samenwerking tussen Agalev/Groen! en Ecolo. In: Oikos. Politiek, milieu, cultur 36: 31-43.

Huyse, Luc (1981): Political Conflict in Bicultural Belgium. In: Lijphart, A. (ed.): Conflict and Coexistence in Belgium. The Dynamics of a Culturally Divided Society. Berkeley: University of California, Institute of International Studies, 107-126.

Luther, Kurt Richard (1999): A framework for the comparative analysis of political parties and party systems in consociational democracy. In: Luther, K. R./Deschouwer, C. (eds.): Party Elites in Divided Societies. Political Parties in Consociational Democracy. London: Routledge, 2-18.

Mazzoleni, Martino (2009): The saliency of regionalisation in party systems: A comparative analysis of regional decentralisation in party manifestos. In: Party Politics 15, (2), 199-218.

Mitchell, James (1998): The evolution of devolution: Labour's Home Rule Strategy in Opposition. In: Government and Opposition 33, (4), 479-496.

Nassaux, Jean-Paul (2001): Le groupe de travail sur les institutions bruxelloises. Deuxième phase et accord. In: Courrier Hebdomadaire du CRISP 2001/11-12, 1716-1717.

O'Neill, Kathleen (2003): Decentralisation as an electoral strategy. In: Comparative Political Studies 36, (9), 1068-1091.

Orte, Andreu/Wilson, Alex (2009): Multi-level coalitions and statute reform in Spain. In: Regional and Federal Studies 19, (3), 415-436.

Pagano, Giuseppe (2002): Le financement des regions et des communautés, 1970-2002. Solidarité, responsabilité, autonomie et concurrence fiscal. Brussels: CRISP.

Pas, Wouter (2002): De door de Grondwet aan de „Wet“ voorbehouden aangelegenheden. Vroeger en nu. In: Alen, A. (ed.): De vijfde staatshervorming van 2001. Brugge: Die Keure, 25-64.

Reynebeau, Marc (2009): Onze kant van het bed. Mythes van de Belgische politieke crisis. Leuven: Van Halewijck.

Sinardet, Dave (2010): From consociational consciousness to majoritarian myth: consociational federalism, multi-level politics and the Belgian case of Brussels-Halle-Vilvoorde. In: Acta Politica. International Journal of Political Science 45, (3), 346-369.

Sinardet Dave (2011): Multilingual democracy and public sphere. What Belgium and the EU can learn from each other. In: Gosseries, A./Vanderborght, Y. (eds.): Arguing about justice. Essays for Philippe Van Parijs. Louvain-La-Neuve: Presses Universitaires de Louvain, 311-321.

Sinardet Dave (2012): Le rôle des médias dans le conflit communautaire belge. Le traitement du dossier "Bruxelles-Hal-Vilvorde“ lors des débats politiques télévisés francophones et néerlandophones en Belgique. In: Perrez, J./Reuchamps, M. (ed.): Derrière les mots. Approches politiques et linguistiques des relations communautaires en Belgique. Brussel: Bruylant.

Sorens, Jason (2009): The partisan logic of decentralisation in Europe. In: Regional and Federal Studies 19, (2), 255-272.

Swenden, Wilfried (2002): Asymmetric federalism and coalition-making in Belgium. In: Publius: The journal of federalism 32, (3), 67-87.

Negotiating the Charlottetown Accord in Canada

Nadia Verrelli

1. Introduction

It took decades of trying by various Canadian governments, but on 17 April 1982, Canada's Constitution – the British North America Act (BNA Act 1867) – was finally patriated; on this day Canada became a fully sovereign country. Despite this, the newly patriated Constitution, now with a domestic amending formula and a Charter of Rights and Freedoms (*Constitution Act 1982*), proved to be unsuccessful and incomplete. First, the Constitution was amended without the consent of the Quebec government – to date, Quebec has yet to "sign on" to the Constitution. Second, recognition of Aboriginal peoples was, simply put, incomplete. The latter, was addressed in a series of constitutional negotiations between the federal government and Aboriginal groups soon after the 1982 patriation. Talks however, broke down when both sides failed to agree on the meaning of Aboriginal self-government. The former was addressed during the Quebec Round in 1987 leading to the Meech Lake Accord where Quebec's demands were met. The Accord, however, was not ratified. Rather than improving the situation, this round of constitutional negotiations worsened the problem as not only did Quebecers feel rejected by Canadians, but the Aboriginal peoples were completely ignored and shut out of the constitutional problem. To add to this, a majority of Canadians outside Quebec resented that the Meech Lake Accord addressed only Quebec's demands.

After the failure of the Meech Lake Accord in 1990, Canadians, mainly those outside of Quebec and the Aboriginal communities, were ready to let the quest for constitutional renewal rest. To their dismay, Quebecers and Aboriginal peoples were neither prepared nor willing to do so. The 1982 Constitution either did not address or fell short of meeting their demands. From their perspective, it remained incomplete and national unity continued to be in question. Canadians in the rest of Canada (ROC) – a term that came into play in the constitutional discourse during the post-Meech Lake Accord period and refers to Canada outside Quebec – had no choice but to re-open constitutional negotiations and attempt to address the grievances of Quebec and the Aboriginal peoples. By this point, ROC was pitted against Quebec and pitted against the Aboriginal peoples. But ROC too was divided; it did not represent one entity with one vision. Rather, it was made up of diverse provinces looking for different things and diverse groups demanding special recognition.

And so the stage was set for a fifth round of mega-constitutional politics in Canada, the Canada Round. It proceeded in three distinct phases: first, public consultations; second, negotiations amongst the federal, provincial, territorial and Aboriginal leaders that eventually led to the signing of the Charlottetown Accord in Charlottetown, Prince Edward Island (PEI) (by its own choosing, the Quebec government joined the negotiations phase late in the process); and finally, the referendum on the Charlottetown Accord held on 26 October 1992, where a majority of Canadians voted No.

Distinguishing the Canada Round from the other rounds of constitutional renewal was first, the extent to which government leaders attempted to be as inclusive as possible with regards to the issues discussed and the number of players at the table. While they remained committed to accommodating Quebec and defining Quebec's place in the federation, first ministers were equally committed to meeting the demands of other interests; national unity was the ultimate goal. Second, distinct and conflicting vision of Canada shaped the discourse. The fact that we have ROC pitted against Aboriginal peoples and ROC pitted against Quebec coupled with numerous interests and demands at the table and the reality that ROC did not speak with one voice, is indicative of how divided the country was. Finally, unlike previous rounds where there was a time lapse between each round, the Canada Round began soon after the collapse of the Meech Lake Accord – governments were responding to a sense of crisis that emerged after the failure of the Accord.

This chapter offers a descriptive analysis of the Canada Round beginning with the constitutional moments leading to the necessity of a new constitutional package and ending with the consequences of the "failure" of this round. In between, the paper offers an account of how this round unfolded starting with the consultations and negotiations and concluding with the referendum on the Charlottetown Accord and what Canadians can take away from this round.

2. The constitutional moment

As indicated above, the 1982 Constitution was perceived to be incomplete by the Quebec government and by Aboriginal groups. To say that there was one event that worked as a catalyst or a defining moment leading to certain issues included in the agenda would underestimate the years of negotiations beginning whole heartedly in the 1960s and ending with the Quebec Round and would underestimate the persistence of both Quebec and the Aboriginal peoples. Quebec continued to pursue recognition of its distinctiveness and expansion of its government's powers and the Aboriginal peoples continued to pursue recognition of their traditional inherent rights.

The Canada Round, therefore, was a two year affair built upon previous rounds of constitutional negotiations and triggered by ongoing events that eventually led to the federal government sitting down with its provincial, territorial and Aboriginal counterparts to 'hammer out' a new, more inclusive constitutional package. However, if we had to pinpoint the events that rendered the Canada Round inevitable, it would have to be the failure of the Meech Lake Accord and, to a lesser degree, the Oka crisis.

2.1 The Oka crisis

In July 1990, the Mohawks at Oka barricaded land designed for a new golf course, claiming it as their own. Lasting throughout the summer of 1990, the Oka standoff began first with the Quebec police and later the Canadian army and ended in mutual consensus. Despite this peaceful ending, the crisis was indicative that the peace between non-Aboriginal Canadians and Aboriginal Canadians was on shaky grounds. Aboriginal demands for a new constitutional order based on mutual consent could no longer be ignored (Russell, 1993a: 155).

2.2 Quebec's reaction to Meech Lake

The day after the Accord 'died', over 20 000 Quebecers, feeling betrayed and rejected by ROC, paraded the streets of Montreal at the annual St. Jean Baptiste festivities chanting "Independence" (Russell, 1993a: 155). In the days following, survey results showed 64% of Quebecers favouring sovereignty over renewed federalism (McRoberts, 1997: 204). ROC could not ignore this.

These two occurrences were coupled with a third element – ROC and the two forces within it: regionalism and Canadian nationalism. Western and eastern provinces wanted to address Ontario and Quebec's central domination of the federation – reforming the Senate to be an equal, elected and efficient institution (triple E Senate) would do just that. Also a growing sense of Canadian nationalism began to take form. But it was divided into three camps: first, the Left who desired stronger social policies, the middle who insisted on a strong central government able to protect their individual rights and deliver strong social policies, and finally the Right, an economic minded group desiring a strong economic Canada.

In short, there were three forces, each with their own perception of Canada, to be dealt with in the Canada Round: Quebec; Aboriginal peoples; ROC. Under the Aboriginal and Quebec perceptions, Canada is viewed as a multination and bination respectively where each nation is regarded as equal to the other. For many English Canadians, Canada is perceived to be one nation that champions provincial and individual equality while celebrating diversity. Both the Aboriginal and Quebec peoples wanted to be included in a renewed constitutional vision. The Aboriginal peoples were looking to constitutionalise their inherent right of self-government; Quebec was looking to constitutionalise its specificity and to increase the powers of the Quebec government in order to protect and enhance its status as a distinct society. For English Canada, a renewed constitution had to address their demands for a reformed Senate and for an inclusive Canada based on provincial and individual equality. To add to the already difficult task facing political leaders, the days of negotiating amongst themselves behind closed doors and outside of public scrutiny were over. Canadians resented the idea that the Meech Lake Accord, a new constitutional package proposing significant changes to the Canadian Constitution, was devised without their participation. The process leading to a new constitutional package therefore needed to be "a more participatory form of constitution-making" (Russell, 1993a: 156). The people *wanted in*. By the time of the Canada Round then, Canada had "entered an acute [unity] crisis, far worse than any in the past" (McRoberts, 1997: 204). By the end, this round proved to be Canadians most exhaustive and exhausting attempt to renew their Constitution.

3. Consultations

Responding to the *people want in*, governments hosted various public constitutional forums. They took place in two solitudes with Quebec and the ROC addressing different questions: Quebec considered "what does Quebec *need* to fulfill its constitutional aspirations?"; ROC explored: "Can the Constitution be reformed to appease *all* Canadians?"

3.1 Quebec

The government of Quebec formed two consultation forums: first, the *Constitutional Committee of the Quebec Liberal Party (the Allaire Committee)*; and second, the Belanger-Campeau Committee. Both focused on Quebec's constitutional future.

3.1.1 The Allaire Committee

The Allaire Committee met with business and union leaders and academic experts to develop constitutional alternatives for Quebec. In assessing options, the Committee considered the necessary political autonomy required for the government of Quebec to develop Quebec's identity. At the end of January 1991, the Allaire Committee released its report, *A Quebec Free to Choose*. In it, the Committee strongly recommended political autonomy, understood as *full autonomy* over social policy and economic development, for Quebec within a strengthened Canadian economy. It devised a list of 22 items that were to be in the exclusive jurisdiction of Quebec (A Quebec Free to Choose, 1991: 38). It should be noted, however, that with the exception of employment insurance, all items listed were already under the province's purview. Nonetheless, the report was a strong reaffirmation of the desire for Quebec sovereignty within a Canadian economic union. The Committee was essentially asking the federal government to step out of the province's jurisdiction. It promised to construct a new Quebec with the French-speaking political and social community of Quebec as the main community.

Soon after the release of the report, the Quebec Liberal government held a party convention. It debated the recommendations put forth by the Allaire Committee with the intent of softening the report's sovereigntist tone. By the end of the convention, almost all of the recommendations were defeated and it was resolved that the report would not be Quebec's final position.

3.1.2 Belanger-Campeau Committee

With the agreement of Jacques Parizeau, then leader of the Parti Quebococis (PQ) and Leader Opposition in Quebec, and Lucien Bouchard, then leader of the Bloc Quebecois (BQ), the Liberal government established the Belanger-Campeau Committee on 4 September 1990. The Committee was made up of 36 members including Parizeau and Bouchard, nine Liberals, six Parti Quebecois, and one member from the Equality Party. It heard from hundreds of individuals, a majority of which favoured either more autonomy for Quebec within a restricted Canadian federation or full out separation. (Russell, 1993a: 157).

In late March 1991, the Belanger-Campeau Committee released the *Report of the Commission on the Political and Constitutional Future of Quebec*. While all the members agreed that Quebec must choose its own constitutional future, they could not define it. They were only able to agree upon a two-track process (Russell, 1993a: 162).

Track one emphasised the need for Quebec sovereignty and resulted in the enactment of Bill 150 (*An Act Respecting the Process for Determining the Political and Constitutional Future of Quebec*) in May 1991. Section 1 of the

Act obliges the Quebec government to hold a referendum on sovereignty between 8 and 28 June or between 12 and 28 October 1992. If the Quebec electorate successfully voted for sovereignty, then Quebec was to acquire it "one year from the date the referendum was held" (*An Act Respecting the Process for Determining the Political and Constitutional Future of Quebec*: 5).

Track two was committed to exploring the federalist option – a strong Quebec within Canada. A legislative committee would be set up to examine offers of a new constitutional partnership presented to Quebec by the federal government. Quebec would not negotiate directly with the federal government, rather, it would respond to the federal government's proposals. Though no referendum was mentioned for the federalist option, the preamble of Bill 150 kept the option open.

Through both reports, Quebecers made it clear that they alone define their constitutional future. And now, a deadline was set. The federal government had until 28 October 1992, to present an acceptable proposal to Quebec in order to avoid a referendum on Quebec sovereignty.

4. The federal government

As indicated, ROC had little desire to reopen constitutional negotiation and even less desire to bend to Quebec's demands. But it was left with no choice. The federal government responded with two forums of its own. The first, the Citizen's Forum on Canada's Future, (the Spicer Commission) established in November 1990, was a forum for all Canadians to voice their opinion on Canada's future. It soon became a forum for Canadians to air out their grievances over the amount of time devoted to constitutional changes while other issues, like the ailing economy, went ignored. The second, the Beaudoin-Edwards Committee, set up in December of 1990, was established to review the constitutional amending process. Both committees were to report back to the government by July 1991.

4.1 The Spicer Commission

The Spicer Commission, hosting town hall meetings throughout the country, heard from over 400 000 Canadians and 300 000 in a special student's forum (*Citizen's Forum on Canada's Future: Report to the People and Government of Canada*). Participation from Quebecers and Aboriginals was, however, low. On 27 June 1991, the Spicer Commission released its final reports and, as was expected, most Canadians expressed a general dislike and distrust of the Mulroney government and of constitutional negotiations taking place without their input. On the issue of constitutional renewal, the Commission was able to reach a consensus – Canada would accommodate the desires and aspirations of Aboriginal peoples and Quebecers as long as they do not compromise Canadian (ROC) values understood as: "a strong central government which will act with resolution to remedy the country's economic ills, help to unify its citizens, and reduce the level of discord among groups or regions" (ibid.: 47). In the final analysis, the report demonstrated just how far apart Canadians were from renewing the Constitution, defining the Canadian political community and from reaching a consensus.

4.2 Beaudoin-Edwards Committee

The Spicer Commission demonstrated that citizens did not trust their leaders to properly renew Canada's Constitution. They preferred a method of either popular ratification or constituent assemblies comprised mainly of non politicians. In light of this, the Beaudoin-Edwards Committee was mandated to consider the amending process and citizen participation and in doing so, it made three recommendations:

First, the current amending formula requiring consent from seven of the ten provinces making up 50% of the population should be replaced with a regional formula. According to the proposal, an amendment to the Constitution would require the consent of the federal government, the governments of Quebec and Ontario, two of the four Atlantic Provinces and two of the four Western provinces (*Report of the Special Joint Committee for the Senate and the House of Commons on the Process for Amending the Constitution of Canada:* 26). Quebec would have a veto, meeting its demand expressed in the Allaire Report, but the western and eastern provinces would have to give up their desire to secure provincial equality. Changing the amending formula, however, would prove difficult and the Committee recognised this. To start, the federal government could not just change the amending process, it would need to address other issues raised by the West and the East or risk portraying that the federal government was catering to Quebec once again. Also, changing the amending formula would require unanimity of the provinces – Meech Lake demonstrated that unanimity is difficult. In light of this, the Committee introduced a recommendation that not only addressed citizen participation, but also, could be effected by a simple act of parliament.

Second, the Committee suggested to introduce legislation that would enable the federal government "to hold a consultative referendum on a constitutional proposal" (ibid.: 42). The new legislation would require a double majority – first, a national majority and second, a majority in each of Canada's four regions. The results of the referendum, though not legally binding on governments, would have political legitimacy and therefore, would render the ratification of a proposed constitutional package easier. During the multilateral negotiations, the federal government introduced and later adopted a referendum law.

Third, the Committee recommended that a parliamentary committee be set up, to hold public hearings on proposals put forth by the federal government and to interact with Aboriginal leaders and provincial and territorial committees set up to consider constitutional issues and proposals (Russell, 1993a: 167). After releasing *Shaping Canada's Future Together*, the federal government established the Unity Committee.

5. The provinces

By the fall of 1991, the other provinces and territorial governments had established committees to explore constitutional options. Not surprisingly, these committees addressed constitutional options through a provincial/territorial lens. However, unlike the two Quebec committees, they were focused on renewing federalism and not only "maximising their own autonomy" (Russell, 1993a: 169).

6. Aboriginal committee

Joe Clark, then Constitutional Affairs Minister, set up a parallel consultation process for Aboriginal peoples in early July 1991. Representatives from the Assembly of First Nations (AFN), the Native Council of Canada (representing non-status Indians), the Métis National Council and the Inuit Tapirisat of Canada consulted with their people and "interacted with the established parliamentary committee [Beaudoin-Dobbie] to discuss the federal government's constitutional options" (Russell, 1993a: 169). This resulted in the Royal Commission on Aboriginal peoples mandated to "examine all aspects of the Aboriginal peoples' condition and to comment on constitutional reform" (Russell, 1993a: 169).

Though this type of consultation process was foreign to Aboriginal peoples since they were not inclined to adopt a top-down approach, but rather a highly consensual form of decision making, they were committed to making it work. For the first time, Aboriginal peoples were included in the constitutional discourse. However, the issue of Aboriginal self-government was difficult for Canadians to grasp and proved to be particularly problematic for Quebec. Similar to Quebec, the Aboriginal peoples wanted their inherent right of self-determination to be constitutionally recognised. But, unlike Quebec, they wanted to exercise this right within Canada, even if Quebec separated. So, while, both Quebecers and the Aboriginal peoples were looking to secure self-determination and self-government, the aspirations of the two, inevitable clashed. The Aboriginals' insistence on staying in Canada potentially threatened the political stability and territorial integrity of Quebec. For the first time, the question of Quebec's borders was on the table.

On 24 September 1991, the federal government revealed its constitutional proposal (devised by a cabinet committee after a process of hearings it held throughout Canada), *Shaping Canada's Future Together*. In it, the federal government made a total of 28 recommendations falling under eight headings: the Canada Clause, distinct society, Charter changes, Aboriginal self-government, Senate reform, the Supreme Court of Canada (SCC), an economic union and the division of powers. It addressed almost every issue on the table, but in doing so, the demands of the interested parties were diluted. Arguably, this was inevitable if the various demands were to be reconciled in compromises. For instance, while Aboriginal self-government was recognised it was not recognised as *inherent* and it would only come into effect ten years after ratification. The proposed Senate reform was a far cry from a triple E demanded by the West and the East. Quebec's recognition as a distinct society was to be confined to the Charter of Rights and Freedoms (Charter). Finally, the federal package would have created a weaker national government. Considering this, most constitutional watchers described the federal package as "something for everyone, but maybe not enough for everyone" (Russell, 1993a: 173).

Unlike past constitutional proposals, this one was meant to continue the conversation rather than being the federal government's final position. In this spirit, it was sent to yet another joint parliamentary committee, the Dobbie-Castonguay Committee (later known as the Beaudoin-Dobbie Committee), also known as the Unity Committee.

7. The Unity Committee

Despite the BQ and the Reform Party growing in popularity amongst the voters in Quebec and in the West respectively, they were not represented on the Unity Committee. Rather the 30 member committee was made up of MPs from the Liberal, Progressive Conservative and the New Democratic Parties of Canada. They would consult first with Canadians in a cross country tour and then with provincial and territorial committees on the federal government's proposal. The committee, however, soon ran into some problems – neither Canadians nor the provinces and territories, still in the process of conducting their own consultations, were prepared to discuss the complex issues raised in the federal package. In November 1991, when few attended the meetings scheduled in Manitoba, the national tour ended (Russell, 1993a: 175). The federal government, in an attempt to salvage the committee, decided to supplement the hearings with five consultative conferences each focussing on one section of the federal package. These conferences were to be organised by non-governmental agencies and were to be a hybrid of Parliamentary committee hearings and constitutional conventions (Young and Brown, 1992: 7).

7.1 The consultative conferences

The first conference, held in Halifax, examined the division of powers. Asymmetrical federalism was considered as an option in an attempt to accommodate the demands of both ROC (provincial equality) and Quebec (distinct society). Prior to this conference, asymmetrical federalism was considered only by academics – now Canadians became familiar with it. Though the participants did not resolve the complications thought to be associated with an asymmetrical form of federalism, for instance, participation of Quebec representatives in central institutions on issues that their government has exclusive jurisdiction, it did succeed in generating this option as a viable one.

The second, held in Calgary, looked at central institutions with the main focus on the Senate. Though participants toyed with the idea of both territorial and social representation, nothing concrete was resolved. In the end, this conference demonstrated that Canadians were not ready to reach a consensus on Senate reform.

The third, in Montreal, looked to combine an economic union with social programs. It resolved that the two were not mutually exclusive; strengthening the economic union and reducing trade barriers between provinces cannot and should not be achieved at the expense of social programs. Thus a strong economic union must be balanced with a social charter.

The fourth, in Toronto, discussed Canadian identity. Participants resolved that they were willing to recognise Quebec as a distinct society. Such recognition, however, did not translate into a dualist conception of Canada. Further they were willing to recognise Aboriginal self-government and that Canada's diversity should be celebrated as the core of Canadian identity.

Finally, in Vancouver, the participants reviewed and synthesised all findings from the previous conferences. Once completed, they handed their report back to the Beaudoin-Dobbie Committee. On 28 February 1992, the Committee released its report, *A Renewed Canada* – a document that came to play an important role in setting up the framework within which the multilateral talks that followed took place.

Notably missing from any of these conferences was a discussion on Aboriginal issues. Joe Clark, recognising this oversight, promised that a special meeting on the topic would be held before 10 April. As mentioned above, the federal government established a Royal Commission on Aboriginal Issues in July 1991.

7.2 A Renewed Canada

As indicated above the Beaudoin-Dobbie Committee released its report, *A Renewed Canada*; in it, it made six recommendations (Beaudoin and Dobbie, 1992):

First, the committee agreed to include a Canada clause defining Canadian identity. In trying to be as inclusive as possible, the committee ultimately diluted most of the values Canadians wished to have constitutionally recognised. For instance, the Quebec distinct society clause was reduced to an interpretative clause applying only to the Charter and not to the division of powers. It was the latter that was most important to Quebec nationalists.

Second, the committee agreed to include Aboriginal inherent right of self-government – a recommendation that reflected the shifting mood of the public and a growing respect for the plight of Aboriginal peoples. Though the details of self-government were to be ironed out at a later date, the committee continued to demonstrate an appreciation of the Aboriginal role in the Canada's evolution by stipulating that no changes to the rights of Aboriginal peoples were to be made without their consent.

Third, on Senate reform, the committee agreed to an elected Senate and to enhancing regional, social and Aboriginal representation. However, it failed to come to a consensus on the powers of a newly elected Senate.

Fourth, on the economic union, the committee departed from the federal proposal and rejected the proposed new head of federal power for positive economic management. Instead, it suggested that a new economic union would be balanced with a social covenant that would establish decent social and environment standards.

Fifth, on the division of powers, the committee called for less decentralisation, answering the calls from Canadians (outside of Quebec) desiring a stronger federal government. It suggested asymmetrical federalism as an alternative to the current relationship between the two orders of government by introducing what came to be known as "make-a-deal federalism". The provinces could opt out of federal programs and negotiate fiscal compensation with the federal government. However, the areas to which it would apply and how it would apply were characterised by uncertain conditions. In the end different and confusing arrangements were proposed for different areas (see Russell, 1993a: 187).

Sixth, on the amending formula, the committee put forth five options, each giving Quebec a veto on changes to the Senate and the SCC. The committee recognised that giving Quebec a veto in these areas, especially over Senate reform, would not sit well with the western and eastern provinces. The alternative of treating Quebec as a province like the others, however, would generate the same, if not greater dissatisfaction amongst Quebec nationalists.

With this report, the committee managed to put together a package that the federal, provincial, territorial and Aboriginal leaders could use to begin the next step. In mid March 1992, Joe Clark launched the multilateral negotiations.

8. Negotiating Charlottetown

After nearly one year and a half of consultations, federal, provincial, territorial and Aboriginal leaders were ready to negotiate a new constitutional package. This next phase took place in three stages: multilateral negotiations; a classical first ministers' conference with the notable exception of Quebec; a First Ministers' conference that included Quebec.

8.1 Multilateral negotiations

The multilateral talks that set the framework for the subsequent two stages of negotiations broke new ground: First, it included many more players. No longer were constitutional negotiations limited to first ministers. Advisors, public servants, consultants were also present. Second, representatives from Aboriginal groups were included – never before had Aboriginal peoples participated in negotiations of such a full range of constitutional issues.

Similar to the previous phase, the participants were confronted with several tough issues including Senate reform, Aboriginal rights, the economic union, the social charter, the division of powers, and Quebec's demands for a constitutional recognition for its distinctiveness and for a constitutional veto over changes to central institutions. To enable the manageability of them, four working groups were set up: first, "unity and diversity" considered the Canada clause, the social and economic union and other matters; second, "institutions" concentrated on the Senate, the SCC and the House of Commons; third, "First Peoples" focussed on Aboriginal self-government and rights; and finally, "roles and responsibility" considered the division of powers (Young and Brown, 1992: 9; Russell, 1993a: 193). Each working group was staffed by two members from each of the 16 delegations (the federal government, the nine provinces, the two territories and the four Aboriginal organisations) and led by two delegates (one from the federal government and one from the provinces), with the exception of the institutions working group which was led by one delegate from the federal government as the provinces were unable to agree upon a co-chair. Though parameters on how to review the issues were not established for the working groups, some groups commissioned studies or papers, while others considered alternative proposals or recruited advisors (Young and Brown, 1992: 9). By early June, the working groups reached a consensus on seven items: the division of powers, the social and economic union, Aboriginal self-government, a Canada clause and recognition of Quebec as a distinct society.

8.1.1 Reaching a consensus

It was obvious in what was agreed vis-à-vis the division of powers, that the provinces dominated the process. Special treatment for Quebec and asymmetrical federalism were out. The agreement retained some of the opting out suggestions, but it was extended to all the provinces. Provincial equality overshadowed asymmetry. On other issues concerning the division of powers, the delegates stayed close to Beaudoin-Dobbie's ideas of "make-a-deal federalism". Finally, the provinces were able to persuade the federal government to abandon and/or eliminate their imperial powers of reservation and disallowance.

On a symbolic level, the consensus reached on the division of powers was not that well received in Quebec (Russell, 1993a: 199). While the federal government agreed to return a lot of powers to the province (powers they lost to the federal government through the use of the spending power), the return depended on negotiations. Quebec was not in the driver seat; and so, Quebec viewed the proposal as not doing enough. Similarly, this consensus was not well received in the other provinces, particularly, "make-a-deal federalism". It was viewed as the federal government giving up too much power to the provinces.

Regarding the Social Charter, the federal government expanded its commitment to economic equalisation and it agreed to discuss changes to equalisation payments with the provinces before introducing them.

Provincial support for the recognition of Aboriginal inherent right of self-government was secured. The participants agreed that the Aboriginal government would be one of the orders of governments in Canada, each sovereign within its own sphere. Self-government would apply to all residents in an area if they choose to participate and would come into effect three years after ratification. Negotiations were to be triggered by the Aboriginal peoples and the federal and provincial governments were constitutionally committed to negotiate in good faith. The participants, however, did not resolve whether the Charter would apply to Aboriginal governments and the fiscal basis of the Aboriginal governments. For treaty Indians, the federal government agreed to interpret treaties in a broad and liberal manner. Also, the federal government agreed to clarify the constitutional inclusion of the Métis and, along with Ontario and the western provinces, negotiate accords with them. Lastly, it was agreed that there would be Aboriginal representation in the Senate and that any changes to the Constitution would require the consent of Aboriginal peoples if amendments affected them.

The Canada clause listed seven fundamental values:

- Parliamentary democracy and Canadian federalism
- The Aboriginal peoples and related rights
- Quebec's distinct society
- Linguistic duality
- Racial and ethnic equality
- Equality of women and men
- The equality of the provinces, while recognising their diverse characteristics.

Applying to the whole Constitution, the clause was a symbolic gesture on the part of the participants to appease the different communities in Canada. However, this caused some controversy as not everyone was included – different ethnic groups began to complain that they were excluded. Multiculturalism was later introduced which led to non cultural groups to complain that they were ignored. Additionally, the recognition of Quebec as a distinct society seemed to be weakened as it was balanced with Canada's other fundamental values – it did not necessarily enjoy the precedence it had in the proposed Meech Lake Accord.

First Ministers' Conferences (FMC) were to be entrenched in the Constitution to be convened once a year. Unlike past FMC where only the federal government and the provinces participated, in future FMC, representatives from the territories and, if the matters concerned them, Aboriginal communities would also participate.

On the issue of reforming how justices are appointed to the Supreme Court of Canada, the participants adopted the process proposed in the Meech Lake Accord – the Prime Minister would choose a justice from a list provided by the provinces; three of the nine Supreme Court justices must have been admitted to the Quebec bar (civil law), guaranteed in the *Supreme Court Act*, was to be entrenched in the Constitution.

Reforming the Senate caused the greatest hurdle for the participants and in the end, no concrete agreement was reached. "A problem complicating the redesign of federal institutions, and particularly the Senate and the House of Commons [...] has been the need to find a balance between adequate representation by population, the interest of smaller provinces, and safeguards for the major linguistic community concentrated in Quebec" (Watts, 1993b: 20). Reforming the Senate meant the domination of Ontario and Quebec in the

House of Commons could be balanced with a Senate based on equal representation; the eastern and western provinces could be significant players in the federation. However, a triple E Senate was not favoured by Ontario, Quebec or the federal government. Under the triple E model, Ontario and Quebec would lose the power they currently enjoy in the Senate. Additionally, a triple E Senate celebrates provincial equality dispelling any claims that Quebec is distinct. The federal government did not support a triple E Senate for two reasons: first, it would weaken the House of Commons and second, the federal government knew it would not be accepted by the Quebec government. Despite this, the parties were able to reach a consensus on how the senators were to be elected (proportional representation) and on some of the powers of the Senate. Eventually though, talks remained deadlocked; "it was the composition and related powers of the Senate that proved to be the most intractable issues" (Watts, 1993b: 24).

On the amending formula, the participants agreed to constitutionalise *opting out with compensation* and agreed that the federal government could create a province by way of a simple act of Parliament. No agreement, however, was reached on extending the unanimity rule to include the Senate or other national institutions. Supporters of the triple E Senate would only agree to this extension on the condition that the triple E Senate model was accepted (Russell, 1993a: 207).

8.1.2 Problems with the multilateral talks

Though this first stage proved groundbreaking, it was not problem-free.

First, the meetings were set up in a way that closely resembled the long-established FMC. This affected the tone of the meetings which spoke to traditional centralised political systems foreign to Aboriginal peoples. In this sense, the negotiation process can be viewed and were regarded by Aboriginal groups as assimilative.

Second, the participation of the Aboriginal peoples proved to be problematic. The problems, however, came mainly from within Aboriginal communities. The AFN for example, refused to endorse the final product arguing that the process in which it was reached catered to traditional western means of negotiations. The fight put up by Native Women's Association of Canada (NWAC), however, proved to be more detrimental to the process than the AFN's objections. NWAC wanted to be included in the negotiations arguing that the concerns of Aboriginal women were not well represented by the four Aboriginal groups invited to participate in the negotiations process. An invitation to them was never extended. It is not surprising therefore, that NWAC did not support the Accord.

Third, the provinces dominated the negotiations more so in this round than in any of the previous rounds. The role of the federal government, where in previous rounds was well defined and strong, was ambiguous. It did not seem to have a clear plan. To add to this, the federal government was not led by the Prime Minister as in previous rounds, but by the Constitutional Minister.

Finally, Quebec, again by its own choosing, was not at the table. Premier Bourassa joined the negotiations late during a subsequent stage of the negotiations process. Despite his absence though, the demands of Quebec were constantly on the minds of the other participants. In addition, some of the leaders, including Bob Rae then Premier of Ontario, kept communication lines with Bourassa open – often relaying Bourassa's views on certain issues to the rest of the delegates (conversation with Ron Watts 12 January 2010).

Despite these problems, the delegates were successful in reaching a consensus and in setting up the next stage of negotiations. Quebec's deadline was the driving force behind all three stages of the negotiations. The participants were well aware that Quebec was committed to holding a referendum on Quebec sovereignty by 28 October 1992. They were thus committed to presenting Quebec with new constitutional package. The participants were also well aware of the backlash that would result if they failed to produce a package for either Quebec or ROC. With this in mind, the second stage of the negotiations began with a lunch at the Prime Minister's house on 29 June. Aboriginal and territorial leaders were not present and Quebec continued to wait for the best offer.

9. First Ministers Conference (without Quebec)

At the lunch, the first ministers agreed to break the impasse on Senate reform and continue negotiating a new constitutional package. Joe Clark was left in charge to represent the federal government while Prime Minister Mulroney attended a G7 meeting in Helsinki. The conference that followed, which included the territories and Aboriginal leaders, took place in Ottawa between 30 June and 7 July. Though all were committed to resolving the impasse, reaching a consensus on Senate reform proved to be difficult for the provincial premiers and Clark as they continued to struggle over how to reconcile a reformed Senate with Quebec's veto over changes to central institutions. Alberta, Newfoundland, Manitoba, British Columbia and Saskatchewan remained firm in their desire for a triple E Senate, while Ontario and Quebec (what was perceived to be Quebec's position) continued to oppose such reform (Russell, 1993a: 205). Nonetheless, the first ministers reached a consensus and on 7 July the Pearson Accord was released.

10. The Pearson Accord

If the Pearson Accord represented the federal and provincial governments' offer to Quebec and ROC, then it failed in two respects. First, from the perspective of Quebec nationalists, the Accord championed provincial equality most evident in the proposed Senate reform. To Quebec nationalists, an equal Senate is the symbolic end of the *deux nations* concept in Canada. Provincial premiers and Joe Clark agreed to reduce the size of the Senate from 102 seats to 84 seats (eight from each province and two from each territory). They also agreed to the possibility of increasing the number of senators to include representation of the Aboriginal peoples – but this was to be determined at a later date. To compensate for the loss of seats in the Senate for the more populous provinces (Ontario and Quebec), they agreed to increase the House of Commons from 295 to 312 seats. The trade off for equal representation in the Senate was representation in the House of Commons that fully realises the principle of representation by population (Watts, 1993b: 30). Finally, the rule of unanimity when amending the Constitution was extended to include changes to the Senate.

In the area of the division of powers, any hint of asymmetrical federalism was out. Anything "gained" by Quebec including the federal government's withdrawal in the area of provincial jurisdiction, was extended to all the provinces. Finally, recognition of Quebec as a distinct society continued to be listed in the Canada clause as one of the many fundamental characteristics of Canada; it was not afforded the special recognition it had demanded in past and the present constitutional rounds.

Second, expressing similar sentiments towards the Canada clause as Quebecers, ROC felt that adding yet another item (respect for individual and collective rights) rendered it less significant. Further, changes to the proposed economic union reduced the federal government's powers to act effectively in the economic realm. Section 121 which would have prevented the "erection of interprovincial trade barriers" was rendered ineffective when 13 qualifications were added, essentially making a mockery of the section. On the Aboriginal front, Aboriginal self-government continued to be recognised. Its coming into effect, however, was extended from three to five years.

In the end, concerns not to isolate Quebec and not to squander the consensus reached in the previous two stages of negotiations kept the talks moving. When Mulroney was presented with the Pearson Accord, he was left with no choice but to work with it and try to get Bourassa on board. Mulroney, however, was skating on thin ice – re-opening negotiations threatened the consensus reached over Senate reform and Aboriginal self-government, but at the same time, both, more so Senate reform, would be a tough sell to Quebecers. To retract on Senate reform, however, threatened to alienate the West.

11. The Final First Ministers' Conference (including Quebec)

On 4 August, talks between the leaders resumed. Deciding that the essence of the Meech Lake Accord was embodied in the Pearson Accord, Bourassa agreed to finally join the negotiations in hopes of working with the federal government to make the Pearson Accord a constitutional proposal acceptable to Quebecers. On 10 August, the second meeting after their initial August 4 one, the leaders all agreed to a full scale constitutional conference. In long negotiations that took place in closed chambers from 18-22 August in Ottawa, a compromise between the players was reached. It was finalised on 27 and 28 August in Charlottetown, PEI.

11.1 The Charlottetown Accord

The final agreement signed on 28 August 1992, and formally known as the Charlottetown Accord had five major elements:

- Unity and diversity
- Institutions
- Role and responsibilities
- First Peoples
- The amending formula

11.2 Unity and diversity

With a commitment to an economic and social union, equalisation payments and the Canada clause, the political actors intended and hoped to secure unity through a celebration of Canada's diversity. However, they fell short; especially with the Canada clause.

Though the non-justiciable policy objectives for the social and economic union were laid out, the mechanism to monitor them were to be established at a later date. The federal government's commitment to the social union was neutral – it neither strengthened nor weakened its ability to provide leadership. On the economic union, it acquiesced to provincial demands. It agreed to include 121 restrictions to a list of matters to be dealt with in the future.

The Canada clause aimed to recognise all parts of Canadian society and *"a shared commitment to building a nation as a whole"* (Schwartz, 1992: 9). It was to serve both a symbolic and an operational function. Symbolically, it suggests that Canada is all things to everyone. Operationally, it indicates to the courts that the Constitution ought to be interpreted with the clause in mind. There were a total of eight enumerated "fundamental characteristics" in the final draft:

1. The Constitution of Canada, including the Canadian Charter of Rights and Freedoms, shall be interpreted in a manner consistent with the following characteristics:
   a) Canada is a democracy committed to a parliamentary and federal system of government and to the rule of law;
   b) The Aboriginal peoples of Canada, being the first peoples to govern this land, have the right to promote their languages, cultures and traditions and to ensure the integrity of their societies, and their governments constitute one of the three orders of government in Canada;
   c) Quebec constitutes within Canada a distinct society, which includes a French-speaking majority, a unique culture and a civil law tradition;
   d) Canadians and their governments are committed to the vitality and development of official language of minority communities throughout Canada;
   e) Canadians are committed to racial and ethnic equality in a society that includes citizens from many lands who have contributed, continue to contribute, to the building of a strong Canada that reflects its cultural and racial diversity;
   f) Canadians are committed to a respect for individual and collective human rights and freedoms of all people;
   g) Canadians are committed to the equality of female and male persons; and
   h) Canadians confirm the principal of the equality of the provinces at the same time as recognising their diverse characteristics (Charlottetown Accord, 1992).

The clause recognising Quebec as a distinct society not only remained one of the eight enumerated "fundamental characteristics" but the parameters of Quebec's specificity were carefully delineated and circumscribed. Distinct society was to be defined as "a French-speaking majority, a unique culture and a civil law tradition. The role of the legislature and government of Quebec to preserve and promote the distinct society of Quebec" was added (ibid.). However, the recognition and affirmation of this role was balanced with a stipulation that Canada and their governments are committed to the vitality and development of both official languages throughout Canada. Further, though the recognition of Quebec's distinctiveness had more reach in this accord than in the Meech Lake Accord (in Charlottetown Quebec distinct society would apply to the whole Constitution and not just the Charter as was the case in the Meech Lake Accord), it was balanced against other fundamental characteristics, thereby watering down not only distinct society, but the other characteristics as well. In the end, the clause became a failed attempt to please everyone.

11.3 Institutions

By the time an agreement on Senate reform was reached "some thirty distinct proposals had been considered" (Watts, 1993b: 24). In the end, the basis of the agreement established in the Pearson Accord was adopted with noticeable exceptions. The leaders agreed to the following: First, senators could be elected directly by the people or indirectly by provincial or territorial assemblies. Second, the powers of the Senate would depend on the type of legislation. Third, measures affecting the French language could be defeated by either a majority of senators or a majority of Francophone senators. Fourth, a provision for Aboriginal representation would be included. Finally, in order to obtain Quebec's consent, the province was guaranteed no less than 25% of the seats in the House of Commons, regardless of its population. While this proved to be the deal-maker for the leaders at the table, helping them overcome the *Senate impasse*, it was the deal-breaker for the people, especially for those in the western provinces. A poll conducted by Angus Reid asking voters "which part of the [Charlottetown Accord] do you particularly dislike?", almost one quarter of those who responded in Alberta and Saskatechewan indicated the guarantee of 25% seats to Quebec (Henry, 1993: 4).

On the SCC – the leaders agreed to constitutionally entrench the SCC as a general court of appeal and the requirement that three of the nine judges belong to the bar of Quebec. Further, they agreed to reform the appointment process – judges are to be appointed from a list of names submitted to the federal government by the provinces and territories. Lastly, the leaders agreed that though the structure of the Court should not be modified in this round, they should consider Aboriginal representation on the Court in a political accord. As well, a clause was put in place stipulating that "the federal government should examine, in consultation with Aboriginal groups, the proposal that an Aboriginal Council of Elders be entitled to make submissions to the Supreme Court when the court considers Aboriginal issues" (Charlottetown Accord, 1992).

A provision requiring the federal government to convene a FMC at least once a year was to be entrenched in the Constitution. Participation in these annual conferences would include the federal government, provinces, the territories and when the issue on the agenda directly affects them, Aboriginal peoples.

11.4 Roles and responsibilities

Including "make-a-deal federalism" in the Charlottetown Accord served the federal government well as it enabled them to appease Quebec without upsetting the principle of provincial equality. At the same time, however, it weakened the federal government's ability to play a strong and leading role in establishing national programs.

On the issue of the division of powers, insignificant changes were proposed. First, the federal government promised to develop a framework for using the spending power in areas of exclusive provincial jurisdiction. Second, the federal powers of disallowance and reservation were eliminated and the use of the declatory power would require the consent of the provinces. These proposals did little to change the relationship between the two orders of government. All three had already fallen into disuse. The proposals to eliminate them then were simply reaffirming what was politically in effect. In this sense then, what was agreed upon in Charlottetown was a far cry from what was demanded by Quebec in the Allaire Report.

11.5 First peoples

One of the most remarkable features of the Charlottetown Accord was the inclusion of the Aboriginal inherent right to self-government. It was to be defined by Aboriginal leaders, the federal government and the provinces by way of treaties, with the onus on Aboriginal leaders to trigger negotiations. Other than stipulating that the Constitution and the Charter were to apply to Aboriginal governments and that Aboriginal governments were committed to providing public services at levels comparable to those established by the federal and provincial governments, the details of self-government would be tailored to the different circumstances of the different Aboriginal communities. Additionally, Bourassa had insisted that clear parameters be established on the recognition of Aboriginal self-governments. First, this recognition was not to create new land rights and second, if Aboriginal laws conflicted with either federal or provincial laws, they would be invalid.

Though a remarkable feat, the recognition of Aboriginal self-government was problematic as it generated great uncertainty. The extent of this recognition, the power bestowed on Aboriginal communities and the extent of the force of federal and provincial laws on Aboriginal communities remained unclear.

11.6 The amending formula

As mentioned, the constitutional amending formula requiring unanimity of the provinces was extended to include the Senate and the SCC with the exception of the nominations of justices to the Court, (changes to the nomination process could be effected by agreement from seven of the provinces making up 50% of the population). Additionally, the amending formulas were expanded to include the Aboriginal peoples; changes to the Constitution that directly affect Aboriginal peoples require their consent. The regional amending formula proposed by the Beaudoin-Edwards Committee was rejected, instead the leaders decided to work with the already established amending formulas. This is not surprising as the current formulas remain true to the principle of provincial equality whereas the regional formula privileges Quebec and Ontario, each with a veto.

12. The referendum

The intent for holding a referendum on the Charlottetown Accord was to discourage individual provincial governments from blocking the ratification of the Accord (as was the case with the Meech Lake Accord). If the public supported the Accord, the provincial governments would be politically obliged to ratify it. However, the federal government's late decision to hold a referendum posed two problems. First, provincial, territorial and Aboriginal leaders were negotiating a new constitutional package full of unfinished business. A few items, including Senate reform and Aboriginal self-government were labelled as "to be determined at a later date." Second, holding a referendum on a document not meant for the public could prove to be disastrous. The participants, when drafting the Pearson Accord, wrote it for heads of government and not for the general public. Had they known, the agreement would have possibly been written in "referendum friendly" terms (conversation with Ron Watts, 12 January 2010). For better or worse, the federal government had committed itself to holding a national referendum. And by the end of this round, a referendum proved to be inevitable for five reasons:

- First, Alberta and British Columbia were legally bound to hold a referendum before their legislatures could consider constitutional changes.
- Second, Quebec was already committed to having a referendum before 28 October 1992.
- Third, the federal government had already committed to holding a referendum on constitutional changes.
- Fourth, after the Meech round, public backlash and six months of closed door negotiations, the democratic legitimacy of a constitutional package would be questioned if the people were not consulted (Russell, 1993a: 219). To a certain extent, Canadians believe that the Constitution belonged to them, so if there are any major changes to it, they ought to be consulted.
- Fifth, a national referendum regardless of the result would provide closure to the ongoing constitutional debate in Canada. A yes vote would be followed by ratification. We need to note, however, that the debate

would not have ended with the referendum or even the ratification of the Charlottetown Accord. There were a lot of "to be negotiated later" clauses that needed to be resolved. A no vote would most likely lead to everyone wanting a break from constitutional talks.

12.1 The campaign

Similar to the beginning of this round with the initial public consultations taking place in two solitudes, the referendum campaign was a *two nations* affair. The federal referendum law governed the referendum in all of Canada except Quebec, where the Quebec referendum law governed. The Quebec law mandated that the National Assembly of Quebec establish two committees: Bourassa and the Liberals led the Yes campaign and Parizeau and the Parti Quebecois the No campaign. Under the federal law, an infinite number of committees were allowed to (and did) campaign. The federal government, the Liberals, and NDP along with provincial governments and various interest groups formed the Yes committee headed by retired politicians and distinguished members of society. The No committee was led by the Reform Party of Canada, the opposition Liberals in British Columbia and a plethora of interest and citizens' groups. Neither law legally bound governments to the results. However, it was understood by all that the results would be politically binding.

Despite the different laws governing the referendum, the question was the same for all voters:

> Do you agree that the Constitution of Canada should be renewed on the basis of the agreement reached on August 28th, 1992 (Russell, 1993a: 220).

The campaign lasted two months and the mood of Canadians during that time quickly turned. Soon after the Charlottetown Accord was signed, polls indicated support at 60%. A month later, however, support dropped by 16% with the most significant drop (20-25%) in the West. Still there remained approximately 40% of undecided voters – it is these voters that the Yes campaign hoped to win over (Henry, 1993: 2). But they never did. Many Canadians were less than grateful for the Accord. They had low faith in all three of their federal political leaders (Brian Mulroney, Jean Chrétien and Audrey McLaughlin) and they resented that the package with 60 proposals in total, was presented as an all or nothing deal. The Accord was a web of concession and agreements – one item or clause could not be approved without the other. On 26 October 1992, 75% of eligible voters made their way out to the polls where 54% rejected the Charlottetown Accord.

12.2 Explaining failure

Many reasons can explain the referendum results beginning with an unorganised and ill-conceived Yes campaign. Conflicts existed amongst the three major federal political parties and between them and citizens groups. Some of the political leaders did not campaign as vigorously as they could have and probably should have (McRoberts, 1997: 216). With the popularity of political leaders, especially Mulroney's, at an all time low, voters were unable to separate their votes from the leaders (Simpson, 1993: 194). The Reform Party, exploiting this, constantly referred to the Accord as the "Mulroney proposals". Further, the advertising campaign was mostly played out on television and the "no vote seemed to have an edge" (Russell, 1993a: 225). The No Campaign was effectively able to portray the No vote as the people's vote. Additionally, no formal legal document was released to the public at the start of the referendum campaign. The No side, capitalising on this, argued that politicians could change the Accord once it passed. Though campaigners for the Yes side denied this, the damage was done. When the legal document was released two weeks before the vote, there was only one major change to the proposed package – Aboriginal self-government would not affect women's rights protected in the Charter. Despite this assurance, Aboriginal women continued to campaign against the Accord.

To add to the growing unpopularity of the Accord, Pierre Trudeau expressed his opposition to the proposed constitutional package in what came to be known as "the egg roll speech". This sent support for the Accord into a downward spiral (McRoberts, 1997: 218). Prior to delivering this speech at the Maison d'Egg Roll in Montreal, Trudeau hinted at his opposition in an essay published in Maclean's magazine in mid September. But, the egg roll speech confirmed this and within days, support for the Accord dropped almost 20 points (McRoberts, 1997: 218). More important than the above reasons, two critical factors can explain the rejection of the Charlottetown Accord by the people: different conceptions of the Canadian political community and the content of the Accord.

For the most part, Quebecers view Canada as a binational or dualist federation made up of two equal political communities, English Canada and French Canada. Central to Quebec's conception of the Canadian political community is the pre-eminence of Quebec for les Quebecois; since a majority of the population in Quebec speak French, the province and its government are regarded as the primary political community for the francophones. Quebec's constitutional aspirations were clearly outlined in the Allaire report – constitutional recognition of Quebec's specificity and expanded powers for the Quebec government that would enable it to protect the Quebec political community and to ensure the flourishing of Quebec's specificity.

Aboriginal peoples viewed Canada as a multinational state where the Aboriginal peoples are regarded as one of the founding nations equal to both the Quebec and ROC nations. Their constitutional aspirations remained rooted in their desires to have their inherent right to self-determination and self-government recognised in the Canadian Constitution.

Over the past two decades, Canada outside of Quebec had firmly become attached to the idea of Canada as its pre-eminent political community. Under this vision, Canada is regarded as one nation with a strong federal government ensuring and protecting national standards, the equality of the provinces and human rights and liberties. It is not surprising then that English Canada did not want this vision to be compromised by a new constitutional proposal.

In order to reach a consensus among those at the table and to make the package palatable to all Canadians, all three projects had to be diluted. "In the end, the political leaders found that in trying to accommodate every group, they had drafted a document that because it required so many compromises made more enemies than friends" (Watts, 1993a: 5).

In the Charlottetown Accord as well as in the Pearson Accord, there was neither an increase nor a decrease of federal powers. Both accords essentially re-affirmed the powers already belonging to the federal government. Yes, Quebec distinct society was recognised in the Canada clause. However, not only was the recognition diluted within the Canada clause, but also it was clear that it would not affect the division of powers since a section was added stipulating that nothing included in the clause derogates from the federal government powers. As indicated, "a general framework to guide the use of the federal spending power and a commitment to negotiate an agreement to coordinate and harmonise the regulation of telecommunication" was included in the Accord, mainly to appease Quebec – though other provinces favoured scrutiny of the federal spending power (McRoberts, 1993: 253). For all intent and purposes, Quebec did not gain much with regards to the proposed restriction on the federal spending power for two reasons: first, the federal government will only withdraw if they are requested to; second, the federal government maintained its role of establishing national standards (Gagnon and Rocher, 1993: 123). Quebec's clearest gain in this round was representation in the House of Commons. The irony of this guarantee was that Quebec did not ask for it nor did it care much for it (McRoberts, 1997: 213). On the other hand, the "25% guarantee" was resented by many in ROC (McRoberts, 1997: 217); it signalled to them that the federal government and provincial governments continued to pander to Quebec.

Though the proposed Senate reform would guarantee equal representation in the Senate, it fell short of meeting the triple E criteria. First, the "25% seat guarantee" for Quebec weakened the headway made by the East and the West to play a significant role in central institutions. Second, many details of the reformed Senate were left unresolved. Other proposals in the Accord, especially those considered to fall under the "make-a-deal federalism" category, while championing the principle of provincial equality, were seen, to the dismay of many in ROC, as potentially weakening the federal government

Regarding Aboriginal peoples, though their inherent right of self-government was recognised, it remained ambiguous. Further, not only were there stipulations placed on it, for instance it would not confer new rights, there was also a delay in the realisation of this right.

By the time the Accord was finalised and all concessions were made, voters had few reasons to endorse it. These reasons were coupled with the electorate's nonchalant attitude towards the potential failure of the Accord. People felt confident that a vote against the Accord would not bring about the dire consequences proclaimed by the Yes side. Voting no, they felt, would not strengthen the desire for sovereignty in Quebec. Rather, rejecting the Accord would signal to politicians that they would have to come up with a better deal (Simpson, 1993: 195).

In the end, the "contradictory motivations of different groups for voting 'No' in the referendum illustrated vividly the continued contradictions of views held by different groups within Canada" (Watts, 1993a: 6).

13. Charlottetown: A success?

Despite the ultimate failure of the Charlottetown Accord, we should not dismiss the immediate and long-term success. First, the Accord represented a consensus reached by the federal government, all ten provinces, the two territories and four major Aboriginal groups and endorsed by three federal parties, major newspapers in English Canada, large and small business communities, women's and multicultural groups. Reaching a consensus and generating endorsement from various players was a feat in and of itself.

Second, 26 October 1992 remains an important date in Canada's political history. "The Canadian people, for the first time in their history as a political community, acted as Canada's ultimate authority – in effect, as a sovereign people" (Russell, 1993b: 211).

Third, up until the Canada Round, constitutional talks were an affair that took place behind closed doors and amongst first ministers. The process leading up to the Charlottetown Accord was much more open with regards to who participated and media reporting. Throughout the process, the media was briefed almost daily. Negotiation meetings were not restricted to first ministers alone. The public, during the initial consultation process, were keenly involved in voicing their interests and demands. Most notable was the active participation of the Aboriginal peoples; no longer were their issues pushed aside. This, coupled with the participation of the people, mark the greatest success of the Canada Round; one that will most likely have a lasting effect on Canadian constitutionalism.

Fourth, the Canada Round had a broader constitutional agenda than previous rounds. Aside from addressing Quebec's place in the federation and attempting to reform central institutions, the public and government leaders gave serious thought to Aboriginal issues and to Canadian identity. Never before have the Canadian people and their governments attempted, in any serious manner, to define who Canadians are as a people and what Canada is as a nation. The result, though an ambiguous and sweeping list of fundamental characteristics embodied in a Canada clause, demonstrates that Canadians are prepared to be more inclusive in their definition of Canada.

We must, however, be careful not to overstate the successful achievements of the Canada Round. Aside from the ultimate rejection of the Charlottetown Accord by the people, deeper problems are associated with it and its aftermath.

First, this constitutional experience demonstrated that reaching a consensus amongst the different players each having a different conception of the Canadian community was and will continue to be a difficult hurdle to overcome. After five rounds, the process of constitutional renewal has become more complex involving more participants and more issues. At the very least, Aboriginal and territorial leaders and their concerns will continue to be included. Further, it is most likely that any future constitutional round will involve the people at levels comparable to this round.

Second, this round demonstrated that sweeping constitutional changes can divide the nation. Though Canada as a whole rejected this package – Canadians continued to resent each other – most notably, English Canada and Quebec. A majority of Canadians outside Quebec felt that Quebec received too much whereas a majority of those in Quebec felt that they did not receive enough (Russell, 1993a: 226). With the failure of the Meech Lake Accord and the disappointment of the Charlottetown Accord, Quebecers felt that the only way to have their desires met was with a strong Quebec government, even if that meant a strong government outside of Canada. This sentiment was well vocalised in the 1995 Quebec referendum on Quebec sovereignty where 50.58% voted against sovereignty and 49.42% voted in favour of it (McRoberts, 1997: 226).

It is important to note that the success of the Charlottetown Accord was that it did not leave Quebec isolated since the Accord was rejected both in Quebec and in ROC. In the year or two after the collapse of the Charlottetown Accord, support for separatism did not spike to over 60% as it did after the failure of the Meech Lake Accord. However, the effect of the 1995 referendum was to confirm Quebec's weariness of constitutional issues and avoidance of the deep divisiveness caused within Quebec society by these issues.

14. Conclusion

If the Canada Round taught Canadians anything, it is that reconciling different and often conflicting agendas is difficult to achieve without diluting them. Everyone had to 'give a little to get a little' and after a long drawn out consultation and negotiation process, few had strong reasons to support the final product and even fewer reasons to engage in another large-scale constitutional renewal process. Ultimately the effect of the Charlottetown Accord was constitutional fatigue and connected to this, subsequent reluctance to try any comprehensive constitutional reform and to turn instead to incremental non-constitutional adjustments.

This is not to say that government leaders will never embark on another mega constitutional round. However, considering the Canada Round experience, it may be safe to assume that barring a real national unity crisis, leaders will continue down the road of incremental non-constitutional changes. Even after the 1995 referendum in Quebec, arguably classifying as a national unity crisis as close to 50% of the electorate in Quebec voted for sovereignty, the federal government, rather than proposing another round of constitutional negotiations, opted to pursue non-constitutional changes.

References

A Quebec Free to Choose (1991): Rep. Constitutional Committee of the Quebec Liberal Party.

Beaudoin, Gerald A./Dobbie, Dorothy (2004): Report of the Special Joint Committee on a Renewed Canada. Rep. Ottawa: Government of Canada.

Charlottetown Accord (1992): Consensus Report on the Constitution. http://www.thecanadianencyclopedia.com/index.cfm?PgNm=TCE&Params=A1 ARTA0010099 [accessed: September 2009]

Citizen's Forum on Canada's Future (1991): Report to the People and Government of Canada. Ottawa: Supply and Services Canada.

Gagnon, Alain G./Rocher, Francois (1992): The Multilareral Agreement: A Betrayal of the Federal Spirit. In: Brown, D./Young, R. (eds.): Canada: The State and the Federation. Kingston: Institute of Intergovernmental Relations, 117-28.

Henry, Shawn (1993): Canada 2000: Towards a New Canada. Rep. Calgary: Canada West Foundation.

McRoberts, Kenneth (1997): Misconceiving Canada the Struggle for National Unity. Toronto: Oxford University Press.

McRoberts, Kenneth (1993): Disagreeing on Fundamentals: English Canada and Quebec. In: Monahan, P. J./McRoberts, K. (eds.): Charlottetown Accord, the Referendum, and the Future of Canada. Toronto: University of Toronto, 249-263.

Report of the Special Joint Committee for the Senate and the House of Commons (1992): A Renewed Canada. Ottawa: Supply and Services Canada, 28 Feb. 1992.

Report of the Special Joint Committee for the Senate and the House of Commons on the Process for Amending the Constitution of Canada. Ottawa: Queen's Printer, 20 June 1991.

Russell, Peter H. (1993a): Constitutional Odyssey: Can Canadians become a Sovereign People? Toronto: University of Toronto.

Russell, Peter H. (1993b): The End of Mega Constitutional Politics. In: Monahan, P. J./McRoberts, K. (eds.): Charlottetown Accord, the Referendum, and the Future of Canada. Toronto: University of Toronto, 211-221.

Schwartz, Bryan (1992): Still Thinking: A Guide to the 1992 Referendum. Rep. Hull. QC: Voyaguer.

Simpson, Jeffrey (1993): The Referendum and Its Aftermath. In: Monahan, P. J./McRoberts, K. (eds.): Charlottetown Accord, the Referendum, and the Future of Canada. Toronto: University of Toronto, 193-199.

Spicer, Keith (1991): comp. Citizen's Forum on Canada's Future. Rep. Ottawa: Government of Canada.

Watts, Ronald L. (1993a): Overview. In: Watts, R. L./Brown, D. (eds.): Canada: The State and the Federation 1993. Kingston: Institute of Intergovernmental Relations, 3-18.

Watts, Ronald L. (1993b): The Reform of Federal Institutions. In: Monahan, P. J./McRoberts, K. (eds.): Charlottetown Accord, the Referendum, and the Future of Canada. Toronto: University of Toronto, 17-36.

Young, Robert/Brown, Douglas (1992): Overview. In: Brown, D./Young, R. (eds): Canada: The State and the Federation 1992. Kingston: Institute of Intergovernmental Relations, 3-26.

The Limits of Flexibility for Constitutional Change and the Uses of Sub-national Constitutional Space: The Case of Spain

César Colino and José A. Olmeda

1. Introduction: the Spanish open federal arrangements and the modes and potential of implicit constitutional change

As is well-known, the Spanish federal system has several peculiarities, which for the sake of brevity may be summarised as five main features:

- The model of territorial distribution of power is not completely spelled out in the constitution, which contains only general principles and a general distribution of powers among levels.
- Its workings are characterised by the existence of strong nationalist movements and parties in two of the autonomous communities, which were recognised in the constitution through extensive and quick devolution and the establishment of some asymmetries.
- It has developed into a relatively decentralised system in terms of public spending and authority, with the dominance of shared powers and revenues.
- It is a devolutionary and evolutionary federalism, which has produced at the same time a dynamic entailing both a centrifugal and differentiating tendency and a centripetal and equalising one.
- It has evolved from an asymmetrical dual equilibrium to a symmetrical cooperative one without one single formal amendment of the very rigid constitution, through a series of mutations or implicit constitutional change effected by political agreements, court interpretation and the amendment of sub-national statutes of autonomy.

In this sense, the Spanish model has been deemed by some as a paradigm of adaptation to the changes in society and to political demands and tensions without having implemented a single constitutional reform, since famously, the constitution was very general and ambiguous on the territorial model and left the Autonomous Communities (ACs) a lot of leeway for negotiating bilaterally their powers with the central government. This system of flexibility and voluntariness, of decentralisation *à la carte* and of multilevel negotiation and sub-constitutional or implicit reform, has been praised and advocated as the best way to accommodate a country perceived by some minorities as multinational and has served so far both the differentiating impulses of some ACs and the equalising aspirations of others (Tudela, 2009).

Recently, from around 2004 to 2011 a round of reforms related to devolution of competences, redistribution of resources and symbolic issues has taken place. Some regional statutes of autonomy have been amended or even drafted anew: Valencia (2006), Catalonia (2006), Balearic Islands (2007), Andalucía (2007), Aragón (2007), Castile and León (2007), Navarra (2010) and Extremadura (2011), have amended their statutes. Some other ACs have debated proposals and drafts, but have not found party-political consensus at the regional level until now, e. g. Canary Islands, Castile-LaMancha, Galicia. In the Basque Country, the reform failed in 2005. Most of the reform process has been triggered and influenced by the initiative and discussion on the Catalan statute reform (on the Catalan reform, see Castellà, 2008; Viver, 2009; Colino, 2009a, 2009b; Corcuera, 2009).

Due to a protracted process of reform and to the final intervention of the Constitutional Court with a landmark ruling on the Statute of Catalonia, this round of reforms has raised many questions about the real reform capacity of the system, on its capacity to achieve integration, accommodation, and adaptation to changing social circumstances and therefore legitimacy and stability without formal constitutional reform. The main political and academic discussion in Spain has revolved around the extent to which this type of reform that has indirectly changed the federal constitution by changing the subnational statutes of autonomy represents a valid way to adapt the general constitution or constitutes an unduly constitutional reform "through the backdoor". There has been debate on the adequacy of a reform of regional statutes prior to a constitutional reform, and on the extent to which it was likely and predictable that implicit reform accomplished through party agreements and without all-party consensus in the negotiation phase would fail at the ratification phase (see Cruz, 2006; Tudela and Kölling, 2009; Garrido, 2009; Sánchez Ferriz, 2009; Tudela, 2010).

As many observers argue, the intervention of the Constitutional Court responding to the challenge by the main opposition party on the Catalan statute (the first time ever that the Court has ruled on the constitutionality of a regional statute of autonomy) has resulted in a failure of the final ratification of many of the original goals of the reform, which have been diluted or annulled by the court. For others, the intervention of the Court has redressed the problems produced by an undue reform, thus safeguarding the previous constitutional consensus. The Court has rejected most of the new interpretations of the 1978 constitution made by the Catalan and the other amended regional statutes of autonomy, thus invalidating the effectiveness of the political pact for implicit constitutional change reached by the majority in the Spanish Parliament. It has also self-empowered itself by clearly reasserting its role in the interpretation of the constitution and the validity of its former doctrine on the distribution of powers and the symbolic recognition of political communities within the Spanish constitution (on the Court 2010 ruling see Albertí, 2010; Barceló et al., 2010; Blanco, 2010; Castellà, 2010; Carreras, 2010; Colino, 2011; Quadra-Salcedo, 2010; Tornos, 2010; Ferret, 2010; Muñoz Machado, 2010a, 2010b; Delledonne, 2011; Solozábal, 2011; López Aguilar, 2011; Tajadura, 2011; Gavara, 2011; Tornos, 2011). This result, apparently not anticipated by many of the political actors involved in the reform process, has caused political turmoil and citizen frustration in Catalonia. It also has led to some legal uncertainty in other ACs, alongside a general feeling of a stalemate in the reform and adaptation capacity of the system, now also under financial and efficiency pressures due to the economic crisis.

This raises the more general question of how to evaluate implicit change in federal systems with rigid constitutions, and particularly in Spain, as a viable strategy of adaptation and accommodation of diversity. More than two years ago one of the authors assessed the reform of the statute of Catalonia as a "paradoxical success" (Colino, 2009a), arguing that "despite disagreements during the negotiation and the remaining conflicts before the Constitutional Court, most of the involved actors and the original advocates of reform claimed to have reached their goals". After the Court's ruling we are rather tempted to speak about a "paradoxical failure". Despite the political agreement reached, the acceptance of the reform by all parties in all ACs except Catalonia, and the basic endorsement of the Court of most challenged articles of the statute, there is the general impression of a failure of all the original goals of the Catalan reform.

In this context, Spain seems to be a good case to study how implicit change works and what are its limits. As has been recently argued implicit constitutional change or mutation may occur through several unilateral or multilateral mechanisms such as political agreements, reinterpretation by the Courts or modernising reforms that formalise previous informal changes in actors' behaviour. All these mechanisms need to be ratified or recognised by all actors to become stable and legitimate, otherwise the Constitutional Court has to intervene if conflicting interpretations persist (see Benz, 2011; Behnke and Benz, 2009; Lhotta, 2010).

The whole outcome of the recent reform in Spain is a good illustration of these mechanisms at work. In the same country and at the same time, we can find successful and failed reforms depending on the unilateral or cooperative initiation of new interpretations of the system rules and institutions. It also illustrates the importance of the ratification phase of implicit constitutional change where, as it has been the case in other countries, agreements among political actors are voted down when the people (through referendums) or the courts (through judicial review of constitutionality) intervene.

In practical terms, the key, and at the same time most puzzling, political and academic question about the final outcome of the recent regional statutes reform process is whether the Constitutional Court with its 2010 ruling has hindered a hard and painfully negotiated solution for guaranteeing the accommodation of reasonable demands coming from several ACs under the current constitution, or whether it has prevented, by safeguarding the traditional interpretation of the constitutional pact, the potentially perverse consequences of the peculiar institutional openness of the Spanish territorial arrangements and its vulnerability to centrifugal and dysfunctional tendencies in terms of cohesion and equity.

This chapter seeks to indirectly address this question. It derives some lessons from the recent reform process about the peculiarities of the Spanish framework and for the future of the Spanish model of federalism. Moreover, it analyses the conditions of success of the peculiar Spanish setting, its reform capacity and what it can teach us about implicit constitutional change and the success of formal reform in countries, such as Spain, with several national identities and considerable sub-national constitutional space given by openness or ambiguity of the federal constitution.

We inquire briefly on these issues and ask whether, given the Spanish political circumstances, the structural constitutional conflicts and the built-in institutional incentives, a failure of this type of reform was to be expected or has been an accident due to the unexpected behaviour of some politicised judicial actors, as some critics have suggested. In sum, we ask who was right: those who said that undertaking the reform of the regional statutes was the only or the best way to accommodate sub-national demands and circumvent the rigidity of the Spanish constitution and the unpropitious party competition; or, on the contrary, those who contended that, without formal constitutional amendment and without inter-party consensus, the attempt to indirectly reform the constitution was inconvenient and too risky. According to this opinion, it turned out to be a waste of political energy, leaving frustration and disaffection (in the form of increasing secessionism) amidst some of the actors who proposed the reform, and raising the sense of a need to start all over again for those who wanted to accommodate their demands.

To discuss these questions and without seeking to go into a detailed description of any of the reform processes, that others and ourselves have described and analyzed elsewhere (Colino, 2008, 2009a, 2009b; Olmeda, 2009; Nagel, 2008; Keating and Wilson, 2009; Orte and Wilson, 2009; Muro, 2009; Tudela and Kölling, 2009), the chapter attempts to establish the potential benefits and potential risks of the Spanish model of implicit multilevel bilateral reform when dealing with a mixture of issues of authority, redistribution and symbols. To that end, we look briefly at the reforms in two autonomous communities and at the conditions under which this type of implicit change or extensive use of sub-national constitutional space are likely to be successful.

After carefully assessing the experience of the Spanish reform processes, we argue that implicit multilevel reform may only work under "favourable winds" conditions. In other words, the unique flexibility of the Spanish system may only work under some very narrow conditions, but may be impossible or dysfunctional in terms of stability and legitimacy under other, more likely conditions. To substantiate this argument within the space limits of this chapter, we proceed to describe briefly the institutional, procedural and strategic characteristics of the previous and recent rounds of reform of the regional statutes of autonomy and the intervention of the Constitutional Court. Then we look at the institutional framework for reform, the incentives it creates for political actors at both levels and its potential benefits and pitfalls. We examine the conditions under which these benefits or pitfalls were likely to occur. The concluding section evaluates the outcomes of reform and looks at the prospects of obtaining these conditions at the foreseeable future and at possible alternative ways to reform the system, which may imply formal amendment of the Constitution or piecemeal agreements on some institutional rules.

2. The goals, process and paradoxical results of the recent round of reform: some examples from Catalonia and Andalusia

For many observers, the recent process of reforms of regional statutes, especially the Catalan one, sought to induce a constitutional mutation without following the logical sequence and the constitutional amendment procedure. To achieve the desired goals it would have been logical to first amend the constitution in order to redesign the federal system, and then to reform the statutes accordingly (Cruz, 2006). But the polarisation of Spanish politics during the first Rodríguez Zapatero's mandate (2004-2008) rendered the constitutional reform impossible, even in the minimalist fashion proposed by the Spanish prime minister in his investiture speech in 2004. This led sub-national actors to explore the possibilities of reform in the sub-national space. The political window of opportunity opened when a left-nationalist coalition was in power in Catalonia and the socialist party governed at the central level. The ideational and technical elements of the reform drew on the notions of both of a forever-open constitution and a constitutional role and status of the regional statutes. Accordingly, it was possible to limit the exercise of central government constitutional competences, and establish a new interpretation of the constitution by changing one statute (Viver, 2005).

That means that although regional statute reforms were technically not a formal constitutional amendment they would imply a reform with constitutional implications for the system. This time the process began with one unilateral regional initiative. This is an extremely important difference with previous rounds of reforms of Spanish federal system where the then two main state-wide parties made political agreements for closing the territorial map in 1981 (UCD-PSOE), and to homogenise the competences of ACs in 1992 (PP-PSOE) in the federal arena. In this recent round, although the two main state-wide parties would agree on all the other regional statutes, the main opposition party was going to be excluded from the agreement both at the Catalan arena, and in the central political scenario regarding the Catalan statute reform. This would cause the intervention by the Constitutional Court at the ratification stage, and consequently the failure of several of the reform goals.

2.1 The Catalan and Andalusian reforms

The main goals of the Catalan initiative were the symbolic recognition of Catalan distinctiveness before the rest of ACs, the reinforcement of competences against encroachment or erosion by the Spanish government and by the transposition of EU directives, and the adaptation and increase of financial resources to growing needs. The new statute was more than a reformed version of the old one. The six main innovations were: the recognition of Catalonia as a nation; the expansion of the politico-legal meaning of Autonomy Statute to acquire the appearance of a proper constitution; the entrenchment of traditional nationalist language policy to strengthen its legal status; the reinforcement of regional competences limiting the central government's ones; the participation in different central constitutional bodies like the Judiciary, the Constitutional Court, and some other independent organisations; the regulation of bodies and procedures for a bilateral relation with the central government (see Blanco Valdés, 2010; Carreras, 2010; Quadra-Salcedo, 2010; Tornos, 2010). By contrast, the reform goals in Andalusia rather aimed at increasing the coordination with and participation within the central government; decentralising competences, especially in the fiscal sector; increasing citizen's entitlements and including social benefits as rights; modernising the institutional design of the AC; increasing responsibilities in justice administration, and at symbolic recognition as a nation in similar terms to that obtained by Catalonia.

Regarding the agenda setting and negotiation phases, both the Catalan and the Andalusian reform, as in other ACs started with deliberation in special parliamentary committees. Here experts and representatives of the civil society were called in for hearings. Furthermore a variety of expert commissions, advisory councils, or legal academic centres intervened with proposals for change. But most of the reform processes were dominated by party political considerations and bargaining. Politicians in regional executive bodies and parliaments may have sometimes used the proposals of experts just as a starting point for political bargaining for their elector's or party's interests, trying to outbid each other for the votes of nationalists or regionalists on the issues of self-government, without much concern for the technical or legal soundness of their proposals (Colino, 2008).

The second phase of the reform of regional statutes usually entailed political negotiations at the national arena. In many cases these negotiations occupied a central place in political and public discussion and attracted the media coverage during months. Apart from the formal meetings of the Constitutional Committee of the Parliament, they implied intra-party and inter-party relations. They involved lengthy negotiating sessions between regional and national party politicians of the same and of different parties lasting several weeks. In the case of the Catalan statute, the proposals were negotiated within the socialist party and between the Prime Minister Zapatero and several Catalan party leaders. They finally reached a decisive agreement with Mas, the leader of the main opposition party in Catalonia, which bypassed the very interests of the Catalan socialist party itself. This agreement was then fed into the formal procedure in the parliamentary constitutional committee (see Colino, 2009b).

In the Andalusian case, there were also sequential negotiations. The regional branch of PSOE in Andalusia (PSOE-A) deliberately sought to distance its proposed reform from the increasingly controversial statute reform projects emerging in the Basque Country and Catalonia, although this attempt to "de-contaminate" the reform proved largely unsuccessful. In fact very high "contagion" from the concomitant statute reform in Catalonia and Valencia occurred, which affected the behaviour of all parties but particularly PP and PA (Andalucist Party) (see Olmeda, 2009). At the national arena, the PSOE needed a pretty radical position from PSOE-Andalusia in order to legitimate the important concessions to Catalan nationalism. Thus it could be said that the pledges made in Catalonia were not so exceptional because a "safe" region, that is, without secessionist political forces like Andalusia, was advancing similar demands as Catalonia. At the same time PSOE-A was interested in pursuing the reform not to lose ground with respect to the increased autonomy reached by other regions with reformed Statutes. It must be remembered that Manuel Chaves, the then Andalusian minister president, was at that time the federal president of the PSOE. Hence he was a real key for the solution of the regional statutes reform puzzle.

The main opposition party (PP) had rejected the reform in Catalonia both in the regional and the national arenas but had accepted Valencia's Statute reform on both levels by agreement with PSOE. The regional PP government sought to fulfil the Valencian demand for increased self-government, but also conformed to the symmetrical model of state organisation supported by the PP national leadership, which sought to contrast the Valencian reform to the asymmetrical proposals emerging from the Catalan parties. In Andalusia, the negotiating solution reached by PP and PSOE consisted in the aggregation of issues instead of an exchange of positions among the different articles using formulas like "according to the Constitution" or "in accordance with the Spanish legal order" in every article. Although posing some kind of problem for PP, this method substantially maintained the text negotiated between PSOE-A and IU-LV-CA and approved by the Andalusian Parliament.

As has been pointed out, the Catalan case was the first regional statute reform since the adoption of the Constitution of 1978 that was undertaken without the agreement of the two state-wide parties. This fact hindered the processing of the reform and paved the way for an appeal to the Constitutional Court by the main opposition party. This possibility was a clear political risk. It could not be discarded in advance that the Court had already established an extensive doctrine on the functioning of Spanish federal state that the new statute was trying to ignore. In case of political disagreements and recourse to the Constitutional Court by the opposition parties, the hard-worked political agreements reached were not to be necessarily validated by the Court, since it had to act on the basis of legal arguments without addressing political or media pressures (Tornos, 2010).

At the end of the process, as is well-known, disagreements on the new Catalan statute led different political actors and other ACs to resort to the Constitutional Court. After its enactment, seven appeals of unconstitutionality were lodged with the Court against the Catalan Statute, by deputies of the main opposition party, the PP, by some central institutions such as the Spanish Ombudsman, and by other ACs. The PP and the ombudsman challenged provisions in the statute regulating issues of citizens' rights and duties, the concept of nation, language policy, jurisdictions, justice, the regional ombudsman, bilateral relations with the central government, and historical rights.

2.2 The role of the Constitutional Court in sanctioning or rejecting implicit change: the 2010 judgment on the Catalan Statute

After almost four years, the Court issued the Judgment no. 31/2010. The ruling was predictable and followed mostly the lines of the Court's previous case-law and doctrine. It declared that, from the 114 articles that the People's Party had challenged, only 14 articles were entirely or partly unconstitutional. The Court proposed a restrictive interpretation of other 27 articles, which were declared as not unconstitutional, insofar as they were interpreted in accordance with what was stated in the judgment. That means that it considered 73 of the 114 challenged articles as constitutional. The court also accepted the provisions in the preamble that described Catalonia as a "nation", but denied the preamble interpretive force and reminded that Spain remained the only nation in a legal-constitutional sense.

Regarding the concrete contents of the judgment (see Colino, 2011), the Court ruled on the role of the regional statutes of autonomy as quasi-constitutional legal instruments with a complementary role to that of the Spanish constitution. It rejected, contrary to the advocates of the reform of the Catalan

Statute and somewhat to its very recent Judgment no. 247/2007, the conception of the regional statutes of autonomy as quasi-constitutional instruments. According to this opinion, the statute is rooted in a political pact and approved through a special procedure, somewhat integrated with the constitution, and therefore able to indirectly define and regulate the distribution of powers and finance. This constitutional view of the statutes of autonomy is considered by the Court in its judgment as having "no other scope than a purely doctrinal or academic one". According to the decision, although many provisions of the Statute may have a constitutional flavour, this does not imply a higher legal force vis-à-vis other national organic laws.

This notion allowed the Court to reassert its role as the only instance, alongside the constitution itself, able to define the *Kompetenz-Kompetenz* and provide authoritative interpretations of the constitution and its provisions concerning fundamental rights or the allocation of legislative powers. In this fashion, the Court "weakens" or deactivates many of the more ambitious provisions of the regional statutes without having to declare their unconstitutionality. Thus, many of the innovative provisions of the Catalan Statute concerning for example the shielding of those areas in which Catalonia has exclusive jurisdiction against central encroachment and those concerning the criteria for the funding arrangements, the participation in central bodies and the deconcentration of the judiciary in Catalonia are not declared unconstitutional but simply deemed the manifestation of political demands that cannot be regulated in the regional statute and need to be regulated in a state organic law by the Spanish Parliament.

Regarding the recognition of the distinctness of Catalonia and its national character and symbolic issues such as historical rights, the ruling accepts the declaration in the preamble of Catalonia as a nation and the use of the adjective national related to the "national symbols" of Catalonia in Art. 8. At the same time, it reminds that since the Spanish legal system is based on the principle of popular sovereignty, the only holder of sovereignty can be the Spanish people at large. This way it deprives these references in the preamble of any interpretive force for the future interpretation of any provision of the regional statute. Regarding historical rights, the Court accepts Art. 5 of the new statute but provided it is interpreted as to avoid any parallels between the Catalan "historical rights" and the constitutionally enshrined historical rights of the Basque and Navarra territories.

The Court also accepts the constitutionality of including a bill of rights in the Catalan Statute but distinguishes them from the fundamental rights contained in the Spanish Constitution. Regarding the language policy and rights, it largely upholds the existing model of Catalan as the language of normal use in the education system – insofar as this does not involve the exclusion of Castilian as teaching language. However, it strikes down the term "preferential" as unconstitutional as applied to the use of Catalan in public administration and media. The Court accepts that the Catalan Parliament, through ordinary legislation, may approve measures of positive discrimination to correct "historical situations of imbalance". Finally, the ruling rejects the general obligation to know the Catalan language, as parallel to the constitutional obligation to know the Spanish language.

Furthermore, the Court rejects the attempts in the new Statute to decentralise competences and to "shield" regional exclusive competences from central encroachment by means of a detailed definition and listing of matters and of definition and limitation of the scope of central framework legislation. It declares that a regional statute of autonomy cannot limit the scope or the substance of central government's competences. According to the ruling, "as the supreme interpreter of the Constitution, only the Constitutional Tribunal is entitled to provide an authoritative – and unquestionable – definition of the constitutional categories and precepts". At the same time, and for the same reason, the Court rejects the attempts to limit the framework powers of the central government so as to represent just the "minimum standards of regulation". In sum, the Court embraces and reinforces a view by which most regional competences have in practice a shared and not an exclusive character.

At the same time, the judgment accepts some innovations in the Catalan Statute suggesting that Autonomous Communities have also something to say in the exercise of central government's exclusive jurisdictions. Following this conception, the court interprets or strikes down a few articles that attributed regional powers, such as the power to call referendums, or some powers on immigration, taxes, and local government regulation. It accepts regional participation in central decisions, for example through the bilateral joint-commissions established in the Statute, the right of initiative to sign international treaties or the right to be informed, through the right to make proposals for the composition of different central state bodies or the participation in the exercise of several exclusive competences of the central government such as economic planning, road communication between several autonomous communities or the determination of the immigrants quota.

Finally, with regard to provisions of the Catalan Statute dealing with the funding arrangements, the Court's ruling also downgrades most of the provisions to mere normative proposals, but in practice most of them have already been incorporated in Spanish legislation in the last reform of the system of regional financing. The Court rejects that the regional Statute may condition the criteria to establish the fiscal contribution of the autonomous communities to the common purse, since that would encroach on the central state competence to "regulate the exercise of financial powers of the autonomous community and set the levels of its contribution to the equalisation system and to solidarity".

3. Unravelling the positive and the negative potential of the system for constitutional change

Looking at the process and the results of these multilevel reform processes at the agenda-setting, negotiation and ratification stages we can try now to abstract several institutional and behavioural determinants that may help to explain the outcomes of these reforms by examining the institutional arrangements and the incentives they create among political actors.

3.1 The institutional framework for reform in Spain and its alleged openness

Regional statutes are quasi-constitutional laws in several respects, but they have the status of organic law. Therefore the same approval requirements as organic laws at the Spanish Parliament apply. Legislatures of the ACs as well as the Spanish Parliament may initiate the regional statute reform and have to intervene jointly in the approval of the amendment of the regional statutes. Therefore amendments may not be unilateral, but have to respond both to regional interests and national interest in the process. The main rules are:

- There is no possibility of unilateral initiative or approval by the centre.
- The concertation between the interests of the AC and the general interests of the central government and other ACs is theoretically assured by the final prerogative of the central parliament.
- The regional statutes of autonomy are thus subject to the majority requirements of organic laws, not to those of constitutional amendment in the Spanish Parliament (the main opposition party may be left out) and to supermajorities in the regional parliaments (more difficult to leave the main opposition parties out).
- The interest of the proposing AC is safeguarded through the inclusion of a delegation of deputies from the proposing regional parliament, which will defend the regional amendment proposals in the discussions of the Committee for Constitutional Affairs of the Spanish Congress of Deputies. This implies bilateral negotiations between the regional and the central parliaments in the form of delegations and joint committee's deliberation.
- In some ACs the population has to approve the final version through binding referendum (for instance in Basque Country, in Catalonia and in Andalusia).
- Finally, there is always the possibility of judicial review even after the referendum has occurred, and several actors are entitled to call on the Constitutional Court.

3.2 The potential positive consequences of this institutional arrangements for reform

These reform rules and procedures may constitute a series of theoretical benefits or advantages for the occasional adaptation of the system that have been recurrently claimed:

- Reform of statutes is easier than explicit constitutional reform or amendment under unfavourable party polarisation in the central parliament.
- These rules encourage deliberation and negotiation and, if successful, may give a sense of updating and re-enacting of the constitutional pact legitimising the constitution.
- They are a way of favouring increased public participation; they support acceptance by citizens and allow for an adaptation of public policies and powers to social reality.
- Reform of statutes may allow responding to particular demands of specific regions, which cannot be attained through formal constitutional reform at the central level, and may thus serve as an escape valve.
- Since the central parliament can veto the regional proposals, it can theoretically safeguard, in the name of cohesion and equity, the interests of the rest of the regions.
- Reform of regional statutes at the initiative of regional parliaments may work as a surrogate of self-determination, weakening secessionist tensions and promoting the adaptation to different aspirations for self-government and recognition of demands.

3.3 The negative flipside of too much flexibility: the possibility of unilateral reinterpretation of the constitution

In practice, the specific reform rules and procedures may have some potentially negative consequences for the stability and legitimacy of the system that may be summarised in several points:

- The unilateral initiated and multilevel negotiated reform process may produce uncoordinated demands from the region in question induced by a competitive outbidding among regional parties on symbolic and redistributive issues. This may lead to increasing polarisation among political actors and deform the reform agenda. As a consequence technically sound and feasible proposals will be displaced by politically opportunistic ones.
- Decision rules may leave the main opposition parties out of the deal in the central parliament and give small opposition parties with nothing to

lose a disproportionate veto power in regional parliaments, and thus an excessive influence on the agenda and the regional demands for reform.

- Party politicisation of reform processes will lead to bargaining oriented towards short-term electoral gains instead of problem solving based on rational solutions to the identified problems for which the reform is initiated.
- Unilateral initiative, regional electoral competition, incentives for bargaining and excessive demands are bound to induce a unilateral reinterpretation of all those provisions of the constitution which are more ambiguous. Thus traditional or consensual interpretations are strained. Additionally, the scope of discretion permitted by the constitution and the role of the statutes of autonomy to effect quasi-constitutional reforms may be reinterpreted.
- Under certain political or electoral conditions, the central parliament may not be able to conciliate or coordinate the contradictory demands of different regions. It will then seek to muddle through or come up with ambiguous agreements that undermine the traditional consensus on the constitution and induce actors to resort to the Constitutional Court. Comparative grievances or emulation and conflict between autonomous communities will weaken the central government as final arbiter of uncoordinated behaviour and demands by all Autonomous Communities following those most profiting from a reform.
- Main opposition parties excluded from the deal at the centre will have incentives to resort to the Constitutional Court in those cases where they do not accept other unilateral reinterpretations of the constitution and in those places where they have nothing to lose in elections at the regional level.
- In consequence, this can result in damages to the constitution and in the transfer to the Constitutional Court of the obligation to adjudicate between competing interpretations of the constitution on political, and not really legal issues.

3.4 What are then the conditions of success and failure of implicit constitutional change?

According to what the experience tells us about the potential positive or negative consequences of the Spanish institutional arrangements for reform of the territorial organisation, these effects could be said to depend on a set of circumstances that we can try to sum up in the configuration of five factors. These conditions may account for the failure in the case of the Catalan Statute of Autonomy and for success in achieving the goals pursued in the other regional statutes. The five factors are the following:

- The goals and philosophy of reform vary considerably: They include symbolic recognition, redistributive demands, devolution of powers, protection against central encroachment, unilateral constitutional reinterpretation, or a mixture of several of them. However, reforms seem to have worked just for decentralisation of competences and the formalisation of existing cooperation mechanisms, but not for issues of recognition or asymmetry and redistribution. By definition unilateral instruments coming from a region do not serve to coordinate and align competing multilateral redistributive demands. On the contrary, this reignites a re-symmetrising spiral in which the less assertive regions try to catch up with those with more powers.
- The strength of the ruling party in central government and the existence and extent of adversarial politics between government and opposition also seem to be two important conditions. If the central government is strong and does not need any parliamentary support from nationalist parties at the national or regional levels, it can manage easily the reform process. On the contrary, if the central government is a governing minority and is dependent on nationalist non-state-wide parties for its survival in parliament, it tends to choose risky strategies. They will put a strain on the constitution and force ambiguous agreements which will be contested by the opposition unless the next condition applies, giving the main opposition party a veto player status.
- The degree of agreement between the two main state-wide parties on the diagnosis of problems and goals to be achieved with the territorial reform seems to be a necessary condition for the success of any effective reform of the territorial organisation and allocation of power. As was revealed during the last round of reforms, constitutional change fails if the governing party at the centre has not counted on the opposition party. The opposition may be unable to block the organic law amending the regional statute, but it can always resort to the appeal to the Constitutional Court as a tool to block or modify the goals and philosophy of a reform. Besides, government and opposition parties do not have to be congruent at the two levels leaving the opposition with more leeway to defend different things in different regions according to its respective electoral interests.
- The political constellations in the regions are a significant condition for success. Strong party competition between non state-wide parties and state-wide parties in the region and the role of junior coalition parties and main opposition parties may induce the regional governing parties to take on most of the regional opposition parties' autonomist or nationalist demands.
- The degree of self-restraint of the Constitutional Court has also significant impact. This restraint will be determined by the degree to which traditional interpretations of the distribution of powers or the symbols of state power go against its traditional doctrine. This self-restraint will tend to be greater if there is a general agreement between the two state-wide parties on the goals and philosophy of reform.

Looking at this set of conditions, we could safely say that the necessary and sufficient condition for success would be the political agreement between the two state-wide parties on the goals and philosophy of reform. The political agreement would minimise the probability of an appeal to the Constitutional Court questioning the aims of the reform and getting its negative ruling. It would maximise the responsiveness of the Court towards new consensual interpretations of the constitutional framework of the system. Without this agreement the political risks of implicit reform seem too difficult to overcome.

4. Conclusion: the problem with implicit change and the limits of flexibility in Spain

Apparently, the Spanish version of federalism is pretty adaptable but its adaptability may have some limits. The recent processes have clearly demonstrated these limits. For some, this is good news, for others, bad ones. If we try to evaluate the results of the reform by considering its original goals, we could argue that the new Catalan Statute has been relatively successful in achieving those goals that did not imply a reinterpretation of the constitutional consensus and doctrine or that reflected an already consolidated institutional practice. These goals include: a) the statutory entrenchment of the language policy model; b) the institutionalisation of relations with the central government by strengthening bilateral relations and by the legal entrenchment of the regional government participation in central and EU institutions, bodies and decision making; c) the decentralisation of some competences in key areas such as immigration, labour inspection and public transportation; d) the establishment of funding arrangements to ensure sufficient resources, as well as a clearer delimitation of the Catalan contribution to the Spanish territorial solidarity scheme. Arguably, the statute reform has been less successful in other original goals that attempted a new, and unilateral, interpretation of the constitutional consensus such as the further national recognition of Catalonia and of the multinational character of the Spanish state, safeguarding exclusive regional competences from central encroachment, and decentralisation or deconcentration of the judiciary in Catalonia. Logically, those statutes of autonomy that followed the Catalan path have also succeeded or failed as to the same goals. Other statutes, which had only pursued some of those goals, have been successful in all of them.

In sum, the reform of the eight statutes of autonomy have brought about increased devolution of competences, some institutional updating or modernising, and some more recognition of identity features as legitimation of regional governments. As regards the traditional nationalists' demands, most of them have not been fulfilled because of their incompatibility with the current constitution. What this six-year exercise of partially failed reform seems to indicate is that the Spanish peculiar version of federalism is not as flexible as has been argued many times, and that under certain conditions the regional statute it is not the best instrument to achieve reform of the territorial organisation, at least for some particular institutional objectives with global constitutional implications affecting all Autonomous Communities.

It is also clear now that there are limits in the Spanish constitutional system to the possibility of imposing a unilateral vision of the constitutional goals in terms of accommodation, recognition and power demands. The partial failure shows clearly that some reforms can only be accomplished through implicit or informal, consensual agreement or through a consensual constitutional amendment. If we try to explain this outcome, we should point out that many of the propitious conditions we have identified for the system to work in a positive way seem to have been absent at this round of reform in the Catalan case. As a consequence even party politicians that had reached an agreement ignored the warnings of many constitutional lawyers and the prospects for intervention of the Constitutional Court at their own peril.

On the positive side, at least for some observers, it seems that no reinterpretation of the constitution on certain issues is easily attainable "through the back door", even if political parties agree on it. The Constitutional Court can be called upon to safeguard the constitution and/or its more consensual interpretations despite the attempts of politicians to advance new reinterpretations which may accommodate certain demands, but may also have perverse effects on the whole system.

On the negative side, other observers deny that an accommodation of certain minority nationalists' demands is possible in the current constitutional frame, no matter how flexible or open it is said to be, unless a previous agreement between the two main political forces in the country is reached. With the benefit of hindsight, it seems now clear that a statute reform that embodied a regional nationalist conception, as the Catalan Statute did, and that unilaterally advanced a new interpretation of the constitution at the same time, ignoring the fact that the constitution has a different conception of the State and the political community, had to have a very difficult time being accepted by the main opposition party at the central parliament and by the Constitutional Court unless a previous pact on recognition is reached or the constitution itself is changed.

Are there alternative paths to implicit constitutional change? The only solution seems to be a constitutional reform agreed by both the main statewide parties and the main regional nationalist parties. In other words, the appropriate way seems to be a renewal of the constitutional pact during the transition period. The problem is how to reach such a consensus in the nowadays extremely polarised political climate.

Some, maybe naïve, proposals could be brought up here briefly: why not a Spanish constitutional convention? The problem with this initiative would be again polarisation. Moreover, this kind of constitutional tool has no fundament in the Spanish political tradition. Besides that, it seems that there is no clear expert consensus about how to solve the usual re-symmetrising spiral produced by the attempt to give satisfaction to assertive demands for asymmetry, recognition and special fiscal treatment by nationalist parties. If this convention method were to prove impracticable, there may still be a repertoire of minor solutions, like raising the majority requirements for unilateral initiatives at the regional parliament, and raising the requirements for approval of regional statutes at the central parliament. Perhaps this could resolve many of the detected potential pitfalls of the present openness of the system. Secondly, another solution could be higher majority requirements within the Court for ruling on these issues, which currently decides by simple majority rule. By requiring more accord, the risk of party politicisation and public delegitimisation of the Court could be reduced. Thirdly and also reasonable seems the reintroduction of the possibility of the Constitutional Court reviewing the constitutionality of amended statutes before the regional ratification referendum takes place. Finally, it seems necessary to devise ways to modernise our constitution through reforms implying, among other instruments, the incorporation of ACs in the constitutional reform procedure (maybe through the previously reformed Senate) with a clear role for them.

But it could well be that all these possibilities are just ways to muddle through because we are dealing here with sometimes intractable political problems without any clear legal solution. Probably a combination of implicit informal change and some small formal reforms is the only way ahead.

References

Albertí, Enoch (2010): El Estado de las Autonomías después de la Sentencia del Tribunal Constitucional sobre el Estatuto de Cataluña. In: El Cronista del Estado Social y Democrático de Derecho 15, 90-98.

Barceló, Mercè/Xavier Bernadí, Joan Vintró (2010): Balanç i perspectives. In: Revista Catalana de Dret Públic, http://www10.gencat.cat/eapc_revistadret.

Behnke, Nathalie/Benz, Arthur (2009): The Politics of Constitutional Change between Reform and Evolution. In: Publius 39, (2), 213-240.

Benz, Arthur (2011): Das Zusammenspiel der Ebenen beim expliziten und impliziten Verfassungswandel. In: Hönnige, C./Kneip, S./Lorenz, A. (eds.): Verfassungswandel im Mehrebenensystem. Wiesbaden: VS Verlag für Sozialwissenschaften, 21-40.

Blanco Valdés, Roberto (2010): El Estatuto de Cataluña y la sentencia de nunca acabar. In: Claves de Razón Práctica 205, 4-18.

Carreras, Francesc de (2010): ¿Es constitucional el Estatuto de Cataluña? In: Claves de Razón Práctica 206, 10-19.

Castellà, Josep M. (2008): Lo Statuto di autonomia del 2006 come (discutibile) strumento per la realizzazione dell'autogoverno della Catalogna. In: Gambino, S. (ed.): Regionalismi e Statuti. Le riforme in Spagna e in Italia. Milano: Giuffrè, 219-244.

Castellà, Josep M. (2010): La sentencia del Tribunal Constitucional 31/2010, sobre el estatuto de autonomía de Cataluña y su significad opara el futuro del Estrado autonómico. Fundación Ciudadanía y Valores.

Colino, César (2008): Den spanischen Autonomiestaat vertiefen oder transformieren? Die neue Reformrunde und die Herausforderungen für den Autonomiestaat. In: Europäisches Zentrum für Föderalismus-Forschung (ed.): Jahrbuch des Föderalismus 2007. Föderalismus, Subsidiarität und Regionen in Europa. Baden-Baden: Nomos Verlagsgesellschaft, 385-403.

Colino, César (2009a): Constitutional Change without Constitutional Reform: Spanish Federalism and the Revision of Catalonia's Statute of Autonomy. In: Publius 39, (2), 262-88.

Colino, César (2009b): Country Profile: Spain – Catalonia. Technische Universität Darmstadt. Unpublished report for project "Patterns of Constitutional Reform in Federal Structures", funded by the German Research Foundation (DFG).

Colino, César (2011): What now for the Autonomic State? Muddling through growing tensions amidst the aftermath of the Court's Ruling and the painful fiscal crisis. In: Europäisches Zentrum für Föderalismus-Forschung (ed.): Jahrbuch des Föderalismus 2011. Föderalismus, Subsidiarität und Regionen in Europa. Baden-Baden: Nomos Verlagsgesellschaft, 309-322.

Corcuera, Javier (2009): Las reformas del modelo territorial en Alemania y en España: dos lógicas diferentes. In: Tudela, J./Kölling, M. (eds.): La reforma del Estado Autonómico Español y del Estado Federal Alemán. Madrid: Fundación Manuel Giménez Abad-Centro de Estudios Políticos y Constitucionales, 43-72.

Cruz, Pedro (2006): La reforma del Estado de las Autonomías. In: Revista d'Estudis Autonòmics i Federals 2, 77-99.

Delledonne, Giacomo (2011): Speaking in Name of the Constituent Power: the Spanish Constitutional Court and the New Catalan Estatut. In: Perspectives on Federalism, 3, 1.

Ferret, Joaquim (2010): Una visió global de la sentencia. In: Revista Catalana de Dret Públic, http://www10.gencat.cat/eapc_revistadret.

Garrido, Vicente (2009): La deconstrucción del estado autonómico. In: Teoría y Realidad Constitucional 24, 383-408.

Gavara, Juan C. (2011): Los efectos de la STC 31/2010 del estatuto de autonomía de Cataluña: las implicaciones para su normativa de desarrollo y los estatutos de otras comunidades autónomas. In: Teoría y Realidad Constitucional 27, 239-290.

Keating, Michael/Wilson, Alex (2009): Renegotiating the State of Autonomies: Statute Reform and Multi-level Politics in Spain. In: West European Politics 32, (3), 534-556.

Lhotta, Roland (2010): „Picking up the slack": Bundestaatsreform durch judizielle Modifikation von Leitideen? In: Blumenthal, J. v./Bröchler, S. (eds.): Föderalismusreform in Deutschland. Bilanz und Perspektiven im internationalen Vergleich. Wiesbaden: VS Verlag für Sozialwissenschaften, 59-94.

López Aguilar, Juan F. (2011): La sentencia más larga repercusiones de la STC 21/2010: política y jurisprudencia. In: Teoría y Realidad Constitucional 27, 221-238.

Muñoz Machado, Santiago (2010): El dogma de la Constitución in acabada. In: Revista Española de Derecho Constitucional 90, sept-dec, 245-266.

Muñoz Machado, Santiago (2010b): Dentro de los términos de la presente Constitución. In: El cronista del Estado social y democrático de derecho 15, 4-11.

Muro, Diego (2009): Territorial Accommodation, Party Politics, and Statute Reform in Spain. In: South European Society & Politics 14, (4), 453-468.

Nagel, Klaus-Jürgen (2008): Die neuen Autonomiestatute in Spanien: mehr Paralyse als Praxis. In: Europäisches Zentrum für Föderalismus-Forschung (ed.): Jahrbuch des Föderalismus 2008. Föderalismus, Subsidiarität und Regionen in Europa. Baden-Baden: Nomos Verlagsgesellschaft, 422-443.

Olmeda, José Antonio (2009): Country Profile: Spain – Andalusia. Technische Universität Darmstadt. Unpublished report for project "Patterns of Constitutional Reform in Federal Structures", funded by the German Research Foundation (DFG).

Orte, Andreu/Wilson; Alex (2009): Multi-level Coalitions and Statute Reform in Spain. In: Regional & Federal Studies 19, (3), 415-436.

Quadra-Salcedo, Tomás de la (2010): Paisajedespués de la batalla. La sentencia del TC sobre el Estatuto de Cataluña. In: Claves de Razón Práctica 206, 20-31.

Sánchez Ferriz, Remedio (2009): Los nuevos estatutos de autonomía en busca de una forma de estado. Entre el Estado Federal y la enésima repetición de la máxima de Lampedusa. In: Teoría y Realidad Constitucional 24, 359-381.

Solozábal, Juan José (2011): La sentencia sobre el estatuto de Cataluña: una visión de conjunto. In: Revista de Estudios Políticos 151, enero-marzo, 203-229.

Tajadura, Javier (2011): El pronunciamiento del Tribunal Constitucional sobre el preámbulo del estatuto de autonomía de Cataluña: nación, realidad nacional y derechos históricos. In: Teoría y Realidad Constitucional 27, 423-448.

Tornos, Joaquín (2010): El Estatuto de Autonomía de Cataluña, y el Estado Autonómico, tras la Sentencia del Tribunal Constitucional 31/2010. In: El cronista del Estado social y democrático de derecho 15, 18-25.

Tornos, Joaquín (2011): Valoración general. In: Tornos, J. (ed.): Informe Comunidades Autónomas 2010. Barcelona: Instituto de Derecho Público, 17-35.

Tudela, José (2009): El Estado autonómico treinta años después: ensayo de una valoración. In: Teoría y Realidad Constitucional 24, 191-242.

Tudela, José (2010): Heterogeneidad y asimetría en un estado indefinido. Una aceptación de la diversidad que es una puerta de futuro. In: Tudela, J./Knüpling, F. (eds.): España y modelos de federalismo. CEPC/Gimenez Abad, 111-149.

Tudela, José/Kölling, Mario (eds.) (2009): La reforma del Estado Autonómico Español y del Estado Federal Alemán. Madrid: Fundación Manuel Giménez Abad-Centro de Estudios Políticos y Constitucionales.

Viver Pi-Sunyer, Carles (2005): En defensa dels Estatuts d'Autonomia com a norms jurídiques delimitadores de competencies. Contribució a una polèmica jurídico-constitucional. In: Revista d'Estudis Autonómics i Federals 1, 97-130.

Viver Pi-Sunyer, Carles (2009): ¿Grandes reformas o pequeños pasos? Una perspectiva desde Cataluña. In: Tudela, J./Kölling, M. (eds.): La reforma del Estado Autonómico Español y del Estado Federal Alemán. Madrid: Fundación Manuel Giménez Abad-Centro de Estudios Políticos y Constitucionales, 31-41.

4. Devolution and Regionalisation in Federalising States

Britain's Constitutional Moment

James Mitchell

1. Introduction: in search of the constitution

In 1999, Peter Riddell of the London *Times* wrote, "The British dislike thinking constitutionally. It is somehow alien to our much-valued pragmatism" (Riddell, 1999). Professor Sir David Edward, former Judge of the Court of Justice of the European Communities, went further in a lecture in 2005. He argued, "We have become constitutionally illiterate, to the extent that we do not understand our own constitution" (Edward, 2005: 9). The reasons for this constitutional illiteracy are not difficult to understand. There is no agreement on what constitutes the constitution. The absence of a formal written document entrenching institutional relationships gives rise to suggestions that the UK has no constitution or that the UK has a "political constitution" (Griffith, 1979), in the sense that the "constitution of the United Kingdom lives on, changing from day to day for the constitution is no more and no less than what happens. Everything that happens is constitutional. And if nothing happens that would be constitutional also" (Ibid.: 19). However, though there may be no capital "c" constitution there is a small "c" constitution (see Johnson, 2004: 18; King, 2001: 3–6). Neil MacCormick suggested one response to the search for the UK constitution, "If a state has at some time been set up, "constituted" by some deliberate act or acts, can these constituent acts be other than constitutions?" (MacCormick, 1978: 1).

MacCormick later described the UK as an "evolved state", one that is "bound to differ from a deliberately constituted one based on a historic constitution" (MacCormick, 1999: 49). An as evolved state, the UK has an historic constitution, as contested and liable to revision as any history. Nevil Johnson argued that the UK has a "customary constitution" which "lays great store by a capacity to leave principles inexplicit, relying instead on what people feel from past experience to be appropriate in the circumstances." (Johnson, 2004: 19). Johnson emphasised the role of the elites in ensuring its legitimacy with a wider public and negotiating political accommodations (Ibid.). One reviewer of Johnson's work remarked that the "customary constitution that Johnson celebrates proves elusive" (Russell, 2005: 457). This elusiveness was what made it attractive to the political elite. But even more elusive than the "inexplicit principles" are any agreed or settled means by which such principles are altered or interpreted contributing to the contested nature of the UK constitution.

Understanding the UK's constitution requires an appreciation of the territorial aspect of the evolved state and it is this that is the subject of this chapter. The UK was the creation of a series of unions over a long period of time, each leaving its distinct legacy. The most important were the unions which created England, creating a centralised and relatively unified polity, the basis of a unitary state. Subsequent unions with Wales, Scotland and Ireland were less complete though each differed and each left its distinct legacy. The nature of this diversity changed over time, as the role and reach of the state changed, but there was a constancy in the state's acceptance of some measure of distinctiveness that ensured that it remained a state of unions in which its components were governed differently in some respects, though a highly centralised state. In the twentieth century, special central government departments and administrative arrangements developed for Scotland and Wales while Northern Ireland was given a measure of home rule (see Mitchell, 2009 for elaboration). Even prior to devolution, the UK was asymmetrical but the form devolution has taken has embedded these asymmetries.

2. The UK's "constitutional moment" and the party system

The UK experienced significant constitutional change after 1997 following the election of a Labour Government. As Robert Hazell remarked, "We are going through a period of unprecedented constitutional change" (Hazell, 1999: 230). New Labour's programme of constitutional reform was, according to Blackburn and Plant, "wider than that of any political party taking office this century" (Blackburn and Plant, 1999: 1). Richard Wilson, Secretary to the Cabinet (1998-2002), maintained, "History may judge that one of the most important and lasting legacies of Mr. Blair's government has been its impact on the British constitution and the institutions of the state" (Wilson, 2005: 281). He outlined the "roll call" of constitutional innovation:

> "devolution to Scotland, Wales and possibly Northern Ireland, human rights legislation, freedom of information legislation, Parliamentary reform, especially of the House of Lords, abolition – or modification – of the role of Lord Chancellor, the setting up of a Supreme Court, possible referendums on the EU constitution and on the euro, hopefully a Civil Service Bill... a mayor for London but no regional assemblies for England so far" (Ibid.).

In an article in 2004, Vernon Bogdanor listed 15 constitutional Acts.[1] Examination of these lists shows that there has been no consistency in how the con-

1 The constitutional independence of the Bank of England; Referendums for Scottish and Welsh devolution (under the Referendum (Scotland and Wales) Act, 1997; Scottish Parlia-

stitution is reformed: some changes followed referendums; others by simple Parliamentary majority, still others without consultation with the Cabinet but through what became known as "sofa government", the informal clique-ish decision-making associated with Tony Blair; some measures were enacted by primary, others by secondary legislation. All, however, required legitimation secured by Parliamentary approval either directly following debates and votes or in attenuated form as the actions of the governing party. Reforming the UK constitution is still ultimately a matter for Parliament at Westminster. Dicey's comments in his *Introduction to the Study of the Law of the Constitution* still hold, "There is under the English constitution no marked or clear distinction between laws which are not fundamental or constitutional and laws which are fundamental or constitutional" (Dicey, 1959: 39). As Dicey himself lamented, parties had come to dominate Parliament, thus making it "really a body of persons elected for the purpose of carrying out the policy of the predominant party" (Dicey, 1890: 504). This was his justification for supporting the referendum. The role of the public and civil society in constitutional change is, therefore, mediated through Parliament.

Party politics plays a significant part in constitutional politics and the absence of entrenchment or special requirements limits the need for cross-party consensus. A simple Parliamentary majority suffices. This also makes some reforms difficult to achieve. This has been evident in the case of electoral reform. While there is some evidence that the British public has long supported electoral reform, opposition from Britain's two main parties, which have alternated in power, has prevented any measure being seriously considered (until now with a coalition that includes the Liberal Democrats). But as well as facilitating constitutional reform, the party system contributes to the legitimisation (or de-legitimisation) of the system. Unlike other areas of public pol-

---

ment (under Scotland Act, 1998); Welsh Assembly (under Government of Wales Act, 1998); Referendum on Belfast Agreement (under Northern Ireland Act, 1998); Northern Ireland Assembly (under Northern Ireland Act, 1998); Referendum on directly elected mayor and strategic authority for London (under the Greater London Authority (Referendum) Act, 1998); Introduction of "proportional representation" for elections to Scottish Parliament; Welsh Assembly; Northern Ireland Assembly and London strategic authority (under various aforementioned Acts); "proportional representation" for elections to the European Parliament (under the European Parliamentary Elections Act, 1999); Requirement that local authorities abandon committee system and adopt a cabinet system, city manager or directly elected mayor – last requiring approval in a referendum with provision for 5% of registered electors to require a referendum on elected mayor (under the Local Government Act, 2000); European Convention on Human Rights enacted (under the Human Rights Act 1998); Removal of all but 92 hereditary peers from the House of Lords (under the House of Lords Act, 1999); Freedom of information (under the Freedom of Information Act, 2000); Registration of political parties, the control of political donations and national campaign expenditure and establishment of the Electoral Commission (under the Political Parties, Elections and Referendums Act, 2000); Abolition of office of Lord Chancellor, removal of Law Lords from House of Lords, and establishment of a new Supreme Court (Bogdanor, 2004: 242-243).

icy, constitutional politics involve "rules of the game", matters which require the consent of winners and losers alike to provide legitimacy. Constitutional politics, as "rules of the game" are thus qualitatively different from other public policies. Both election winners and losers need to consent to rule changes to maintain legitimacy (Anderson et al., 2005). Indeed, the losers are central to this. This raises problems in a system in which constitutional politics are determined in the same way as other public policies, through simple Parliamentary majority.

The concept of "losers' consent" is useful in understanding these issues. There are likely to be winners and losers in any constitutional order and similarly with any changes to a constitutional order. While it might be possible to adopt some institutional form of Rawls' "veil of ignorance" (Rawls, 1972) after some radical disruption or the founding of a new state, this is more difficult in an "evolved state". Anderson et al. discuss the implications of what they refer to as the "winner-loser gap" – "the difference in opinions and attitudes between winners and losers" in discussing electoral systems (Anderson et al., 2005: 10). Any such gap cannot be dismissed if the legitimacy of the liberal democratic state is to be maintained. Short-term or intermittent periods as "losers" may be acceptable to "losers" within a system perceived to be operating fairly. A loss of specific consent need not undermine diffuse consent (Easton, 1975). However, a tipping point may come when losers perceive systemic biases and unfairness to be the cause of their inability to win leading them to withdraw consent, undermining the legitimacy of the established constitutional order. If losers are geographically concentrated and constitute a majority within an existing distinct polity, this may give rise to a shift in allegiance from the existing territorial constitution to a new or nascent territorial constitutional order. Geographical concentrations of losers may not be enough alone. Geographic concentrations of losers require a credible alternative political authority. If losers are concentrated geographically but without a sense of community or in an area that has little or no recognised boundaries, then the losers may fail to have an alternative community to which to shift allegiance.

The idea of losers' consent is useful when considering devolution. Problems of legitimacy arose in each case as minorities felt marginalised by the system of government marginalised. Devolved government reflected the asymmetry in keeping with the UK as a state of unions. The state evolved though its essential nature remained the same. In the remainder of the chapter, the background to and nature of devolution will be explored before considering whether this response may have simply displaced an existing problem rather than solved it.

Public pressure and civil society activity needs to focus on Westminster and win a mandate for reform there. Advocates of reform are unable to change the constitution until such time as they command a majority or can force concessions. These were reforms initiated by a party that had been out of office for many years and thereby capable of viewing the constitution more as an outsider coming into office than as one awaiting its turn to govern. In essence, Labour's view of its role was less as part of the Establishment elite that presided over the customary constitution than might previously have been the case. Many of these reforms were resisted by other parties or at least the Conservatives, the main opposition party.

As Bogdanor comments, any single item on this list would constitute a radical change but taken together

> "they allow us to characterise the years since 1997 as a veritable era of constitutional reform comparable with the 1830s and period immediately before 1914 though the list includes no single item which is as dominant or significant as the Great Reform Act of 1832 or the Parliament Act of 1911" (Bogdanor, 2004: 243).

Robert Hazell described the five themes of the new "constitutional settlement":

> "A highly centralised system of government is being replaced by a form of quasi-federalism; this and other changes will lead to more checks and balances on the UK executive; parliamentary sovereignty is likely to be further eroded; there will be tighter rule of law, with a shift of power to the courts; and our majoritarian, two-party system will be replaced by more pluralist forms of democracy" (Hazell, 1999: 230).

Dawn Oliver noted the absence of a "master plan or coherent programme for reform of the UK constitution… No coherent 'vision' of democracy or citizenship or good governance or constitutionalism" but that the reforms were "pragmatic responses to political pressures and perceived problems, on an ad hoc, incremental basis" (Oliver, 2003: 3). Pat McFadden, one of Tony Blair's specialist advisers, noted:

> "Some constitutional reformers criticised Labour for implementing some changes but not others. But blueprints are not compatible with the competing interests and pressures of real politics. Moreover, Labour faced the difficult task of decentralising power, while trying to respond to public pressure to sort out big domestic and international issues, pressure which demands a strong centre. Many of the advances of which Labour is most proud – the NHS and welfare state – were driven by strong *central* governments. The same pressures for action from the centre are driving the reform of public services today" (McFadden, 2002: 11).

The absence of a coherent constitutional programme, far less a coherent constitutional doctrine, was perhaps an inevitable consequence of a general perception that change was necessary, combined with a reluctance to be seen to be too radical and certainly to avoid accusations of revolutionary change. New Labour politicians and disappointed supporters of coherent and comprehensive reform can join with Nevil Johnson, arch-sceptic of New Labour's reforms, in viewing New Labour's constitutional reforms as "well within what is widely believed to be the British tradition of pragmatic adaptation" (Johnson 2004: 284).

2.1 Northern Ireland

Northern Ireland had been the one part of the UK with experience of devolution. A directly elected Assembly, modelled on Westminster, had governed Northern Ireland from 1922 to 1972. The simple plurality electoral system resulted in majority community dominance which undermined its legitimacy in a system of government that discriminated against the minority. As Richard Rose remarked, the "chief political institutions" of Northern Ireland were "institutions of discord" (Rose, 1971: 113). Northern Ireland lacked a "loyal opposition", a "*sine qua non* for fully legitimate regimes" (Ibid.: 447). Members of the minority community campaigned against Stormont's policies and procedures. For most of Stormont's existence, Westminster kept its distance, refusing to intervene in internal Northern Ireland affairs. However, the civil rights movement in the 1960s and civil unrest forced the UK Government to intervene. This culminated in Stormont being prorogued in 1972 by Parliament at Westminster. Following prorogue, British Governments sought a system of government that satisfied majority opinion but also had minority consent. In a deeply divided society, this would prove a difficult, protracted and iterative process.

In late 1973, an "unprecedented meeting" (Rose, 1975: 30) took place at Sunningdale Civil Service College in England bringing together Ministers from the UK and Irish Governments and leaders of three political parties in Northern Ireland involved in a power-sharing executive. They agreed to establish an all-Ireland Council and consultative Assembly; that Northern Ireland's status could only be changed with the consent of its people; and agreed a range of law and order, judicial, extradition and policing policy. The *Sunningdale* Agreement's collapse followed opposition from the majority community in Northern Ireland who feared being losers either as a minority within Ireland as a whole or having decisions imposed on them as a minority within the UK.

The following quarter of a century saw a series of efforts, pursued with varying degrees of commitment, to revive devolution according to these power-sharing ideas. There were important milestones along the way. In March 1991, the UK Government launched three strands of talks: on relations within Northern Ireland; on relations between the people of the island of Ireland; and on relations between the Governments of the UK and Ireland. It was agreed that these should progress on the basis that "nothing is agreed until everything is agreed" (Cochrane, 1997: 276). This initiative itself failed but contributed to the process that led to the *Belfast* Agreement in 1998. The Belfast Agreement had three "strands": democratic institutions for Northern Ireland, a North-South Ministerial Council, and a British-Irish Council and Intergovernmental Conference. It also included sections on rights, safeguards and equality of opportunity, arms decommissioning, security, policing and justice, and prisoner release. Each element was important but the process required a fine balance taking all into account. Devolution was only one part of the agreement.

The process leading to the Agreement necessitated high-level, confidence-building politics. Much of this was inevitably done in secret. It was elite driven with the public in Northern Ireland playing an important role in challenging the legitimacy of the constitutional order and ultimately sanctioning change, including devolution, but otherwise largely excluded from the process. Seamus Mallon, leading Irish constitutional nationalist, described the Agreement as "Sunningdale for slow learners" (*Irish Times*, 2 April 1997), a reference to the 1973 discussions. The Belfast Agreement has been subject to considerable debate both amongst politicians and within the academic community.

Brendan O'Leary has described the key features of the Agreement as consociationalist (O'Leary 1999; McGarry and O'Leary 2006a and b). Consociationalism was defined by Arend Lijphart (1977) as having four key elements designed to create stable democracy in divided societies: cross-community executive power-sharing; proportionality rules applied throughout the relevant governmental and public sectors; community self-government (or autonomy) and equality in cultural life; veto rights for minorities. Central to consociationalism has been elite accommodation. Lijphart himself argued that the 1995 Framework Agreements, precursors of the Belfast Agreement, were consociationalist (Lijphart, 1996) with an "important external dimension" (Ibid.: 68), notably the links with the North-South strand and relations with the Irish Republic. At least as important were policies on policing, prisoner release and decommissioning of paramilitary arms. Others have described it as having a "consociational lineage, but with ostensibly confederal arrangements knitted into the pattern" (Wilford and Wilson, 2001: 87). Some scholars have argued that these structures have entrenched and polarised communal differences (Taylor, 2001; Dixon, 2005). Four aspects in particular have been identified as having "entrenched rather than palliated division": acceptance of the "either/or constitutional choice of the United Kingdom or a United Ireland"; Single Transferable Vote which encourages candidates on small core votes and discourages cross-communal preference formation; communal registration by Assembly Members; and election of the Executive using a proportional formula (Wilford and Wilson, 2003: 100). The Agreement works to "encourage and reward those who pursue strategic ethno-national group calculations and interests – and to have thereby reinforced and politicised ethno-national group divisions – in ways that run counter to promoting liberal politics" (Taylor, 2006: 218). This is done primarily through group designation in the Assembly, Executive formation and the electoral system (Ibid.).

The challenge in Northern Ireland was to create institutions of consensus to replace the "institutions of discord" (Rose, 1971: 113) of the past by winning the consent of Protestant "losers". This could not be achieved by devolution alone but required other institutions and policy changes. The majority Protestant unionist community in Northern Ireland feared their position as a minority within a united Ireland and a minority within the UK as a whole while the Catholic nationalist community feared their position as a minority within Northern Ireland. Losers' consent, therefore, required responses to each of these fears. The implications for the rest of the UK of devolution in Northern Ireland, the smallest polity within the state of unions and where a separate party system operated, were less significant than devolution elsewhere. Achieving peace was a victory which made any constitutional asymmetries seem trivial.

2.2 Scotland and Wales

The background to devolution in Scotland and Wales was similar though the form devolution took in each differed. Scotland and Wales had territorial departments of state (Scottish and Welsh Offices) to take account of distinctiveness, headed by Ministers appointed by the Prime Minister. This highlighted the limited support for the Conservatives in Scotland and Wales when the party was in power. The governing Conservative Party's support declined in both polities after 1979. Over the eighteen years of Conservative Governments, a perception grew that London was insensitive to Scottish and Welsh distinctiveness. The case for devolved government was articulated in terms of "democratic deficit".

Between 1987 until the Conservatives were defeated in 1997, the political head of the Welsh Office did not even represent a Welsh constituency in the Commons. When William Hague, a Yorkshire Tory MP, became Welsh Secretary in 1995, opposition MPs boycotted his first Welsh Questions session in the Commons. Devolutionists argued that the array of Welsh quangos, appointed by the Welsh Secretary, contributed to a democratic deficit (Morgan and Roberts, 1993). In 1991, the Secretary of State for Wales was responsible for 1,400 appointments to 80 quangos with a combined budget of £1.8 billion (Ibid.: 56). The appointment processes and crises in the Welsh Development Agency (WDA) made quangos particularly controversial in Wales as compared with Scotland. Weak regulation resulted in the WDA being accused of malpractices, including appointments that were perceived to have been made on the basis of party political considerations rather than merit (Ibid.: 57-63).

The Labour Party was central to developing support for Welsh devolution. Having been deeply divided on the issue in the 1970s, it edged towards support over the course of the Conservatives' period in office. Ron Davies, Labour MP for Caerphilly and the key figure in Welsh Labour's support for as Assembly, later wrote that the re-emergence of devolution onto Labour's agenda was "fuelled by the impact of successive election losses and facilitated by the pressure for local government reform" (Davies, 1999: 4). Support emerged almost surreptitiously: devolution was accepted by the party under the guise of local government reform. Morgan and Mungham describe this as the "smuggler's road to constitutional change: an elected Wales-wide body was, quite consciously, smuggled into being via the provisions for local government reform in Wales, a stark contrast to Scotland, where an elected parliament was openly demanded as an expression of national identity" (Morgan and Mungham, 2000: 86). It was presented as part of "regional" reform throughout the UK and not as an important policy in its own right, though proposals for English regional reforms were a shadow of what was being discussed for Wales. Devolution was not adopted by the party with any great enthusiasm: it was a "peripheral issue and was presented in largely structural terms; no connection was made between an Assembly and Labour's vision for societal change" (Davies, 1999: 5). The deepening of Labour's commitment to Scottish devolution shored up its Welsh commitment. In its 1997 manifesto, the Labour Party promised a referendum on a Welsh Assembly which would have "secondary legislative powers and will be specifically empowered to reform and democratise the quango state" elected by an additional member system (Labour Party, 1997). In September 1997, Wales voted very narrowly for an Assembly. The greatest challenge in the early years of devolution was to embed it in the system of UK government and win over sceptics in Wales.

Similar developments were occurring in Scotland. The decline of the Conservatives and perception that unpopular policies were being imposed on Scotland fuelled demands for a Parliament. This culminated in the introduction of the "poll tax", a flat rate head tax, to fund local government that provoked strong opposition after it was legislated for at the end of the 1983-87 Parliament and implemented in the early part of the next Parliament. The Scottish Conservatives had lost half of their Parliamentary representation in Scotland at the 1987 election, contributing to the sense that the system of government marginalised Scotland. In both Wales and Scotland, the language of democratic deficits was used but what became evident was a legitimacy deficit. The withdrawal of consent came from those who lost out under the constitutional arrangements.

In 1988, a Constitutional Steering Committee of "prominent Scots" was set up by the Campaign for a Scottish Assembly (CSA), a home rule pressure group, to draw up plans for a Constitutional Convention. In July 1988, the Committee produced the "Claim of Right for Scotland" which proposed a Convention without statutory or official authority. Its legitimacy would derive from its membership. The "Claim of Right" offered a critique of the system of government and challenged the traditional notion of Parliamentary sovereignty, marking a significant shift in thinking,

> "There is a constitutional flaw in the present machinery of Scottish government: it can work only within a limited range of election results. Providing a Scottish Ministerial team, Scottish Whips and Government representation on Standing and Select Committees, requires a certain minimum number of Government party MPs from Scottish constituencies. There is no guarantee of such a number being elected…"

> "Within the United Kingdom the Scots are a minority which cannot ever feel secure under a constitution which, in effect, renders the Treaty of Union a contradiction in terms, because it makes no provision for the safeguarding of any rights or guarantees and does not even require a majority of the electorate to override such rights and guarantees as may once have been offered" (Campaign for a Scottish Assembly, 1988: 3, 4-5).

The authors of the "Claim of Right" rejected an elected convention as impractical and proposed a body that was partly indirectly elected, consisting of all Scottish MPs as well as representatives of Scottish local authorities, and various elements of Scottish "civil society". While the "primary responsibility for taking the lead" rested with Scottish MPs, the MPs "should be supplemented by members nominated by or on behalf of parties so as to address some of the party imbalance resulting from the 1987 election" (CSA, 1988). The aim was to produce a scheme that would win widespread support, particularly the support of the Labour Party which had won 50 of Scotland's 72 seats at the 1987 election.

The Conservatives refused to participate and the SNP chose not to do so. This meant that the two main participants were the Labour Party and the Liberal Democrats. The Scottish Greens participated for a period and the Democratic Left, formerly the Communist party, was involved. The Greens suspended membership in November 1991 when the Convention refused to agree to a multi-option referendum on Scotland's constitutional status or commit itself to a clear timetable to select a voting system.

There were seven full meetings of the Convention between 1989 and 1992. An Executive Committee provided leadership and started meeting regularly from April 1989. The Convention agreed to operate by consensus and that

> "When a vote is proposed it shall be open to any one of the designated political groups to indicate that the matter is of such fundamental importance to that group that it could not be bound by an adverse vote. In such circumstances no vote shall be taken" (NAS GD 489/1/2).

Much work was done in working groups:

- Powers of Assembly or Parliament
- Financing of Assembly or Parliament
- Constitutional Issues
- Women's Issues
- Publicity and Public Involvement.

The culmination of this process was a Convention meeting on St Andrews's Day, 30 November 1990 when *Towards Scotland's Parliament* was issued. This was described as a "report to the Scottish people" (Constitutional Convention, 1990). There remained a number of gaps in the document. Its conclusions largely followed the Labour Party's existing policy on devolution but differed in arguing for a more proportional electoral system for the Scottish Parliament. Following the 1992 election, the Convention established a Commission which considered the electoral system and other outstanding business. The Commission proposed using the Additional Member System (AMS) in place of simple plurality. The electoral system was supported amongst those who feared that a Scottish Parliament would be dominated by the Labour Party elected under simple plurality. This work provided the basis of the Labour Government's devolution proposals outlined in a white paper in 1997 (Scottish Office, 1997). The UK Government accepted the Convention proposals in broad outline though much detail still needed to be worked out, especially in how devolution was financed. It also proposed to define those matters that would be retained at Westminster instead of defining what would be retained. These proposals differed from those for Wales in that the Scottish parliament had legislative powers and some very limited tax varying powers and responsibility for a wider range of matters. Scots gave overwhelming support for devolution in a referendum in September 1997.

Devolution's most significant success in Wales and Scotland has been the restoration of consent to the system of government. Constitutional debate continues but within the context of acceptance of the legitimacy of devolved government. Further important changes have occurred. In February 2011, Wales voted for legislative powers for the Assembly in a referendum and further development of Scottish devolution are in process. However, resolving one problem of legitimacy has potentially given rise to new problems of legitimacy elsewhere in the UK constitution as a consequence of the *ad hoc* nature of constitutional change.

2.3 England and devolution

With 85% of the UK's population, England is by far the largest component of the United Kingdom and is now the only part without devolution. England, Richard Rose argued, claims no distinctive institutions of governance "though it acquires these, if only by default, when Scotland, Wales, and Northern Ireland opt out of specific policies" (Rose, 1982: 31). In other words, an English dimension emerges simply because it is what is left, albeit the largest part of the state, after special provisions are made for Scotland, Wales and Northern Ireland. Robert Hazell has pointed out that the English Question has resulted from the programme of devolution and regionalism since 1997. He described it as a "portmanteau heading for a whole series of questions about the government of England" (Hazell, 2006: 1) and that England is the "gaping hole in the devolution settlement" (Ibid.). But there had been plans for English devolution. There was no England-wide sense of a "democratic deficit" as developed in Scotland and Wales, not least because the Conservatives were the largest party across England as a whole throughout the period when that party was in government. There were, however, parts of England where the Conservatives consistently had little support. In these areas, it was thought that there might be some demand for devolution of some sort. Labour's 1997 manifesto noted:

> "Demand for directly elected regional government so varies across England that it would be wrong to impose a uniform system. In time we will introduce legislation to allow the people, region by region, to decide in a referendum whether they want directly elected regional government. Only where popular consent is established will arrangements be made for elected regional assemblies" (Labour Party, 1997).

Greater emphasis was placed on functional regions, the organisation of central government machinery in the regions. A rolling programme of elected regional Assemblies in England came to an abrupt halt when the first region to be consulted – the North-East – overwhelmingly rejected the idea in late 2004: 78% voted "No" on a turnout of 48%. There had been debate over many years in the North East of England on the need to have a stronger voice and the referendum had been preceded by the usual consultation but the proposals for devolution came from the centre. The only exception was London where a directly elected mayor and directly elected Assembly – the Greater London Authority – were supported in a referendum in May 1998. London differed from the rest of England in that it was the capital city and had had its own authority – the Greater London Authority – until Margaret Thatcher's Government had abolished it following a commitment in the Conservatives' 1983 election manifesto. The decision to get rid of the GLC was hasty and rooted in a "history of conflicts" (Flynn et al., 1985: 9). Opinion in the capital in favour of a reconstituted elected authority hardened in subsequent years.

England had emerged by default as a consequence of devolution to Northern Ireland, Scotland and Wales. The problem is that devolution was conceived for these other parts of the UK in isolation with little consideration of the UK-wide implications and the potential consequences for the legitimacy of government. To date, the English Question has remained more an academic than practical concern. However, the UK-wide implications of devolution and the "English Question" remain issues in the background. These unresolved issues of devolution focus on two areas in particular: the funding of devolution with accusations that devolution has entrenched existing biases in favour of devolved areas and the "West Lothian Question"[2], the

2 This issue became known as the west Lothian Question in the 1970s after the constituency of Tam Dalyell, the MP who raised it persistently in devolution debates at that time.

asymmetrical consequences of devolution in the House of Commons whereby English matters that have been devolved are still the subject of votes by all MPs whereas comparable devolve matters are no longer voted on by MPs. Though these have not yet become politically salient, they have the potential to become contentious in the event that the majority community within the UK are mobilised in opposition to perceived unfairness of devolution. If the English public or its political leaders are mobilised in opposition to a system that might be seen as disfavouring them then a serious problem of losers' consent, comparable to those that devolution was designed to address in Scotland and Wales, may arise.

3. Devolution's impact on constitutional evolution – continuation of constitutional moment

Referendums were held separately in Scotland, Wales, Northern Ireland (and simultaneously in the Irish Republic), London and the North-East of England. These had a number of consequences. Though formally consultative, there was little prospect that Parliament would ignore the outcome of the referendums. In Northern Ireland, a clear majority backed the Agreement including a majority of the Unionist community who were deemed least likely to support it. In Scotland, substantial majorities voted for a tax-varying Scottish Parliament but in Wales only a narrow majority on a low turnout backed devolution. In London, a large majority on a low turnout voted for the Greater London Authority.

The rejection of devolution in North-East England not only killed off devolution there but across all of England's regions. But there were other consequences. The subsequent legislation for Scottish devolution passed through Parliament relatively unscrutinised as compared with similar legislation in the 1970s. The decisive majority for devolution undermined opposition to and the scrutiny of devolution legislation in the Commons and Lords. Having a pre-legislative referendum would appear to minimise opposition at least so long as there is a substantial majority in the referendum. There was relatively more scrutiny of the Welsh devolution legislation which passed through Parliament separately. Key provisions affecting the UK as a whole were paid little attention in each case when devolution was being established, including the financing of devolution and relations with London.

Devolution has been successful as a response to particular problems of legitimacy in components of the UK. However, the unintended consequences and spillover effects of devolution were paid scant attention. Again, issues of finance and intergovernmental relations (IGR), especially financial IGR, are evidence of an absence of coherent thinking. But the fundamental problem is that of partisan approaches to constitutional change. Devolution has potentially only displaced the problem of legitimacy rather than resolving the problem in the asymmetrical system that exists in the UK. It is conceivable that in time the implications of devolution will provoke a backlash in England. As Rose remarked, England acquires distinctive institutions of governance "only by default, when Scotland, Wales, and Northern Ireland opt out of specific policies" (Rose, 1982: 31). Devolution highlights asymmetries in ways that may call into question the legitimacy of English governance especially in period of public financial constraints.

The UK constitution can be amended as any other non-constitutional policy change can be enacted. This creates the possibility that constitutional change is subject to the vagaries of adversarial party politics. This was highlighted in February 2011 during a House of Lords debate on the Coalition Government's proposals for a referendum on the Alternative Vote. A former Labour Minister complained about the manner in which constitutional change was brought about:

> "My point is that, as I face the Chamber, the two oldest political parties in the country [Conservatives and Liberal Democrats] are joining together to rewrite our constitution on a daily, as-you-go-by basis. In other words, we do not know what is happening next. This cannot be the right way to operate; it cannot be the right way in which to bring in a major constitutional change of the first ever binding referendum in the UK. There is no big picture by which we may judge this part of the constitutional changes – we know that there are others on the conveyor belt – and that is a major difficulty" (Rooker, 2011).

Lord Rooker's observation could equally have been applied to the "constitutional moment" after 1997 discussed above when he served as a Labour Government Minister. Normal politics, especially adversarial party politics, have been intimately linked to UK constitutional politics. When party advantage becomes the main driver of change, then systematic losers are likely to emerge. This can give rise to a situation in which, as has happened with devolution, resolving one problem involved simply creating a new problem elsewhere in the constitution.

References

Primary source:

NAS GD 489: Papers of Scottish Constitutional Convention, National Archives of Scotland, Edinburgh.

Ackerman, Bruce (1993): We The People: Foundations. London: The Belknap Press of Harvard University Press.

Ackerman, Bruce (1984): The Storrs Lectures: Discovering the Constitution. In: Yale Law Journal 93, 1013-1072.

Anderson, Christopher/Blais, André/Bowler, Shaun/Donovan, Todd/Listhaug Ola (2005): Losers' Consent: Elections and Democratic Legitimacy. Oxford: Oxford University Press.

Blackburn, Robert/Plant, Raymond (eds.) (1999): Constitutional Reform: The Labour Government's Constitutional Reform Agenda. London: Longman.

Bogdanor, Vernon (2004): Our New Constitution. In: Law Quarterly Review 120, 242-262.

Campaign for a Scottish Assembly (1988): A Claim of Right for Scotland. Edinburgh: CSA.

Constitutional Convention (1990): Towards Scotland's Parliament. Edinburgh: SCC.

Davies, Ron (1999): Devolution – A Process not an Event. Cardiff: Institute of Welsh Affairs.

Dicey, Albert Venn (1890): Ought the referendum to be introduced into England. In: Contemporary Review 57, 489-511.

Dicey, Albert Venn (1959): Introduction to the Study of the Law of the Constitution. London: Macmillan, 10th edition.

Easton, David (1975): A Re-Assessment of the Concept of Support; In: British Journal of Political Science 5, (4), 435-437.

Edwards, David (2005): Thinking about Constitutions. http://www.fedtrust.co.uk /admin/uploads/Essay_34.pdf [accessed: 22 November 2011]

Flynn, Norman/Leach, Steve/Vielba, Carol (1985): Abolition or Reform?: The GLC and the Metropolitan County Councils. London: George Allen & Unwin.

Griffith, J.A.G. (1979): The Political Constitution. In: Modern Law Review 42, (1), 1979.

Hazell, Robert (1999): The New Constitutional Settlement. In: Hazell, R. (ed.): Constitutional Futures: A History of the Next Ten Years. Oxford: Oxford University Press, 230-247.

Hazell, Robert (2006): Introduction: What is the English Question?. In: Hazell, R. (ed.): The English Question. Manchester: Manchester University Press, 1-23.

Johnson, Nevil (2004): Reshaping the British Constitution. Basingstoke: Palgrave Macmillan.

King, Anthony (2001): Does the United Kingdom still have a Constitution?. London: Sweet & Maxwell.

Kingdon, John W. (2003): Agendas, Alternatives, and Public Policies. London: Longman (2nd ed.).

Labour Party (1997): Britain Will Be Better With New Labour. London: Labour Party.

Lijphart, Arend (1977): Democracy in Plural Societies. New Haven, CT: Yale University Press.

Lijphart, Arend (1996): The Framework Documents on Northern Ireland and the Theory of Power Sharing. In: Government and Opposition 31, (3), 267-275.

Low, Sidney (1904): The Governance of England. London: T. Fisher Unwin.

MacCormick, Neil (1978): Does the United Kingdom have a Constitution? Reflections on MacCormick v. Lord Advocate. In: Northern Ireland Legal Quarterly 29, (1).

MacCormick, Neil (1999): Questioning Sovereignty. Oxford: Oxford University Press.

McFadden, Pat (2002): Federalist Fun. In: Prospect, (74). http://www.prospect-magazine.co.uk/2002/05/federalistfun/ [accessed: 22 November 2011]

McGarry, John/O'Leary, Brendan (2006a): Consociational Theory, Northern Ireland's Conflict, and its Agreement. Part 1. What Consociationalists can Learn from Northern Ireland. In: Government and Opposition 41, (1), 43–63.

McGarry, John/O'Leary, Brendan (2006b): Consociational Theory, Northern Ireland's Conflict, and its Agreement. Part 2. What Critics of Consociation can Learn from Northern Ireland. In: Government and Opposition 41, (2), 249–277.

Mitchell, James (2009): Devolution in the United Kingdom. Manchester: Manchester University Press.

Morgan, Kevin/Roberts, Ellis (1993): The Democratic Deficit: A Guide to Quangoland. Cardiff: Cardiff School of City and Regional Planning, no. 144.

O'Leary, Brendan (1999): The Nature of the British Irish Agreement. In: New Left Review I/233, 66–96.

Oliver, Dawn (2003): The Project: Modernising the UK Constitution. In: Oliver, D. (ed.): Constitutional Reform in the United Kingdom. Oxford: Oxford University Press, 3-27.

Rawls, John (1972): A Theory of Justice. Oxford: Oxford University Press.

Riddell, Peter (1999): The Times. 18 January 1999.

Rooker, Lord Jeff (2011): Speech in House of Lords. 16 February, http://www.publications.parliament.uk/pa/ld201011/ldhansrd/text/110216-0001.htm#11021657000085 [accessed: 29 November 2011]

Rose, Richard (1971): Governing Without Consensus: An Irish Perspective. Boston: Beacon Press.

Rose, Richard (1975): Northern Ireland: A Time of Choice. Basingstoke: Macmillan.

Rose, Richard (1982): Understanding the United Kingdom. London: Longman.

Russell, Meg (2005): A Constitution by any other name… (Book Review). In: The Political Quarterly 76, (3), 457-459.

Sandford, Mark (2005): The New Governance of the English Regions. Basingstoke: Palgrave Macmillan.

Scottish Office (1997): Scotland's Parliament. Edinburgh: HMSO, Cm.3658.

Taylor, Rupert (2006): The Belfast Agreement and the Politics of Consociationalism: A Critique. In: The Political Quarterly 77, (2), 217–226.

Tomaney, John/Hetherington, Peter (2004): English Regions: The Quiet Revolution?, In: Trench, A. (ed.): Has Devolution Made A Difference?. Exeter: Imprint Academic, 121-140.

Tremblay, Luc B. (2003): General Legitimacy of Judicial Review and the Fundamental Basis of Constitutional Law. In: Oxford Journal of Legal Studies 23, (4), 525-562.

Wilford, Rick/Wilson, Robin (2003): Northern Ireland: Valedictory?, In: Hazell , R. (ed.): The State and the Nations: The Third Year of Devolution in the United Kingdom. Exeter: Imprint Academic, 79-118.

Wilson, Richard (2005): Constitutional Change: A Note by the Bedside. In: The Political Quarterly 76, (2), 281-287.

Wilson, Robin/Wilford, Rick (2001): Northern Ireland: Endgame. In: Trench, A. (ed.): The State of the Nations 2001: The Second Year of Devolution in the United Kingdom. Exeter: Imprint Academic, 77-106.

Federalising a Regionalised State. Constitutional Change in Italy

Franco Bassanini

1. The rise of constitutional politics

Italy changed the territorial structure of its state in a long process of constitutional change. While regional units have been established before 1970, later reforms gave way to the creation of a regionalised state, which meanwhile turned into a kind of a federal state. This process gathered momentum since the 1980s, but until present did not end with a final result. Still Italian federalism is an unfinished project, and recent reforms revealed a stop and go in constitutional policy.

Up to the end of the 1970s, the issue of constitutional reform remained on the sidelines of the Italian political debate and out of the spotlight of media attention and public opinion.

This was mainly due to three factors:

- the persistent, widespread bipartisan (or multi-partisan) support for a Constitutional Charter that had been approved at the end of 1947 by a very large majority of the Constitutional Assembly: in effect, the Constitution of 1948 was the product of a teamwork that involved all the anti-fascist political forces (even though they were already divided – in the spheres of foreign, social and economic policies – by a dramatic confrontation between the pro-Western parties led by the De Gasperi's *Democrazia Cristiana* and the pro-Soviet communist and socialist parties led by Togliatti and Nenni);
- the significant delays in implementing the new constitutional measures (the Constitutional Court began working in 1956 and Italy's 15 ordinary Regions only in 1970): consequently, until the mid-1970s the political debate and the public opinion remained focused on the implementation of the new institutional measures introduced by the Constitution, which still had to be tested and clearly could not yet be assessed;
- the remarkable success of the government policies in the 1950s and 1960s, particularly in post-war reconstruction, consolidating Italy's NATO membership, starting up European integration and building a modern social market economy (with the economic boom of the 1960s and the development of a modern universal welfare state). Therefore, one of the key triggers of every constitutional reform, i.e. the need to create

new institutional instruments to overcome the failure or inadequacy of existing public policies, was then completely absent.

During the 1980s, the issue of constitutional reform returned to the surface of the political debate. This was due to some relevant changes which occurred in the country's policies and economy, such as:

- the slackening of the galloping growth that characterised Italian economy in the 1950s and 60s, slackening due to the oil crisis, the public spending boom and rising public debt[1], the abnormal expansion of economic sectors shielded from competition and the market (public or private monopolies), and the increases in regulatory and bureaucratic costs;
- the increasing cost of welfare state, not followed by improvements in public services, owing to poor public sector efficiency;
- the Italian economic and productive model, characterised by low-tech manufacturing and business dwarfism (many micro and small businesses, few large companies), unsuited to adapt to changes in the global economic scenario (consolidation of a service-related and information economy, new technologies, increased international competition).

These developments in economy and their impact on public policies opened a debate that basically involved two positions:

- On the one hand some politicians and opinion makers believed that solving these problems should require a radical change in public policy (economic and social reforms, privatisation and market deregulation, investments in infrastructures and human resources, modernisation of public administration, reductions in tax pressure on businesses and employment, etc.) rather than institutional reforms;
- On the other hand, many argued that, on the contrary, the roots of the crisis were primarily in political instability and ineffective decision-making at national and local level. Therefore it should be first of all necessary to review the country's constitutional structure, strengthening the executive stability, accelerating the policy-making processes and improving the tools to implement public policies decisions.

The first position garnered support mainly from the left wing and amongst the liberals[2]. But the recipes proposed by the left wing and the liberals were partially discordant. The second position found its supporters in the centre and right wings and prevailed in the 1980s, focusing attention of public opinion on the Constitution. Institutional reforms were presented as necessary and

1 The public debt to GDP ratio increased in Italy from 41% in 1970 to 97% in 1990.

2 The liberal-democratic faction in Italy spans all the political parties, but is normally in the minority. Even if for short periods – e.g. in the second half of the 1990s – it gains a leading role, it did manage to rally cross-party majorities.

primary measures to achieve more stable national and local governments, backed by cohesive majorities and with more effective decision-making and implementing tools. However, the reforms proposed mainly concerned government institutions (such as electoral laws and parliament-government relations at the central and local level) rather than the territorial structure of the state. Reforming the powers and responsibilities of the Regions and local authorities was not yet considered as crucial, also because the Regions had only been established in 1970 and only in 1977 their powers and responsibilities had been defined.

The key moments of this phase were[3]:

- the setup of a Parliamentary Commission for institutional reforms, led by Aldo Bozzi (1983-1985), which submitted a project for the review of 44 articles of the Constitution;
- numerous parliamentary debates[4], party congresses, conventions and conferences on constitutional reform, all tending to target the reinforcement of state and local government stability and powers;
- the approval by a large majority of a number of laws[5] to strengthen the stability and powers of local governments (direct election of mayors, majority vote electoral laws, automatic wind-up of local councils after a vote of no confidence). This model was later extended to Regional governments (Constitutional Act N. 1/1999).

The Bozzi Commission proposals were never followed up. In this respect it should be remembered that the Italian Constitution (art. 138) requires special procedures to amend the Constitution[6] which makes it difficult to approve a controversial reform; moreover there was in Italy – until the start of the 1990s – a strong conviction that, in any event, constitutional reforms should be the result of a wide consensus among the parliamentary majority and the opposition (or at least most of it).

---

3 Of the following reforms, we are interested here only in those referred to under point c). Like the others, these aim to strengthen government stability and executive powers, but in effect they also represent a precondition for awarding greater powers and responsibilities to regional and local governments

4 First and foremost in the Lower Chamber on 18 May 1988 and in the Senate on 19 May 1988.

5 First of all, Acts N. 142/1990 and 81/1993.

6 According to art. 138 of the Constitution, constitutional amendment laws need two consecutive approvals by each of the Chambers. For the second approval, absolute majority of both Members of Parliament and Senators is needed. When an absolute majority is reached, but not a two-thirds majority, the reform goes then to public referendum if requested by one fifth of Members of Parliament, by one fifth of Senators, by five Regional Councils or by 500,000 voters.

2. From regionalisation to federal reform

In the early nineties, the political and economic scenario changed yet again. The Italian economy loses competitiveness and the budget crisis got worse, with an annual deficit-GDP ratio exceeding 10% and a debt-GDP ratio increased from 97% in 1990 to 124% in 1994. Proof of widespread corruption and swindling came to light (culminating in the so-called "Tangentopoli", a clientelist relation between private and public actors as evidenced in the Milan public prosecutor's "Clean Hands" inquiry). The Italian North-South divide widened. Local protest movements spread especially in the North fuelled by the conviction – technically unfounded but no less widespread – that strong tax pressure on business and employment was mainly due to the high cost of public aid for underdeveloped areas of the South. Public mistrust in politicians increased; and finally a strong crisis of representativeness and legitimacy of the institutions arose.

The tendency to overestimate the role of institutional reform became stronger, especially as for reforms strengthening majority cohesion and stability and executive powers (a reform of the "*government form*" in Italian constitutionalist jargon). This was confirmed by a public referendum in 1993. It abolished the proportional representation system in force for political elections since 1945, and led to a subsequent adoption of an electoral system largely based on the first-past-the-post plurality voting system (for the 75% of the parliamentary seats).

But at the same time we observe an increasing spread of the conviction that a more extensive and all-inclusive reform is required. It was deemed to aim at the overall institutional architecture, i.e. at a reform of the "*form of the State*" in Italian constitutionalist jargon including:

- a redefinition of the mission of public institutions, with downsizing to the bare essentials (according to the principle of subsidiarity);
- a drastic cut of central powers, launching an institutional reform in the federal sense, with a strengthening of the autonomy and sovereignty of regional and local authorities and a wide reallocation of powers, responsibilities and resources;
- a radical reorganisation of public administrations, focused on public service quality according to the principles of liability, merit, assessment and user satisfaction.

Therefore a reform of the constitutional structure was set on the agenda. Through greater independence and self-governance of regional and local authorities, it was to lead to better public services, lower public spending and tax burdens, and give the public more direct control over the management of public resources.

Most observers agree that this shift in opinion has been mainly triggered by the electoral success of the *Lega Nord* (Northern League), a regionalist/independence-oriented party (which at first ran on a single-issue programme wavering between a federal reform and the secession of Northern Italy).

Confined to a regional dimension covering mainly Lombardy throughout the 1980s (0.48% of votes at the 1987 elections), the League suddenly leaped to 8.65% at the 1992 national elections (obtaining 24.3% of votes in Lombardy, 17.3% in Veneto and 17% in Piedmont). In 1994 the League confirmed its advance with 8.36% of votes, but most of all proved to be a determining factor for the electoral success of the coalition led by Silvio Berlusconi and for the building of his first government. In the meantime, the adoption of the first-past-the-post electoral system had in fact pushed the political and electoral weight of the League upwards thanks to its strong roots in the highly populated regions of Northern Italy. And it had driven the major political forces to assess which policies' concessions they could make to the League in order to keep the door open to an alliance crucial to electoral success.

But the favour for a federalist model, in fact, had much more ancient roots in Italy. As it does in Germany – unlike France, Spain and the UK – the unification of Italy dates back only to the second half of the 19th century, and even then many authoritative politicians (from Carlo Cattaneo to Giuseppe Mazzini) supported the federal model, as more consistent with a political and administrative tradition whose origins lie in the independence of the mediaeval municipalities. The federal model had then many supporters in the Constitutional Assembly, especially among the Christian Democrats, but also from isolated socialist (Lussu) and communist (Laconi) constituents. Yet, finally a compromise between the unitary and the federal model prevailed which experts defined as a "regional state" (vesting to Regional Governments legislative powers in various matters, but in accordance with basic principles set by national outline laws and in compliance of the national interest).

However the effective implementation of the regional reform envisaged in the Constitution met resistance and obstacles in the 1950s and 1960s. They delayed its entry in force by twenty years and imposed then a very strict interpretation of powers vested to the Regions. In practice, state acts continued to regulate in detail matters in which the Regions should have autonomous legislative powers, de facto downsizing regional law to secondary regulation; and the Regions' administrative measures were subject to in-depth preventive checks.

Therefore many hopes of improving public and government services that had been vested in regional reform, remained unfulfilled, fuelling further disappointment and protests. But the underlying cause of the failure of regional reform was identified in this mutilation of the constitutional plans for a regional state. The ensuing protest roused a widespread demand for a real federal reform which gained ground even among the left-wing parties. In 1989, much earlier than the Northern League's consolidation, most of the regional conferences of the Italian Communist Party approved resolutions in favour of a federal reform of the State, overcoming the party's traditionally centralist approach.

This turnaround showed itself in the mission assigned to a new Parliamentary Commission for constitutional reform set up in 1992 by the two Houses (known as the De Mita-Iotti Commission). By constitutional law[7], the commission was then assigned the task of preparing proposals on electoral system reform and an organic bill for reforming the entire Part II of the constitution. The "form of the State" reform was therefore included in the commission's mandate, along with reviewing the form of government, the electoral laws and the constitutional guarantee system. In effect, the commission easily reached an agreement on the reforms of the form of State and of the form of government: the final report on both issues (drafted by two Constitutional Law professors, both MPs – the socialist Labriola and myself as left-wing democrat) was approved by a wide majority and submitted to the Chambers on 11 January 1994. In contrast, the reforms of the constitutional guarantee system and of the Senate's composition met with a certain amount of dissent and were not included in the final report.

The approved project involved:

- an extensive reform of the relations between the State and the Regions, which reversed the criteria for assigning powers (with strict definition of the State's legislative powers and the devolution of all other legislative powers to the Regions)[8] and introduced new guarantee tools for regional autonomy;
- a wide reform of the government structure following the "neo-Parliamentary" pattern, which envisaged a direct investiture of the Prime Minister by Parliament, gave to the Prime Minister exclusive power to ap-

7 Const. Act N. 1/1993.

8 The central state retained power over functions considered essential to guaranteeing its unity and sovereignty, i.e. its responsibilities for foreign, military, justice and finance policy. It also retained the right to define the essential contents of individual freedom and civil, ethical, social, economic and political rights based on provisions in Part I of the Constitution. The Regions were to have legal and administrative responsibility for all other matters. The strict list of state-regulated matters can be summarised as related to the following sectors: foreign policy and international relations; national defence and public security; individual civil rights; justice policy; monetary policy; State accounting and finance; general economic planning and rebalancing; industrial, energy, transport and national communications policy; environmental protection and public hygiene; scientific and technology research and the protection of artistic, literary and intellectual property; welfare and general law on ensuring safety in the workplace; general education and higher education laws and planning; general rules on administrative organisation and procedures; electoral matters; profession-related laws; statistics, weights and measures; arms and explosives; post office and telecommunications matters; sport-related laws of national interest.

point and remove ministers, and introduce the so-called "constructive no confidence vote" by the two Houses;
- the introduction of new rules on budgets, urgent decrees, de-legislation, regulatory powers of the Government, public administration organisation;
- a big increase of the Houses' powers of inquiry.

As for the "form of government", it was the clear intention to introduce many of the parliamentary democracy streamlining tools, as successfully tested in the German Federal Republic. But also for the "form of the State", though cautiously repeating its definition as a regional state, the model proposed by the Commission was in fact very similar to cooperative federalism as it exists in Germany.

Unfortunately, Parliament did not have enough time to examine and approve the De Mita-Iotti Commission's bill, because of the two Houses' dissolution of 16 January 1994, three years earlier than the end of five planned by the Constitution.

The 1994 elections produced many relevant political innovations. Among the traditional political forces, only the left-wing Democratic Party – born of the transformation of the strongest communist party in Western Europe – continued to have a significant representation in Parliament. The Socialists all but disappeared, the ex-Christian democratic People's Party was strongly downsized, and a very narrow majority was obtained by a hitherto unheard-of centre-right coalition formed by a new party (*Forza Italia*, founded just a few months earlier by Silvio Berlusconi), the Northern League and a national-conservative party born of the transformation of the neo-fascist *Movimento Sociale Italiano.*

The governing coalition was improvised and very disparate in terms of its political-program. However, for the first time, the majority was formed by political forces that had not contributed to the drafting and approval of the 1947 Constitution, and were therefore more willing to support a program of radical constitutional reform, rather than merely updating, tweaking and integrating a constitutional charter considered basically sound. Yet, at the time, the centre-right coalition was also split on matters of institutional culture. The "Northern League" lead by Umberto Bossi was anti-centralist and anti-state, undecided between the idea of a federal state and the idea of a confederation of independent regions. Fini's post-fascists were centralist, pro-state and historically supporter of a presidential reform. Last but not least, the supporters of *Forza Italia*, i.e. the new party founded by the tycoon Silvio Berlusconi were wavering between liberalism in principle, pro-state for their own interests, an agnostic pragmatism, and a kind of "populist peronism", So the coalition failed to enact any constitutional reform and collapsed within a few months, giving way to a technical government supported by the centre-left opposition and by the League.

This new government, led by Lamberto Dini, former Bank of Italy's vice-governor, had no significant reform program of its own. In effect, it depended on a working parliamentary majority based, besides the League, on centre-left parties loyal to the 1948 Constitution.

A bipartisan attempt to open a new season of constitutional reform was made at the beginning of 1996. An agreement between the leaders of the three main parties (Berlusconi, D'Alema and Fini) led to the establishment of an informal committee of "four wise men", experts in constitutional law but also prominent Members of Parliament, two belonging to the centre-right (Giuliano Urbani and Domenico Fisichella) and two to the centre-left (Cesare Salvi and myself). The draft this committee prepared followed the guidelines of the De Mita-Iotti Commission project, and was therefore based on the German model ("neo-parliamentary" pattern, with a strong leadership of a Prime Minister having exclusive power to appoint and remove ministers, and a "constructive no confidence vote" by the Parliament). It was appreciated by D'Alema and Berlusconi, but was rejected by Fini, loyal to the presidential model.

A later attempt to form a new government led by Antonio Maccanico, with a program including a constitutional reform aiming at the French semi-presidential model, failed even before the start of a real debate on these new lines of constitutional reform. So after just two years Italy was again faced with an early general election.

3. Reform attempts of the Prodi government

The 1996 elections brought the centre-left parties (gathered together in the *Ulivo* coalition) back to power. The new majority, led by Romano Prodi, rejected any upheaval of Constitution, considering its principles and values still valid and current, but was convinced that some updating and modernisation of the 1948 Charter were nevertheless needed.

The electoral program of the *Ulivo* coalition in fact included significant institutional reforms to modernise the form of government and the form of state, for the most part reiterating the proposals of the bicameral De Mita-Iotti Commission. But the *Ulivo* coalition had not an independent parliamentary majority in the Chamber of Deputies. The Prodi government held firm because of external support by *Rifondazione Comunista*, an extreme left party strongly opposed to any strengthening of the executive power and to any federal reform. So a highly complex political problem arose: The parliamentary influence of *Rifondazione Comunista* was slight, and therefore not sufficient for avoiding a constitutional reform eventually supported by a wide bipartisan majority; but *Rifondazione Comunista* could have provoked, in this case, a government crisis by withdrawing its decisive external support to the government.

A temporary solution was found by adopting a sort of double-track process. The power to set up a reform bill was vested to a new Parliamentary Commission totally independent from the Government and chaired by the leader of the main majority party (the former communist Massimo D'Alema). The Cabinet's action in the institutional issues was focused, on the contrary, on reform's bills not requiring amendments to the Constitution: these bills could have had a quite large impact, given the flexibility of many of the constitutional provisions.

For doing so, the Prodi government opted for an innovative and brave path, by asking Parliament to merely approve some enabling acts establishing only the general outlines of the reform program. Two acts approved at the beginning of 1997 and commonly known as the I and II "*Bassanini*" Acts, enabled the Government to enact from 1998 to 2001 many legislative delegated decrees, providing 1) a general reallocation of administrative powers among central, regional and local governments according to the subsidiarity and decentralisation principles; 2) a strong reduction of central government's control on regional and local governments; 3) a significant increase of regional and local organisational autonomy; 4) a strong downsizing of central administrative organisation following the reduction of national functions (e.g. by cutting the number of ministries from 18 to 12); 5) a general program aiming at reducing regulatory onus and red tape, the beginning of a process of systematic simplification of administrative procedures and the introduction of the analysis of the impact of regulation; 6) the start up of a far-reaching public administration reform envisaging temporary office for public managers, performance review and appraisal, executive liability for results, and linking public managers' remuneration to performance.

All the related delegated decrees were unanimously agreed by Government, regions and representatives of local and provincial governments. The result was: a strong increase of the sectors and services assigned to regional and local administrative responsibility, for the first time including industrial and labour policies; an effective strengthening of regional and local regulatory power in the same sectors; the introduction of vertical and horizontal subsidiarity principles; the allocation of new financial resources to the regional and local governments (though still insufficient to cover all the cost of transferred functions). In this way, it was introduced in Italy – as, many scholars wrote using a technically incorrect but effective term – a sort of *administrative federalism by keeping the constitution unchanged (i.e. without amending constitutional law)*. After this reform, actually, the administrative and political powers of the Italian Regions are quite similar to those of the German *Länder*.

However the Bassanini reforms could not replace a constitutional reform, still necessary for vesting greater legislative powers to regional and local authorities, to adjust their financial resources, to consolidate the new distribution of administrative functions established by law[9], and to adapt the constitutional organisation to the new structure of the State (with the transformation of the Senate, now a duplicate of the Lower Chamber, into a federal Senate). So a new bicameral commission on institutional reform was set up by a Constitutional Act (no. 1 of 24 January 1997), with the task of "preparing reform projects of the Part II of the Constitution, particularly concerning the State structure ("form of the State"), the government organisation ("form of government"), the bicameral system and the guarantees system". Moreover, the commission should try to obtain the support of a wide bipartisan majority within the commission and later in the two Assemblies for such a project.

The proposals submitted to the commission were generally more radical than those approved by the two previous commissions. As for the form of state, they explicitly adopted the federal model. Regarding the form of government, they worked on two alternative scenarios – the first based on the French semi-presidential model, the second based on a parliamentary model tailored to include direct public election of the Premier and a strong strengthening of his powers (so strong that the proposal provoked widespread fears for a "premier dictatorship")[10].

The decision to adopt the federal model was not directly influenced by the Northern League, because the League's Members of Parliament deserted the works of the commission for many months, as a sign of protest against the election for president of the commission of the leader of the left-wing democratic party, the former communist Massimo D'Alema. While the League was away, the debate inside the commission was focused on the different patterns of federal state. The outcome was that the cooperative model, closer to the German than the American one, prevailed with a wide majority. But the proposal strongly emphasised the role and powers of local authorities, particularly the municipal ones, consistently with the Italian tradition dating back to Middle Ages, according to which local identity has much stronger roots than regional and national ones. Some elements were very noteworthy:

1. the recognition of the equality and the same constitutional dignity of the central, regional and local governments;
2. the strong importance given to the subsidiarity principle (both vertical and horizontal subsidiarity[11]);

---

9 If the administrative federalism in fact has represented an important anticipation of to the federal reform of the State, it had nevertheless a strong structural limit: implemented under ordinary legislative procedure, it could be repealed at any time by a new ordinary act approved with a simple parliamentary majority. It was clear that only a constitutional reform could overcome this limit.

10 This solution was presented by its supporters as an Italian version of the "Westminster model" used in the UK. Its denigrators instead claimed that it was effectively related to the model unsuccessfully tested in Israel at the end of the 1990s.

11 See the first two paragraphs of the art. 56 of the Commission's draft: "The functions that cannot be adequately performed anymore by private individuals shall be split up among lo-

3. the constitutionalisation of the redistribution of administrative powers pursuant to Bassanini laws;
4. the suppression of central power of preventive legitimacy check on regional laws;
5. the assignment of general legislative responsibilities to Regions, while the central state kept the exclusive legislative competence only in some areas – primarily its "regalian" functions (defence, security, justice and foreign affairs)[12];
6. the supremacy of central law when necessary to protect "indispensable/essential national interests".

The D'Alema Commission's draft was approved by a large majority on 30 June 1997. During the following months, each Member of Parliament had the right to submit amendments to the draft. Taking into account these amend-

---

cal authorities (Municipalities and Provinces), Regions and the State, according to the principle of subsidiarity and differentiation, in compliance with functional autonomies as recognised by law. Control of the functions shall be the responsibility of authorities closest to the public interest, in accordance with the criterion of standardisation and suitability of organisational structure with respect to such functions. Municipalities shall be assigned regulatory and administrative functions in general, also in relation to matters on which the State or Regions have legislative powers, except for functions specifically assigned to Provinces, Regions or State under the terms of the Constitution, constitutional laws or ordinary law, without function duplication and with the identification of related responsibilities".

12 See the first two paragraphs of art. 59 of the project: "The State shall have legislative powers in reference to: a) foreign policy and international relations; nationality, immigration and legal status of foreigners; European Parliamentary elections; defence and Armed Forces; monetary affairs, protection of savings and financial markets; b) State constitutional and institutional bodies and related electoral laws; State referendums; budget, tax law and related accounting regulations; State principles of organisation and administration; coordination of information, statistics and electronic nature of State, regional and local administration data; public order and personal safety; civil and criminal law, legal authorities and related jurisdiction; electoral laws and legislation governing local and provincial government bodies; c) general rules on production and trading of goods and services; general regulations on education and higher education, related qualifications and their professional use; general law on science and technology research; setting minimum common levels for services regarding civil rights and health protection; general measures on health treatment; general laws on occupational safety and protection; environmental and ecosystem protection; cultural and environmental heritage protection; large transport networks; postal services; energy production, transport and national distribution; national law on communications; general law on civil protection; national law on sport-related matters; decisions on compulsorily standard requirements and technical parameters to be adopted throughout the country; the manufacture and sale of drugs, narcotics and poisons; dietary matters and the control of food substances. The State shall also be responsible for legislative powers assigned as a result of other constitutional measures and for the protection of prominent and imperative national interests. The State may issue laws delegating regulatory functions to the Regions on matters referred to under the first paragraph. Each to the extent of their jurisdiction, the State and Regions shall issue laws governing the promotion and organisation of cultural activities. Regional governments shall have legislative power in all matters not expressly attributed to State legislative powers.

ments, the D'Alema Commission approved finally the constitutional bill that was submitted to the Chamber of Deputies on 4 November 1997. Concerning to the form of the State, the corrections introduced were numerous but unsubstantial. With regard to the distribution of legislative competences between central state and regions – still the most controversial matter – the new text added a central responsibility for competition law, while it decided that, on environmental protection, central government could set only general guidelines. The supremacy clause remained unchanged ("The State shall also have legislative power to protect prominent and imperative national interests").

The parliamentary discussion of the bill started on January 1998. Criticism, perplexity and dissent quickly emerged. The communist extreme left was strongly against, since they believed that the project endangered the unity of the country and the principles of parliamentary democracy. Also against the draft was the Northern League, since they considered the project as inconsistent with the proposal to build a true federal state. Berlusconi and *Forza Italia* Members of Parliament were almost as critical, mainly because of the insufficient powers assigned to the President (who, following the bill, would have been directly elected by Italian people): the new form of government – they claimed – resembled the Austrian or Portuguese model more than the one of the French Fifth Republic[13]. Both in the centre-right and centre-left ranks, many MPs were perplexed by the reform proposals concerning the form of the State. But, within the same parliamentary groups, there were those who criticised the bill for its excessive federalism, and those for its excessive centralism[14].

Nevertheless, the project as a whole was still supported by a transversal parliamentary majority, including D'Alema's left-wing democrats, Marini's People's Party (former Christian Democrats) and Fini's *Alleanza Nazionale*. This majority was, however, politically and culturally too heterogeneous and

---

13 See Hon. Berlusconi's speech at the session held on 28 January 1998 ("The new constitutional physiognomy of the President of the Republic still remains uncertain. His powers, limits and functions are not clear, so we could have a constitutional figure that is legitimised by millions of votes and therefore of strong political impact, but with a lack of real powers. A President that is elected by the people must be responsible for government policy direction and must have the tools to implement it. It will not be possible to successfully complete the reform process without solving this problem, which determines political and institutional balance"). In Berlusconi's assessment what actually had an even greater influence were justice-related issues ("separation of the careers for public prosecutor and judges – that is a prerequisite for truly fair and efficient justice – still seems far from happening").

14 See the Hon. Berlusconi's speech, again during the session held on 28 January 1998 ("However, it is on the issue of federalism that the gap between needs of the country and the text of the reform as agreed by the bicameral Commission seems widest. Of course, steps forward have been made. The regions will have some legislative independence and local authorities will have financial, tax and organisational independence in sectors which directly affect citizens' lives. But this autonomy, based on the bicameral proposal, could be suspended by central government at any time. Can we define this as federalism?")

in any case not large enough to achieve success for such a complex project. Even before moving on to examine the provisions on the form of the State, and therefore, on the federal reform, the *casus belli* arose about the powers to be assigned to a President of the Republic directly elected by the people. After a sort of ultimatum by Silvio Berlusconi[15], the presidency of the parliamentary commission on constitutional reform was forced to acknowledge that "the political conditions to continue the debate on the reform project do not exist anymore" (9 June 1998). In other words, the commission recognised that the launch of a general reform of the whole second part of the Constitution with such a slight parliamentary majority was impossible.

4. Federal reform of the D'Alema government

A few months later, in autumn 1998, the political scene changed again. *Rifondazione Comunista* left the majority, Prodi resigned and a new government led by Massimo D'Alema was established. It was supported by the centre-left parties and by a new centre party of former Christian Democrats which had been elected in the centre-right ranks two years earlier. In the new cabinet, a highly prestigious political member, former Prime Minister Giuliano Amato, was appointed as minister for constitutional reform.

On a proposal by D'Alema and Amato, the government considered it appropriate to restart the parliamentary debate on federal reform, mainly for two reasons. On the one hand, it seemed necessary to consolidate and complete the evolution towards a federal form of government started by the Bassanini reforms (which the D'Alema government was implementing). On the other hand, the centre-left majority – which had also achieved good results in terms of fiscal consolidation, accession to the European Monetary Union and

15 In his speech during the parliamentary session held on 27 May 1998, after strong criticism for the text as approved thus far ("The figure of President of the Republic as emerges from the text approved so far seems nonsensical; a President that is elected by the people but still has powers which remain weak, uncertain, definitely not proportionate to the source of legitimisation. Why inconveniencing the sovereign people to elect such a President? Who will solve inevitable conflicts which will arise with the Prime Minister who is elected by the people?"), Berlusconi dictated the terms to carry on with the debate ("a truly political federalism, together with an advanced fiscal federalism, that can allow a correct allocation of resources; a strong statement of freedom of initiative in the economic and social sector, supported by effective restrictions on state and public institution powers; a system to protect citizens' rights in line with Europe through the transposition of the principles of the Strasbourg Convention into our Constitution: presidentialism. If, as it seems, the strength of the decisions already made compel us to vote on this inconsistent, contradictory and dangerous presidentialism, we would not hesitate to say "no". A decisive "no" that, also valid for other observations, would involve the whole reform project we are looking at now").

the reform of public administration – regarded it as unwise to face the next elections (in 2001) without having approved the federal reform that the majority of Italians (at least in the central and northern areas) were clamouring for[16]. Therefore, a new project was submitted by the government to Parliament, concerning only the Fifth Title of the second part of the Constitution[17]. Significantly entitled as "Federal Framework of the Republic", it followed in general terms the corresponding section of the D'Alema Commission project, with some important differences, most of which aimed at gaining the consent of the supporters of federalism that were in the ranks of the parliamentary opposition. The main differences concerned:

- the suppression of the "supremacy clause" that would have allowed Parliament to legislate in the sectors of regional competence if proved necessary "for the protection of pre-eminent and imperative national interests";
- the extension of concurrent legislation (in which case the national legislator can only set out "general provisions") to some highly important sectors that the D'Alema Commission had reserved to national legislation: large transport and navigation networks; communications law; production, transportation and national distribution of energy; cultural and environmental heritage protection. Vice versa, legislation on higher education passed from concurrent to exclusive competence of the State;
- the suppression of the recognition of vertical and horizontal subsidiarity principles (the substance remaining only for the first, not for the second);
- the preference for a presidential form of government for the Regions, unless the regional statute did not decide otherwise.

The Government explicitly aimed at a wide consensus to be reached through parliamentary debate. All previous attempts of constitutional reform after the Second World War were driven by the conviction that amendments of the constitution would have needed in any case a wide agreement. In fact, all previous reforms, and even the unsuccessful attempts – included those not mentioned in this paper – had had the support of transversal political forces not congruent with the parliamentary majority. But this was not the case for the Title V reform: the parliamentary process, in fact, was characterised by a bitter clash between majority and opposition. Nothing could avoid it, neither the adoption of the text approved by the D'Alema Commission with a large majority, nor the addition of amendments proposed by the opposition (one of them reintroduced the principle of horizontal and vertical subsidiarity). In

16 In fact, the impasse on the reform project proposed by the D'Alema Commission had not been related to the federal reform, which had been supported – at least verbally – by all the political forces (with the exception of the extreme left-wing communists).

17 Constitutional Bill no. 5830, *Ordinamento federale della Repubblica* (Federal framework of the Republic), presented on 18 March 1999.

fact, in the opposition ranks, the renewed alliance between the centre-right parties and the Northern League kept until the end. And until the end the opposition denounced the inadequacy of steps made by the bill towards the federal model[18], the vacuity of the provisions on horizontal subsidiarity, the *sine die* postponement of the transformation of the Senate into a Chamber of Regions, the inadequate formulation of the rules on fiscal federalism and on taxation powers of regional and local authorities, and, above all, the claim to change the constitution by relying only on majority votes. Until the last minute, the centre-left majority internally debated on the opportunity to set the controversial precedent of a constitutional reform approved only by a very narrow parliamentary majority. In the end, electoral considerations (the aim to limit room for opposition propaganda in the central and northern areas) and, above all, the strong support provided to the reform by regional and local governments (including most of the centre-right governments), were decisive.

As promised, the centre-right opposition immediately launched a people's referendum (as provided under the constitution when a reform project does not reach, at second reading, at least a two-thirds majority from MPs). But the referendum, held on 7 October 2001, despite of a low turnout (34% of the electorate), led to the success of the reform, that was approved by 64% of voters.

The outcome of the referendum was the confirmation of some specific features of the Italian constitutional process in the eighties and nineties: first of all the strong support of the large majority of public opinion for a federal reform conceived as a tool for modernising the country, bringing the institutions closer to citizens, reducing the bureaucratic centralism and improving the self-governance of local communities. And so, in the referendum of 2001, the supporters of the old centralised state and the supporters of a more radical federal reform (Northern League) were both clearly defeated.

Indeed, in support of a federal but not radical reform (therefore following the model of cooperative federalism) a vast and somewhat unusual convergence was recorded during the nineties: It included the major trade unions (CGIL, CISL and UIL) and employer organisations (*Confindustria*), the most influential newspapers, the vast majority of public opinion and scholars of constitutional law. But public support for the federal model, very wide in the mid-nineties, began to decline at the end of the decade, and in any case expressed, rather than an adherence to a well-defined constitutional model, a general request for modernisation and cutting red tape.

---

18 The Northern League leader, Umberto Bossi, spoke of "Stalinist federalism". Sen. La Loggia, the spokesman for Forza Italia senators, was equally critical, ("There is no serious reference to the principle of subsidiarity in a horizontal and social sense. The Chamber of regions is not really established. There is no structural reform of the Constitutional Court. There is no authentic fiscal federalism").

In the constitutional process as described, the support for federal reform was naturally strong among the vast majority of the regional and local governments and local political class. But their role was generally marginal. In constitutional reform decision-making process the role of the national political class has always been predominant. This was mainly due, in my opinion, to three reasons:

- the centralised structure of Italian political parties (the result of their historical evolution, especially in the case of the left-wing parties, linked to the Leninist model, and of the Northern League, which that model had consciously copied);
- the lack of vision and long-term strategies of the regional political elite, mostly projected towards national political roles and responsibilities;
- the divisions and conflicts that have almost always opposed the local representatives to the regional representatives: the distrust of mayors and presidents of the provinces towards the regional political elite, and their fear of falling from the frying pan of the centralised state into the fire of a new regional centralism.

These factors have weakened the bargaining power of the front of autonomy against the central government and administrations.

In fact, until the approval of the 2001 reform, Regions, Provinces and Municipalities, rather than helping to build a culture of forward-looking reform and to define and implement a comprehensive project for modernising the institutions, engaged in an action to claim more powers and resources. After the approval of the reform, the quality of their action has not changed much. The claim of more powers gives way to the request for implementing a reform that has now already given to the regions and local authorities, at least in theory, the powers and responsibilities typical of a regional or local institution in a federal state. What remained unchanged – and today not yet satisfied – was the request of adequate resources, i.e. the request of implementation of the tax autonomy recognised by the new Article 119 of the Constitution.

5. The failed "reform of the reform"

The new Title V entered into force as reformed on 8 November 2001, after the referendum. In the meantime, the centre-right and the Northern League won the 2001 general elections. Thus, the political forces that had fought against the reform became the new parliamentary majority. The new majority immediately declared its intention to approve as soon as possible a "reform of the reform" intending to establish an "authentic federalist form of the state". Moreover, it refused to consider the form of the state introduced by the 2001 reform as accepted and shared. Waiting for questioning it and replacing it with another process, the majority blocked the completion/implementation of the reform that still needed approval for

- the reform of the Senate, transforming it into a Chamber of regional and local authorities (similar to the German *Bundesrat* model or on the French *Sénat* one)[19];
- the definition of the key functions of local and provincial governments, and the transfer of functions and resources from the State to local authorities;
- the definition of public service standards, in order to ensure equality for citizens in the exercise of their fundamental rights;
- the reform of public finance law in accordance with the principles of fiscal federalism, needed to convert the mechanisms of finding resources from a system based on transfer from the central state to the regional and local governments, to one based on local and regional government responsibility (by rebuilding the relationship between revenues and responsibility for expenditure, as required for a well-balanced functioning of any federal system).

During the 14th legislature (2001-2006) none of these measures was approved. Therefore, the implementation of the reform remained paralyzed. Amongst other things, the result was a strong increase of disputes before the Constitutional Court: Regions were claiming powers and financial resources as assigned to them by the reform of Title V, while the State was refusing to hand them over in absence of adequate implementing measures.

In 2005, after a hard battle with the centre-left opposition, the centre-right majority approved a new, global reform of Part 2 of the Constitution. This reform was based on the one hand on a hyper-presidentialist model, on the other hand on the new "totem" chosen by the Northern League: the "devolution" of exclusive legislative powers to the regions.

The reform:

- almost completely cancelled the separation between executive and legislative powers, by assigning to the Prime Minister – directly elected by the people – unlimited powers to influence Parliament's legislative decisions;
- returned to the exclusive legislative competence of the central state some sectors which Title V had made concurrent between the state and the regions (like, e.g. work safety; transport and navigation networks; communications; intellectual professions law; and national energy production transport and distribution);

---

19 Though non-federal, the French Senate seems to better respond to the need – that is based on solid historic, political and cultural rationales – to represent not only the Italian Regions, but also the Municipalities and the Provinces.

- assigned to the exclusive competence of the Regions some sectors previously included under concurrent legislation, such as health care and organisation, regional administrative police, school organisation, school management and the definition of education programs of specific interest for the region ("devolution" in common journalist jargon);
- assigned to the Parliament (triggered by a government proposal) a sort of discretional veto power over regional laws considered to be against the national interest;
- set up a "federal" reform of the Senate, according to the US Senate model.

Apparently the winner was Berlusconi. The reform assigned unlimited powers to the Prime Minister, so that, according to the opposition, a sort of majority dictatorship, or rather a premier dictatorship had been set up. Moreover, it introduced a sort of "accordion" federalism, almost confederal in vesting exclusive legislative powers to the Regions, but strongly neo-centralist in assigning "a posteriori" veto powers to central government and Parliament in order to stop regional laws considered as against the national interest.

However, on June 2006, the reform bill wanted by the Berlusconi government was rejected by people in a referendum, with a wide majority of the 61.7% of the voters.

6. Outcomes and achievements

In recent years the political clash on the Title V reform decreased. A sort of widespread reassessment seems to be ongoing. Even many of those who in 2001 criticised it, seem now to discover many merits of the reform. After the rejection by the electorate (as mentioned earlier) of the clumsy attempt to introduce a federalism coming close to the confederal model, for many the "new" Title V came back to mean the maximum innovation possible for a federal reform.

The reform's implementation process vigorously restarted with the approval by a wide majority of the bill on fiscal federalism (Law 62/2009). The debate on this law confirmed that the Title V provisions on regional and local finance (art. 119) are today generally appreciated. Moreover, all agreed on the need for regional and local governments to become firmly responsible for their public spending and to fight tax evasion. Likewise, almost all agree on the need to adopt a caring, cooperative federalism model in which every regional and local government must have sufficient resources to guarantee essential public services, without discrimination among the various areas of the country.

Implementation of the fiscal federalism will take several years and will have to overcome considerable technical and political difficulties, aggravated by the effects of the economic and financial crisis; the crisis implies of course that additional funds are not available for facilitating the implementation of the reform. But at least on this point the way has been paved.

On other Title V provisions, too, the criticism has either disappeared or has at least died down. As for the distribution of powers between the central state and the Regions, the Northern League seems to have given up on its claim to exclusive regional legislative powers in healthcare and education in favour of its request for a rapid and consistent implementation of the fiscal federalism reform. A widespread consensus is emerging between the majority and the opposition on two amendments to article 117[20], both of which aim to downsize the legislative powers of the Regions. The first concerns a decrease in the list of sectors assigned to concurrent competences of state and Regions, by returning to the state important competences such as work safety, large transport networks, energy production and power grid, laws on communications and the professions. The second amendment, long suggested by scholars, consists in adding to the constitution a provision following the model of art. 72 of German *Grundgesetz*. It awarding to the central legislative the power to intervene in matters covered by regional legislation, where required to protect the legal or economic unity of the federal state or the equality of citizens in exercising their constitutional rights. It is well known that this supremacy clause can be found in all federal systems, either explicitly written in the constitutional law, or established by a settled interpretation of the constitutional court, so much so as to justify the conclusion that it is one of the structural elements of a federal state, and actually, one of the distinctive features of the federal system as compared to the confederal system.

The introduction of a supremacy clause would also solve the problem of "variable geometry" federalism, as envisaged in article 116, subsection 3 of the Constitution[21]. In fact, all, or almost all, are ready to accept that a certain degree of variable geometry is imposed by the marked differences in economic and social conditions, and in cultural political and administrative traditions that characterise Italy. However some fear that this provision could con-

20 These are the same corrections that, in autumn 2000, the Senate wanted to make to the Title V reform approved on first reading by the Chamber of Deputies. However, any amendment would have forced a return of the text before Parliament and it would therefore have been impossible to approve the law before the end of the legislature. Therefore the Senate was forced to give up.

21 Under article 116, final subsection, individual Regions could obtain by "law approved by the absolute majority of members of the Chambers" … "further forms and special conditions of autonomy" and in particular exclusive legislative powers in sectors assigned under article 117 to concurrent responsibility of State and Regions (including health, energy, infrastructures, research and local government), in addition to matters concerning education and environmental protection.

stitute a kind of Trojan horse to demolish the unity of the Republic and the very principles of cooperative federalism. The introduction of the supremacy clause would give national Parliament the necessary powers to intervene to protect general and national interests, in sectors that the constitution fully or exclusively assign to regional legislation (and therefore also in sectors assigned to the competence of a single region, under article 116, subsection 3).

Nevertheless, we cannot underestimate the fact that, in federal systems, the supremacy clause is mostly accompanied by suitable guarantees to prevent its misuse by federal institutions – in other words to avoid its power being used as a means to squash regional autonomy as recognised under the constitution. For this reason, the supremacy clause envisaged in article 72 *Grundgesetz* of the Federal Republic of Germany is balanced by the *Bundesrat's* participation in the approval of the federal laws issued to protect the legal and economic unity or to guarantee equivalent living conditions across the entire federal territory.

The addition of a supremacy clause to the Italian constitution should therefore go together with a reform of the Senate, in order to make this Chamber representative of the Regions (or, more likely, of the whole system of local authorities). On this point there seem to be a total consensus at least on the principles. In practice, the solutions differ, wavering between various models: the US Senate, the German *Bundesrat*, the French Senate or a combination of these different models.

Thus, the reform of Title V is therefore far from complete. The transition from the old constitutional organisation to the new will be lengthy and difficult.

Decentralisation and Territorial Reforms in France: How Constitutional Constraints impact Strategies for Reform

Patrick Le Lidec

1. Introduction

The debate on the right balance to strikc between constitutional rigidity and flexibility and on how to organise relations in multilevel systems has become a problem for governments and a major object for academic research in federal states. One of the common beliefs in federal countries is that unitary states have chosen to be constitutionally less stable but more flexible in exchange for a lesser protection of minority rights or of certain territorial interests. Unitary states are supposed to be gifted with more resilient constitutional structures which in turn favour their capacity to adapt to change. The analysis of the French case provides an interesting opportunity to discuss the long term effect of binding strategies through constitutionalisation (Elster, 1995), by which actors, at a given time, build institutional arrangements with the purpose of shielding certain aspects of government from democratic change.

In fact, contrary to appearances, France is confronted with constitutional blockages (not necessarily perceived or debated as such) which seriously handicap the modernisation of the territorial organisation and the vertical sharing out of responsibilities. The French case confirms that the capacity to adapt to change does not necessarily reduplicate the usual dichotomy between unitary and federal states, underlining the need to go beyond such a rigid perception of the way systems work (Baldi, 1999). France is probably still viewed abroad as a very unitary system and a centralised country with an impotent parliament and a strong executive which can change things at will, alter the sharing out of competencies, reshuffle financial resources between the various levels of authority, even do away with an entire category of local government. That reputation is partly true and partly false. Considered as a so-called unitary system, the French centre is in fact more constrained by local governments than commonly imagined. In fact, even if we leave aside paraconstitutional variables (which are of great importance within the French system) and focus on the constitutional variables, the French reality appears to be mixed: very flexible and pliable in places, very rigid in others.

On one hand, the constitution vertically seems very flexible and the distribution of power between state and sub-national authorities is quite easy to change. The article 72 of the constitution stipulates that "In the conditions provided for by statute, local communities shall be self-governing through elected councils and shall have power to make regulations for matters coming within their jurisdiction", thus giving actors a good amount of leeway to change the vertical distribution of power by changing the ordinary law and enhancing their capacity to adapt to changing political circumstances and environments. The changeover from a very centralised France in the 1960s to decentralisation in the 1980s – *e.g.* the laws of 1982 which apportioned greater resources, power and legitimacy to all tiers of sub-national government – took place without a single word of the constitution being changed. Thwarted by the impossibility to change the constitution, the Socialist governments in the early 1980s (between 1982 and 1986) resorted to 33 pieces of ordinary legislation to decentralise France.

On the other hand, the horizontal architecture and balance of powers at a local level are extremely rigid and difficult to modify. The constitution contains an explicit list of the existing categories of territorial communities so that eliminating one was hardly possible without modifying the text. That horizontal rigidity may explain why France has retained an extraordinary patchwork of municipalities many of which are tiny: nearly 40% of all the municipalities in the European Union are in France alone, a serious drawback that prevents decentralisation from progressing there. Contrary to a large number of European countries who went on to merge municipalities and rationalise their territorial architecture, France has not managed to do so. The horizontal architecture of local authorities and the ways they relate to each other are very difficult to change. The original constitutional design of 1958 is in fact much more restrictive than is usually imagined.

That horizontal constitutional rigidity appears closely linked to the constitutional veto detained by the Senate. While the Senate readily poses (and is perceived) as the champion of decentralisation and the representative of grass-roots organisations, I argue that it has become the main hurdle in the way of modernising local government and a stumbling block in the way of decentralisation. Though it is obviously not the only element to be taken into consideration[1], the place occupied by the Senate within the French constitutional framework is particularly inhospitable to large-scale decentralisation. To make any headway today, decentralisation would first require extensive local reforms – but these run up against the Senate veto.

---

1 When explaining the French trajectory we deliberately leave aside certain very important institutional factors such as multiple mandates, associations of local government representatives or committees of joint decision making between levels of governments. Our decision on how to expose the situation is justified by the importance we attach to a reasoning that follows the order of historical sequences. Multiple mandates developed quantitatively after the Senate was created, not before. For further analysis of the weight of multiple mandates in recent reforms, see esp. Le Lidec (2008; 2009).

One of the aims of this chapter is to contribute to the debate surrounding the evolutionary processes and dynamics of change in multilevel systems, whether they be reputed or labelled unitary or federal, by taking into account the weight of historical legacies (Benz, 2010; Broschek, 2010). Between the Jeffersonian view which tends to underline the benefits of flexibility and the Madisionian view which tends to underline the need for strong precommitments entrenched within rigid constitutional rules (Elster, 1995), we would like to argue in favour of the former in the light of the French experience.

In an attempt to account for the weight of historical legacies, this chapter underlines how constitutional choices made under given circumstances can have very (negative and unintended) long term impacts. Based on an historical-institutionalist perspective, the central thesis is that the creation of a demos-constraining Senate, originally designed to counterbalance direct universal suffrage – therefore over-representing rural communities and empowered by its constitutional veto – moulded French politics and institutions to a large extent. The political decisions made during the particular circumstances of the birth of the Third Republic were crucial and gave way to a path-dependent process. The Senate has acted as a major institutional veto point to inhibit explicit constitutional change. Therefore, over the past thirty years, constitutional changes have not been undertaken principally by implementing explicit constitutional policies; to the extent it was mastered by political actors, the result of institutional development in France has been rather to accumulate micro-changes, a series of adjustments spread out over long periods of time that ended up by transforming the French territorial framework.

In a nutshell: due to their incapacity to initiate the necessary constitutional reforms, or because they feared a second failure like the one of 1969, successive governments decided to promote constitutional evolution through limited legislative reform, sometimes followed by a constitutional amendment of validation. Such constitutional rigidity (and the failure of the unique authoritative attempt to replace it) explains why the French territorial style of reform might be considered pragmatic (Ashford, 1982). The French case thus offers an interesting opportunity to discuss the efficiency of policies of incremental change and the dynamic interplay between implicit and explicit constitutional reforms in multilevel systems.

To demonstrate my point, I shall first recall the fact that the French constitution includes a bias of territorial *status quo*: the actor who controls the formal constitutional amendment process under the Fifth Republic (in place since 1958) – *i.e.* the Senate – has absolutely no interest in favouring territorial change. To grasp the reasons why such a curious and rigid system was established in France, I argue that one must reconsider the political history of the constitution by revisiting the birth of the Third Republic. Reviewing our historical heritage allows us to visualise the architecture of the French constitution and understand the central role the Senate was supposed to fill. I argue that at a given point in time, granting the Senate the power of veto seemed reasonable to the actors in the face of the chronic constitutional instability of a country marked by repeated revolutions. The French Senate was initially conceived as a "demos-constraining" chamber and a cornerstone of constitutional stability. To guarantee it, the founders of the Third Republic invented a chamber comprised of representatives of an overwhelming majority of small townships logically renowned for their conservative leanings. By making the Senate the "grand council of French municipalities" and granting it the constitutional veto, the founders of the Third Republic won their wager, since its longevity is unsurpassed. The problem, however, is that the constitutional design which they acted upon gave way to institutional "lock-in": though clearly poorly adapted to the altered economic and social environment, the Senate has become extremely difficult to do away with. It has become a major instrument for the preservation of the territorial *status quo*, that being the only way it could assure its own survival. Its original design had structural effects on the development of French institutions, considerably hindered by the Senate's composition and constitutional prerogatives which slow down the process of territorial reform and prevent decentralisation from progressing. The failure of the unique attempt at explicit constitutional reform has led to making implicit reform the main road to change. Since the traumatic failure of 1969, explicit constitutional reforms have been undertaken and met with formal success but they only minimally altered the blueprints of the government's architecture. Significant blockages caused actors to develop a policy of incremental constitutional evolution and to enter into an era of "hidden politics" of territorial reforms, the effects of which we will finally rapidly present and discuss.

2. The rule of constitutional amendment controlled by the Senate

Under the Fifth Republic, constitutional drafting is particularly restrictive. The amendment rule is embodied in a single paragraph (§ 89) and provides for only one method of change: a constitutional law must be adopted in exactly the same terms by both chambers[2]. Formally speaking, the French bi-

2 According to paragraph 89, "the President of the Republic, on the recommendation of the Prime Minister, and Members of Parliament alike shall have the right to initiate amendments to the Constitution. A Government or a Private Member's Bill to amend the Constitution must be passed by the two Houses in identical terms. The amendment shall take effect after approval by referendum. However, a Government Bill to amend the Constitution shall not be submitted to referendum where the President of the Republic decides to submit it to Parliament convened in Congress; the Government Bill to amend the Constitution shall

cameral system looks perfectly symmetrical, since the indirectly elected upper house appears to have the same prerogatives as the assembly directly elected by the people. However, the system is asymmetrical with the balance of power leaning towards the Senate, a direct legacy from the Third Republic.[3] While the General Assembly is at permanent risk of being disbanded by the President of the Republic, the President is helpless against the Senate. Nor can any organic laws concerning the Senate be adopted without its consent.[4] These rules signify that constitutional power is largely in its hands and that it can oppose any amendment.

3. The French Senate as a "demos-constraining" chamber and cornerstone of constitutional stability: the constitutionalisation of a "rotten boroughs" compromise

In a "reactive sequence" (Mahoney, 2000: 527), the Senate was imagined as an institution to oppose constitutional change. When the Third Republic was founded, the Senate was not conceived as a chamber representing territorial interests but as a moderating or "demos-constraining" chamber (Stepan, 1999). When the French constitution was being drawn up, in reaction to the chronic instability of the revolutionary events of 1789, 1830, 1848 and 1871 which marked the political and constitutional history of 19th century France, a stabilising function was assigned to the Senate. Build on a precommitment strategy, its role was to prevent the political consequences of a new revolutionary outburst and guarantee the stability of the political regime.

During the troubled times following the fall of the Second Empire and the crushing of the revolutionary episodes of the Paris Commune (Hanson, 2010), creating the Senate was the fruit of a compromise between certain Republican and certain Monarchist leaders. Instituting the Senate was accepted in exchange for recognising the Republic. The birth of the Third Republic followed the vote of constitutional law of 24 February 1875 that created the Senate and made it the keystone of the regime. That first constitutional law established a system of checks and balances based on an overall egalitarian bicameralism: senators and deputies elected the President of the Republic and shared constitutional power. It was the prerogative of the Chamber of Depu-

---

then be approved only if it is passed by a three-fifths majority of the votes cast. The Bureau of the Congress shall be that of the National Assembly".

3 The constitutional law voted on 24 February 1875 had already created an imbalance favourable to the Senate.

4 The Senate cannot be disbanded. Any organic law concerning the Senate, either directly or indirectly, must be approved by the upper house.

ties to be first to examine and vote the budget, or to be able to impeach the President of the Republic, but the Senate enjoyed others privileges: it could for example officiate as Court of Justice to judge the President or its ministers. When the two chambers come together to form the National Assembly, the bureau shall be that of the Senate. The President of the Republic can disband the Chamber of Deputies but only with the official approval of the Senate which cannot itself be disbanded. In many respects, the Senate appears a bulwark against mayhem.

To allow it to exert its function of stabiliser effectively, the Senate was placed at the far end of the constitutional chain, safe from the eventual upheavals that might affect the majority, precisely because the Senate was devised as the central element that locks the entire constitutional edifice in place. Senators were elected for nine years and one third was renewed every three years. As a result of the original compromise, they were elected by départemental colleges, composed of one delegate from each of the 36,000 municipalities, deputies, and general and district councillors. The design of the electoral college made sure that urban zones were under-represented, by virtue of the principle that cities had always been the hotbed of previous revolutions and that they fostered the left-wing vote more than rural zones.

Although municipalities descend from the parishes of the ancient regime, using their municipal zoning as a basis for senatorial elections in no way implied the intention to turn the Senate into a chamber of representatives of subnational units. Creating a second chamber was not meant to acknowledge and protect the "rights of territorially organised groups" either, as is the case in federal countries. On the contrary, it was meant to protect the main part of the French population from the political influence of urban populations, and counteract the agitations of a minority in Paris or of a Paris threatened by revolutionary eruptions. A touch of federalism was deliberately introduced in order to dilute the principle of civic equality. Applying a system of municipal delegates was in fact an a-democratic way of steering away from the democratic "one person, one vote" principle. Given the overwhelming number of rural communities in France, using the municipal format was a practical way of setting up a conservative chamber capable of counterbalancing the chamber elected by direct universal suffrage.

The over-representation of the rural world harks back to 1875 and was not challenged by the parties left of center when they won the majority in the Senate. In 1884, they were content with bending that over-representation to their own advantage, by increasing the weight of municipalities from 500 to 3,500 inhabitants to be represented in the senatorial colleges, preventing the radical left, best embedded in the urban centres, from reaching positions of power. "Henceforth, instead of each community having just one delegate, a sliding scale was introduced in 1884, linked indirectly to the population through the size of municipal councils" (Smith, 2010: 19). The over-representation of rural citizens remained very high since senators had both a vested interest in perpetuating their own positions and the power to do so.

4. The consequence of the "demos-constraining" compromise: making a degree of municipal federalisation constitutional

That "demos-constraining" political-institutional compromise generated effects of institutional "lock-in" and set up forces or complementary institutions that have caused the compromise to be perpetuated in the long term. Doubtless it fulfilled its stabilising function[5] but it also produced unwitting consequences that were not clearly perceived.

The indirect role attributed to the municipal councils during the senatorial election in the context of a fledgling Third Republic produced effects of "increasing return" (Pierson, 2000) and largely shaped the future development of French institutions. The municipal system thus became the foundation of the institutional pyramid (with the Senate at the apex) around which French territorial development unfolded. Though it was not at all the intention of the actors of the 1875 constitutional compromise to turn France into a federation of municipalities, adopting the municipal framework as the foundation upon which to build the institution was to have far-reaching consequences. It drew France away from the ideal type of unitary state and injected a touch of federalism into its constitutional makeup. The territorial representation introduced a strong "center-constraining mechanism" (Baldi, 1999) within the French unitary polity.[6] It had another unintentional consequence: that of congealing the municipal map of France. When, after the Second World War pressures were brought to bear to merge small municipalities in order to adjust the French territory to the developing welfare state, France was incapable of adapting her institutions, while modernisation was ongoing in most of the other Western countries. The incapacity to modernise the French territorial system and its impossibility of launching a massive consolidation of small towns – which would have permitted attaining the critical mass required to manage the local public services then in full swing – led the French state to develop its own decentralised, territorial network in order to compensate for the shortcomings of the local authorities.

---

5 According to Steven Hanson (2010), "the fact that the Third Republic managed to maintain genuinely democratic institutions for seven decades seems a nearly miraculous achievement".

6 This element was compounded with a second "center-constraining mechanism", i.e. multiple mandates.

5. The Senate as an agency to preserve the territorial *status quo*

A new territorial model could have emerged in 1946, after the external shock caused by the Second World War. In 1946, the Constitutional Assembly was dominated by three forces: the Communist party, the Socialist party and a Centre-Left catholic party called MRP. Communists and Socialists worked together to adopt a unicameral constitution and to abolish the Senate. They also shared the intention to decentralise France and to create a special status for cities. The MRP opposed these projects and saved the upper house. Born from a compromise between these opposite tendencies, the constitution of the Forth Republic first considerably weakened the Senate and renamed it the *Conseil de la République*. Later, the fall of the Iron Curtain and the breaking of the communist-socialist alliance in 1947 helped the second Chamber to regain some of its prerogatives under the Forth Republic. Despite certain vicissitudes linked to external shocks (WWII, the Algerian war) which caused the collapse of the Third and the Fourth Republics, the Senate largely recuperated its initial form and prerogatives in 1958. In 1958, the fear of Communism and its strength mainly in large urban centres favoured the "demos-constraining model". In order to camouflage and justify a dubious choice, Article 24 of the Constitution of the Fifth Republic specifies that "the Senate shall be elected by indirect suffrage. The Senate shall ensure the representation of the territorial communities of the Republic".[7] Though the inherited network of townships was denounced by General De Gaulle's collaborators as being a management freak (Le Lidec, 2001), it was nevertheless used as the basis on which to once again lay the foundations for the Senate in 1958. "Three elements in the Senators' electoral system combine to warp the indirect suffrage system into a distorting mirror for the electorate that gives rural areas too much importance: the overwhelming preponderance of the French "communes" within the constituencies; unbalanced representation between rural and urban populations which gravely affects the sociological image of over 75% of the "*départements*"; and majority vote in the predominantly rural "*departments*" where the rural majority thus enjoys nearly total exclusiveness. Consequently this leads to a constant and one-way distortion of the Senate's political representativeness which hardly helps carry out its regulating mission and sometimes even brings about serious malfunctioning in the bicameral system. As a matter of fact, the very nature of the senatorial institu-

7 The expression is ambivalent and contradicts articles 1 and 3 of the Constitution which read "France shall be an indivisible Republic … National sovereignty shall be vested in the people, who shall exercise it through their representatives and by means of referendum. No section of the people nor any individual may arrogate to itself, or to himself, the exercise thereof".

tion should normally lead to a way of finding out a better-balanced and pluralist representation system that would ensure the right of expression for the various territorial, sociological and political parties and be better fitted to the specific function of the Senate while maintaining its most distinctive feature, i.e. the particular bond that exists between the Senators and France's rural population" (Grangé, 1997).

Despite minor changes since 1958, the Senate is still elected by a college in which 96% are municipal councillors or their delegates (Grangé, 1990). Mal-apportionment has given centre and right-wing senators a permanent majority and until 2011 prevented the left from winning a majority in the Senate. This electoral mode has created a right-wing bias, an artificial imbalance amounting to a difference of from 10 to 20 points between the results of senatorial and general elections.

The rule has created considerable political disparities and motivated those who benefit from them to forcefully defend them. When functional reasons (political stability) for preserving the system disappeared, bringing along the need to encourage urban development and merge small towns so as to enlarge the size of sub-national units, it became very difficult to do so because it would have modified the distribution of power entrenched within the Constitution. Though the system of 36,000 municipalities has proved dysfunctional, a large coalition of actors driven by senators up for re-election still has a vested interest in safeguarding it. They have taken advantage of their constitutional veto to block constitutional reforms that would allow modernising the territorial system and have used the ordinary legislative channels to delay change. In order to protect their own existence and prerogatives, Senators have made it their business to maintain the territorial structure of 36,000 communes and 100 *départements* against all attempts at reform. Since they find no electoral advantage in promoting territorial change, they are content with adaptations that are only peripheral and best protect the base of their own power. Such electoral concerns have heavily impacted the roads to decentralisation France has chosen to follow and the gamut of reforms undertaken. That unique institutional design, along with the Senate's capacity for obstruction explains France's particular style of territorial reform.

6. The importance of a very costly precedent: the failed 1969 referendum

The only major effort to eliminate the Senate and reform the constitution was undertaken by Charles De Gaulle in 1969. He used what along with Arthur Benz (Benz, 2008: 4) one might term a revolutionary procedure. As he had already done in 1962, De Gaulle disregarded the constitutional amendment procedure codified by Paragraph 89 of the Constitution which provides that "a bill to amend the Constitution must be passed by the two Houses in identical terms". He considered that he could use a direct referendum procedure to impose a constitutional change, bypassing the constitutional veto power of each chamber, and especially that of the Senate.[8] The use of such a procedure could at least be considered as highly controversial, since it did not follow the formal requirements of the Constitution, the Constitutional Council having expressed misgivings regarding the means of the reform in 1962. Nevertheless, using a revolutionary procedure was the only way to overcome the constitutional veto of the Senate. The Senate would have never agreed a government bill aiming at abolishing itself. Aside from the fact that it was rejected by a small majority, presenting the referendum as an attempt to launch a process of decentralisation and regionalisation was problematic, because De Gaulle in reality had two other aims in mind: first, to use the referendum as a plebiscite for reasserting his own legitimacy after the events of May 1968 and secondly to make the upper chamber simply consultative. The failure of the referendum had a negative impact from the point of view of the procedure as well as on a more fundamental level. None of the future presidents would dare to use the referendum as a way to amend the constitution and to bypass the Senate's constitutional veto. The 1969 failure froze the constitutional status quo. Since then, explicit constitutional reforms have been ventured but the Senate's constitutional veto has strongly limited their frequency and scope.

7. Explicit but ineffective constitutional reforms

Two other formal reform attempts were aimed at changing the territorial framework but, though formally crowned with success, by and large they can be considered ineffective. The results of the first were very disappointing. The reform of 28 March 2003 aimed first of all to give constitutional backing to the way legislation had evolved over the past twenty years, thus validating the *fait accompli*. By stipulating in article 1 of the Constitution that "France shall be organised on a decentralised basis" the law constitutionalised the decentralisation carried out twenty years earlier. Some of the amendments which were passed thus entrenched former practices or principles into constitutional law. But the Senate also passed amendments directly aimed at blocking further development. To protect the municipalities and *départements* it

8 In 1962, the use of a referendum procedure had been denounced by political opponents such as Gaston Monnerville, the president of the Senate, as "a deliberate, conscious, premeditated and outrageous violation of the constitution of the Fifth Republic".

represented and oppose the regionalisation, the Senate entrenched into the Constitution the principle that precludes subordinating one sub-national level of government to the other. The Senate's influence on constitutional reform had other negative effects as well. The Senators initiated new constitutional provisions relating to the financial autonomy of local bodies whose role was to protect their own tax revenue. However, the compromise arrived at by the government had the contrary effect. Not only did the texts finally adopted do nothing to increase the fiscal autonomy of local governments and keep it from declining, they actually aggravated the situation. They also introduced new constitutional constraints which paradoxically tend to block the advance of decentralisation: by stipulating that all new transfers of competence must not further reduce the local authorities' previous ratio of fiscal autonomy (tax revenue), the 2003 reform hampers the decentralisation process. In short, the reform introduced over-regulation and produced adverse effects.

The only positive aspect of the 2003 revision is the introduction of a touch of horizontal flexibility. Henceforth, it is feasible to create territorial bodies with particular status, *sui generis* authorities that can replace, if necessary, one or several of the categories listed in the Constitution. Officially meant to explore institutional solutions for problems in the Overseas territories and Corsica, the amendment was also introduced (like a virus) to allow replacing old categories of local government (*communes* and *départements*) by new ones (*intercommunalités* and *régions*). After fifty years of layering and overlapping of tiers, it might allow vertical merging to take place. To make sure the amendment would be adopted, the Government had to promise reluctant parliamentarians (especially Senators) that constitutional law would allow only a few vertical mergers, limited in number, and would not be used to eliminate a category of local government.

The new horizontal flexibility was obtained in exchange for a new privilege for the Senate. "The constitutional reform enhanced the Senate's prerogatives by amending Article 39-2 of the Constitution to give the upper chamber first view of all legislation concerning local government, and decentralisation" (Smith, 2010: 81). The Senate made the government pay its power to veto all constitutional reform dearly for. As Tsebelis and Money have shown, granting first view to one of the houses always increases its influence on the legislation passed (Tsebelis and Money, 1997). From a procedural standpoint, the government did nothing to avoid falling hostage to the Senate and to overcome distributive conflicts. The process was the result of a "package deal", a compromise arrived at by government and Parliament (under the dominant influence of the Senators) in behind-the-scenes bargaining.

A second constitutional reform was initiated by President Sarkozy in 2008, with the explicit aim of modernising the institutions of the Fifth Republic and to even out the balance of powers between parliament and government. To avoid the senatorial veto and a text which would exclusively reflect arrangements arrived at in private conversations, a constitutional commission composed of jurists and politicians (including Senators and Deputies of both the left and the right) was set up, chaired by ex-Prime Minister Balladur and charged with suggesting reforms. It was the first constitutional commission since the Vedel Commission in 1993. To enhance its autonomy with regard to parliament and help overcome classical distributional issues the commission was urged to hold public hearings. Though it was not its explicit mission, it came forth with a series of recommendations that would thoroughly modernise the Senate and the territorial system. One of its first recommendations was that "the composition of the Senate's electoral college should more accurately reflect demographic realities". To insure the respect of equal voting rights, it also suggested "setting up an impartial procedure to re-define the electoral districts periodically (every ten years) so as to account for population shifts". To loosen up constitutional proceedings, the Commission also suggested instituting a "referendum upon popular demand, *i.e.* upon the demand of one fifth of members of Parliament and one tenth of registered voters". It also proposed abolishing the Senate's right to veto in constitutional matters and replacing it by an automatic recourse to a referendum so that disagreements between the two houses would be systematically resolved by the people. It also spoke up for abolishing the system of multiple mandates that systematically puts Parliamentarians in positions of conflict of interests. None of these recommendations were retained however and the renovation of the Senate fell through.

Had he wanted the general good to prevail, the President could have announced his intention to have constitutional reform approved by referendum, thus bearing down on Parliament, especially Senators, forcing them to give in and discuss matters rather than resort to their traditional blackmail. But it didn't happen. The President preferred to withdraw the propositions liable to alienate the Senate rather than risk jeopardising all of his constitutional reform. The result was that the 24th reform of the Constitution adopted on 23 July 2008 did not solve any problems. Creating a "loosely coupled arena" in charge of constitutional negotiations was not sufficient for change to take place. The procedure didn't prevent Senators from successfully defending their own interests. Overcoming distributive logics for the benefit of the general good supposes political commitment and risk-taking.

8. Incremental constitutional evolution and the hidden agenda of territorial reforms

To overcome the deadlock of constitutional reforms due to the Senate veto, each of the French governments has decided to promote institutional change through ordinary legislation, what Benz calls "evolution". Important changes have in fact come about since the beginning of the 1970's without modifying the written Constitution, particularly in the case of local government reform. An explicit constitutional reform would have been far too costly. A good number of legal changes were accomplished by addition rather than subtraction. Instead of trying to do away with time-worn, inherited institutions, the strategy known as "layering" (Hacker, 2004; Mahoney and Thelen, 2010) consisted in creating new institutions, in the secret hope they would someday replace the old. Instead of dismantling the old structures that framed senatorial elections, a new layer of intermunicipal and regional government was created and gradually evolved over the past thirty years.

Faced with the Senate's reluctance to merge the 36,650 municipalities, central governments have preferred to drain them gradually and transfer their competences and resources to intermunicipal governments. For such a change to succeed and in order to minimise the political price to pay, the governments have applied two strategies: obfuscation and compensation (Pierson, 1994: 19-24). The obscuring strategy meant concealing the real objectives and stretching the progress of intermunicipalities out over a lengthy period. Spreading the consequences of the reform over long periods of time made it possible to overcome the resistance of mayors and Senators. At the same time, in order to surmount opposition, the central government injected more money to buy consensus and the good will of mayors and Senators. Creating intermunicipal governments without at the same time eliminating municipalities also allowed for an increase in the number of positions of power to hand out. In this way, central governments have advanced little by little, the rhythm being stepped up by the laws of 1992 and 1999. The number of intermunicipalities rose from 104 in 1972 to 1,577 in 1998, levelling off at 2,599 in 2011.

The success of intercommunality has thus grown out of a profoundly ambiguous situation: locally elected officers and Senators saw it as a primary means of preserving small towns in the face of a changing environment while the central government saw it as a way to prepare their future demise. The central government is counting on the fact that, by carrying out incremental intermunicipal reforms thanks to a multiplication of legal measures, the reforms will end up by becoming constitutional, a major, explicitly acknowledged and therefore legitimate change (Le Lidec, 2009).

A quite different though relatively comparable strategy was used to endorse regions to the detriment of *départements*. Regions were first created in 1972 in the minor form of public entities with extremely limited powers and little autonomy. In 1982, they were upgraded, becoming fully fledged local authorities – regional councils are directly elected by the people. But the old system resisted successfully. Article 59 of the law of 2 March 1982 restricts the regions' sphere of competence by specifying that they must "respect the integrity, autonomy and attributions of the Départements and Municipalities". An electoral rule which considerably penalised the regions was also adopted, the regional councillors being elected in *départemental* constituencies by full proportional representation, with a very low barrier of 5% threshold to obtain a seat. Using *départements* as the electoral constituencies weakened the regional character of the elections and maintained *départements* as the main level of identification and the favourite road for politicians to parliament. The use of the proportional representation rule with a very low threshold made it very difficult to build majorities within regional assemblies. Very often presidents of regional councils lacked working majorities. Such an electoral rule also made regional careers more risky than the départemental ones. Départemental careers were considered much safer by politicians: the single member district system used for the départemental elections within very small electoral districts (the cantons), helped them to develop a personal vote and to secure their careers.

Despite such initial limitations, all the governments have tried to strengthen the regions by transferring to them an increasing number of competences and resources. In 2003 regions were granted constitutional status. The regional electoral law was also reformed in order to strengthen the regional executive and to build strong regional working majorities.

The result of the layering policy is a very complex territorial system. As a consequence, the French sub-national system is composed of four tiers of government, none of which detains exclusive prerogatives or fiscal bases. Their complex interrelations are not organised according to any clear-cut hierarchy: on the contrary, they are supposedly on an equal footing and governed by the constitutional principle (introduced by the Senate) that no local government may exercise hierarchical authority over another. Over-administered and under-regulated, such a system of local government implies high transactional costs and lengthy procedures (Le Lidec, 2005).

Nevertheless, from the middle of the years 2000, in a mounting context of budgetary restrictions and ever-growing public deficits, the overhead expenses generated by the four-level system increased the pressure to overhaul the territorial organisation from top to bottom. Official reports repeatedly reiterated the need to make the best of the accumulation of incremental changes since 1969 and speed up territorial reforms so as to insure the changeover towards a different system in which regions and intermunicipalities would become the principal protagonists (Le Lidec, 2009). The Commission chaired by former Prime Minister Balladur was supposed to prepare a territorial "big bang" thanks to a strategy of constitutional erosion. It came forth with a radical proposal consisting in setting up, within the highly populated cities, eleven *sui generis* metropolitan governments, called "*Métropoles*" that would organise a vertical merger and replace the municipalities, intermunicipalities and *départements*. The idea was to take advantage of the new horizontal flexibility included in the 2003 constitutional revision and use the *Métropoles* as a virus to swallow up the old local authorities. But the Senate surgically amended the government's project, reduced its impact and managed to preserve the integrity of the old local authorities' senatorial electoral college. Under the influence of the Senate, the *Métropoles* failed to be transformed into territorial authorities and remained ordinary intermunicipal public entities. The law of 16 December 2010 is thus a compromise that hardly lives up to the ambitions of the "big bang" advocated by the Balladur Commission. It provides that all municipalities must be included in an intermunicipality by the year 2014 and that intermunicipal councils be elected by direct universal suffrage. The ultimate objective of the entrepreneurs of change remains to use the ambiguity inherent to institutions to prepare a conversion (Mahoney and Thelen, 2010) of intermunicipal governments into supra-municipal governments.

The law also ventures to merge *départements* and regions without prior modification of the constitution by amalgamating their elected representatives: by 2014, regional and départemental councils are to be made up of the same councillors. The government's strategy was to blend *départements* and regions through normal legislation, wagering that once the merging of regional and départemental representatives would become a *fait accompli*, the Senate will end up agreeing to ratify the change and make it legitimate through explicit constitutional reform. As Minister Xavier Bertrand admitted, once the law being passed, in order to abolish the *départements* "we would have had to modify the constitution, it would have been mandatory to have a 3/5 majority in Parliament ...we'd never have made it... The simplest and most intelligent solution was actually to amalgamate the elected representatives of each"[9]. Erosion (Benz, 2008: 4) has been applied here by entrepreneurial agents as the main method to bring about constitutional change. As one law professor put it, having "départemental and regional affairs managed by a single category of elected personnel – territorial councillors – isn't that a rather fictitious way of preserving two moral entities, in other words a procedure that could be termed anti-constitutional?" (Chavrier, 2009). The Constitutional Council decided to approve such erosion, probably considering that it was the only way to surmount the constitutional barrier ahead on the road to the modernisation of the French territorial model.

9. The persistently ambiguous effects of the hidden agenda of territorial reforms

Whether such a layering strategy – based on a wager and part of a "hidden politics" (Hacker, 2004) of territorial reform – has been a success or not, still

9 Acteurs Publics, février 2010, p. 80.

remains at this stage an open question since its effects must be assessed over the long term. One can nevertheless recall that the layering strategy was not conceived as an end in itself but as a transitional way to counteract the Senate veto. It is clear that institutional entrepreneurs who sought to reduce the number of territorial layers after having rescaled them, have not yet met with success. For the moment, the outcome of such a strategy remains unclear or mixed. It may well be that this result will finally come to pass in the long run.

On one hand, there is no doubt that the "domestic institutional adaptation" through layering has been a formal success. Crucial institutional changes have taken place over the past three decades, despite the overall stability of the formal constitutional framework. The development of regions and the generalisation of intermunicipal governments, which will cover all of France in 2014, have profoundly altered the ancient territorial meshing. Certain observers feel that such a strategy of gradual reapportionment of power to the benefit of intermunicipal and regional governments has been successful, that the loyalty of major political actors to municipal and départemental echelons has considerably waned.[10]

In the same vein, we must also observe that with the recent regionalisation of state services, pressures to destabilise the former system have become more insistent. The reforms of 2004 and 2010 considerably upset the balance of power within state territorial networks: the regional level has become stronger to the detriment of the départemental level and regional prefects have finally become the hierarchical superiors of *département* prefects (Bezes and Le Lidec, 2010: 940). The imbalance between the state framework which gives priority to the regional level and the electoral framework still structured by sub-départemental constituencies such as the canton and the municipality, creates an asymmetry in favour of the state. The regionalisation of state services should thus bring yet more pressure to bear on regionalising the system of local authorities in the years to come.

These changes might give the impression that the modernisation process will soon generate constitutional feedback. According to the reasoning of "entrepreneurial agents", the accumulation of incremental changes already in place, combined with a deepening of budgetary restrictions, may end up by creating an effect of numbers by 2020 and swing into another system in which intermunicipal governments and regions would become the more powerful levels. That scenario would mean bottom-up changes and have a boomerang effect on the Senate.

On the other hand, the change is much less striking if one considers the evolution of styles of governing, electoral rules or policy outcomes. One of the objectives of layering was to change the mechanisms of the aggregation of interests by increasing the size of municipalities and break with the "traditional

10 Fifty Senators out of 343 henceforth preside intermunicipal governments.

pattern" of allocating public resources based on the sprinkling of credits and pork barrelling. However, for the moment, these objectives have not been met. To make it short, changes have been more quantitative than qualitative (Le Lidec, 2008: 263-268). Institutions inherited from the past like a system composed of mayors, general councillors and Senators have resisted well and partly managed to filter the strong pressures of the environment in favour of institutional change. Rather than doting new institutions with new mechanisms of aggregation of interests, "status-quo defending actors" have managed to build the new institutions upon the old electoral rules, which has also allowed them to colonise them. Creating two new institutional levels has not overturned the pattern of political careers or the local distribution of power; politically regions and intermunicipalities remain largely controlled by départemental and municipal elites. Intermunicipal councils reproduce the system of under-representation of the urban populations and remain to a large extend under mayors' control. The mandate of départemental councillor remains a focal point of the local political system and the main access to Parliament. In the Senate, the presidents of départmental councils are still seven and a half times more numerous than the presidents of regional councils (30 *vs.* 4).

The new institutional layers have not transformed the formal constitutional framework all that much and have failed yet to generate formal constitutional feedback. The Senate has resisted well and remains as it was. This evolution illustrates the strength of path-dependence and the difficulty to part with a historical institutional arrangement in the absence of an external shock.

Such a mixed picture globally fits in with the "gradual institutional change" theory (Mahoney and Thelen, 2010) in the sense that the reforms actually implemented combine both elements of change and a large measure of inertia. The answer to the question whether the layering strategy has been a failure or success depends on the time scale applied and the post of observation (Benz, 2010: 13). Even if it is not possible to give a precise or detailed estimate here, we may at least stress that layering has driven up the number of civil servants, increased the public debt and deficits while at the same time considerably enfeebled accountability within the political system. Nevertheless, such a modality of change by ripple effects has by now been theorised by those in charge as being the only way to reform the French territorial system. Confronted by the great number of veto points and by the difficulty to accept the "transaction costs of path change" outright, they practice institutional reform as if it were a game of billiards with voluntary ripple effects. Changing the French territorial system thus proceeds by a series of destabilising fits and starts that have reciprocal consequences. As Hacker (2004: 246) puts it, "instead of single-use tools, institutions are usually versatile multitaskers, and this versatility is itself a crucial variable shaping the strategies of actors who wish to change them".

10. Conclusion

All in all, the French experience confirms that in case of explicit constitutional obstruction, an implicit road to constitutional change does in fact exist. By necessity for some, by choice for others, French leaders have since 1969 taken the way of a slow and silent evolution, thinking they might in the end, through a policy of incremental change, place the Senate before the *fait accompli* and force it to capitulate. It may be too soon to tell if they are right or wrong. The failure of the constitutional revolution attempted in 1969 was partly compensated by an evolution but without going the whole way and the cost may already be considered exorbitant. One might well think that evolution is only a lesser evil or an escape at great expense to the national community. It implies a transition, potentially a very long transition, during which citizens will have to make do with a very confusing institutional setting and much inconvenience.[11]

References

Ashford, Douglas (1982): British Dogmatism and French Pragmatism. Central-Local Policy-Making in the Welfare State. London: Macmillan.

Baldi, Brunetta (1999): Beyond the Federal-Unitary Dichotomy. Working paper. Institute of Governmental Studies: University of California, Berkeley.

Bezes, Philippe/Le Lidec, Patrick (2010): L'hybridation du modèle territorial français. RGPP et réorganisations de l'Etat territorial. In: Revue française d'administration publique 136, 919-942.

Benz, Arthur (2008a): Unsuccessful reform and successful non reform – constitutional policy in Germany and Canada. Paper presented at the conference "Die Verfassung der Demokratien", 21-23 November 2008, Osnabrück.

Benz, Arthur (2008b): From Joint-decision Traps to Over-regulated Federalism – Adverse Effects of a Successful Constitutional Reform. In: German Politics 17, (4), 440-456.

Benz, Arthur (2010): Reform, adjustment and historical evolution. Understanding dynamics of federal systems. 82nd annual conference of CPSA.

Broschek, Jörg (2010): Federalism and Political Change: Canada and Germany in Historical-Institutionalist Perspective. In: Canadian Journal of Political Science 43, (1), 1-24.

Chavrier, Geraldine (2009): Les conseillers territoriaux: questions sur la constitutionnalité d'une creation inspirée par la Nouvelle-Caldéonie. In: Actualité Juridique Droit Administratif, 21 décembre, 2380-2384.

Elster, Jon (1995): Forces and Mechanisms in the Constitution-Making Process. In: Duke Law Journal 45, (2), 364-396.

11 A great help in translation has been provided by Gabrielle Varro.

Grangé, Jean (1997): Le poids des campagnes au Sénat. Effets et problèmes de la surreprésentation rurale. In: Economie rurale 237, 22-26.

Grangé, Jean (1990): Les déformations de la représentation des collectivités territoriales et de la population au Sénat. In: Revue française de science politique 40, (1), 5-45.

Hacker, Jacob S. (2004): Privatising Risk without Privatising the Welfare State: The Hidden Politics of Social Policy Retrenchment in the United States. In: American Political Science Review 98, (2), 243-260.

Hanson, Stephen E. (2010): The Founding of the French Third Republic. In: Comparative Political Studies 43, (8-9), 1023-1058.

Le Lidec, Patrick (2008): La réforme des institutions locales. In: Borraz, O./Guiraudon, V. (eds.): Politiques publiques 1. La France dans la gouvernance européenne. Paris: Presses de Sciences po.

Le Lidec, Patrick (2009): Réformer sous contraintes d'injonctions contradictoires: l'exemple du Comité Balladur sur la réforme des collectivités locales. In: Revue Française d'Administration Publique 131, 477- 496.

Le Lidec, Patrick (2005): La relance de la décentralisation en France. In: Politiques et Management Public 3, 101-125.

Money, Jeannette/Tsebelis, George (1997): Bicameralism. Cambridge: Cambridge University Press.

Mahoney, James (2000): Path Dependence in Historical Sociology. In: Theory and Society 29, (4), 507-548.

Mahoney, James/Thelen, Kathleen (2010): A Theory of Gradual Institutional Change. In: Mahoney, J./Thelen, K. (eds.): Explaining Institutional Change. Ambiguity, Agency, and Power. Cambridge: Cambridge University Press, 1-37.

Pierson, Paul (1994): Dismantling the Welfare State? Reagan, Thatcher, and the Politics of Retrenchment. Cambridge: Cambridge University Press.

Pierson, Paul (2000): Increasing Returns, Path Dependence, and the Study of Politcs. In: American Political Science Review 94, (2), 251-267.

Smith, Paul (2009): The Senate of the Fifth French Republic. Basingstoke: Palgrave Macmillan.

Stepan, Alfred C. (1999): Federalism and Democracy: Beyond the U.S. Model. In: Journal of Democracy 10, (4), 19-34.

5. Processes of Ratification

Constitutional Amendment Rules in Federal and Unitary States

Markus Kaltenborn

1. Introduction

There can be different reasons for amending the rules or sets of rules contained in a constitution. Besides the particular problems inherent in each legal system, developments at the international or supranational level often induce the constitutional reform process, for example, most notably, with respect to European constitutional law and the compliance with EU or EC laws.

Additionally, the accelerated globalisation of economic relationships exerts pressure on national constitutional law. Increasingly, states – and their legal systems – are competing for investments, tax revenue and jobs. The constitution as a cornerstone of each legal system and its ability to adapt and to efficiently fulfil state responsibilities is seen as a factor in this competition. Whether it aims at overcoming budgetary problems, the efforts of "young" democracies to strengthen the rule of law in their countries, the fight against unemployment, or the expansion or restructuring of the social security system – each of these political reform projects requires effective decision-making processes. Frequently, constitutional amendments (or even major constitutional reforms) are seen as necessary in order to support policy reforms or to make them possible at all. Recent examples of this include the reforms of German federalism (Häde 2006, 2010; Ipsen, 2006; Meyer, 2008) and the second constitutional reform in Italy – defeated in a referendum in 2006 though (Panizza, 2006). According to the driving political powers behind these reforms, constitutional amendments are supposed to render decision-making more efficient by reorganising the current allocation of powers between a central government and its constituent units, or between individual constitutional bodies.

By and large, governments and legislative bodies seem to be equally affected by the political pressure exercised by impulses from Europeanisation and globalisation. To what degree, however, the specific legal systems are adequately prepared, depends on their respective constitutional frameworks, which vary significantly between individual states. This applies not least to the rules of constitutional amendment: The provisions relating to the responsibilities and powers of actors and those guiding procedures of constitutional reform processes – including smaller modifications to the constitutional wording – clearly differ from one country to another. The differences become evident not only regarding the formal decision rules but also regarding the substantial restrictions on constitutional amendments. Below are a few examples of constitutional amendment rules that reflect the different legal requirements (Wieser, 2005: 85-97; Masing, 2005; Weber, 2010, 45-61; see also Häberle, 1998: 267-282; Moderne, 2006). It is clear that federal states, when compared to centralised states, have specific rules, but that these are set in a variety of ways.

2. Right to initiate constitutional amendments

An important, formal feature is the right to initiate amendments. The procedure to introduce a constitutional amendment reveals which constitutional body has the right to initiate an amendment. The constitutional amendment process can only start if the constitutional body in this key position is convinced that a constitutional provision requires an amendment. Indeed, in the process of negotiation and decision-making, other bodies may feel entitled to take part and, therefore, influence the new constitutional provision to be elaborated. However, the content of the constitutional change will be dictated in large extent by the intention of the initiating constitutional body.

Even when comparisons are made at this level, the diversity of the various constitutional laws is obvious: The right to initiate a constitutional amendment often is assigned to the members of parliament or to one specific parliamentary chamber along with various qualifications of majority rules (Wieser, 2005: 91). In some countries (e.g. Austria, Spain and Russia), the government has the right to introduce a constitutional amendment procedure. In other countries, this right is awarded to the president (e.g. Poland, also France, with some restrictions). Furthermore, in some European monarchies, the king or queen is entitled to take part in the constitutional amendment initiative (e.g. Belgium and the Netherlands). In Switzerland and Austria, the people can also initiate a constitutional amendment if they are able to prepare a proposal supported by a specific number of voters.

In federal states, in general, only federal bodies may initiate a constitutional amendment. Exceptions exist where the federal constitution grants regional bodies the right not to comply with federal regulations. For example, the Spanish constitution allows autonomous communities to propose a constitutional amendment (Art. 166 and Art. 87 II of the Constitution of the Kingdom of Spain). Otherwise, constituent states can only initiate an amendment of their own constitution and must, in the process, take the framework of the federal constitution into consideration.

3. Majority requirements and other stabilising methods

The continued existence of the current constitutional law is protected first and foremost by the fact that an amendment of its provisions must always be supported by a broad consensus. The restrictions for the political majority within the constitutionally instituted representative bodies are stricter than in the ordinary legislative process. The old order is privileged in a way by the right of the minority to veto changes (Masing, 2005: 4). To some extent, the constitution also provides for a quorum, for example, in Belgium, Austria and Germany.

But in specific instances, there are also exceptions to the requirement of a qualified majority. According to Art. 89 of the French constitution, a draft amendment or proposal must be passed by both chambers and, following this, adopted through a national referendum. A qualified majority among the participating constitutional bodies is only required if the constitutional amendment is put before Parliament by a decision of the President. In this case no national referendum is held, but the draft must receive a majority of at least three fifth of the votes cast (regarding the constitutional amendment process in France, see Favoreu et al., 2009: 686, 772-784; Gicquel and Gicquel, 2008: 180-183). In principle, qualified majorities are not required to amend the constitution in Italy, either. However, Art. 138 of the constitution provides for a national referendum based on the initiative of members of the legislative bodies, or voters. Such a referendum is not allowed if the amendment law has been adopted by more than two thirds of the members of each chamber (Modugno, 2008; Amirante, 2007: 311-313; Carmeli, 2001: 136-138). In the US, an official amendment of the American federal constitution requires the approval of three fourth of the states (Art. V of the Constitution of the United States of America). This high legal hurdle in the official amendment process explains the particular weight given to the jurisprudence of the Supreme Court in the "upgrading" of constitutional law in the US (Quint, 1986: 620-621; Brugger, 2002: 26, 183; Masing, 2005: 6; Vile, 1994: 35-54; von Hoff, 2008; for a critique of the role assigned to Congress in the amendment process, see Dellinger, 1983; Tribe, 1983; regarding the Supreme Court jurisprudence with respect to Art. V of the constitution, see Paulsen, 1993).

Aside from these special majority requirements, there are other stabilising methods that relate to the constitutional amendment process. In Europe, one striking example is to be found in a country that has a non-federal constitution: In Greece, to protect the constitution against amendments made in rapid succession and the related risk of destabilising the political system, new amendments are not allowed during the five years following the adoption of the most recent amendment (Art. 110 VI of the Constitution of the Greek Republic). In addition, the resolution to amend the constitution must be voted on repeatedly by the respective constitutional bodies with a specific period of time having to be passed between the votes. A comparable requirement exists in Italian constitutional law (Art. 138 of the Italian constitution). This particular method helps to make decision-making bodies cautious against making decisions too hasty.

In federal systems that have two legislative chambers, both are generally involved in the decision to amend the constitution. The crucial prerequisite for a constitutional amendment is usually the consent of both chambers, either with an absolute majority (e.g. Spain, Australia and India), or a qualified majority (e.g. Germany, Belgium, Austria, USA, Argentina and Brazil, in case of a complete revision also Spain). Moreover, in some countries (e.g. USA, Canada, Russia and India) the consent of the state or provincial legislatures is required in specific instances.

4. Instruments to reinforce legitimacy

The different rights to initiate and the majority requirements already offer an impressive image of the diverse legal systems when it comes to such a politically significant instrument as a constitutional amendment. Beyond that, the legal situation becomes completely heterogeneous if the instruments provided by constitutional legislators to legitimise each amendment procedure are considered, too (Wieser, 2005: 91-96; Masing, 2005: 7-10). For example, the above mentioned method of repeated votes on an intended constitutional amendment can be used not only to tie the amendment closer to existing constitutional law, but also to reinforce democratic legitimacy. In the Netherlands (Art. 137 I, III, IV of the Constitution of the Kingdom of the Netherlands; see also Kortmann 2008: 101-104; Van der Pot 2006: 196-200) and in Belgium (Art. 195 II-IV of the Belgian Constitution; also Van Damme, 2008: 61-68; Mercier, 2004; Delperée, 2000: 79-85, 2003), the dissolution of one or even both chambers is mandatory following the first debate of a constitutional amendment. After (as in the Netherlands) the second chamber has been re-elected, or after (as in Belgium) the two new chambers have convened, the resolution is finally passed by the new representative bodies. In Spain, a comparable procedure exists to completely or partially amend the constitution with respect to basic rights, the rights of the crown and significant constitutional principles (Art. 168 I, II, Constitution of the Kingdom of Spain; regarding the Spanish constitutional reform process Aragon Reyes, 2009: 201-212; Ruiz Robledo, 2006: 64-72, 277; von Kuhlberg, 2000: 27-71; de Vega, 1993; regarding, in particular, the constitutional commitment of the integration power according to Art. 93 of the Spanish constitution, see Fischer 1999: 243-253). Greece's legal situation is similar: In accordance with Art. 110 III of the Constitution of the Greek Republic, only a newly elected Parliament can pass a resolution to amend the constitution as proposed by the previous Parliament. The election of parliament should occur in knowledge of the intended amendment as is the case in the Netherlands and Belgium. In this way, the incumbent Parliament cannot alter a constitutional provision on its own. Only the newly elected Parliament can adopt the amendment, while being barred from defining its content.

One instrument widely used to reinforce legitimacy is the appeal to the sovereign power of the people. In this way, the voters decide in a referendum on the substance of the constitution, even if the decision on "when" and "how" the referendum is initiated often remains the prerogative of Parliament (Masing, 2005: 9). In Europe, referendums are provided for in the constitutions of Austria, France, Italy, Poland, Spain and Switzerland, as well as in the still relatively new constitutions of the Baltic States. Accordingly, a referendum is held when it is demanded, as in Italy and Spain, by a specific number of the members of the legislative bodies (Art. 138 II of the Constitution of the Republic of Italy; Art 44 III 1. of the former Austrian Federal Constitutional Law; Art. 167 III of the Constitution of the Kingdom of Spain) or if, as in Poland, Austria and, once again, Spain, specific constitutional provisions are affected, or a total revision of the constitution is to be decided upon (Art. 235 VI of the Constitution of the Republic of Poland; Art. 44 III 1. of the former Federal Constitutional Law; Art. 168 III of the Constitution of the Kingdom of Spain).

In France, there are two different procedures for amending the constitution: ordinarily, a referendum is mandatory. However, should the President of the Republic decide that the amendment is supposed to follow the simplified procedure, a referendum is not required, and the National Congress decides instead with a majority of three fifth of the votes cast in a joint session (Art. 89 II and III of the Constitution of the French Republic). This second procedure is intended for minor amendments or technical revisions whose content leaves the public indifferent (Mathieu and Verpeaux, 2004: 224-225). The absence of direct legitimacy through the sovereign power of the people in this case is balanced, at least in part, by the convening of the National Congress in Versailles and the requirement of a qualified majority.

Referendums are held in federal as well as in unitary states. In federal states, the people of the constituent states are, to some extent, of particular importance. In Switzerland, for example, the constitutional amendments must be approved by the double majority at the federal level and at the canton level (Art. 140 I a, 142 II of the Federal Constitution of Switzerland). In Canada, some individual provinces provide for regional referendums to approve a change to the federal constitution. These rules merely prove the rich variety of amendment rules that exists and underline the lack of any perceived systematic differences between federal and unitary states.

5. Exclusion of core principles from amendment

Besides the formal rules that have to be taken into account when making constitutional amendments, some requirements concerning the substance of a constitution must also be considered to some extent (Weber, 2008). Barriers to a constitutional amendment prohibit changing individual constitutional provisions or a group of constitutional provisions that express, for the most part, the core principles of each constitution. They represent the strongest means of safeguarding the existing constitutional law, and they have to be distinguished from those provisions that either constrain changing a selected central constitutional rule – a typical example is the American constitution, according to which no state can be deprived of an equal voting right in the Senate without its approval (Art. V of the Constitution of the United States of America; see also Bothe, 1977: 118) – and those that determine that a change to a fundamental principle can only occur as part of a total revision of a constitution.

Exclusion of core principles can be found, for example, in the provisions contained in some European constitutions which, during times of war and crisis, completely ban any amendments (examples can be found in Art. 196 of Belgium's constitution, Art. 169 of the Constitution of the Kingdom of Spain, and Art. 89 IV of the Constitution of the French Republic). Other variations are the "guarantee of perpetuity" of Art. 79 III of the German Basic Law, according to which specific constitutional principles may not be abrogated, or the law contained in Art. 193 IV and 194 II of the Swiss federal constitution to hold inviolable the mandatory provisions of international law (Arnold, 2000). Further examples include the protection of the constitutionally enshrined rights of the king during his reign according to Art. 197 of Belgium's constitution, or the guarantee of the republican form of government in France's constitution (Art. 89 V; see also Wittekindt, 2000: 120-151) and in Italy's constitution (Art. 139). Moreover, in some states there are unwritten restrictions on the content of a constitutional amendment that must be taken into account (Wieser, 2005: 88-89; generally also Winterhoff, 2007: 175-182; regarding the legal situation in Austria, in particular, Hiesel, 2002; regarding the constitutional situation in Spain, von Kuhlberg, 2000: 79-85).

This brief overview illustrates that the type and the scope of the exclusion of particular norms from a constitutional amendment clearly vary. Moreover, not all constitutions contain such restrictions on the amendment process. Presumably their existence expresses a specific constitutional tradition of the state in question. This often applies, not least, to those safeguards which are used to preserve the federal order. However, the reasons for choosing specific guarantees of inviolability sometimes may lie elsewhere. The relatively broadly applied guarantees of the German Basic Law in the form of the "perpetuity clause", for example, do not stem from tradition, but rather from the fear of the constitutional legislators of the abolition of the democratic system by extreme political powers (for the history on its origins see Dreier, 2006: 1799-1802). In contrast, the Constitution of the Kingdom of Spain avoids the exclusion of constitutional provisions from amendment, although this country, like Germany, experienced a lot of upheaval during the previous century, including the change in the form of government. Therefore the existing political system is protected by a process of total revision which is rather complicated compared to other European constitutions (von Kuhlberg, 2000: 57-70). The dissolution of the elected representative bodies and new elections following, provided for in the case of Spain, are also provided for in the Netherlands and in Belgium. Yet only the Belgian constitution erected additional hurdles which – as mentioned earlier – declare the inviolability of the right of the king during his reign, which is not present in the constitutional laws of either the Netherlands or Spain. Therefore, specific barriers and their interaction with the demands on the constitutional amendment process are not always seen simply as a reaction to historical events or as formative elements of a particular constitutional tradition.

6. Conclusion

All in all, a comparison of constitutions shows that the right to amend a constitution exhibits a great variety of constraints and procedures. Differences can be found in the right to initiate an amendment and in the majority requirements, as well as in other procedural hurdles that must be taken into account by legislators if they wish to implement changes to the constitutional foundations of the state structure. At the same time, it could also be demonstrated that no systematic differences exist between federal and centralised states with respect to the formal rules entrenched in constitutions that govern constitutional amendments.

References

Amirante, Carlo (2007): Diritto pubblico. Torino: G. Giappichelli.

Aragón Reyes, Manuel (2009): Estudios de derecho constitucional. 2nd ed. Madrid: Centro de Estudios Políticos y Constitucionales.

Arnold, Pascal (2000): Ius cogens als materielle Schranke der Verfassungsrevision. In: Fleiner, T. et al. (eds.): Die neue schweizerische Bundesverfassung. Basel et al.: Helbing & Lichtenhahn, 53-69.

Behrendt, Christian (2003): La possible modification de la procédure de révision de la Constitution belge. In: Revue francaise de Droit Constitutionnel 54, 279-298.

Bothe, Michael (1977): Die Kompetenzstruktur des modernen Bundesstaates in rechtsvergleichender Sicht. Berlin / Heidelberg / New York: Springer.

Brugger, Winfried (2002): Demokratie, Freiheit, Gleichheit. Studien zum Verfassungsrecht der USA. Berlin: Duncker & Humblot.

Carmeli, Sara (2001): La procédure de révision dans la constitution italiènne. In: Revue de la recherche juridique – droit prospectif 2001-1, 131-139.

van Damme, Marnix (2008): Overzicht van het grondwettelijk recht. Brugge: Die Keure.

Dellinger, Walter (1983): The Legitimacy of Constitutional Change: Rethinking the Amendment Process. In: Harvard Law Review 97, 387-432.

Delpérée, Francis (ed.) (2003): La procédure de révision de la Constitution. Bruxelles: Bruylant.

Delpérée, Francis (2000): Le droit constitutionnel de la Belgique, Bruxelles: Bruylant.

Dreier, Horst (2006): Kommentierung des Art. 79 III GG. In: Dreier, H. (ed.): Grundgesetz. vol. 2. 2nd ed. Tübingen: Mohr Siebeck.

Favoreu, Louis (2009): Droit constitutionnel. 12th ed. Paris: Dalloz.

Fischer, Robert (1999): Die Offenheit des Grundgesetzes und der spanischen Verfassung für den Fortgang der europäischen Integration. Konstanz: Hartung-Gorre.

Gicquel, Jean/Gicquel, Jean-Éric (2008): Droit constitutionnel et institutions politiques. 22nd ed. Paris: Montchrestien.

Häberle, Peter (1998): Verfassungslehre als Kulturwissenschaft. 2nd ed. Berlin: Duncker & Humblot.

Häde, Ulrich (2006): Zur Föderalismusreform in Deutschland. In: Juristenzeitung (JZ) 61, (19), 930-940.

Häde, Ulrich (2010): Die Ergebnisse der zweiten Stufe der Föderalismusreform. In: Archiv des öffentlichen Rechts 135, 541-572.

Hiesel, Martin (2002): Gibt es in Österreich unabänderliches Verfassungsrecht?. In: Österreichische Juristen-Zeitung (ÖJZ) 57, 121-127.

von Hoff, Stefanie (2008): Die Rolle des US-Supreme Court im Prozess der Verfassungsänderung in den Vereinigten Staaten von Amerika. Frankfurt a.M.: Peter Lang.

Ipsen, Jörn (2006): Die Kompetenzverteilung zwischen Bund und Ländern nach der Föderalismusnovelle. In: Neue Juristische Wochenschrift 59, (39), 2801-2806.

Kortmann, Constantijn A. J. M. (2008): Constitutioneel recht. 6th ed. Deventer: Kluwer.

Kuhlberg, Alexander von (2000): Änderung und Revision der spanischen Verfassung vom 29. Dezember 1978. Frankfurt a.M.: Peter Lang.

Masing, Johannes (2005): Zwischen Kontinuität und Diskontinuität: Die Verfassungsänderung. In: Der Staat 44, (1), 1-17.

Mathieu, Bertrand/Verpeaux, Michel (2004): Droit constitutionnel. Paris: Presses Universitaires de France.

Mercier, Jacques (2004): De la révision de la Constitution. In: Verdussen, M. (ed.): La Constitution Belge: lignes & entrelignes. Bruxelles: Le Cri ed., 448-450.

Meyer, Hans (2008): Die Föderalismusreform 2006, Berlin: Duncker & Humblot.

Moderne, Franck (2006): Réviser la Constitution: analyse comparative d'un concept indéterminé. Paris: Dalloz.

Modugno, Franco (2008): Legge di revisione costituzionale e altre leggi costituzionali. In: Mangiameli, Stelio, Diritto costituzionale. Milano: Il sole-24 ore, 294-304.

Panizza, Saulle et al. (2006): La riforma della parte II della Costituzione sottoposta a referendum oppositivo. In: Il Foro Italiano 131, 117-145.

Paulsen, Michael S. (1993): A General Theory of Article V: The Constitutional Lessons of the Twenty-seventh Amendment. In: The Yale Law Journal 103, (3), 677-789.

Pot, Combertus Willem van der (2006): Handboek van het Nederlandse Staatsrecht. 15th. ed. Deventer: Kluwer.

Quint, Peter E. (1986): Amerikanisches Verfassungsrecht – ein aktueller Überblick. In: Juristenzeitung 41, (13), 619-623.

Ruiz Robledo, Agustín (2006): Compendio de derecho constitucional español. Valencia: Tirant lo Blanch.

Tribe, Laurence H. (1983): A Constitution We are Amending: In Defense of a Restrained Judicial Role. In: Harvard Law Review 97, (2), 433-445.

de Vega, Pedro (1993): Das Verfahren der Verfassungsänderung in der spanischen Rechtsordnung. In: López Pina, A. (ed.): Spanisches Verfassungsrecht. Heidelberg: Müller, 91-116.

Vile, John R. (1994): Constitutional Change in the United States. Westport: Praeger.

Weber, Albrecht (2008): Der Schutz der Verfassung durch Revisionsverbote und Notstandsregime in vergleichender Sicht. In: Fischer-Lescano, A. et al. (eds.): Frieden in Freiheit. Festschrift für Michael Bothe. Baden-Baden: Nomos, 1229-1241.

Weber, Albrecht (2010): Europäische Verfassungsvergleichung. München: Beck.

Wieser, Bernd (2005): Vergleichendes Verfassungsrecht. Wien/New York: Springer.

Winterhoff, Christian (2007): Verfassung – Verfassungsgebung – Verfassungsänderung: zur Theorie der Verfassung und der Verfassungsrechtserzeugung. Tübingen: Mohr Siebeck.

Wittekindt, Christoph (2000): Materiell-rechtliche Schranken von Verfassungsänderungen im deutschen und französischen Verfassungsrecht. Frankfurt a.M.: Peter Lang.

Constitutional Rigidity and Procedures for Ratifying Constitutional Reforms in EU Member States[1]

Carlos Closa

1. Introduction

When constitutional actors choose institutional rules, they do so following the very rational assumption that they can *predict* the future outcomes of the application of these rules. However, failures to predict the whole range of all possible outcomes seem inevitable in rational decisions, since unintended consequences seem to be co-substantial to institutional choice. Within constitutions, the design of specific rules for amendment is particularly important since it is perceived that the amendability defines the stability of the system. Leaving aside the weight of contextual factors (such as historical and cultural factors), actors will choose a procedure trying to calculate whether the rules permit to amend the constitution. This decision derives from beliefs on the necessity to protect minorities, not to bind living generations to the will of passed ones, etc.

If facts matched actors' expectations, the logical result would be that the more rigid rules will make the occurrence of amendment rarer than the more flexible ones which permit a large number of amendments. However, scholars who have tested the hypothesis on the relation between amendments and rigidity have obtained mixed results: Lutz (1994) argued that the degree of rigidity of a constitution affects the amendment rate in a cross-national analysis. Ferejohn (1997) failed to replicate Lutz's result and restored to the disaggregation of Lutz´s index and composed a category called legislative complexity (defined as the requirement of special majorities *or* separate majorities in different legislative sessions, *or* bi-cameralism) which, in his analysis is the key variable to explain amendment rate (…). Ferejohn concludes that *legislative complexity* is a good predictor of amendment rate whilst he finds that "there is no evidence that a ratification requirement, whether involving states or a popular referendum, has any significant impact on amendment

1 This research has been carried through with the support of the MICINN project *Instituciones nacionales e integración europea: la ratificación de los tratados de reforma de la UE* CSO2009-06971. Patricio Galella provided research assistance for this paper and Pablo Castillo run and revised endless statistical tests whilst Rubén Ruiz provided valuable comments. I am particularly indebted to Peter Bussjäger for his very kind assistance in identifying Austrian constitutional amendments in form of "constitutional laws".

rates" (Ferejohn, 1997: 523). Whilst he differentiated veto players from parliamentary ratification, the category "legislative complexity" is so extensive that it comprises almost all cases and hence it has only marginal discriminatory value *vis a vis* referendums or states' ratification (outside the sample selected which includes US-states). Rasch and Congleton (2006), however, found that the empirical relationship between stringency and amendment rate found by Lutz and Ferejohn is not robust. Instead, they proposed controlling the influence of veto players with the result that the number of veto players and veto points has systematically effects on the amendment rates. Amendment rates fall as the number of veto players increases and with the requirements for intervening elections and/or referenda. The requirement of supermajorities in the legislatures and the age of the constitution have no systematic effect within their sample. In contrary sense, Lorenz (2005); Roberts (2009) and similarly Anckar and Karvonen (2002) do not find strong evidence of the influence between rigidity and amendments.

This chapter tests again the hypothesis of the relation between rigidity and amendment procedures. Firstly, it presents the theoretical bases that inform the choice of amendment rules and it then proceeds to assess whether it holds empirically true that rigidity implies a minor amendment rate whilst flexibility permits a higher amendment rate.

2. Theoretical reasons for choice of amendment rules

Formal constitutional amendment is one of the mechanisms for constitutional change among others (for instance, jurisdictional interpretation). The assumption behind is that where the constitution is taken seriously, important modifications in the operation of political systems need to be reflected by the constitution. This view seems to have prevailed in the contemporary technique of constitutional design, since almost all national constitutions include articles that provide for partial or total change in their constitutions. According to the date of the Comparative Constitutions Project, more than 80% of all constitutions between 1850 and 2008 had amendment clauses.[2]

Formal constitutional change results from the interaction of three effects (Lutz, 1994): every political system needs to be modified over time; in parallel, all constitutions require regular, periodical modification, whether through amendment, judicial or legislative alteration or replacement and, more importantly, in serious constitutional systems, important modifications in the operation of political systems need to be reflected by the constitution. Thus, the

2 See Comparative Constitutions Project, Option Reports: Constitutional amendment 22 May 2008, www.constitutionmaking.org.

commonly shared assumption behind the plain existence of amendment rules is that constitutional change is permissible and possible since it derives from the principle of popular sovereignty. If the constitution emanates from people's consent, then, it seems obvious that the same subject can modify the original pact: if a constitution rested on popular consent, then, the people could also replace it with a new one (Lutz, 1994: 355).

2.1 Two views on constitutional reform

Beyond the common assumption on the desirability of constitutional amendments, the design of specific ratification procedures results from the agreement, on a variable point, between two competing theoretical approaches on constitutional reform.

2.1.1 The Jeffersonian view

One approach favours flexible constitution and the extreme version of this view would be the Jeffersonian interpretation: law is the codified rule of past generations, and as such its effects on the present generation could be arbitrary and even despotic. Viewed in this light, a constitution becomes especially suspect if it is made difficult to amend. By placing fundamental issues beyond the control of ordinary majorities, a constitution will protect the *status quo*, perpetuates injustices and subordinates the interests and vision of the present generation to ossified expressions of past legislatures (Ferejohn, 1997: 502). Jefferson believed that every constitution (and most other laws, for that matter) should expire after 19 years, a figure that he based on an estimate of how long a majority of adults alive at any time would expire according to European life expectancies.[3] Thus, changing constitutions is not a requirement for marginal adaptation of a more or less perfect document but rather is an essential mechanism to counteract a potentially fallible document which, in American constitutionalism, derives from three premises (Lutz, 1994: 356): the doctrine of popular sovereignty (which can remove previous bonds), the belief in an imperfect human nature; a parallel belief in the efficiency of the deliberative process and a distinction between normal legislative and constitutional matters.

A number of practical requirements concur with the normative argument strengthening the case for constitutional reform. Firstly, drafters are fallible human beings and the original document may have, plainly, mistakes. Secondly, constitutional rules and institutional arrangements may produce unintended, unwanted, unexpected consequences which require their change.

3 Thomas Jefferson to James Madison 1789 ME 7:459 Paper 15:369; quoted in Elkins et al., 2008.

Thirdly, old contents may require their updating to changing circumstances, in particular, changes in the environment and changes in the value system distributed across the population. Fourthly, constitutions may need to reflect the cumulative effects of decisions made by legislatures and/or through jurisdictional adjudication. Fifthly, constitutions may need to be changed to reflect the changes in the international arena: the EU in particular has been one of the single more important sources triggering constitutional reform among EU Member States. Finally, there is a pragmatic argument: constitutional binding may be simple impossible. As the Venice Commission, an official advisory body of the Council of Europe put it, it is impossible for drafters of a constitution to create a text which is eternal, and which can serve society through processes of development and transformation (Venice Commission, 2010: 17).

In particular, this Jeffersonian view on constitutional reform and its belief in the necessity of a flexible amendment procedure to cope with change seems to be closely associated with federal systems since the inherently dynamic nature of the relation between two levels of government seems to call for increased processes of change. Constitutional flexibility has also been perceived as an essential requisite in transition to democracy in order to deal with the changes taking place (Holmes and Sunstein, 1995). In fact, Roberts (2009) concludes that the evolution of constitutional reforms in Eastern European states seems to vindicate Holmes and Sunstein recommendation since, contrary to conventional wisdom, the amendments that have been passed typically reduced executive powers, better guaranteed human rights, and ensured integration into international bodies. Even authors showing a preference for more rigid constitutions (e.g. Harding, 2007: 406) nuance their approach to the medium long term future: Constitutional amendment should be made difficult, once the constitution has settled into its foundations (Harding, 2007). And concurring with Holmes and Sunstein, he also concedes that developing countries should be allowed flexibility in constitutional development up to the point at which the constitution can be said to have settled into its foundations (Harding, 2007: 407)

From an empirical base, Elkins et al. (2008) concur with this argument: they argue that adaptability is crucial for constitutional survival and durability is closely associated with the ease of the amendment process (plus the existence of proper constitutional review and their emergence under conditions characterised by an open, participatory process – conditions that confer legitimacy upon the document, encouraging enforcement of its terms).

2.1.2 The Madisonian view

These strong arguments in favour of constitutional reform are balanced against the requirements of the Madisonian view of constitutionalism. The kind of constitutional choices made at constitutional moments is far reaching and affects the long term stability of the regime. Thus special issues treated in special moments must have a special protection in constitutions:

> "By separating constitutional from ordinary law, troubling fundamental issues can be dealt with once (or at least, rarely), and the business of ordinary government can proceed in a less passionate atmosphere." (Ferejohn, 1997: 503)

This separation serves the end of creating pre-commitments in the constitution: the compromise with certain essential elements and their non amendability (or a very difficult one) reinforces the credibility of the pact. In particular, the pre-commitment strategy affects to two main areas: the protection of individual (fundamental) rights and minority rights and interests and the protection of democratic procedures and the independence of certain institutions. This later aim is particularly important for constitutional rigidity. Thus, in 2007 a resolution from the Parliamentary Assembly of the Council of Europe invited to examine constitutional amendments to find "whether the current national arrangements for changing the constitution require a sufficient high approval level to protect abuses of democracy".[4] The study carried out by the Venice Commission however did not prescribed an ideal degree of rigidity, less so a favoured amendment procedure.

Arguments from political economy emphasise similarly the importance of commitments or "pre-commitment" whose origin can be detected in "libertarian" constitutionalism (Buchanan and Tullock, 1962). By restricting the ability of officials to renege on agreements, a constitution may permit a government to make credible commitments to repay its debts, to maintain stable money supply, and to make believable threats of retaliation (Ferejohn, 1997: 503). Germany and Spain, for instance, have introduced in their constitution the prohibition of public deficits which has also become a demand for the reform of the constitution of euro member states.

Pre-commitments are associated with higher values and with the function of providing legal stability as a pre-condition for justice and republican (i.e. democratic) government. There are two basic institutional instruments for securing the pre-commitment strategy, being the first the *entrenching* certain provisions whose mere existence is perceived as essential for the existence of the constitution itself. In particular, two sets of rights should be strongly entrenched (Holmes and Sunstein, 1995): a specified list of individual rights should be made immune to revision and, secondly, some of the broad outlines of the institutional arrangements might safeguard against too easy a change. There are, of course, authors that think that it may be politically impossible actually to entrench constitutional provisions (Ferejohn, 1997: 513) since later interpreters faced with governmental necessity, or just ordinary tempta-

4 Chapter II no. 9; http://www.venice.coe.int/docs/2010/CDL-AD%282010%29001-e.asp?Print [accessed: 19 July 2011].

tions, will develop modes of interpretation that can defeat any attempt to fix constitutional meanings once and for all.

A second mechanism for securing credible commitments is constructing *stringent amendment procedures* that made very difficult to change the original compromises. In this way, constitutional rigidity is associated with constitutional stability (and this, in turn, with regime stability). Stability occurs when relatively few formal and informal amendments are adopted. The more difficult the formal amendment procedure, the less dependent formal constitutional stability is on the existence of a continuous political consensus of relevant policy makers (Congleton, 2003: 15). Although this view associates stability with permanence and durability of the laws, empirical research, as mentioned above, (Elkins et al., 2008) comes to the conclusion that in fact flexible amendment procedures (*inter alia*) concur to decrease the mortality of constitutions. Furthermore, authors warn on extreme rigidity: A perfectly rigid constitution might not accommodate widespread demands for reform, and in limiting cases, a very costly civil or revolutionary war might be the only possible method of "amendment" (Rasch and Congleton, 2006: 323). Moreover, rigidity/flexibility of amendment procedures also influences other mechanisms of constitutional change, first and foremost, change by judicial interpretation: If the methods of securing formal amendment are difficult (as in the USA), there may be pressures to adapt the constitution through judicial interpretation (Elkins et al., 2008). These authors argue that constitutions that lack either flexible formal amendment or effective mechanisms of informal reinterpretation may not adapt to changing environmental conditions. They predict that "such constitutions will force actors to take extra-constitutional action when faced with environmental changes and will then die young" (Elkins et al., 2008: 19).

Thus, the central question in designing procedures for constitutional amendment is to strike a balance between flexibility and rigidity. Almost all constitutional theorists seem to agree that the proper position should reasonably blend both the Jeffersonian and the Madisonian view. The design of the rules for ratification and the determination of their eventual rigidity seek precisely to obtain the correct balance and blend between both given specific circumstances in different countries. If the choice goes in favour of a system with high capacity for constitutional reform, choice of rules will go in favour of not highly demanding ones. On the other hand, if preferences go for preserving certain constitutional values, procedures will tilt in direction of more stringent ones. According to Elkins et al (2008) the optimal level of flexibility is not universal, but determined in any particular constitutional situation by both exogenous factors (such as the role of technological or environmental change) and endogenous factors (such as the level of responsiveness of political institutions under the constitution, and the endowment of legitimacy at the outset of the constitutional system). In ideal terms, to avoid the extremely high costs of civil warfare, while securing the advantages of stable constitutional governance, the amendment process should ideally be difficult enough to prevent temporary partisan interests from securing a permanent constitutional advantage, but not so difficult as to eliminate the long-term advantages of constitutional reform (Elkins et al., 2008: 16).

Thus, calculating the amendability of a given constitution seems to be a crucial constitutional choice and actors hence may be expected to use mechanisms that produce the expected result of their eventual calculation. Contrary to this expectation and in line with most research, this chapter will show that ratification rules by themselves are not good predictors of constitutional amendability.

2.2 Writing a constitution and ratifying it: the subject of popular sovereignty

The intervention of parliaments in the ratification process raises two types of questions. The first refers to the very relationship between constituent and constituted powers: parliaments' approval of constitutional reform turns them into the body exercising the "constituent power" blurring thus the distinction between constituent and constituted powers which is central to constitutional theory.

Constitutional theory normally grants or at least accepts that drafting new constitutions corresponds to *ad hoc* bodies, particularly in what could be termed "constitutional moments". These have specific functions, limited in time. In particular, the American and French revolutionary experiences have distilled the model of conventions or constituent assemblies as the ones legitimated for exercising this function. Noticeably, the US model departs from the idea that the ordinary legislative (the Congress) could exercise this constituent power (not least, of course, because of the very practical reasons that the scarce operativity of the Congress was one of the targets of the constitutional process itself). A similar desire to mark a "constituent moment" underlies to the Convention method followed by the EU convention in 2002-2003 to amend the EU Treaties. In contemporary Europe, to the extent that such "constitutional moments" can be identified, as the 1970s for Southern Europe or the 1990s for the Central and Eastern European states, newly elected legislative assemblies drafted new constitutions although they assumed also, in most cases, legislative powers for the duration of the constituent process.

The identification of specialised bodies as well as parliamentary drafting of a new constitution in "constitutional moments" goes hand in hand, in most cases, with a strict separation between drafting and ratification: in the US revolutionary constitutionalism, ratification was referred back to the states. These, by and large, adopted the mechanism of State Ratifying Conventions and, in few cases (such as Rhode Island) referendums, giving thus practical sense to the idea that normal legislature and constituent power were different. In the European cases associated with constitutional moments, eliciting popular consent for the new text was considered essential and hence, the constitution was ratified also by referendum. These were the cases, for instance, of Spain (1978) or Poland (1997). Next to these "ordinary" constitutional moments, a number of countries followed a more evolutionary path of constitutional "substitution". Two cases (Sweden, 1974 and Finland 2000) have totally replaced their respective constitutions without calling for a referendum whilst outside the EU Switzerland (1999) approved its new constitution by referendum.

The use of a distinctive *ad hoc* body is not a common feature of constitutional amendment procedures. The right of initiating amendments and (formally at least) the power of drafting them, belongs almost universally to parliaments even though other actors may intervene in constitutional negotiations via formal and informal channels and the competence may be functionally delegated. The only constitutionally established different body is the Bulgarian Grand National Assembly which has to be convened although only for drafting a new constitution or amending special provisions. In some other cases, *ad hoc* bodies are being created for the specific task of drafting (for instance, the Austrian convention) whilst the French Congress has exclusively a ratifying function of the amendments approved by parliament.

In parallel, a significant number of ratification procedures have moved away from the requirement of a compulsory referendum and towards forms of rigidity organised around parliament involvement. In the EU, no less than 13 countries do not contain an explicit or explicit mandate for constitutional reform referendums. Given also the largely absence of the regional bodies in most EU states, drafting and the ratifying body have in practice coincided.

Of course, good reasons advice to trust in parliaments: they guarantee the representativeness requirement expected from a constituent body whilst, at the same time, the premise of parliamentary work (in ideal terms) is that they apply deliberation as the method of work (even though, again, negotiation is a pragmatic component of constitution making). Not surprisingly, the Venice Commission Study (2010) considers that the main arena for procedures of constitutional amendment should be the national parliament as the institution best placed to debate and consider such issues). In parallel, this melting of functions has positive effects for the ratification of constitutional reforms: there are relatively few cases of failure at the ratification stage and, when they are logically linked to the existence of an external actor with veto players (referendums). Ireland provides a case where several constitutional reform processes have been voted down in referendums. Equally, in France, a second attempt of constitutional reform via the contested article 11 failed in a referendum. Not surprisingly, there are not documented failures of constitutional reforms by means of a parliamentary vote at the ratification moment. Obviously, negotiating parties, knowing beforehand the possibilities of ratification, would avoid a vote with no chances to be won although some cases in this volume illustrate precisely failure without reaching ratification stage.

However, there are also downturns to this dynamic. By entrusting the amending function to parliaments, it serves both as an ordinary legislator and as the constitutional legislator and this brings the risk that the mixture of constitutional amending functions with the normal legislative ones pollutes the former with the dynamics of the second. This may create additional difficulties for achieving constitutional agreements, for instance in Germany reforms were negotiated without differentiating the arena of constitutional politics from that of normal politics and in a committee, reproducing structures of intergovernmental and party political bargaining (Behnke and Benz, 2009) and this may account partly for its failure. More importantly, this introduces an additional problem: "design actors" (Heritier, 2007: 51) are fully identical with actors affected by constitutional change and, hence, they have vested interest in a specific outcome precluding thus options for reform.

3. The effect of ratification rules on amendment rates

The empirical substance of this chapter is to test the hypothesis of the relationship between rigidity of amendment procedures and ratio of reform. The rational expectation is that the more rigid ratification procedures, the lower the amendment rate and, contrariwise, the less rigid, the higher the amendment rate. Political scientists have tried to identify the eventual relationship between the rules for constitutional reform and the number of occurrences of change. Lutz study in 1994 may be considered the pioneer and hence a number of others have followed (Ferejohn, 1995; Anckar and Karvonen, 2002; Lorenz, 2005; Rasch and Congleton, 2006; Roberts, 2009). A common shortcoming of all these studies is that they treat each constitution as a single case. This neglects the totally essential fact that constitutions have often more than one reform procedure and that this reflects a conscious decision to distinguish with more or less rigidity different parts of the constitution. Thus, differently to any other previous study, this chapter treats every procedure as a case, a decision which is common, for instance, in the study of electoral systems.

This chapter aims at testing again the thesis of the relationship between rigidity of rules and amendment rate for the universe of EU member states (i.e. 26 countries since the unwritten UK constitution cannot be treated through the parameters used in the research design). There is certainly an inflation of European based research on constitution and constitution making but this merely reflects the fact that Europe is a densely populated constitutional environment. The issue of delimiting what part of the written law is the constitution is relevant in one case: In Sweden, there are four documents which are together considered the constitution: the *Instrument of Government* (1974); the *Act of Succession* (1810) (amended 10 times), the *Freedom of the Press Act* (1766) (amended 39 times) and the *Fundamental Law on Freedom of Expression* (1991) (amended 3 times). Following the convention (Congleton, 2003), only the *Instrument of Government* will be considered.

The utilisation of the EU as the universe has some advantages: the automaticity of the selection, whilst other research designs had to rely in *ad hoc* criteria. Thus, Rasch and Congleton (2006) use advanced democracies/OECD as their sample, whilst Roberts, 2009 examines constitutional change in 17 Eastern European countries (a case of geographically delimited sample). Lorenz (2005) uses more systematic criteria: cases which have been fully established, peaceful democracies between 1993 and 2003. She selects 39 countries which, additionally, fulfil the criteria of being covered in at least two other samples. In the case of EU member states, the group of states is predetermined from their membership of an organisation that *requires (as a precondition) democratic credentials* from its members. Being democracy is a constant requirement in the construction of samples and, thus, EU membership cancels the search for *ad hoc* characterisations on the level of democracy. The universe is also internally diverse; it comprised constitutions with very different duration (measured in years); federal, regional and unitary states and different (territorial and population) sizes. The universe is fairly homogenous from the point of view of the type of regime since almost all the EU countries can be considered parliamentary democracies and, certainly, in all cases (with the exception of France), the Head of State has no role in constitutional amendment procedures. The sample permits also neutralising additional intervening variables such as colonial origin or difference in geographical area which had explanatory value in Anckar and Kervonen (2002). Additionally, the group of countries have been stable democracies either after 1945 or after completing their respective transitions to democracy and, hence, they have not, by and large, experimented the kind of "precipitating events" (shocks and crisis) described by Elkins et al. (2008) who granted these exogenous variables capacity for explaining change. Finally, this group of countries shares one of the most formidable sources of demands for constitutional amendment: EU membership. Hence, an eventual source of demands for constitutional change can be held constant in the research and this allows a better appreciation of the eventual effect of the rules (and other factors) on constitutional reforms. This strengthens the explanatory value of design variables.

3.1 The dependent variable: the amendability of constitutions

By and large, most of these studies take as their dependent variable "constitutional change", normally identified with constitutional stability and measured either in absolute terms as the *number of amendments,* or in relative terms, as the *rate of amendments* (amendments divided by the years of existence of the constitution). This paper adopts the second way of expressing amendability, i.e. *rate of amendments*.

Amendments are formal changes to the original document following the amending procedure whilst "replacements" are changes without following such procedure (Elkins et al., 2008). *Prima facie*, distinguishing amendments seems an obvious operation but there are two states at least, in which this is not such a straightforward operation. In Austria, any legislative rule may be raised to constitutional rank simply by declaring it expressly a "constitutional law" (*Verfassungsgesetz*) or a "constitutional provision" (*Verfassungsbestimmung*) and voted by a two-thirds majority. Rules of substantively "constitutional" character (*materielles Verfassungsrecht*) such as the structure of the state are generally – though not always (sic) – enacted as constitutional law in formal sense (*formelles Verfassungsrecht*). But many other provisions have been also passed in the form of constitutional law and constitutional provisions merely in order to provide them with greater protection against subsequent change (Hausmaninger, 2003: 22, 24-25). The rule does not need to be incorporated into the text and, thus, next to the formal amendments included in the constitution (108), there exist approximately 1000 constitutional provisions floating outside the constitution proper. Sweden also presents some peculiarities in relation to what amendments exactly are. Accordingly to Congleton (2003: 18-19), not all major constitutional reforms are incorporated into Sweden's instrument of governance and this is sometimes a source of confusion. After 1975, the IG began to include many details of policy having little to do with fundamental governmental procedures or constraints. The Swedish case presents a puzzle since, on paper, its amendment procedure does not seem comparatively as the most flexible one and, nevertheless, the number of amendments (40) and amendment rate (1,08) is quite high and some authors argue that the procedure is very flexible (Congleton, 2003).

Defining amendments as changes to the written document following established procedures for constitutional reform does not permit to discriminate between the importance of the amendment comprising all of these from a single word to total change of the constitution (provided that the amendment procedure is respected). Roberts (2009: 103) proposes an alternative way to ponder amendments by pondering the number of constitutional articles changed – added, altered or deleted – in each country per year. He argues that the number of articles changed is not a perfect measure of significance (some are more or less consequential) but is a relatively objective gauge of the extent of change. Whilst Roberts' proposal sounds reasonable, it does not again capture the importance of the amendment. Thus, this paper sticks to the definition that emphasises the procedural dimensions. In practical terms, amendments are counted (when they are not a self-evident occurrence) following the information provided by authoritative sources (mainly, national parliaments).

Next to amendments, the second indicator to construct the amendment rate is the *duration of a constitution* on which the sample is particularly varied. Establishing the duration requires in turn identifying the constitution's "birth date" which is easily spotted if it coincides with a constitutional moment, for instance, USA in 1789 or Spain in 1978. This applies to countries in which their constitution resulted from transition to democracy either after WWII or after the second and third waves of democratisation and a significant number of states in the EU belong to either of these categories. But long standing constitutions subject to permanent and ongoing processes of changes present more challenging difficulties. A way to measure the "age" of a constitution is to make it equal to the period in which its original rules of amendment have been followed (Rasch and Congleton, 2006: 20). This rule raises only the question of measurement in the cases in which total amendment happens (i.e. instances of total renovation of the regime). In the group of EU member states, there are relatively few cases; i.e. Sweden, 1974 and Finland, 2000 (whilst, outside the EU, Switzerland is considered as a successful process of constitutional substitution). The new 2000 Finnish Constitution cannot be considered at all a revolutionary, *ex novo* creation and in fact, it was drafted by means of the existing amendment procedures. However, since the aim was precisely to update the old document and, in this way, render less necessary constant amendment and change, the new constitution is taken as an additional case. On the other hand, Hungary amended its existing constitution in 1989-1990, but since it changed totally (according to Roberts, 2009: 102) the new amendments left it totally unrecognizable) and it is considered to be a new one also because the regime changed totally. As for Sweden, the consensus seems to be, like in the Hungarian case, to take the 1974 amendment as a case of a "new constitution" (Congleton, 2003). Conversely, Belgium presents something of a puzzling case: its constitution dates back to 1831 but it has suffered at least three major reforms: 1970, 1988-1989 and 1993 which have totally and dramatically changed the structure of the regime. In particular, the 1993 reform used the so-called "coordination mechanism" which allows for changes in the structure, subdivisions and articles of the constitution.

Table 1: Amendments and duration of constitutions

Country	Promulgation date	N° of procedures	N° of amendments	Lifetime of the Constitution (years)	Amendment rate
Austria	1920	3	109	91	1.1978
Belgium	1831	1	31	180	0.1722
Bulgaria	1991	2	4	20	0.2
Cyprus	1960	1	5	51	0.098
Czech Republic	1992	1	7	19	0.3684
Denmark	1849	1	4	162	0.0246
Estonia	1992	3	1	19	0.0526
Finland	1919	2	44	82	0.5432
Finland	2000	2	2	11	0.1818
France	1958	2	24	53	0.4528
Germany	1949	1	57	62	0.9193
Greece	1975	1	3	36	0.0833
Hungary	1990	1	34	21	1.619
Ireland	1937	1	24	74	0.3243
Italy	1947	2	14	64	0.2187
Latvia	1990	2	10	21	0.428
Lithuania	1992	3	7	19	0.3684
Luxembourg	1868	1	37	143	0.2587
Malta	1964	3	20	47	0.4255
Netherlands	1815	1	21	196	0.1071
Poland	1997	2	1	14	0.0714
Portugal	1976	1	7	35	0.2
Romania	1991	1	1	20	0.05
Slovakia	1992	1	8	19	0.421
Slovenia	1991	2	5	20	0.25
Spain	1978	3	1	33	0.0303
Sweden	1974	1	40	37	1.081

Source: own elaboration

The analysis of data shows a strong association between the duration of a given constitution and the number of reforms it has experienced (for this analysis, the cases are states, not procedures and, hence, N=26). This confirms a basic intuition: older constitutions are amended more than younger ones.

Duration and number of reforms

Diagram 1: All cases

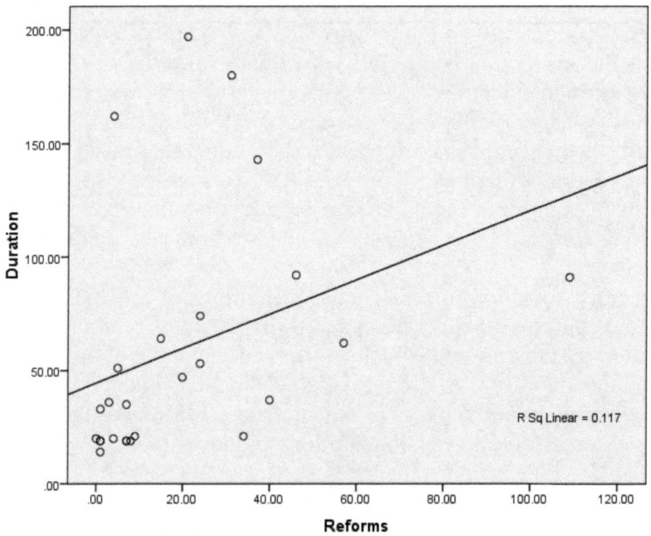

Diagram 2: Without outliers

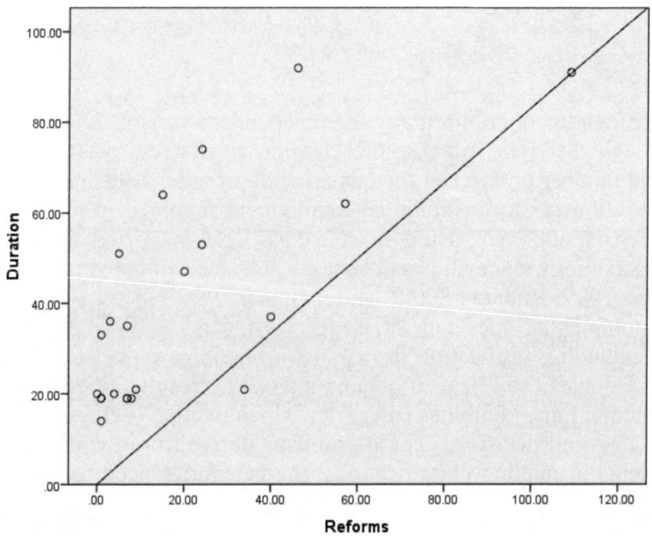

The diagram for all cases (diagram 1) reflects a strong association between duration in years of the constitution and the number of reforms. However, the parametric correlation between both variables (which assumes a homogeneous distribution of cases) is not statistically significant (Pearson Correlation coefficient 0.342). However, if a non-homogeneous distribution of cases is assumed, then, the association is not only statistically significant at 99% but also extremely strong (Spearman's rho 0.623). The lack of statistical significance for *all cases* is caused by 4 constitutions (Belgium, the Netherlands, Denmark and Luxembourg) which are older than 100 years (three of these, older than 150 years). If these very "old" constitutions are not taken into account (diagram 2), then both the parametric and non-parametric correlations show very strong associations (.737 and .701) and in both cases, they are significant at 99%.

However, no association appears between number of amendments and the rigidity index and this leads to the conclusion that if this relation exists, it may be mediated by the duration of constitutions. Hence, the option in order for measuring amendability is to use rate of amendments which combines duration of the constitution and number of amendments. Taking the states as the unit of analysis, the sample of EU constitutions produces an average amendment rate of 0.196 with extreme values 0.0248 (Denmark) and 1.7 (Hungary) being the average 0.38. As it will be discussed below, this chapter takes procedures as the unit of analysis rather than states. This means that a country may count as more than one if more than one constitutional amendment procedures exist.

3.2 The independent variables: the rigity index

The rules for amendment are normally the independent variable and they are presented in two different formats: the creation of discrete classifications with a reduced number of cases or the construction of indexes that grant pondered value to all and any institutional requirement involved in ratification processes. The first approach, using discrete classifications, offers the advantage of their parsimony since all possible cases presented fit between 4 (Lutz, 1994; Lijphart, 1999; Roberts, 2009[5]) and 6 (Lane, 1996; Elster, 2000) categories. But complexity does not sit easily with parsimony; simplicity is achieved by excluding ratification devices with potential explanatory value. For instance, Lijphart (1999), who obtains interesting results, does not consider referendums; Lane combines categories which overlap (delays and confirmation by a second decision). These problems derive from the parsimonious requirements in making classifications: the categories need to highlight

5 Roberts (2009) applies a four categories scale from 1 (easiest) to 4 (hardest) but he does not clarify how they have been constructed.

one central aspect of the ratification procedure missing the point that rigidity may result from the specific combination of different devices. By not considering all possible mechanism, discrete classifications assume an implicit arbitrariness and bias which normally derive from their tailoring to the sample of countries selected.

Because of these limitations, a number of authors have oriented towards the use of indexes of rigidity which attempt to integrate in a measure all the intervening devices of a ratification procedure. This is a superior measurement instrument since all eventual mechanisms for creating rigidity are accounted for. Lutz pioneered this path and he defined 68 actions to initiate and approve a constitutional reform. He concluded that the amendment rate can be explained by the interaction of the length of the document (in words) and the rigidity of the amendment procedures. However, Ferejohn (1997) and Lorenz (2005) failed to replicate Lutz´s results. Lorenz wrote:

> "I personally failed to apply the Lutz index to measure the rigidity in countries which are not mentioned by him because he had not offered scores for many of the procedural devices." (Lorenz, 2005: 342)

She concludes that "apparently, concepts of rigidity have to be left open for the endless creativity of constitutional engineers" (ibid.). She used an index contained in a former (2004) publication in German.

There is a strong argument in relation to the utilisation of an index: it reflects better the assumption on control of outcomes of constitutional drafters. The combination of different devices seeks to graduate the intensity of the rigidity of the amendment procedure (irrespectively of the eventual accuracy in their calculation). In this respect, it allows a better measurement of the underlying questions: do institutions for constitutional reform matter for easing it or making it more difficult?

3.2.1 Preliminary considerations: entrenchment and the existence of more than one constitutional reform procedure

Entrenchment is a relatively common provision among the constitutions of EU Member states. In the EU, the constitutions of 10 member states (Belgium, Czech Republic, Cyprus, France, Germany, Greece, Italy, Luxembourg, Portugal and Romania) include clauses forbidding constitutional reform in specific domains. Entrenchment techniques follow two alternative varieties: in few cases, constitutions identify explicitly specific provisions as non-amendable. However, more commonly, constitutions preserve from amendment certain principles and this permits a certain degree of change as long as the core elements of the principles protected are maintained. Among the special principles protected are: fundamental democratic or republican form of government, federal/territorial structure, sovereignty, territorial indivisibility. In some other cases (for instance, France and Lithuania *inter alia*), constitutions contain clauses for *temporal entrenchment*: specific circumstances in which a constitution cannot be amended (war or invasion, for instance). Finally, an additional form for securing entrenchment is to grant constitutional courts the power of reviewing amendments which may conflict with general and fundamental principles of the constitution (Italy).

The most extended technique for signalling specially protected clauses is the introduction of different (i.e. more stringent) procedures for amending specific parts of the constitution. A majority of EU member states (15) have only one modality of amendment, whilst 11 have two or even three possible avenues. The existence of more than one procedure is highly revealing since it indicates the wish of constituent drafters to create a hierarchy of constitutional clauses according to their importance.

The existence of more than one procedure is methodologically crucial. Former research has unanimously opted by choosing between one of several procedures for each country when more than one existed. Lijphart (1999) and Anckar and Kervonen (2002: 14) count only the most stringent procedure whilst Lorenz (2005) opts for the easiest one. Opting for counting one procedure per country converts the later in the unit of analysis but it misses also a very important issue in relation to constitutional design: Does the difference of procedures within the same constitution matter? It also neglects a very important and preliminary issue: countries may change their amendment procedure and chose a more rigid/flexible one. For instance, Austria added in 1984 the requirement of a two-thirds majority in the *Bundesrat* for constitutional reforms affecting *Länder* competence (article 44.2 Austrian Constitution).

In order to generate evidence able to respond this question, this chapter treats every different amendment procedure (understood as the combination of prescribed constitutional devices) as the unit of analysis. Whilst this option differs from former research, it comes closer to the standard technique, for instance, in analyzing electoral systems. The result within the EU is 44 different cases.

3.2.2 Indicators and scores for parliamentary requirements

Amendment procedures typically involve two rules: the ones related to the actor legitimated to initiate the procedure of constitutional reforms and the ones referred to ratification. Whilst all constitutions (in the sample and almost everyone universally) detail the rules for ratification, the requirements for initiation are not necessarily made explicit in a number of constitutions. This absence means that initiation of constitutional reform, when not constitutionally determined, is assumed to be similar to initiation of legislation. As for the requirements for parliamentary ratification, they include a number of devices that seek to differentiate it from the approval of normal legislation. They comprise qualified majorities, parliamentary procedural requirements, such as a second or third vote and delays, and, eventually, the threat of using a referendum to validate the parliamentary vote. For the elaboration of the index, internal logical consistency in the scores can be achieved within each of these three categories; however, the consistency of the scores between categories remain (for example, the index ponders 1 any veto player and 0.75 for a four-fifths majority but the relation between them is totally random).

In all cases among EU member states, ratification of constitutional amendments involves always at least a vote in parliament even if a referendum is compulsory. Parliament is never excluded. The only contentious and marginal exception to this rule was the application of Article 11 in the French V Republic which requires a referendum called by the President of the Republic. The parliamentary majorities are the following:

Majorities
The main purpose and effect of a qualified majority requirement is a) to ensure broad political consensus and thereby strengthen the legitimacy and durability of the amendment; b) protect the interests and rights of the political opposition and minorities. Such a requirement in effect gives a minority (of a certain size) a veto on constitutional amendments (Venice Commission, 2010: 19). If not strong majorities are required for constitutional reform, then, it may be assumed that governmental majorities have a solid possibility to model the procedures to their own tastes. In the case of EU member states, the dominant requirement is two-thirds majority of the chamber(s) (equivalent to 66% approximately). In a considerable number of cases, simple majority is the procedure although, as it will be discussed below is almost always associated with strong veto points/players. Tree-fifths (60%) is less common whilst four-fifth (80%) is rare although there exist cases. As mentioned above, Ferejohn (1997: 523) reclaimed the explanatory value of majorities: the requirement of special majorities or separate majorities in different legislative sessions or bicameralism is the key variable to explain the amendment rate. In other words, Ferejohn suggests that special majorities in the legislature may be both necessary and sufficient to achieve a moderate amendment rate.

Delays and second votes
Time delays force that amendments eventually constructed on the political passions of a certain moment may only survive if they endure continued consistent support through time. Delays also enlarge the opportunities for extra-parliamentary actors to engage with the process, increasing their options to influence the outcome. *Prima facie*, it could be presumed that enlarged time offers the opportunity for improving deliberation.

A specifically minority protecting mechanism: The threat of referendum
In some cases, a certain number of members of parliaments, or voters or external bodies such as regional assemblies can call a referendum once the par-

liament has voted a constitutional amendment. This device introduces an element of risk and uncertainty that political actors need to calculate in their decision to reform the constitution.

3.2.3 Indicators and scores for veto players

An index cannot qualitatively discriminate between the different instruments used within a given amendment procedure (as classifications do). This however, reduces the option of pondering the eventual relevance of veto players. In his revision of Lutz's 1994 analysis, Ferejohn (1997: 523) concludes that *there is no evidence that a ratification requirement (whether states or referendums) has any significant impact on amendment rates*. Rasch and Congleton (2006) dispute these conclusions and on the basis of their own sample conclude that the results suggest that the number of veto players and veto points have systematically effects on the amendment rates of (OECD) countries. Amendment rates fall as the number of veto players increases and with the requirements for intervening elections and/or referenda. This index accepts the hypothesis that veto players may have an influence on amendment rates. There are three types of veto players: the intervention of a second chamber, the intervention of voters by means of a referendum or the requirement of ratification by the vote of a second, different legislature.

Second chambers

Typically, all constitutions require that both chambers of parliament vote the constitutional amendment although in some cases with the caveat that second chamber voting may be restricted to the matters of their competence. And, in all cases, the majorities required are symmetrical (with the exception of Spain where the original requirement of three-fifth for both chambers changes to two-thirds for the Congress and simple majority for the Senate in case of lack of agreement between them). None of the empirical studies on amendment rules grant explanatory power to the vote in the second chamber, despite the fact that they may be elected and composed by different criteria; i.e. normally, second chambers have not acted as an alternative veto player. Austria presents a specific evolution of the role of the second chamber: until 1984, the *Nationalrat* could approve "constitutional laws" by a two-thirds majority and the *Bundesrat* had only the option of a suspending veto which could nevertheless be overruled by the *Nationalrat*. After the reform of constitutional amendment rules in 1984, a two-thirds majority of the *Bundesrat* is required for constitutional reforms that restrict *Länder* competences.

Referendums

Using referendums for ratifying constitutional amendments is consistent with the theoretical consideration of the people as the constituent subject. Within the EU states this is not the dominant procedure: it is the only procedure in Denmark, Ireland and Romania. However, a number of other states use it for selected constitutional provisions (normally, the most important ones) and in a number of countries is an optional procedure.

Intervening elections and parliamentary dissolution

Intervening elections associate voters to the constitutional amendment process and introduce also the requirement of a second vote by the newly elected parliament. Similarly to referendums, these cases associate citizens to the process of constitutional amendment. However, differently to referendums, citizens' choice on constitutional amendments is diluted in the choice among the competing political parties. Ten cases of the sample contain an intervening election. For Greece, Sweden, Belgium, Luxembourg and the Netherlands it is the only procedure (even though in the Greek case, there are two different combinations). In several of these cases, the majorities required from the first and second legislatures diverge.

A more stringent variety appears in several cases, in which the parliament is dissolved after a total or selected revision of the constitution (Bulgaria, Estonia, Lithuania, Spain). Parliamentary political parties need to calculate the eventual electoral costs and benefits associated with the procedure of constitutional reform.

3.2.4 Federal versus non-federal states

These mechanisms combine within each state one or several different procedures. Whilst the variety is large, there are however some common traits within the group of 25 EU member states. Differently to the US model and despite the existence of several federal or quasi-federal states, *in Europe*, only the Swiss Constitution (not included in this study) contains provisions for the intervention of the regional level either via regional legislature or referendum. Federal states require ratification by the lower tiers of government, being these three quarters of states legislatures or state conventions (USA), a referendum delivering a majority of votes in the entire federation concurrent with a majority of votes in a majority of states (Switzerland and Australia) or approval by both chambers of parliament and three-fifth of provincial legislatures representing at least 50% of the population (Canada).

Within the EU, in no federal system regional units intervene directly in the ratification of constitutional amendments. Regions or constituent states intervene through their participation in the second chamber in the cases in which they have a role in their formation (Austria, Belgium, Germany and Spain). Belgium, however, presents an interesting peculiarity: most of the detailed provisions concerning federalism, including the distribution of powers and financial arrangements, are to be found in "special laws" rather than the

Constitution itself. The amendment of special laws requires not only the approval of a two-thirds majority in each house of parliament, but also a majority in each language group: *In practice this means that the governments of the regions and communities must accept the proposal* (Deschouwer, 2005: 72).

3.2.4 Summary: A European model of constitutional amendment procedure?

The Venice Commission (2010: 62) argued that a fairly widespread model typically requires a certain qualified majority in parliament (most often two-thirds) and then, one or more additional obstacles. When the procedures are aligned along the required parliamentary majority, the constellation is as it follows: out of the 44 cases, 24 require a two-thirds majority, 11 require a simple majority, 8 a majority of three-fifths and 1 a super qualified majority of four-fifth. What is interesting is how these majority requirements combine with other instruments: out of the 24 cases of two-thirds majority, 9 add a veto player: an intervening election (5) or a compulsory referendum (4), whilst a further 3 offer the threat of a referendum. Among the 11 cases of simple majority, 7 require a referendum and 3 intervening elections. Only a Maltese procedure allows constitutional reform ratification by means of simple majority with no added veto player.

Table 2: Rigidity Index

Parliamentary majority	Vote after intervening election	Veto players and veto points	Delays and successive votes	Referendum threat
Single majority=0 3/5 majority (60%)= 0,25 2/3 majority (66%)= 0,5 3/4 majority (75%)= 0,75	Single majority=0 majority=0.25 3/5 majority= 0.5 2/3 majority= 0.75 3/4 majority= 1	Additional chamber=1 Joint sessions (specialised body)=0,25 Intervening election=1 (plus either 1 for an extra Camera or the rate for the required majority) Compulsory referendum=1	Delay=0,25 Successive vote=0,25	=0,25

3.3 Independent variables: the length and detail of constitutions

Some authors have assigned explanatory value to the length of constitutions (see Lutz, 1994; Ferejohn, 1997; Elkins et al., 2008; Roberts, 2009). The assumptions that can be derived from the length are totally antagonist: on the one hand, it may be assumed that long constitutions which regulate in detail political life may require frequent amendment. On the opposite side, it may be expected that documents painted with broad brush strokes would seem more amendable to change than those that make very specific commitments and run a greater risk of constraining executives (Elkins et al., 2008). They conclude, though, that contrary to (their) expectations, longer constitutions, which they expected to be less adaptable, are slightly more durable than shorter ones.

Different authors seem to agree on the same measurement procedure (i.e. counting the number of words in the English translation), which has the undoubtedly advantage of reducing all legal text to a single language. However, standardisation comes with a cost: it also may reduce the nuances of legal expression in the vernacular. In any case, the advantages seem to outweigh the costs and hence, this chapter counts the words on the English language version. A second issue in the counting is the moment when it is made: in this chapter, measurement is done on the original constitution at the registered moment of its approval. This permits standardising the count for all cases eliminating the possible variance that amendments themselves may introduce in the number of words (particularly important in cases such as Austria or Sweden).

Length in words is a proxy for the level of detail. Different topics tend to be regulated in different constitutional provisions and, hence, a second measure is added: the number of articles which is a more appropriate measurement of length (as different to detail). The differences between both (words and articles) may be large; for instance, the Hungarian constitution has 78 articles and 12000 words, whilst the Polish constitution has 243 articles in 20000 words. Additional, transitory and final dispositions have not been included since they are accessory to the main body of the constitution (and, hence, they are normally the object of amendments) and, on the other hand, they are not a widespread constitutional device. Only 5 states among the 27 have these types of provisions. An additional indicator created is the rate between words and articles. In any case, counting words and provisions does not say much about the substantive contents of the constitution which may be at the root of reform requirements. As an example, the German 1871 Constitution dedicated 11 of 78 articles to detail the aspects of the railroad and telegraph system (Elkins et al., 2008).

The results are totally disappointing since there is no evidence of association between the length of constitutions measured either in words, articles or ratio between both and the reforms, measured either in absolute terms or as a ratio of amendments per year. This finding is totally counterintuitive and challenges basic assumptions on long constitutions. Naturally, this statement has to be nuanced in relation to the existence of alternative forms of constitutional change.

4. The relation between rigidity and constitutional reform: results of empirical analysis

One of the findings, reported above, is the strong association between duration in years of a constitution and number of amendments. This confirms a basic intuition: older constitutions require more amendments than more modern ones and this happens regardless of the procedure for constitutional reform applied. However, the confirmation of other obvious *a priori* expectations does not find the same degree of support; in particular, the amendability of the constitution. Using the EU sample as the universe, the data show a relation between the degree of rigidity and the rate of constitutional amendment in the expected direction (i.e. the more rigid, the lesser the amendment rate) but this relation is not statistically significant. This coincides with the findings of authors using different samples (Lorenz, 2005; Roberts, 2009 and resonates with Anckar and Karvonen, 2002). In principle, this may mean that rigid amendment procedures are not a full predictor of amendability and this may raise questions on the ability to design constitutional institutions whose effects can be calculated *a priori*. This finding must be nuanced in relation to some additional observations on the impact of the constitutional design.

Firstly, the average rate of reforms is much larger in the cases in which only legislatures intervene than in the cases in which an additional actor (either an intervening election or a referendum) also intervene. Differences are statistically significant between the procedures that only require parliamentary vote and those in which a referendum or referendum and elections are required. This means that veto players do matter in coincidence with Rasch and Congleton (2003) results. The only exception which is not statistically significant is the difference between ratification with legislatures only and ratification involving also an intervening election. This helps to place the large exception that represents Belgium, which has a very rigid procedure according to the index's scores and nevertheless implemented a large number of reforms. Diagrams 3 and 4 below present the data. The dot marks the average and the lines the corresponding deviations.

Type of actors and ratio of reforms

Diagram 3:

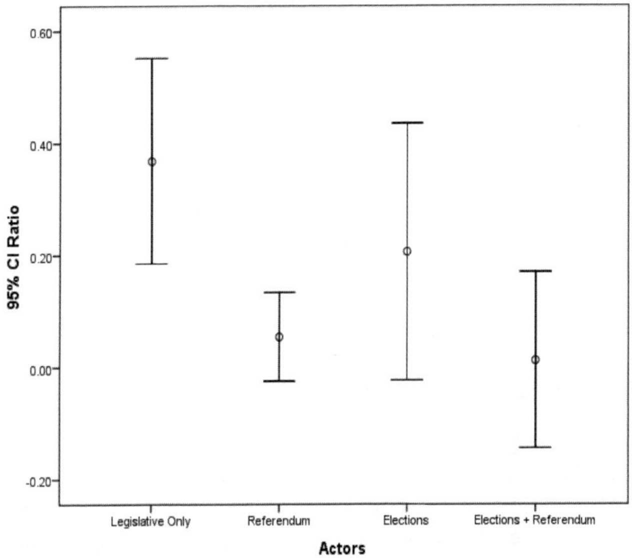

Diagram 4:

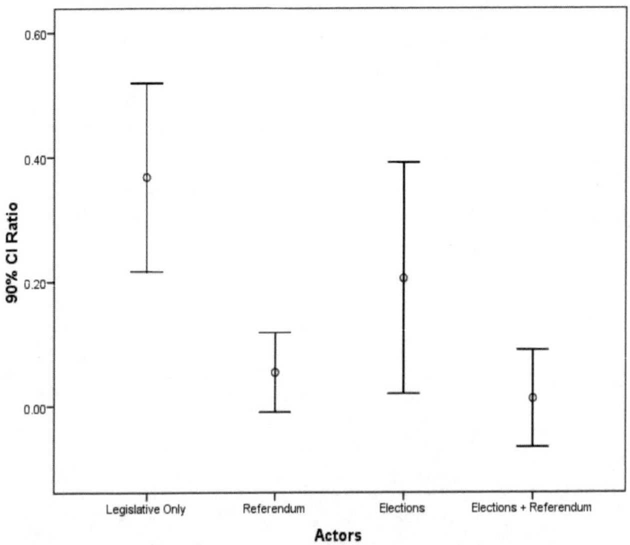

If the procedures with more than one actor intervening are reduced to a dichotomic classification, then the differences appear clearly: average amendment is superior in procedures in which only the legislative intervenes and this difference is significant at 90%.

Type of actors (legislatures vs. additional players)

Diagram 5:

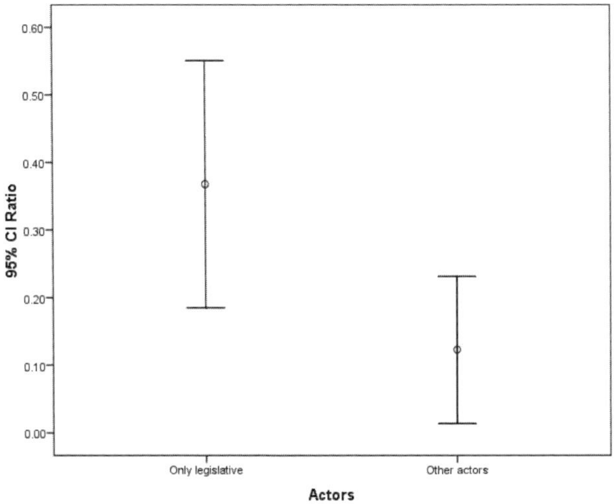

Diagram 6:

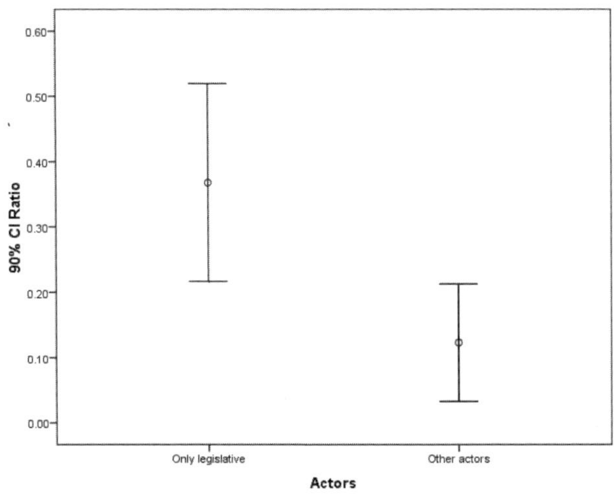

Then, among countries having more than one procedure, amendment rates are superior when only the legislature intervenes than when veto players (either an intervening election or a referendum) are added. Statistical significance exits at 95%.

Number of procedures and ratio of reform

Diagram 7:

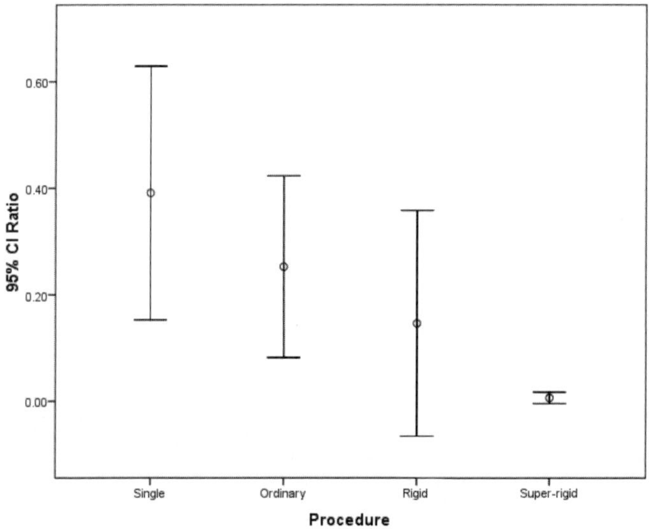

Table 3:

Spearman's Rho

	Ratio	Procedure
Correlation Coefficient	1.000	-.539**
Sig. (2-tailed)	.	.000
N	43	43

**. Correlation is significant at the 0.01 level (2-tailed).

Finally, looking only to parliamentary majorities required (i.e. 50%, two-thirds; three-fifth; four-fifth), the trend seems to go in the opposite direction to the one logically expected: those procedures requiring aggravated majorities have, in fact, a higher tendency towards higher amendment rates (with the exception of the 75% majority of which only a case exists). This tendency, however, is meaningful bearing in mind that lower parliamentary threshold are more commonly associated with additional strictures in the ratification procedure and, in particular, with the addition of veto players.

Size of parliamentary majority and ratio of reforms

Diagram 8:

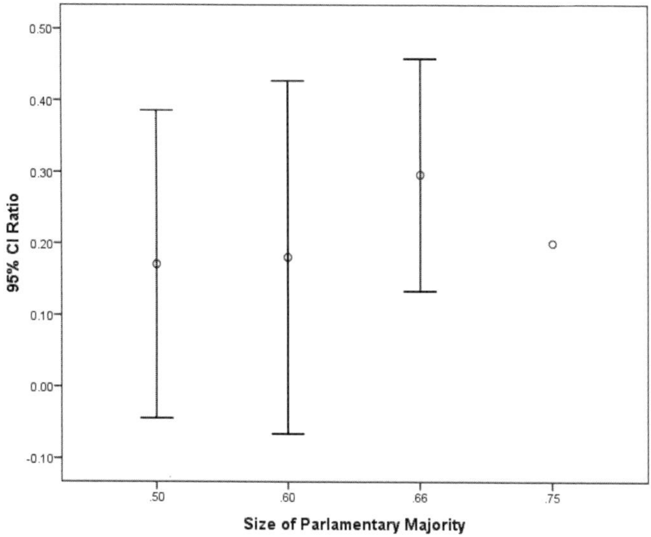

Diagram 9:

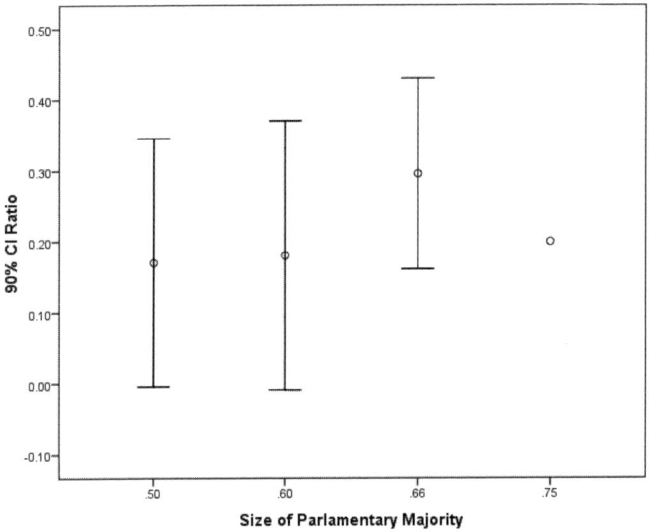

5. Some preliminary conclusions

The data shows some interesting conclusions, in particular in reference to veto players and duration as variables with explanatory power. This chapter has considered the *factual application* of formal ratification procedures. In the current volume, however, there are several examples of failed constitutional amendment processes which did not reach the ratification stage. This means that, apart from the actual strictness of the amendment procedure, other factors and, in particular, the relations between political parties may be essential to explain reform. The cases of Germany, Belgium and Spain may illustrate this point. In Germany, the process of constitutional reform went nowhere until the "Grand coalition" between CDU and SPD included it as part of the government program (See Hofmann, in this volume). In Belgium, political parties' leaders were able to agree constitutional reforms among themselves in five days. Parliamentary ratification was a mere formalisation of the agreement. In Spain, lack of agreement between parties precluded even starting negotiations for the process of constitutional reform that the government proposed in 2004. Contrariwise, in Sweden, a country with an *a priori* very rigid procedure for reform and a surprisingly high constitutional amendment rate, changes in the constitution are normally the result of cross-party negotiations: in 2010, all the seven parliamentary parties voted in favour of constitutional reform in the *Riskdag*. This means that constitutional reform, once approved by the first legislature, will not become an object of dispute in the electoral campaign in the ensuing election before the second parliamentary vote on constitutional reform. Thus, in summary, institutions may ease or make it more difficult to amend a constitution. But in the absence of powerful external veto players, it seems that political parties' agreements may sail through even the most stringent constitutional reform procedure, particularly when its duration requires regular actualisation.

References

Anckar, Dag/Kervonen, Lauri (2002): Constitutional amendment methods in the democracies of the world. Paper presented at the XIIIth Nordic Political Science Congress. Aalborg, Denmark, 15-17 August 2002.

Behnke, Nathalie/Benz, Arthur (2009): The politics of constitutional change between reform and evolution. In: Publius: The Journal of Federalism 39, (2), 213-240.

Buchanan, James M./Tullock, Gordon (1962): The Calculus of Consent: Logical Foundations of Constitutional Democracy. Ann Arbor: The University of Michigan Press.

Cheibub, José Antonio/Gandhi, Jennifer/Vreeland, James Raymond (2010): Democracy and dictatorship revisited. In: Public Choice 143, (1-2), 67–101.

Congleton, Roger D. (2003): Improving Democracy hrough Constitutional Reform. Some Swedish Lessons. The Hague: Kluwer Academic Publishers.

Deschouwer, Kris (2005): Kingdom of Belgium. In: Kincaid J./Tarr G. A. (eds.): Constitutional Origins, Structure, and Change in Federal Countries. Kingston/Montreal: McGill-Queen's University Press.

Elkins, Zachary/Ginsburg, Tom/Melton, James (2008): The lifespan of written constitutions. Mimeo available at http://www.gwu.edu/~igis/assets/docs/Elkins_paper.pdf [accessed: 7 March 2011]

Elster, Jon (2000): Ulysses Unbound. Studies in Rationality, Pre-commitment, and Constraints. Cambridge: Cambridge University Press.

Ferejohn; John (1997): The politics of imperfection: The amendment of constitutions. In: Law and social inquiry 22, (2), 501-530.

Hausmaninger, Herbert (2003): The Austrian Legal System. Wien: Manzsche Verlags- und Universitätsbuchhandlung.

Heritier, Adrienne (2007): Explaining Institutional Change in Europe. Oxford: Oxford University Press.

Holmes, Stephen/Sunstein, Cass (2005): The politics of constitutional reform in Eastern Europe. In: Levinon, S. (ed.): Responding to Imperfection: The Theory and Practice of Constitutional Amendment. Ewing: Princeton University Press, 275-306.

Lane, Jan-Erik (1996): Constitutions and Political Theory. Manchester: Manchester University Press.

Lijphart, Arend (1999): Patterns of Democracy: Government Forms and Performance in Thirty-Six Countries. New Haven: Yale University Press.
Lorenz, Astrid (2005): How to measure constitutional rigidity. Four concepts and two alternatives. In: Journal of Theoretical Politics 17, (3), 339-361.
Lutz, Donald S. (1994): Toward a theory of constitutional amendment. In: American Political Science Review 88, (2), 355-370.
Rasch, Bjorn Erik/Congleton, Roger D. (2006): Amendment procedures and constitutional stability. In: Conglento, R. D./Swedenborg, Birgitta (eds.): Democratic Constitutional Design and Public Policy: Analysis and Evidence. Cambridge: MIT Press, 319-342.
Roberts, Andrew (2009): The politics of constitutional amendment in post-communist Europe. In: Constitutional Political Economy 20, (2), 99-117.
Venice Commission (2010): Report on Constitutional Amendment. Study n. 469/2008 CDL-AD(2010)001.

Regional Actors' Participation in Constitutional Reform: Opportunities, Limits and Risks

Jörg Kemmerzell and Bettina Petersohn

1. Introduction

Changes in the territorial organisation of a state or in the distribution of power and resources between different levels of government usually require a constitutional reform. Federal theory assumes that in federal systems both levels of government participate in those constitutional reforms in one way or another (Watts, 2008; Burgess, 2006; Elazar, 1987). Since these reforms usually affect the allocation of power between all levels of government, involvement of regional actors seems to be essential. Firstly, non-involvement or weak involvement may disadvantage sub-state entities, be it *Regions, Provinces, Länder* or *Kantone*, in terms of losing power in areas of autonomous or joint decision-making. Fields of jurisdiction might also be granted to or downloaded on them without the necessary financial resources to adequately exercise these competences. In order to have any influence on the outcome of territorial reforms some kind of participation for regional actors ought to be provided for. Secondly, participation of regional actors may enhance the legitimacy of reform results, i.e. a new territorial order or changed distribution of power, thus contributing to the long-term stability of a federal system. However, despite the necessity or desirability of regional participation increasing the number of veto players may have adverse effects on reform negotiations or results. According to veto player theory, actors agree on a reform only if the gains outweigh transaction costs for each of them. Increasing the number of veto players delimits the prospects of constitutional reform because the "winset" of possible reform solutions will be narrowed by the higher the number of players (Tsebelis, 2002). Since redistributing power between different levels of governments is always contested, reform attempts may be jeopardised by enlarging the influence and veto-points of regional actors.

Even if one agrees to the necessity of regional involvement, the following questions still remain: what determines the roles and power of regional actors in constitutional reform processes? Which regional actor is provided with what kind of power in reform negotiations? Who has to consent to a reform according to the amendment rules, all sub-state entities or only several? Empirical observations show that reform processes display a variety of organisational forms with large differences in the roles adopted by sub-state entities or regional actors.

Applying a veto player framework, this chapter inquires into the roles of regional actors in constitutional reform processes and the ambivalent consequences of increased veto options at the sub-state level. In a first step, main arguments of veto player theory are elaborated with reference to constitutional reforms. Secondly, we discuss existing options of how regional actors participate in reform processes using empirical examples from selected countries.[1] Finally, the consequences of these alternatives on reform negotiations and reform results are analysed. The comparative analysis reveals that veto-power granted to sub-state parliaments or governments are indeed endangering the success of constitutional reforms. Contrary to theoretical assumptions however, veto power does not primarily cause constitutional deadlock but rather advances the ratification of ineffective reforms based on the lowest common denominator. In multinational contexts where negotiations on constitutional territorial reforms tend to be contested between different national communities, these ineffective results can also accelerate federal disintegration. Increasing the opportunities for regional actors may thus be desirable for reasons of legitimacy but may also have unfavourable effects on the overall stability of the federal system.

2. Veto player theory and constitutional reform processes

Rules of constitutional amendment usually set high thresholds for cross-party consensus and give veto players a particularly strong position. Empirical studies have however convincingly demonstrated that high thresholds are not generally reducing the likelihood of constitutional reforms (Lorenz, 2005) but that they may become an obstacle for the reform success if matters are contested among negotiating partners (Bryde, 1982). Basically, amendment rules define the procedures of ratifying a constitutional reform. They constitute certain actors as veto players and enhance the complexity of the reform process having an impact on the negotiations themselves. Even if they are not determining the probability of ratification we assume that rules of amendment affect the opportunities for regional actors to participate and shape the outcome of territorial constitutional reforms.

With regard to Tsebelis' veto player approach, one can distinguish between institutional and partisan veto players (Tsebelis, 2002: 19). The veto

1 The comparative analysis is based on a research project funded by the German Research Foundation (DFG) in which the following cases of constitutional territorial reforms have been analysed: Austria, Constitutional Convention (2003-2005); Belgium, State Reform (2000-2001); Canada, Charlottetown Accord (1992); France, Decentralisation Acte II (2002-2003); Germany, Federalism Reform I and II (2003-2009); Italy, Reform of Title V of the Constitution (2001); UK, Devolution (1998); Switzerland, Neuer Finanzausgleich (1994-2008); and Spain: Constitutional Change induced by Statute Reforms in Catalonia (2006) and Andalusia (2007).

power of institutional veto players is vested in formal requirements while the veto power of the latter depends on specific political circumstances, e.g. the actual distribution of votes and a party's ability to control government decisions. But even partisan veto players are sometimes constituted by formal rules of amendment, like the necessity of special majorities for constitutional reform. In case of parties controlling majorities necessary for amendment, institutional veto players get absorbed by partisan veto players. This holds true particularly for two-chamber systems with vertical integrated party systems (for the concept of vertical integration of parties see Thorlakson, 2009). Party integration covers what Tsebelis refers to as *cohesion* of veto players. According to veto player theory, the "policy stability" of a political system increases due to the cohesiveness of the veto players.

Rules for constitutional amendment usually constitute institutional veto players at the national or state-wide level assigning veto power to the first chamber of parliament and to the second chamber if it holds equal powers. In a two-chamber system with different parties or party coalitions controlling the respective chambers we might expect deadlock or reforms to be less innovative and limited in scope. Congruent majorities in both chambers enhance the probability of more definite reform steps. Whilst constitutional amendment needs the agreement of special majorities in most countries, full control of both houses by one party rarely occurs. The importance of partisan veto players is highlighted e.g. by the case of the German Federalism Reform I. Even though many controversial topics, like the fiscal constitution, have been excluded right from the beginning, a small-scale reform was not adopted until a Grand Coalition at the federal level temporarily moderated the rigidity resulting from party confrontation (Burkhart, 2009).

Before we explain these assumptions in greater detail, it should be mentioned that veto player analysis is applied not in its strict formal version but as a heuristic concept intended to structure our inquiry. Our approach is interested in identifying and specifying *regional* veto players and to study opportunities available to exert influence on processes of territorial reform.

3. Types of regional actors and their role in ratification processes

Regional actors are defined by their reference to the sub-state level. They represent interests of specific territorial entities and act according to specific regional needs. Actors may be composed of members of regional governments or regional parliaments as well as the people of a territorial entity that gets involved by a regional referendum. Organisations of civil society can theoretically also pursue specific regional interests. However, they are usually more influential in initiating reform processes and shaping the reform agenda (see Banting and Simeon, 1985) whereas in ratification of constitutional agreements they usually play a limited role. Rules of ratification for constitutional amendments largely define the actors involved in ratifying constitutional reforms as well as their powers. Empirical observations illustrate that variations in the organisation of the reform process nevertheless take place within one state and under the same ratification rules. However, institutions of sub-state entities are rarely given an explicit veto. For the assessment of the roles of regional actors in constitutional reforms, electoral outcomes and composition of both chambers are of equal importance.

Engagements of regional actors are affected by different provisions (Marks, Hooghe and Schakel, 2010: 26-29): regional referenda or a national referendum with special regional quotas grant more power to the regional population; regional parliaments or regional governments can exercise a more powerful position in parliamentary processes; and strong regionalist parties[2] put pressure on negotiating partners in case their votes are required to meet special majorities. In reality, regional referenda mostly can be found in multinational federations[3] whereas regional parliaments are rarely involved in ratifying constitutional reforms.

Within our case selection regional referenda can be found in Great Britain, Spain and Canada. During the devolution processes in Scotland and Wales, the facultative referenda were supposed to give the Scottish and Welsh people an opportunity to express their opinion on the future territorial organisation of the state. Similarly, the decision of some Canadian provinces to hold regional referenda prior to provincial consent on the negotiated constitutional reform was intended to involve the regional population and enhance the legitimacy of the reform (O'Neill, 2000; LeDuc and Pammett, 1995). Despite the assertion of proponents of a regional nationalism, the regional population does not constitute a homogeneous actor but has diffuse and heterogeneous interests in a popular referendum. Although confined to a territorial entity, regional population behave as "multiple actors" and more than one opinion materialises in the popular vote as has been demonstrated by studies of the 1992 Charlottetown Referendum in Canada (Noël, 1994; Johnston et al., 1993) or the referendum on sovereignty in Quebec in 1995 (Massicotte, 1997). Therefore, a failed regional referendum on further decen-

---

2 Regionalist parties are defined by an electoral success that relies on a certain regional territory. At least two common characteristics unite them: the reference to a sub-state territory, and the assertion of an exclusive group identity of the population, respectively a part of the population of that sub-state territory (Deschouwer, 2009; Türsan, 1998).

3 Referenda can be mandatory and binding, or they can be consultative, leaving formal power of constitutional amendment to the legislature. In this case, they are not binding. In practice, this distinction has limited relevance since governments or parties cannot ignore the result of a consultative referendum. Usually, a government and its majority in parliament initiate a referendum with the explicit claim to hear the voice of the people and accept a majority vote.

tralisation cannot automatically be equated with the rejection of an increase in regional autonomy as well as a passed regional referendum doesn't mean unconditional consent to it. In Switzerland, the population is involved in constitutional reforms by means of an obligatory national referendum and a popular initiative. The populations of the cantons are taken into consideration due to special majorities required for final approval.

Compared to the frequency of referenda, regional parliaments serve only rarely as ratifying authorities in constitutional reforms. They are more involved in cases of reforms of regional statutes. In Spain, these statute reforms constitute by now a common pattern of changing the allocation of power between the levels of government. Reforms of the Catalan Statute of Autonomy are partly initiated at the regional level and require a two-thirds majority of consent in the Catalan parliament before the reform draft is sent to the *Cortes Generales*. The final reform is then accepted or rejected by a regional referendum. Changing the Statute of Autonomy in Andalusia follows a similar pattern. Regional actors, especially regional parliamentarians, gain a powerful role in drafting and negotiating the reform whereas the regional population plays a role in the final ratification (Keating and Wilson, 2009).[4] In contrast, British devolution failed to provide analogous patterns for further federal changes after its implementation in 1997. The involvement of the Scottish Parliament and the Welsh Assembly in future reform steps has not been regulated in any way, so that minor reforms are likely to be pursued in bilateral processes between the devolved bodies and Westminster. Major steps of reform, like a general revision of the devolved competences or the abolition of them, will probably be subject to further referenda but this has not been made a formal requirement (Jeffery and Palmer, 2000: 328).

Among the countries under scrutiny, regional parliaments are directly involved in ratifying reforms of the federal constitution only in Canada. Depending on the subject, all or a majority of the provincial legislative assemblies have to consent beside the federal parliament in order to pass a constitutional amendment changing the federal system. If governments control parliamentary majorities, the federal government as well as several or all provincial governments gain a veto in federal constitutional reforms. Together with the regional referendum required in some provinces, the threshold of consent for constitutional reforms is comparatively high in Canada or even too high, eventually reducing the likelihood of future reforms altogether (Russell, 2004: 239). Furthermore, the premiers of the provinces gain a particular powerful role in pooling and representing regional interests in constitutional reform processes. At the same time, they are more vulnerable to electoral defeat because they can be held responsible for the results of reform negotiations, as the defeat of the

4 Apart from the opportunity of initiating a reform by the autonomous community, reforms of the statutes of autonomy require bilateral negotiations and the consent of both levels of government (see Colino and Olmeda in this volume).

Meech Lake Accord (1987-1990) clearly demonstrated. This case confirms the assumptions of veto player theory about the relation between the number of veto players and the likelihood of ratification. The veto options available for the provinces have been successfully invoked to block the passing of the reform despite the consensus found earlier in the negotiations.

In a majority of our cases, delegates in second chambers indirectly represent regions in decisions on constitutional amendments. Hence, the authority of regional actors to exert influence depends on the composition of second chambers and their formal powers. Directly elected in regions (e.g. in Switzerland and partly in Belgium and Italy), and provinces (partly in Spain), indirectly elected in the *départements* (France), appointed by the federal government (in Canada), delegated by regional parliaments (like in Austria or for a certain number of senators also in Belgium and Spain) or by regional governments (as is the case in Germany), they participate in constitutional reform processes in several ways (see Riescher, Ruß and Haas, 2010 for details on the election, composition, and powers of second chambers). Their power, however, is not only determined by these institutional rules reflecting differences in governmental systems and political culture. Institutional rules unfold differently and the effects depend on the political context and the existence of regionalist parties. Members of second chambers representing distinct regional interests can play a role in parliamentary decisions or joint parliamentary committees, take influence on positions of national governments or exert veto-power jointly if approval in the second chamber is a necessary requirement in passing constitutional amendments.

When comparing these variations in composition and power of second chambers, the roles of regional actors differ significantly across our cases. Whereas the appointment process in Canada leaves the Senators rather powerless in ratifying constitutional reforms and without a specific regional basis or democratic legitimacy, members of the German *Bundesrat* can exercise a powerful role if representatives of several *Länder* are cooperating with each other. Since constitutional reforms require a two-thirds majority of the votes in the *Bundesrat*, one third of the members can veto a reform proposal. However, empirical observations of several reform processes in Germany demonstrate that the institutional veto of the *Bundesrat* is usually absorbed by partisan veto players. Due to a strong vertical integration of parties in Germany and incongruent majorities in both houses of the legislature, the *Bundesrat* more often reflects the divide between government and opposition than regional cleavages (Lehmbruch, 2000; Thorlakson, 2009: 167). For the use of the veto granted to the *Bundesrat*, the distribution of seats between the parties thus becomes more important than distinct regional interests on reform issues. Particularly in Germany, regional interests are also represented within political parties. Regional branches, parliamentarians and members of *Länder* executives regularly influence the position of the federal party. A similar situation can be identified in other cases, where party affiliation dominates regional allegiances or both houses are controlled by the same majorities (e.g. in Belgium and Spain).

Ratification rules, therefore, do not solely determine the effective power of regional actors, but the interplay of ratification rules and party system characteristics seems to be essential in parliamentary ratification processes. Regions gain a stronger position if their interests are not represented only by state-wide parties but if additional parties exist with a special connection to one or several sub-state entities. Regionalist parties usually focus on certain regions creating asymmetric conditions for reform processes. The entirely regionalised party system of Belgium certainly represents an exceptional case but we find strong regionalist parties in the UK, in Spain or Canada that have been a driving force in constitutional reform processes. Regionalist parties are often considered as representatives of autonomy movements following the purpose of protecting and preserving a regional culture. In reality however, they pursue different goals, depending on electoral strength and institutional circumstances. Large or dominant parties which control or could control regional governments, like the Scottish National Party (SNP), *Convergència i Unió* (CiU) in Catalonia or the *Parti Québécois* (PQ) in Canada, often claim for the extension of cultural and political autonomy. On the contrary some small parties, like the *Partido Andalucista,* concentrate on the transformation of Spain into a federal structure with equal autonomy for all communities as well as a better system of financial transfers for Andalusia (Montabes et al., 2006: 218-219).

Overall, a comparative view reveals a great variety of represented regional interests and opportunities for regional actors to participate in constitutional reform processes but only few cases in which regional actors are able to veto reform proposals unconditionally. Rules of constitutional amendment shape but not completely determine the power of regional actors. Other factors, like the composition of second chambers and the party system are of particular importance in parliamentary processes of ratification. Although high hurdles of amendment are not reducing the chances of ratifying a reform successfully, they have a significant impact on decision-making in reform processes. The following table highlights these different forms of regional involvement and categorises our selected cases along the type of veto player (institutional or partisan) and the influence of regional actors. For this purpose, we intend to assess whether regional veto players exist at all, and to specify weak and strong regional veto players.[5]

As the table indicates, regional actors can have a strong influence on ratifications of federal reforms but this influence is not necessarily guaranteed by rules of amendment. Second chambers bestow only limited power on regional actors although they are in most cases established to represent substate entities and interests. In contrast, regional referenda, mandatory or fac-

5 It should be mentioned that categorisation is supposed to serve for illustration only, but cannot refer to clear-cut measurement.

ultative, constitute regional populations as influential veto players. In Scotland and Catalonia, we find a combination of strong institutional and partisan veto players. This affects the negotiation results as well as territorial developments. Both cases feature significant similarities, in that territorial reforms were successful in terms of agenda fulfilment. Likewise, reforms in both cases strengthened federal asymmetry remarkably. Overall, our units of analysis display most of the possible constellations of regional veto players. To explain the degree of regional involvement we might attach greater importance to national contexts and party system characteristics as well as differences in reform types. Nevertheless, both types of veto players have an impact on constitutional negotiations and reform results.

Table 1: Regional actors in territorial constitutional reforms

Case	Regional institutional veto player	Regional partisan veto player
Austria: Constitutional Convention 2003-05	None	None
Belgium: Lambermont Accord 2000/01	Weak: *Sénat* (several senators elected by community parliaments; Senate widely absorbed by community parties)	Strong: parties in the regionalised party system
Canada: Charlottetown Accord 1992	Strong: provincial governments; in some cases people of the provinces	Generally weak, strong only in Quebec: PQ
France: Decentralisation Act II 2002/03	Weak: *Sénat* (rather committed to local level)	None
Germany: Federal Reform I + II, 2006, 2009	Weak: *Bundesrat* (*Länder* interests balanced and/or superimposed by party competition)	None (Bavarian CSU bound in cooperation with federal CDU)
Italy: Reform of Title V of the Constitution 2001	None	None (*Lega Nord* restricted to agenda setting)
UK: Scotland Act 1997	Strong: people of Scotland (referendum), but subject to Westminster legislation	Strong: SNP
UK: Wales Act 1997	Strong: people of Wales (referendum), but subject to Westminster legislation	Weak: *Plaid Cymru*
Spain: Reform of the Statute of Catalonia 2006	Strong: Parliament of the Autonomous Community (draft of reform proposal), people of Catalonia (final referendum)	Strong: support of oppositional CiU indispensable for reform approval
Spain: Reform of the Statute of Andalusia 2007	Strong: Parliament of the Autonomous Community (draft of reform proposal), people of Andalusia (final referendum)	Weak: PSOE dominant party, able to choose partners among several smaller parties
Switzerland: NFA 1994-2008	Weak: cantonal interests represented by coequal *Ständerat*; double majority requirement in referendum	None

4. Impact of amendment rules on constitutional negotiations

Political actors are effectively constituted as veto players by the formal procedure of constitutional amendment. In this regard, actors' powers do not rest upon their ability to affect the content of constitutional reform but to accept or reject an already negotiated proposal. In negotiations, participants have to anticipate the preferences of those actors with veto power and include their demands in order to propose amendments that, in the end, are acceptable to them. Hence, the influence of regional actors on negotiations largely depends on whether distinct agents at the negotiating table can be bound to particular regional positions. The agent, on the other hand, has to persuade the negotiating partners that the collective regional actor represented by him will follow his advice and consent to an agreed compromise.

If we consider the types of regional actors distinguished previously, the impact on negotiations differ considerably. A regional population can be represented in negotiations only by members of their governments or parliaments without being able to check on their behaviour or adherence to agreed positions. At the same time, voting in regional referenda seems to be more or less unpredictable. In the cases of Andalusia and Catalonia we observe a comparatively close coupling between the parliamentary and the referendum arena where the outcomes of the referenda approximately resembled the strength of the respective party camps. While supporters of parties backing the reform proposals largely approved, those of the opposition rejected the reform or abstained from participating in the referenda at all (Colino, 2009a; Olmeda, 2009). In the British cases of devolution, party affiliation similarly determined the outcomes of the referenda. But, even though the Labour Party headed the negotiations in both regions, it took different courses in Scotland and Wales. In Scotland, the cross party and consociational *Constitutional Convention* dominated debates about devolution at the beginning of the 1990s and framed the general matters including suggestions from various social and political groups (Mitchell, 2009: 15-17). The extent of public involvement and public discussion reached in Scotland was not matched in Wales. Here, negotiations only included representatives of the Labour Party, so that the devolution proposal in Wales essentially became the product of internal Labour policy development (Bradbury, 2010: 7). However, the strong Scottish National Party together with a more vibrant social society were successful in putting pressure on negotiating parties, which eventually resulted in a significantly larger scope of devolution proposals in Scotland than in Wales. Similarly, statewide referenda in Switzerland are expected to end with approval if all parties gather behind a reform proposal and campaign in favour of it (Freiburghaus, 2005).

Nevertheless, representatives of regions cannot rely on an automatic ratification of a negotiated consensus in a popular referendum. If a referendum is required in order to pass a constitutional reform, it affects negotiations in a rather diffuse way without exercising any direct influence on actors' positions. Particularly regional governments may be induced to insist on their demands for decentralisation and autonomy in case a regional referendum is required for ratification. Consequently, finding a consensus in negotiations can get more difficult because of unpredictable behaviour of certain participants. Outright failure however cannot be identified more often when compared to reforms without regional referenda. Strong arguments can be made that regional referenda induce changes in communication strategies and open the process for public consultations. Negotiating parties have to communicate the final consensus to citizens in order to win the popular vote. More opportunities for public participation, deliberative forums or hearings as well as a continuous dialogue between the negotiating parties, the public and organisations of civil society raise the visibility and legitimacy of the on-going reform process. These features may also enhance the feasibility of successful ratification without being any guarantee as illustrated by the example of the lost referendum on the *Charlottetown Accord* in Canada in 1992. Here, despite extensive public consultation at the beginning, the population did not accept in the final referendum the compromises negotiated afterwards in intergovernmental conferences behind closed doors (Stein, 1993; Chambers, 1998).

As explained previously, the influence of regional parliaments on constitutional reforms varies depending on the composition of second chambers and the strength of regionalist parties. Regional negotiators are strengthened if the consent of regional parliaments is required for final ratification like in Canada or in Spain, where reform drafts require the approval of two-third (Catalonia) or three-fifth (Andalusia) majorities in the legislatures of the autonomous communities before being discussed at the national level. Therefore, negotiations follow an intergovernmental pattern where package deals and intergovernmental bargaining dominate the process. The leeway of action for regional representatives depends on their ability to control majorities in the regional parliaments or their reliance on other parties for final approval. Territories with strong regionalist parties representing national minorities may turn into key actors in constitutional reforms as in Great Britain with the SNP as well as in Canada where the PQ put pressure on negotiations to deal with accommodating specific interests of the province of Quebec. In both cases, parties threatened with separation if reforms would not meet their demands. That these threats were not purely theoretical became obvious during the campaign for the referendum on sovereignty in 1995 in which the Quebec population voted to continue as a Canadian province only by a margin of less than one per cent (Government of Quebec, 2001). Otherwise, the credible "threat" of regionalist parties can also contribute to the quality of reform results, as may be the case with Scottish devolution.

If ratification procedures include a special majority in parliament, regionalist parties can influence negotiations and focus on regional demands if their votes are required for ratification. In Belgium the *Volksunie* played that game successfully and pushed for further decentralisation until its final break up over the state reform of 2001 (De Winter, 2006). The pivotal role of the oppositional Catalan CiU might also serve as a good example for the establishment of partisan veto players through formal rules of amendment. During the reform of the Catalan Statute of Autonomy, the oppositional, moderate nationalist CiU was able to significantly influence the text of the new statute. The Catalan Socialists as the leading party of the Catalan coalition depended on CiU's consent. Consequently, the passed reform proposal came closer to the preferences of the CiU than to the PSC and its coalition partners in government. CiU continued its pivotal position when negotiations moved to the national and then back to the regional level, since the Socialist led Spanish government was committed to find accordance with the CiU in the referendum (Colino, 2009a).

The influence of single regions is comparatively weak if their specific interests are represented only by certain members in second chambers. In second chambers for example, unsettled majorities may be fixed by slight modifications of reform proposals as it may happen in two-chamber systems like Germany, Italy or France where "post-negotiation negotiations" in the legislature are feasible. In comparison, decision-making processes between regional parliaments are less flexible, and referenda do not allow at all for the subsequent forming of majorities. Thus, constitutional reformers are compelled to consider two crucial aspects pointed out by veto player theory: firstly, the significance of the median voter's position which should be covered by the proposal; secondly, the spoiling potential of a multiplicity of actors, may it be parties or public interest groups, who are able to mobilise for a *No*-campaign leading to the failure of a reform. Generally, referenda are disposed to a significant degree of uncertainty, regardless of whether they take place state-wide or at the regional level. The risk of failure is extended in divided societies, where identity conflicts superimpose a reconciliation of interests. Ratification in second chambers appears to be effortless in contrast. If negotiations between both chambers are conducted in a joint commission, like in Germany, ratification of bargaining results seems to be guaranteed. But two aspects have to be considered in this regard. First, the necessity of a vertical integrated party system, which provides the basis for smooth ratification of negotiation results; and secondly, that successful ratification does not guarantee the quality of a constitutional reform. In fact, constitutional bargaining confined to the intergovernmental arena tends to lead to compromises on the lowest common denominator without contributing significantly to solving the constitutional problem.

5. Impact on reform results and federal developments

When discussing the impact of regional actors on reform results we must first distinguish between rather *regional* and *federal* reforms. In regional reforms focusing on selected constituent entities, regional actors find it easier to influence the process and can focus on their specific region without the necessity of balancing other regional interests. A common impact of all regional reforms upon the federal level is a tendency towards asymmetrical decentralisation. Although devolution processes in Scotland and Wales were linked with each other, negotiations took place separately leading to significantly different outcomes in these regions: the Scottish Parliament exhibits full legislative and some tax-varying powers, whereas the Welsh Assembly is responsible for decisions on executive and administrative matters only (Keating, 2004). Asymmetries in Spain had been enshrined in the constitution during the democratic transition at the end of the 1970s. But after failed attempts of amending the Spanish Constitution in the new millennium, autonomous communities one by one extended their competences by reforming their statutes, with the agreement of the national government achieved in intergovernmental negotiations. Revisions of autonomy statutes are now pursued as a substitute for a general federal reform but without fully achieving the intended results (Colino, 2009b: 264). Consequentially, such piecemeal approach improves conditions for regional actors to participate while it deepens divergence between the regional units. Attempts by the Spanish state to reintroduce a symmetrical distribution of power have led to an overall increase in the level of competences of the autonomous communities (Maiz et al., 2010).

A similar pattern of asymmetric development has been established with Scottish and Welsh devolution in the UK. These asymmetries are particularly embodied in the divergence of the devolved institutions concerning the distribution of powers and competences. Reasons for this divergence were not only historical path dependencies but also the higher extent of Labour control of the devolution process in Wales, the strength of the SNP in Scotland in comparison to the much weaker *Plaid Cymru* in Wales, and the greater significance of devolution in the Scottish public. In view of the whole territorial structure these factors accounting for divergence have rather been strengthened during the devolution process, because of increased political opportunity structures for regional actors. In this regard, one might consider for example the SNP led minority government in Scotland since 2007, which used the new institutions in order to strengthen the arrangement of self-rule. Meanwhile, at the Scottish regional election on 5 May 2011, the SNP succeeded in securing an overall majority of parliamentary seats.

In contrast, federal reforms covering all sub-state entities more often provide for a symmetrical distribution of power even if national minorities demand special rights or the transfer of particular competences. Due to the entitlement of several or all provinces in Canada to decide upon major federal reforms, a consensus has to be found that reflects the interests of all provinces and of the federal level and balances different regional particularities at the same time. Looking at negotiating results, political actors have been far more reluctant in accepting asymmetrical arrangements than in the UK or Spain. But at the same time, ratification has also been less successful than in other cases. The number of veto players together with the diversity of regional interests caused a constitutional deadlock after decades of constitutional negotiations (Russell, 2004). Federal change below the constitutional level and without veto positions for every province was the answer to the impasse in the Canadian case (Lazar, 1998). Although not entircly accommodating Québec's demands they allowed for some non-constitutional, asymmetrical arrangements without accelerating centrifugal tendencies of the federal system.

In Belgium, the two large linguistic communities hold a veto position in constitutional and territorial reforms. During the transformation into a federal state compromises were reached and successfully ratified at the expense of the national level (Hooghe, 2004). Changed economic circumstances delimited the leeway of action and tightened the federal budget, but at the same time stimulated demands for further reforms on the Flemish side. As a consequence, negotiations ended repeatedly without results and bred a government crisis. Since the consent of both communities is not only required for constitutional reforms, but for all revisions of institutional and federal arrangements enshrined in special majority laws, the deadlock encompasses a wide range of political decisions and blocks the development of the federal system as a whole (Swenden, 2006; Petersohn, 2011). The veto positions of the two communities in Belgium have thus not prohibited the successful ratification of any constitutional reform, but they have caused a greater long-term impasse than the failed ratification of negotiation results in Canada. Although the probability of ratification is reduced in Canada due to the number of veto players, the substance of the negotiating results in terms of solving the underlying constitutional problem seems to be higher than in Belgium where different ways of splitting the country are repeatedly debated (for a comparison of reform outcomes see Behnke et al., 2011).

Furthermore, many federal reforms do not solely focus on regional matters but are dominated by procedures of national policy-making as well as by conflicts and cleavages at the federal level. In this regard, Switzerland, where regional and societal actors have been involved at all stages of constitutional policy-making, establishes an exceptional case (Braun, 2009). In addition, rules of the Swiss referendum democracy empower the population to act simultaneously as "*demos*" and "*demoi*" in every referendum. This might have contributed to the stability of the diversified Swiss Federation while simultaneously maintaining reform capacity in the long run. In contrast, negotiations on constitutional reforms in Germany are closely coupled to the arena of ordinary policy-making without giving regional actors any significant influence. As outlined above, the *Bundesrat* represents members of *Länder* governments but is often captured by partisan interests both in ordinary and constitutional politics. Negotiation results are predominantly ratified successfully but they rarely tackle the underlying constitutional problems. The German federal system, therefore, stays within the constraints of the joint-decision-trap without being capable of agreeing on significant federal reforms reducing the existing inefficiencies (Benz, 2008, 2011; Scharpf, 2009).

In Austria and Italy (with the exception of the regions of Aosta and South Tyrol-Trentino), the influence of regional actors is rather weak and absorbed by party-dominance. In both cases, we can nonetheless detect a pattern of regional party elites influencing national party politics from within, without entailing a rearrangement of the overall vertical integrated party systems so far. In Italy, the *Lega Nord*, which might be expected an important actor, largely rejected to participate seriously in reform negotiations and remained merely an agenda setter. A noticeable pattern has been developed in France, where partisan veto players are widely absent and the *Sénat*, as the potential institutional veto player to pursue regional interests, is rather committed to the local level. Dominated by local notables the *Sénat* is important with regard to local representation and therefore rather reluctant towards reform steps meant to strengthen the regional level (Le Lidec, 2009).

In comparison, involving regional actors to a substantial degree in constitutional reform processes does not necessarily increase the risk of ratification failure; regional actor involvement might limit capacities to reform the territorial organisation of the state in multilateral intergovernmental negotiations. However, it also may facilitate the solution of constitutional problems related to territorial dynamics like in Scotland, Switzerland, Catalonia, or to a lesser degree in Canada and Wales. Nevertheless, the tendency in former unitary states to mainly bilateral intergovernmental negotiations often ends in an asymmetrical distribution of power and may stimulate centrifugal forces. Bilateral negotiations offer the best opportunities for regional actors to pursue their interests, but they put the federal development at the same time at risk.

6. Conclusion

The comparison of regional actors in selected cases of constitutional reform demonstrates opportunities but also risks of different types of involvement. In all cases, regional actors took part in reform negotiations in one way or the other, via members of regional governments or parliaments or representatives of regionalist parties. The rules of ratification define only the broad framework and constitute relevant actors as veto players up to a certain degree. Equally important seems to be the type of reform and features of the party system. Regional reforms, on the one hand, provide better access for regional actors, as could be seen to different degrees in Spain and the UK, than federal reforms where access to negotiations and ratification is rather channelled by national institutions. Any influence on the outcome therefore remains limited. Sub-state entities are rarely constituted as veto players in the final ratification of constitutional reforms. On the other hand, federal reforms usually perpetuate symmetrical structures while regional reforms strengthen asymmetric arrangements. Thus, the types of reform differ not only in the opportunities for regional actors but also in their impact on the overall development of the territorial structure.

Furthermore, federal reforms are usually dominated by the federal level and reproduce existing conflicts of ordinary policy-making. Switzerland and Canada are the exceptions, where the culture of direct democracy, particular institutional requirements and constitutional conventions shape the procedures. In both cases various opportunities for regional actors exist to influence constitutional reforms in different phases. In Canada, tensions occurred between the traditional consensual style of intergovernmental negotiations and competitive politics without the moderating impact of vertical integrated parties. Deadlocks in negotiations on constitutional amendments have been a repeated pattern in Canadian history. At the same time, the involvement of the provinces at the stages of negotiation and ratification has also contributed to the accommodation of national and regional diversities. In Switzerland, constitutional reforms take place against the backdrop of amendment requirements setting high thresholds for consent and stipulating a final referendum. However, the two cases also demonstrate that high hurdles of consent for constitutional amendments including enhanced influence for regional actors have not only negative effects on negotiations and reform outcomes as assumed by veto player theory. Switzerland and Canada have been rather successful in solving constitutional problems and accommodating diversity compared to other cases under scrutiny. Increasing veto points in order to enable broad participation of regional actors or sub-state entities may jeopardise the smooth progress of constitutional negotiations but at the same time improve the long-term quality of reform results. In comparison, limited opportunities for regional actors to influence constitutional reform processes may lower the risk of ratification failure like in Germany. But the dominance of party competition reduces the opportunities of solving the inefficiency problems inherent in the system of joint-decision-making.

In order to assess the degree of influence of regional actors, the veto player approach provides a good starting point. Without any veto options, regional actors do not get involved in constitutional reform processes to any substantial degree. If veto rights are at their disposal, their influence is determined firstly by the institutional configuration: single veto opportunities of sub-state entities, joint opportunities for several entities, or an institutional veto of the second chamber. Secondly, certain types of reform and characteristics of the party system allow for more influence of regional actors beside the provisions of the ratification rules. However, these opportunities are not entirely institutionally granted and depend on electoral outcomes and situational factors. Therefore, they can only be invoked under specific conditions hardly providing a basis for strategic policy considerations.

References

Banting, Keith G./Simeon Richard (1985): Introduction: The Politics of Constitutional Change. In: Banting, K. G./Simeon, R. (eds.): The Politics of Constitutional Change in Industrial Nations. Redesigning the State. London, Basingstoke: Macmillan Press, 1-29.

Behnke, Nathalie/Petersohn, Bettina/Fischer-Hotzel, Andrea/Heinz, Dominic (2011): Measuring success and failure of constitutional reforms. In: Regional & Federal Studies 21, (4), 443-473.

Benz, Arthur (2008): From Joint-decision Traps to Over-regulated Federalism – Adverse Effects of a Successful Constitutional Reform. In: German Politics 17, (4), 440-456.

Benz, Arthur (2011): Escaping joint-decision traps: National and supranational experiences compared. In: Falkner, G. (ed.): The EU's Decision Traps: Comparing Policies. Oxford: Oxford University Press, 199-216.

Bradbury, Jonathan (2010): Country Profile: UK – Wales. Technische Universität Darmstadt (unpublished report for project "Patterns of Constitutional Reform in Federal Structures", funded by the German Research Foundation).

Braun, Dietmar (2009): Constitutional Change in Switzerland. In: Publius: The Journal of Federalism 39, (2), 314-340.

Bryde, Brun-Otto (1982): Verfassungsentwicklung. Stabilität und Dynamik im Verfassungsrecht der Bundesrepublik Deutschland. Baden-Baden: Nomos.

Burgess, Michael (2006): Comparative Federalism. Theory and Practice. London, New York: Routledge.

Burkhart, Simone (2009): Reforming Federalism in Germany. Incremental Changes Instead of the Big Deal. In: Publius: The Journal of Federalism 39, (2), 341-365.

Chambers, Simone (1998): Contract or Conversation? Theoretical Lessons from the Canadian Constitutional Crisis. In: Politics & Society 26, (1), 143-172.

Colino, Cesar (2009a): Country Profile: Spain – Catalonia. Technische Universität Darmstadt (unpublished report for project "Patterns of Constitutional Reform in Federal Structures", funded by the German Research Foundation).

Colino, Cesar (2009b): Constitutional Change Without Constitutional Reform: Spanish Federalism and the Revision of Catalonia's Statute of Autonomy. In: Publius: The Journal of Federalism 39 (2), 262-288.

De Winter, Lieven (2006): In Memoriam the Volksunie 1954-2001: Death by Overdose of Success. In: De Winter, L./Gómez-Reino, M./Lynch, P. (eds.): Autonomist Parties in Europe: Identity Politics and the Revival of the Territorial Cleavage. Barcelona: Institut de Ciències Politiques i Socials, 13-45.

Deschouwer, Kris (2009): The Rise and Fall of the Belgian Regionalist Parties. In: Regional & Federal Studies 19, (4-5), 559-577.

Elazar, Daniel J. (1987): Exploring Federalism. Tuscaloosa: The University of Alabama Press.

Freiburghaus, Dieter (2005): Bedingungen für eine gelingende Föderalismusreform: Die Neugestaltung des Finanzausgleichs und der Aufgabenverteilung zwischen Bund und Kantonen in der Schweiz. In: Europäisches Zentrum für Föderalismus-Forschung Tübingen (ed.): Jahrbuch des Föderalismus 2005. Baden-Baden: Nomos Verlagsgesellschaft, 506-515.

Government of Québec (2001): Resolution of the Québec National Assembly on the 1995 referendum question and an extract of the Official Report of the Directeur général des élections (results). In: Government of Québec (ed.): Québec's Positions on Constitutional and Intergovernmental Issues. Doc. 31, Québec City, 465-466.

Hooghe, Liesbet (2004): Belgium. Hollowing the Center. In: Amoretti, U. M./Bermeo N. (eds.): Federalism and Territorial Cleavages. Baltimore: John Hopkins University Press, 55-92.

Jeffery, Charlie (2009): Devolution in the United Kingdom: Problems of a Piecemeal Approach to Constitutional Change. In: Publius: The Journal of Federalism 39, (2), 289-313.

Jeffery, Charlie/Palmer, Rosanne (2000): Das Vereinigte Königreich – Devolution und Verfassungsreform. In: Europäisches Zentrum für Föderalismus-Forschung Tübingen (ed.): Jahrbuch des Föderalismus 2000. Baden-Baden: Nomos Verlagsgesellschaft, 321-339.

Johnston, Richard/Blais, André/Gidengil, Elisabeth/Nevitte, Neil (1993): The People and the Charlottetown Accord. In: Watts, R. L./Douglas M. B. (eds.): Canada: The State of the Federation 1993. Kingston: Institute of Intergovernmental Relations, Queen's University, 19-43.

Keating, Michael (2004): The United Kingdom. Political Institutions and Territorial Cleavages. In: Amoretti, U. M./Bermeo, N. (eds.): Federalism and Territorial Cleavages. Baltimore: John Hopkins University Press, 155-179.

Keating, Michael/Wilson, Alex (2009): Renegotiating the State of Autonomies: Statute Reform and Multi-level Politics in Spain. In: West European Politics 32, (3), 536-558.

Lazar, Harvey (1998): Non-Constitutional-Renewal: Toward a New Equilibrium in the Federation. In: Lazar, H. (ed.): Canada: The State of the Federation 1997. Non-Constitutional Renewal. Kingston: Institute of Intergovernmental Relations, Queen's University, 3-35.

LeDuc, Lawrence/Pammett, John H (1995): Referendum Voting: Attitudes and Behaviour in the 1992 Constitutional Referendum. In: Canadian Journal of Political Science 28, (1), 3-33.

Lehmbruch, Gerhard (2000) Parteienwettbewerb im Bundesstaat. Stuttgart: Kohlhammer Verlag (3rd ed.).

Le Lidec, Patrick (2009): Réforme constitutionnelle du 28 mars 2003. Technische Universität Darmstadt (unpublished report for project "Patterns of Constitutional Reform in Federal Structures", funded by the German Research Foundation).

Lorenz, Astrid (2005): How to Measure Constitutional Rigidity. In: Journal of Theoretical Politics 17, (3), 339-361.

Loughlin, John (ed.) (2001): Subnational Democracy in the European Union. Challenges and Opportunities. Oxford: Oxford University Press.

Maiz, Ramon/Caamaño, Francisco/Azpitarte, Miguel (2010): The Hidden Counterpoint of Spanish Federalism: Recentralisation and Resymmetrisation in Spain (1978-2008). In: Regional & Federal Studies 20, (1), 63-82.

Marks, Gary/Hooghe, Liesbet/Schakel, Arian H. (2010): The Rise of Regional Authority: A Comparative Study of 42 Democracies. New York: Routledge Chapman & Hall.

Massicotte, Louis (1997): Référendum: le « n'oui » des Québecois. In: Jaumain, Serge (ed.): La réforme de l'Etat ... et après? L'impact des débats institutionnels en Belgique et au Canada. Bruxelles: Editions de l'Université de Bruxelles, 177-195.

Mitchell, James (2009): Scotland's Constitutional Moment. Technische Universität Darmstadt (unpublished report for project "Patterns of Constitutional Reform in Federal Structures", funded by the German Research Foundation).

Montabes, Juan/Pérez Nieto, Enrique G./Ortega, Carmen (2006): The Partido Andalucista: from Autonomy to National-Federalism and Government. In: De Winter, L./Gómez-Reino, M./Lynch P. (eds.): Autonomist Parties in Europe: Identity Politics and the Revival of the Territorial Cleavage. Barcelona: Institut de Ciències Politiques i Socials, 199-226.

Noël, Alain (1994): Deliberating a Constitution: The Meaning of the Canadian Referendum of 1992. In: Cook, C. (ed.): Constitutional Predicament. Canada after the Referendum of 1992. Montreal, Kingston: McGill-Queen's University Press, 64-81.

Olmeda, José A. (2009): Country Profile: Spain – Andalusia. Technische Universität Darmstadt (unpublished report for project "Patterns of Constitutional Reform in Federal Structures", funded by the German Research Foundation).

O'Neill, Michael (2000): Great Britain: From Dicey to Devolution. In Austin, D./O'Neill, M. (eds.): Democracy and Cultural Diversity. Oxford: Oxford University Press, 69-95.

Petersohn, Bettina (2011): Konfliktakkommodierung bis zur Selbstaufgabe? Stabilität und Dynamik der Verfassungsentwicklung in Belgien. In: Politische Vierteljahresschrift 52, (2), 195-219.

Riescher, Gisela/Ruß, Sabine/Haas, Christoph M. (eds.) (2010): Zweite Kammern. München: Oldenbourg (2nd ed.).

Russell, Peter H. (2004): Constitutional Odyssey. Can Canadians Become a Sovereign People? Toronto: University of Toronto Press.

Scharpf, Fritz W. (2009): Föderalismusreform. Kein Ausweg aus der Politikverflechtungsfalle?. Frankfurt a.M., New York: Campus.

Stein, Michael B. (1993): Tensions in the Canadian Constitutional Process: Elite Negotiations, Referendums and Interest Group Consultations, 1980-1992 In: Watts, R. L./Brown, D. M. (eds.): Canada: The State of the Federation 1993. Kingston: Institute of Intergovernmental Relations, Queen's University, 87-116.

Swenden, Wilfried (2006): Belgischer Föderalismus 2005: getrennt zusammenleben oder zusammen auseinanderfallen? In: Europäisches Zentrum für Föderalismus-Forschung Tübingen (ed.): Jahrbuch des Föderalismus 2006. Baden-Baden: Nomos Verlagsgesellschaft, 303-317.

Thorlakson, Lori (2009): Patterns of Party Integration, Influence and Autonomy in Seven Federations. In: Party Politics 15, (2), 157-177.

Tsebelis, George (2002): Veto Players. How Political Institutions Work. Princeton, NJ: Princeton University Press.

Türsan, Huri (1998): Introduction. Ethnoregionalist Parties as Ethnic Entrepreneurs. In: De Winter, L./Türsan, H. (eds.): Regionalist Parties in Western Europe. London & New York: Routledge, 1-16.

Watts, Ronald L. (2008): Comparing Federal Systems. Montréal, Kingston: McGill-Queen's University Press (3rd ed).

6. Evolution after a Constitutional Reform

Austria after the Austrian Convention

Christoph Konrath

1. Introduction

In Austria, no other debate on federal and constitutional reform has enjoyed such a lasting effect than the Austrian Convention. When its President Franz Fiedler presented the Convention's report along with his own proposal for a new Federal Constitution in January 2005, many commentators perceived this as "failure of the Convention" (Wiederin, 2008). But when politicians, journalists and the public deplore the want of institutional and economic reform in Austria today, they still refer to the Austrian Convention. They like to present the Convention's report as a blueprint for reforms or as a treasure chest full of good ideas. The then-President of the Convention is still regarded as one of the pre-eminent experts on constitutional and administrative reform and is a regular contributor to public debates.

It is, however, interesting that almost no one refers to the Convention process, and hardly anyone discusses the actual proposals of the Convention or its members.[1] What seems to have had an impact is the impression that it is possible to formulate substantial and workable reform proposals "even in Austria" and a general view that a lot of the problems the Austrian state faces – foremost such of the federal order – are grounded in a flawed constitution.

Apart from the Convention and the specific public it generated, other (comparatively closed) debates on constitutional reform and especially on federalism have continued. Those debates among specialists have had a lot of influence and they have also set the tone and themes since the end of the Convention. From the constitutional perspective of the Convention the debate has more and more shifted to issues of administrative reform and efficiency of public institutions. This is, however, an issue that had already prevailed in the Convention itself (Wutscher, 2008). At the same time and at a different level, the traditional attitudes of Austria's political parties towards federalism have been blurred. The decade-long stand-off between the conservative and

---

1 The current bibliography (Konrath, 2011) of the Austrian Convention and constitutional reform debates in Austria comprises appr. 450 entries (ranging from pamphlets to legal reviews) of which only 45 are – at least partly – concerned with procedural issues, about 20 articles offer an analysis of the Convention procedures, actors and strategies.

federalist *Österreichische Volkspartei* (Austrian People's Party) and the centralist stance of the Social Democrats is no longer valid.

In this paper I will argue that the Convention has been an example of a new and different mode of discussing matters of federal and constitutional reform, but it has not initiated a change of paradigm. I hold that if we want to understand what has happened after the Convention we have to know how issues were framed and how debates were held before and outside of the Convention. Thus, I will emphasise the instrumental understanding of constitutional law in Austrian political discourse and the specific way of piecemeal constitutional reform. In order to do so I will propose three steps of analysis: an overview of the long-lasting patterns of constitutional reform in Austria (2.), a survey of the developments parallel to and since the Convention (3.) and a concluding attempt to evaluate the state of Austrian federalism today (4.).

2. Prevalent modes of debating, preparing and drafting constitutional and federal reforms

Since the foundation of the Republic of Austria in the wake of the First World War, the federal organisation has been a matter of forceful debates and political divisions. The Federal Constitutional Law of 1920 established a rather weak federal and strong central state. To be more precise: it transformed the remnants of the Habsburg Empire, which had been a highly decentralised unitary state, into a republic that called itself federal (Wiederin, 2004). Thus, it took until 1925 to reach an agreement on the allocation of power between the federation and the *Länder* governments. In some areas – especially in all matters relating to school organisation and education – the political actors could not achieve a solution until 1962. Furthermore, it was not before 1948 (after the disruption caused by an authoritarian federal state 1934 to 1938 and the "*Anschluss*" to the Third Reich 1938 to 1945) that governments could agree on the principles of fiscal federalism as specified in the "*Finanz-Verfassungsgesetz*" (Fiscal Constitutional Act). This has resulted in an extremely detailed and complex distribution of competences and an extreme rigidity of formulations and definitions. Along with other features of the constitution this has caused a lot of discontent with the federal system which can – according to the general understanding – not be adapted to current demands (Dachs, 2007). Since the 1980s federal reform has been on the political agenda. The accession to the EU has made the problems even more obvious as it is hard to match the Austrian allocation of powers and competences with the demands of European integration and EU-law (Öhlinger, 2002a: 90ff.).

These debates on constitutional and federal reform have followed traditional modes of preparing, negotiating and drafting. They can be characterised by piecemeal reforms and an instrumental understanding of the constitution, the nomination of expert groups and political bargaining.

2.1 The ongoing change of the Federal Constitution

The Austrian Federal Constitution is an extremely flexible, fragmented and complex constitution and it is unique in its way to incorporate international legal acts and international influences. Its flexibility is, at the same time, paired with a strange kind of rigidity insofar as it is considered necessary to regulate a lot of issues in a constitutional law and in a very detailed manner (Öhlinger, 1992; Wiederin, 2007a: 403f.). Legally, it is comparatively easy to amend the Federal Constitution or any other so-called constitutional law: To pass a constitutional act or amend federal constitutional laws, all what is necessary is to secure a two-thirds majority in the *Nationalrat* (Austrias's first national parliamentary chamber), which is the main chamber of the legislature, and to specify the act explicitly as "constitutional provision". Any law can have formal constitutional quality, without needing to be part of or incorporated into the main constitutional document, the *Bundes-Verfassungsgesetz* (Federal Constitutional Law; B-VG). Neither the B-VG nor legal scholarship demands any further criteria. The only exception is a "*Gesamtänderung*", i.e. a "total revision" of the Federal Constitution, which would also need the consent of a majority of the electorate in a mandatory referendum. It is not easy to identify a "*Gesamtänderung*", and the term has caused debates and has been at the centre of the development and construction of fundamental constitutional principles in Austria (Öhlinger, 2009: 54ff.).

In our context it is important to note that the abolishment of the federal system would surely be regarded as a "*Gesamtänderung*". However, substantial changes, which were proposed in and after the Convention, might not suffice, regardless of the political effects and demands. Also, some argue that piecemeal reform could – in the end – be qualified as an evasion of the procedure required in case of a "*Gesamtänderung* and thus be used to minimise the influence of *Länder* representatives.[2]

When we look at constitutional politics it is important to distinguish two sides of constitutional development in Austria at least until the Convention: The constitution, its continuous application and development had a more or less instrumental but not fundamental character in the Austrian consocia-

2 For the arguments of the members of the Department of Public Law at the University of Innsbruck see their opinion in the assessment procedure of the first draft-package of the "Expert group 2007/08" (see infra III. b.) 42/SN-94/ME at www.parlament.gv.at. Note that this department is known for its strong federalist stance.

tional political system since 1945 (Öhlinger, 2002b). There were hardly any, and certainly no wider public debates on constitutional politics (Schaller, 1997). Along with the instrumental aspect went the technical-legal character in the tradition of Austrian legal positivism. In this view there are only gradual differences between constitutional laws and ordinary laws. For a long time constitutional scholars and practitioners in the administration and at the courts have fostered an understanding of constitutional laws that places the emphasis on structures and not on content and concepts. Following traits from the administrative tradition of the late Habsburg monarchy, a technical and seemingly apolitical view of constitutional law that required expert knowledge made the constitution a domain of legal professionals, while political scientists and others did not engage in the debate or were not recognised as equal partners. This is even more noteworthy as Hans Kelsen and Adolf Merkl, who were among the most influential commentators of the Federal Constitutional Law and its theoretical background in the 1920s, emphasised the political and democratic aspect of the constitution (Wiederin, 2007c; Ehs, 2011).

The flexibility and the instrumentalist approach do not demand substantial constitutional debates and major reforms. They make continuous and piecemeal adaptations possible and they secured a steady development of the constitution and its key concepts, i.e. the *Rechtsstaat* and fundamental rights (Pernthaler, 2000; Khol and Konrath, 2005: 202ff.). In the light of the constitution's theoretical background this can be an asset, as it does not constrain contemporaries unnecessarily. In the context of a consociational approach to the Austrian diversity and paired with a predominantly legal-technical approach that sees no necessity for broader debates or knowledge, this can however lead to deadlock (Ehs and Konrath, 2010).

This is reflected in the fact that there were no major reform projects of the Federal Constitution or of the federal organisation as such until the Austrian Convention. With "major reform projects" I refer to initiatives that aim to evaluate and discuss the constitution and federalism in a holistic approach and that have broad political and institutional support and try to generate public participation (Schaller, 1997; Khol and Konrath, 2005).

2.2 Expert commissions and governmental initiatives

While there are no traditions of wider and substantial political debates, there are two important traditions of constitutional reform talks in Austria that bore heavily on the proceedings of the Austrian Convention and that are of central importance for everything that has followed since: attempts for constitutional and federal reform have so far been initiated by the executive branch of government. The Austrian Convention is singular insofar as it was – at least to a considerable extent – initiated by the then Presidents of the *Nationalrat* and the Federal Council along with leaders of the opposition party and the President of the Court of Audit (Khol and Konrath, 2004).

Attempts from the executive branch of government come in two forms: either by appointing an expert commission composed of academics and high-ranking civil servants or by launching negotiations between the Federal Government and *Länder*-governments (Khol and Konrath, 2005: 207ff.). The huge bulk of questions regarding the federal system has so far been the domain of negotiations between the Federal Government and State Governments thus reflecting the Austrian type of cooperative federalism. The most important example is the comprehensive agreement on federal reform that was concluded before EU-accession but dropped by the *Länder* after general elections and concessions made to the opposition on the federal level (Wiederin, 2007b: 96ff.). On the other hand, expert commissions had been assigned to prepare a reform of fundamental rights, new models for the allocation of powers between the federation and the *Länder* or the introduction of administrative courts on *Länder* level (Khol and Konrath, 2005: 207ff.). Recently, an inter-ministerial expert commission prepared a far-reaching comprehensive budget reform that was passed unanimously in parliament – which is certainly an exception (Steger, 2010).

In our context we observe tensions between expert talks and political negotiations that remained more than once unresolved. Neither have starting positions and targets usually been defined, nor has it often been clear whether experts could and should act on their own or as speakers for political or administrative interests. Furthermore, it has often remained unclear whether experts have been able to satisfy demands, i.e. whether they have had enough insider knowledge of administrative and political practice to meet the expectations of their counterparts (Konrath, 2005: 354). We also should note that both types of negotiations have not aimed at public involvement, often not even at informing the public. They either have created the impression that a highly controversial topic is actually the domain of – and this is crucial in the Austrian case – legal experts or they have suggested that just another bargain among politicians is on its way. Again, the only exception seems to be the recent budget reform, which has been and still is the domain of economists in the civil service.

2.3 Parliamentarians and citizens?

Even from this sketch we can see that until the inception of the Austrian Convention, substantial attempts for constitutional and federal reforms remained the domain of political and/or administrative leaders and of – in fact – a rather small group of experts. Parliaments on federal or *Länder* level were usually not involved and more often than not did not even consider participating. The same applies to the involvement of the general public. Until the mid

1990s legal scholars and high-ranking civil servants even surmised that the involvement of citizens would only cause confusion (Holzinger, 1991: 493). This points to another characteristic of federal and constitutional reform in Austria: the absence of any attempts to facilitate public discourse. Apart from a general positive attitude towards federalism there is an obvious lack of knowledge about federalism in particular, its mechanisms and values. It is often paralleled by a negative and unappreciative coverage of federal issues in Austria's leading papers and magazines and a failure of politicians to improve this situation (Dachs, 2007: 58ff.).

Constitutional and federal reform remained the domain of governments. And in the case of Austrian federalism it is even dominated by the *Landeshauptleute*, i.e. the heads of governments of the *Länder*. Their position is rather special: they are governors of the Land, they fulfil the leading role in the specific Austrian system of indirect federal administration in the *Länder* – and this is from where governors draw their real power. Additionally, they not only chair the party organisation of their respective *Land* but usually occupy high positions in the respective federal party organisation. As a consequence, a rather unique situation of overlapping territorial and partisan interests has so far proved crucial in most reform attempts. Unlike expert debates and the possibilities of mediation in parliamentary procedures, Austrian cooperative federalism has been strongly influenced by complex party political interests and claims of self-legitimisation by the actors involved. Any attempt to federal reforms has to deal with a multitude of interests that cannot be reduced to an aligning of interests between two levels. They will always have to include coordination within the *Länder*, between the *Länder* governments and within political parties (Fallend, 2003: 17, 24ff.).

3. Developments after the Convention

The Convention has been a turning point with regard to previous reform efforts: the connection to parliament and parliamentarians, the aim to bring academics, leading figures of the administration and politics together and to get the media and public involved formed a completely new approach (Khol and Konrath, 2005). However, the design of the Convention contained a lot of shortcomings and pitfalls, as Peter Bußjäger explains in this volume.

Yet there is another point that we should add, which is not only crucial for the question of success or failure of the Convention but also for everything that followed: It is interesting that the traditional modes of debating and bargaining about issues of constitutional change and federal organisation were carried on in parallel to the Convention proceedings and apart from them. Key actors and especially the *Landeshauptleute* relied on their ways of dealing with things and did obviously not trust in the Convention with its specific demands for transparency and publicity.

3.1 Parallel worlds

While the Convention was still discussing reforms of the allocation of powers or competences between the Federation and the *Länder*, a long-lasting debate on the competence for animal protection was concluded in May 2004. An amendment to the Federal Constitutional Law transferred the legislative jurisdiction to the federation and provided for homogenous regulations all over Austria. Also, major reforms of the organisation of police authorities, the federal railway system, the Austrian postal system and the so-called "Austrian Power Solution" securing closer cooperation between the main producers of electric energy and providers of power grids were accomplished. All of them crucially affect the position and interests of the *Länder* in the context of the Austrian federal system. Finally, the Convention proceedings were also accompanied by three *Länder* elections in 2003 and two in 2004 of which especially those in Salzburg attracted interest as the conservative governor was replaced by a Social Democrat (Institut für Föderalismus, 2005).

But the most important developments beside the Austrian Convention were the negotiations about the Intergovernmental Fiscal Relations Act (*Finanzausgleich*) for the period of 2005 to 2008 which were held between April and October 2004 (Institut für Föderalismus, 2005: 118ff.). Remarkably, while the representatives of the Federation, the *Länder* and the municipalities committed themselves to continue administrative reform as proposed in the Convention, they did not refer in any way to the debates about federal and fiscal reform in the Convention. This is all the more noteworthy as most of the people who participated in negotiations on fiscal relations had been also members of the Convention.[3]

In this context, it is crucial that intergovernmental fiscal relations are organised in an interconnected way (*Verbundsystem*) in Austria (Matzinger and Pröll, 2010). The *Länder* governments hardly legislate on or collect any taxes. Thus, their organisation and the exercise of their powers depend to a high degree on the funds allocated to them on the basis of the Intergovernmental Fiscal Relations Act. The scheme of fiscal relations is not congruent with the allocation of powers between the federation and the *Länder*. The traditional input-orientated system of fiscal relations, which prevails until today, stands also in conflict with the change to performance-based budgeting that has started in 2008 (Matzinger and Pröll, 2010: 104ff.).

---

3 See the positions of the Länder as contained in the parliamentary materials, 702 d. B., XXII. GP at www.parlament.gv.at.

Another aspect is worth to be considered: Fiscal federalism is an example of the executive-level negotiations mentioned above. It is also governed by long-lasting patterns of interaction and achieved positions, which will usually not be altered or abandoned by governments in current negotiations. This entails that every attempt to reform the federal system will, at some point or another, conflict with previous or concurrent negotiations about fiscal relations. In the end, a simple law, the Intergovernmental Fiscal Relations Act will thus determine to a very high degree the constitutional playing field with regard to federalism.

3.2 Keeping the reform on the agenda

Following the Austrian Convention, the governing coalition formed by the conservative People's Party and the „Alliance for the Future of Austria“, a split-off from the right-wing Freedom Party, set up a "special committee" of the *Nationalrat* to discuss the Convention's report. This was a rather unusual move aimed at keeping the issue of constitutional reform on the agenda. If the report would have been debated in the constitutional committee led by a social democrat, it would most probably have died very quickly. Even so, it seemed as if everyone was waiting for the general elections to be held in October 2006 (Khol and Konrath, 2006). For the time being, only one – though important – amendment of the B-VG was passed, namely a new codification of the principles of school education (Schnizer, 2005).

After six years, the general elections brought the return of a Grand Coalition between the Social Democrats and the People's Party and invested them with a two-thirds-majority in the *Nationalrat*. However, bargaining between the two parties turned out to be difficult. Additionally, the new coalition was confronted with a lot of scepticism from the beginning. In this situation the party leaders resorted to the announcement of major constitutional and federal reforms. They claimed that only a Grand Coalition could solve major problems. The parties used this as a legitimising concept for their endeavour. This way they refuted the attempt of the Convention to initiate constitutional reforms without a safe constitutional majority in parliament (Wiederin, 2008: 22).

In its program, the coalition government announced constitutional reforms on the basis of the debates and proposals of the Austrian Convention. It emphasised a new allocation of powers, the strengthening of the constitutional autonomy of the *Länder*, and new constitutional parameters for administrative organisation including procedures as a basis for major administrative reforms. Moreover, the government's program ruled out a total revision of the federal constitution. An expert group was supposed to prepare those reforms and present results within six months.[4] At this point it became clear

4 Regierungsprogramm für die XXIII. Gesetzgebungsperiode (Government Program for the XXIII. Legislative Period), Vienna 10 January 2007, 23ff.

that the broad and partly inclusive approach of the Convention had obviously been an interlude in constitutional evolution. Constitutional and federal reform was again in the hands of the Federal Government.

3.3 Restoring the participation of experts

Members of this expert group included the former president of the Austrian Convention, two members of the Convention's presidium, Andreas Khol and Peter Kostelka, which both also formerly had leading positions in the coalition parties. Other members were the head of the Constitutional Service in the Federal Chancellery, Georg Lienbacher, a leading scholar of constitutional law, Theo Öhlinger, and two *Landeshauptleute*: Gabi Burgstaller of Salzburg represented the Social Democrats, while Herbert Sausgruber of Vorarlberg, a spokesperson for stronger federalism, represented the People's Party. The latter did not participate in the discussions in person and nominated permanent representatives, Ewald Wiederin and Jürgen Weiss. The members of the group were nominated by the two parties in government. They were expected to cooperate in a more effective way with political leaders than the experts in the Convention had done. However, as further developments made obvious, the group members including the senior politicians worked independently from the political parties. Instead of opening their discussion to parties or the public, the experts conducted their work in private, just like other expert groups had done before (Lienbacher, 2008).

Actually, the year 2007 could have been an appropriate time for achieving a far-reaching constitutional reform. Firstly, another expert group entered the final phase of long work on a comprehensive reform of the federal budget rules. All five parties represented in the *Nationalrat* supported this process and voted unanimously for this fundamental transformation which introduced performance-based budgeting later that year. From 2013 onwards this reform will have significant consequences for the federal administration and will certainly have effects on the budget rules of the *Länder*, too (Steger, 2010). Secondly, the *Länder* governments called for early negotiations on the Intergovernmental Fiscal Relations Act since a number of measures proposed by the government program and deemed without alternatives could not have been implemented without *Länder* support.[5] Thirdly, the political constellations in the *Länder* and on the federal level provided favourable conditions for a reform: Social Democrats and Conservatives were almost on an equal level in the *Nationalrat*, and each of them held the majority in four *Länder* parliaments after the People's Party had lost its majority in Styria in March 2005.

5 For the positions of the *Länder* see the parliamentary materials, 289 d. B., XXIII. GP at www.parlament.gv.at.

However, patterns already known from the Austrian Convention recurred. While the expert group was working on draft papers, the Federal Government and the *Länder* governments agreed on fiscal relations and sealed them until 2013. Thus, anything the expert group proposed was met with reasoning referring to the existing Intergovernmental Fiscal Relations Act and the necessity for revisions.

The Federal Government had announced in its government program to present comprehensive proposals in July 2007. But plans were modified. After a series of minor amendments concerning electoral laws (Stein and Wenda, 2007), only a first "package" was presented in July. One of its main points was the introduction of administrative courts in the *Länder*. This topic had been discussed at least since the 1980s and had for long been rejected by the *Landeshauptleute*, who feared losing their influential role in administrative procedures (Grabenwarter, 1998). The Convention had, however, changed attitudes. Indeed, the *Länder* representatives submitted unanimous and reasoned positions in the following assessment procedure in which they appreciated the introduction of administrative courts (Institut für Föderalismus, 2008).[6] At the same time, they made clear that they would not be willing to pay for restructuring administrative procedures and organisations. This was an important issue that had never been touched in the Austrian Convention. Although many proponents had spoken of savings and efficiency gains that would be possible with a new constitution, no one had mentioned the costs that would certainly have to be paid for adaptations. Also, it was unclear what would happen with those administrative units that had so far regulated and decided on matters determined to be transferred to administrative courts. The problems connected with knowledge transfer or with specific functions a court is unable to fulfil had not been touched, either.

In the end, the Federal Government submitted a bill without proposing regulations for administrative courts. Instead, it presented a draft for a new "Federal Asylum Court", which caused a lot of outrage as it had not been subject of the assessment procedure. Since then, no one mentioned administrative courts anymore, and no one gave reasons why they had been abandoned. Three more aspects of this amendment should be mentioned: it comprised a number of important changes concerning the approval and incorporation of state treaties, a new general rule for the establishment of independent bodies and agencies and it provided for a – highly disputed – constitutional basis for the Austrian "social partners", the pillars of the traditional consociational/corporatist system. Furthermore, the amendment led to a first consolidation of the immense number of constitutional provisions in Austrian laws, a technical, though very important measure (Lienbacher, 2008).

6 For the joint position of the *Länder* see the assessment procedure following the presentation of the expert group's draft, 45/SN-94/ME, XXIII. GP at www.parlament.gv.at.

Two more aspects deserve to be noted: As a matter of fact, the *Landeshauptleute* were represented in the expert group, but they rejected major parts of the proposal. As in the Convention, one could get the impression that they had never been consulted. So firstly, they did not endorse the process once more and it remains unclear in which way the experts nominated by the two *Landeshauptleute* involved in the group had sufficient discretionary power. Secondly, long-term views on federalism itself shifted within the parties. Federalism had been the domain of the People's Party for a long time whereas the Social Democrats favoured centralist approaches. Of course, there had always been tensions and conflicts of interest within the political parties at the different levels, and representatives at the federal level would always have supported more homogenous policies and regulation by federal authorities (Fallend, 2003). Yet as debates in the Convention revealed influential groups in the realm of the People's Party did no longer share the traditional views on federalism and pursued a more centralist approach (Konrath, 2005: 352ff.). At the same time, the Convention made the case for a closer cooperation between the *Länder* governments regardless of the incumbent party alliances, in particular since the Social Democrats had now a much more influential position on the *Länder* level. These alliances were strengthened after the Convention. They became obvious in the orchestration of a high number of opinions in the assessment procedure by the *Länder* administrations. The sheer number of critical statements certainly had an impact and might have been responsible for the fact that no public political debate about administrative courts was continued after the assessment procedure (Institut für Föderalismus, 2008).

3.4 The last proposal for comprehensive reforms

The expert group continued its work and submitted a proposal for a fundamental reform of the allocation of powers between the Federal Government and the *Länder* governments. As became known only later, the group had submitted its draft to the Federal Chancellor in January 2008 but the latter did not present it for pre-parliamentary assessment procedures until March of the same year. Also, the Federal Chancellor did not adopt it as "his" ministerial draft but marked it explicitly as "experts' proposal". This was a rather unusual step since a minister usually takes sole responsibility for a draft.[7] Again, a lot of institutions participated in the assessment procedure, which lasted until June. As the presentation coincided with disputes about education reform aiming at the complex system of school administration and authorities in Austria, a lot of attention was devoted to the parts of the draft regulating these issues. Thus, the debate focused on the power of the *Landeshauptleute*

7 See 168/ME, XXIII. GP at www.parlament.gv.at.

with regard to school personnel, the supposedly bloated school administration in the *Länder* and the fear that education and schools might henceforth be the domain of the *Länder*. This was clearly reflected in the high percentage of opinions in the assessment procedure that dealt (almost) exclusively with aspects of school administration.[8] The debate shifted to issues of administrative reform and efficiency, and federalism received rather bad responses at least as regards education.

Even before the assessment procedure ended in June, most leading politicians on the federal and the *Länder* level had distanced themselves from the draft. Even the expert group had explicated that they hadn't reached full consensus (Konrath, 2008). After the coalition had broken up in July 2008, the draft was no longer discussed and did not lead to a bill. While even the draft of the "first package" on administrative courts, independent bodies and the consolidation of the constitutional law stimulated an academic debate (Journal für Rechtspolitik, 2007), in politics no one has bothered to discuss the proposals of the "second package" in more detail (Lienbacher, 2009).

This has been the last proposal for a substantial federal reform so far, and it can certainly serve as model, even though a negative one. It is based on a three-tier-model developed in the Austrian Convention (Konrath, 2005: 358ff.). The extremely complex and detailed regulations of the present federal constitution were simplified and summarised, and there should just be exclusive competences of the Federation, exclusive competences of the *Länder*, and mixed competences in a third tier in the future. The third tier is deemed necessary as even the best solution cannot prevent overlapping and concurrence of competences. Inevitable conflicts should be resolved by political negotiations (another model, proposed in the Convention, had favoured conflict resolution by the Constitutional Court), and thus, the expert group proposed a reform of the *Bundesrat*, the second chamber of the Austrian Parliament, which is considered as extremely weak. Instead of the existing representation of the *Länder* by members of their parliaments ("*Landtage*"), the expert group suggested a mixed institution composed of the *Landeshauptleute* and members of the *Landtage* (Lienbacher, 2009).

This model met with a lot of criticism from the spokespersons of the *Länder*, who feared that the proposal would invest the Federal Government with much more power. Instead, they proposed to shift more powers to the *Länder* and to introduce a system of double majorities on decisions concerning the third category of mixed competences: They should require a majority of votes in the *Bundesrat* and a majority of the *Länder*. On the other hand, influential institutions like the Chamber of Commerce or the Association of Industrialists feared that the Federal Government would lose powers and issued warnings about irrational federalism. However, as mentioned above, even the

8 See i.e. 2/SN – 7/SN-168/ME, 70/SN-168/ME etc. at www.parlament.gv.at.

Länder focused on the complex system of school administration and made clear that their interests were also devoted to administrative issues.[9]

3.5 Recent developments

The early general elections in 2008 again resulted in a coalition formed by the Social Democrat and the People's Party. But these parties lost the constitutional majority. The new coalition has abandoned plans for major constitutional and federal reforms. But it promised to carry on with administrative reforms in the context of budget consolidation. This time, the *Rechnungshof* (Court of Audit) and economists were asked to prepare reform proposals.[10] So far, the group is known to have met only once in a while and it has not presented any significant results or proposals yet.[11] Also, the Constitutional Committee of the *Nationalrat* established a sub-committee that was assigned to debate matters of administrative reform from July 2009 to November 2010. This sub-committee set out with an ambitious program and held a number of expert hearings. But its members did not reach any conclusions and the majority voted for a closing of the committee.[12] So far, there has been no new attempt to discuss matters of constitutional or federal reform as before. Still, the success of any attempt for necessary reforms regarding public finances, education and health services will depend on adjustments of the federal system.

However, 2010 saw important changes of the federal system that were passed almost unnoticed by the general public: The Court of Audit, which is by the way one of the most influential and highly trusted institutions in Austria, was invested with new powers and may now carry out audits in municipalities with more than 10.000 inhabitants. Before that, it could only audit a small number of municipalities with more than 20.000 inhabitants.[13] Also, this amendment aimed at clarifying the competences of the (federal) Court of Audit in the *Länder*. Thus, it has led to a reassessment of Federation-*Länder*-relations in the realm of financial control. This change was favoured by many political parties, and its effect on federalism was therefore not discussed in detail. It is noteworthy that this amendment was filed as private members' motion. That means that there was no pre-parliamentary assessment procedure and, therefore, no possibility for the *Länder* governments to issue reasoned opinions (which deprived them of the opportunity to voice discontent in a rather "formal" way).

---

9 See the examples in footnote 8.

10 Regierungsprogramm für die XXIV. Gesetzgebungsperiode (Government Program for the XXIV. Legislative Period), Vienna 2 December 2008, 264 n.

11 Salzburger Nachrichten, 7 April 2011, 2.

12 See 2/A-VF and the detailled report 989 d. b., XXIV. GP, at www.parlament.gv.at.

13 1187/A at www.parlament.gv.at.

The second change came with the implementation of the Lisbon Treaty. The *Länder* and the *Bundesrat* had been fierce advocates of subsidiarity control for a long time. Now they lobbied to achieve the same constitutional rights as the *Nationalrat* in EU-matters, which includes the power to bind the Federal Government in Council negotiations.[14] This comparatively strong position of the *Nationalrat* is moderated as the Federal government controls a majority in the responsible committee. But the government might not be able to control the *Bundesrat* in the same way. In the end, the *Bundesrat* did not get a stronger right to bind the Federal Government but was set on equal footing with the *Nationalrat* in decisions on subsidiarity control and treaty revisions. This is an innovative development since the *Bundesrat* has been – according to the Federal Constitution – in almost any context much weaker than the *Nationalrat* (Öhlinger and Konrath, 2012).

4. Federalism after the Convention

Austria is often considered as one of the most successful and stable member states of the EU. But there is a growing awareness that stability and prosperity depend on a number of structural reforms in the educational and healthcare sector, the tax system, the pension system and public administration. A number of major reforms can only be achieved along with federal and constitutional reform. But these come obviously with high political costs for the parties involved and affected, as the story of federal reforms in Austria suggests. The current Federal Government has made clear that it is not willing to start talks about such reforms as it will not be able to find agreement with the *Länder*. Since the Federal Government does not have the support of a constitutional majority in the *Nationalrat* any reform attempt would also face demands from opposition parties. Thus, it is trying to achieve administrative reforms that do not depend on constitutional amendments.[15] As I have showed in this paper, constitutional and federal reform can not be successful without a reform of fiscal federalism and especially of the intergovernmental fiscal relations. As long as both systems are not aligned with each other, fiscal relations will always trump any reform attempt. Changes might be stimulated by the new federal budget rules, but it is hard to predict how they will be received in the *Länder*.

14 See the opinions 68/SN, 69/SN, 72/SN, 73/SN, 75/SN, 77/SN, 81/SN, 88/SN to the draft 978/A, XXIV. GP, at www.parlament.gv.at

15 This stance has been reinforced by the Federal Chancellor Werner Faymann at several occasions, i.e. when he answered questions on administrative reform in the 79th session of the National Council on 5 Oct 2010. See pp. 24 ff. of the records of this session at www.parlament.gv.at.

4.1 No changes of the Federal Constitution

The constitutional basis of the Austrian Federation and its interpretation has hardly been touched since the days of the Austrian Convention. What meanwhile has changed, however, is the general perception of the federal constitution. Before the Convention, the constitution had received not much attention in the public and media discourse. The debates about constitutional reform that led to the Convention and the Convention itself coincided with the perceived end of the "old" Grand Coalition governments and their grip on the constitution. Now, the constraints for political actors that are entrenched in the constitution became more obvious. On the one hand, a lot of reform projects of the new coalition could not be achieved without constitutional amendments; on the other hand, constitutional laws and especially fundamental rights were used by the opposition and leaders of civil society as arguments to trump government proposals. After the presumably failed Convention, the impression that something is wrong with the federal constitution and that this might be a cause for continuous political deadlock apparently has remained. This became obvious in 2010 when the 90th anniversary of the adoption of the Federal Constitutional Law (B-VG) was commemorated. Academics, journalists and politicians alike appreciated the democratic core and stability of the constitution but re-iterated the metaphors of a ruinous or flawed constitution and the structural problems of the constitution's federal regime that prevents change (Ehs and Konrath, 2010).

4.2 Reminiscences

In retrospection, the Austrian Convention (with all its shortcomings) was an episode, and the traditional modes of constitutional change and expert discussions have proved to be stronger. Neither the subsequent coalition governments nor other political actors have called for a broad debate or participatory approaches. Assessment procedures are, of course, open to a wider public, but they receive little attention in the media and are more often than not considered as experts' fora. The attempt to discuss at least issues of administrative reform in parliament did also not lead to solutions or even agreements or debates that could be considered as "milestones". Still, the Convention serves as a kind of reminiscence and rhetorical figure. Whenever one deplores political deadlock or suggests fundamental reforms he or she will refer to the Convention. But it can be doubted if the proposals (and the small number of actual drafts) will still serve today's needs.

The general attitudes about federalism do not seem to have changed. As before, people tend to be rather proud of their *Land* and favour a federal system (Bußjäger et al., 2010). But – as has been claimed by Ewald Wiederin, a leading constitutional scholar and expert on federalism – Austrian federalism seems to be a "feel-good federalism" (*Föderalismus für's Gemüt*) and not a federalism based on differences and conflicting interests (Wiederin, 2004). Maybe it has, over time, also become a "Dinner for one"-federalism, as every year politicians utter reform proposals but never expect anyone to start a debate. The best example may be the presidents of the *Bundesrat*. Each of them starts her or his half-year term with a speech proclaiming the importance of the second chamber they chair. But so far, none of them has ever discussed the proposals of the expert group that would reform the *Bundesrat* and increase its powers significantly.[16]

Public debates, commentaries and media coverage follow the same old trails, too, as Herbert Dachs has stated already in 2007 (Dachs, 2007). Even in view of demands for reform and of – at times – massive criticism of the federal system there seems to be no attempt to explain and justify federalism in public debates. Apart from general appraisals of federalism neither politicians in general or declared federalists in particular have ever tried to counter prejudices and false claims. This is even more interesting as the *Länder* nowadays form stronger alliances across party lines and stand against federal institutions in a number of politically important confrontations. In such a situation it could be expected that they ask for support and present well-reasoned arguments in the interest of federalism.

References

Bußjäger, Peter/Karlhofer, Ferdinand/Pallaver, Günther (2010): Föderalistisches Bewusstsein in Österreich. Regionale Identitätsbildung und Einstellung der Bevölkerung zum Föderalismus. Innsbruck: Institut für Föderalismus.

Dachs, Herbert (2007): Neue Bundesstaatlichkeit im Spannungsfeld zwischen B-VG, Realverfassung und Utopie. In: Steger, F. (ed.): Baustelle Bundesstaat. Wien: Braumüller, 57-64.

Ehs, Tamara/Konrath, Christoph (2010): 90 Jahre Baustelle Bundesverfassung. Die Furche 35, 12.

Ehs, Tamara (2011): Verfassungspolitologie. Zur Bedeutung des B-VG aus politikwissenschaftlicher Sicht. In: Journal für Rechtspolitik 19, (1), 3-14.

Fallend, Franz (2003): Föderalismus – eine Domäne der Exekutiven? In: Dachs, H. (ed): Der Bund und die Länder. Über Dominanz, Kooperation und Konflikte im österreichischen Bundesstaat. Wien: Böhlau, 17-68.

Grabenwarter, Christoph (1998): Auf dem Weg zur Landesverwaltungsgerichtsbarkeit. In: Journal für Rechtspolitik 6, (3), 269-286.

Holzinger, Gerhart (1991): Grundrechtsreform in Österreich. In: Machacek, R./Pahr, W./Stadler, G. (eds.): Grund- und Menschenrechte in Österreich. Band I: Grund-

16 See the speeches in the 765th, the 781th, the 786th and the 793rd session of the *Bundesrat*.

lagen, Entwicklungen und internationale Verbindungen. Kehl am Rhein-Strasbourg-Arlington: N. P. Engel Verlag, 459-498.

Institut für Föderalismus (2008): 32. Bericht über den Föderalismus in Österreich (2007). Wien: Braumüller.

Journal für Rechtspolitik (2007): Schwerpunktheft zum „Entwurf eines Bundesverfassungsgesetzes, mit dem das Bundes-Verfassungsgesetz geändert und ein erstes Bundesverfassungsrechtsbereinigungsgesetz erlassen wird (94/ME, XXIII. GP)“. In: Journal für Rechtspolitik 14, (4).

Khol, Andreas/Konrath, Christoph (2006): Bilanz des Österreich-Konvents und Fortsetzung der Verfassungsreform. In: Khol, A./Ofner, G./Burkert-Dottolo, G./Karner, S. (eds): Österreichisches Jahrbuch für Politik 2005. Wien-München: Verlag für Geschichte und Politik – Oldenbourg Wissenschaftsverlag, 431-445.

Konrath, Christoph (2005): Dann bleibt es eben so: Föderalismus und Kompetenzverteilung als Themen des Österreich-Konvents. In: Österreichische Zeitschrift für Politikwissenschaft 34, (4), 351-365.

Konrath, Christoph (2008): Föderalismus für's Gemüt; Die Furche, 23/2008: 24.

Konrath, Christoph (2011): Literatur zum Österreich-Konvent, www.konvent.gv.at

Lienbacher, Georg (2008): Staatsreform. Die Ergebnisse der Expertengruppe 2007. In: Lienbacher, G./Wielinger, G. (eds.): Öffentliches Recht. Jahrbuch 2008, Wien/Graz: Neuer Wissenschaftlicher Verlag, 23-44.

Lienbacher, Georg (2009): Staatsreform. Die Ergebnisse der Expertengruppe 2008. In: Lienbacher, G./Wielinger, G. (eds.): Öffentliches Recht. Jahrbuch 2009, Wien/Graz: Neuer Wissenschaftlicher Verlag, 9-34.

Matzinger, Anton/Pröll, Gerlinde (2010): Finanzausgleich. In: Steger, Gerhard (ed.): Öffentliche Haushalte in Österreich. 3rd ed. Wien: Verlag Österreich, 63-109.

Öhlinger, Theo (1992): Stil der Verfassungsgesetzgebung – Stil der Verfassungsinterpretation. In: Funk, B.-Ch./Klecatsky, H. (eds.): Staatsrecht und Staatswissenschaften in Zeiten des Wandels, Festschrift für Ludwig Adamovich zum 60. Geburtstag, Wien 1992, 502-514.

Öhlinger, Theo (2002a): Die Europäisierung der österreichischen Verfassung. In: Neisser, H./Puntscher-Riekmann, S. (eds.): Europäisierung der österreichischen Politik. Wien: Facultas, 82-99.

Öhlinger, Theo (2002b): Verfassung und Demokratie in Österreich zu Beginn des 21. Jahrhunderts. In: Brünner, Ch. et al. (eds.): Kultur der Demokratie. Festschrift für Manfried Welan, Wien: Böhlau, 217-235.

Öhlinger, Theo (2009): Verfassungsrecht. 8th ed. Wien: Facultas.

Öhlinger, Theo/Konrath, Christoph (2012): Artikel 23g B-VG. In: Korinek, K./ Holoubek, M. (eds.): Österreichisches Bundesverfassungsrecht. Textsammlung und Kommentar (forthcoming).

Pernthaler, Peter (2000): Verfassungsentwicklung und Verfassungsreform in Österreich. In: Wieser, B./Stolz, A. (eds.): Verfassungsrecht und Verfassungsgerichtsbarkeit an der Schwelle zum 21. Jahrhundert. Wien: Verlag Österreich, 67-116.

Schaller, Christian (1997): Demokratie- und Verfassungs(reform)-Diskussionen in Österreich. Endbericht-Projekt Nr. 5584 des Jubiläumsfonds der Österreichischen Nationalbank, Wien.

Schnizer, Johannes (2006): Schulreform und Verfassung. Zur Interpretation der neuen Bestimmungen des Art 14 B-VG. In: Journal für Rechtspolitik 13, (3), 197-206.

Steger, Gerhard (2010): Die Haushaltsrechtsreform des Bundes. In: Steger, G. (ed.): Öffentliche Haushalte in Österreich. 3rd ed. Wien: Verlag Österreich, 483-506.
Stein, Robert/Wenda, Gregor (2007): Die Wahlrechtsreform 2007. In: SIAK-Journal 4, 61-75.
Wiederin, Ewald (2004): Bundesstaat neu. In: Österreichische Juristenkommission (ed.): Der Österreich-Konvent: Zwischenbilanz und Perspektiven. Wien-Graz: Neuer Wissenschaftlicher Verlag, 49-77.
Wiederin, Ewald (2007a): Grundlagen und Grundzüge staatlichen Verfassungsrechts: Österreich. In: von Bogdandy, A. et al. (eds.): Handbuch Ius Publicum Europaeum. Band I: Grundlagen und Grundzüge staatlichen Verfassungsrechts. Heidelberg: C. F. Müller, 389-449.
Wiederin, Ewald (2007b): Bundesstaatsreform in Österreich. In: Merten, D. (ed.): Die Zukunft des Föderalismus in Deutschland und Europa. Berlin: Duncker und Humblot, 87-117.
Wiederin, Ewald (2007c): Denken vom Recht her. Über den modus austriacus in der Staatsrechtslehre. In: Schulze-Fielitz, H. (ed.): Staatsrechtslehre als Wissenschaft. Die Verwaltung Beiheft 7. Berlin: Duncker und Humblot, 293-317.
Wiederin, Ewald (2008): Verfassungsrevision in Österreich. In: Thaler, M./Stolzlechner, H. (eds.): Verfassungsrevision. Überlegungen zu aktuellen Reformbemühungen. Wien: Jan Sramek Verlag, 17-26.
Wutscher, Werner (2008): Wird Österreich gut verwaltet? Einige kritische Thesen zu den Reformen der letzten Jahre. In: Khol, A./Ofner, G./Halper, D. (eds.): Österreichisches Jahrbuch für Politik 2007. Wien: Böhlau, 127-133.

Constitutional Change in Canada after Charlottetown

Marc-Antoine Adam and Martin Fournier[1]

1. Introduction

The Charlottetown Accord of August 1992 was an effort by the Canadian federal government and the governments of the ten provinces and two territories[2], as well as four national Aboriginal organisations[3], to substantially modify the Constitution of Canada. As part of a series of constitutional negotiations from the 1960s to the 1990s, the "Canada" or "Charlottetown" Round was a direct follow-up to the preceding round of negotiations, the "Québec Round". The Québec Round had been an attempt to bring Québec back into the "Canadian constitutional family" after its isolation from the major constitutional reforms of 1982[4] (Mulroney, 2007; Russell, 2004; Pelletier, 2008). It ended in failure in June 1990 when the Meech Lake Accord did not obtain the approval of all the legislatures required for its ratification[5]. Essentially, the Meech Lake Accord was seeking to address a number of Québec concerns relating to federalism which had been left aside in the *Constitution Act, 1982*[6] (recognition of Québec as a distinct society, limitation of the federal spending power, Supreme Court appointment process reform, devolution of immigration responsibilities and tightening of the amending formula).

The Charlottetown Accord proposed a significant number of modifications to the Constitution of Canada. It incorporated many of the elements contained in the Meech Lake Accord and added numerous others, including major changes in federal institutions, the House of Commons, the Senate and the Supreme Court, recognition of the inherent right of self-government for

---

1 The authors are writing in their personal capacity.

2 At the time, the Canadian North included two federal territories in addition to the provinces. Today, following the subdivision of one of them, there are three.

3 Assembly of First Nations, Native Council of Canada, (today: Congress of Aboriginal Peoples), Métis National Council and Inuit Tapirit Kanatami.

4 From a legal perspective, the Constitution Act, 1982, like the entire Canadian Constitution, still applies to Québec despite its refusal to recognise it.

5 For a more complete portrait of constitutional evolution in Canada since 1987, see Russell (2004). For an historical overview of the positions and recommendations adopted or formulated by different Québec governments on Québec's status and constitutional powers, see Québec – Gouvernement du Québec (2001), whose third edition, published in 2001, covers the period from 1936 to 2001.

6 Schedule B of the Constitution Act, 1982, 1982, c. 11 (U.K.).

Aboriginal peoples leading to the creation of a third order of constitutional government in Canada, revision of the federal distribution of powers, and increased formalisation of intergovernmental relations (Canada – Government of Canada, 1992a).[7]

In response to critics who faulted the process leading up to the Lake Meech Accord for its lack of transparency and public involvement (Johnston, 1993), the Canada Round was distinguished by, among other things, extensive prior public consultations, a negotiating table expanded to NGOs, regular public reports on the subjects discussed and a double "consultative" referendum, in Québec and in the rest of Canada, designed to have the Accord approved by the entire country, a first in Canadian history (Watts, 1993).[8]

Despite these efforts the Charlottetown Accord was rejected by the population on 26 October 1992, both in Québec and in other parts of Canada.[9] A number of factors have been suggested to explain this result: voter conservatism in democratic countries vis-à-vis constitutional matters (Johnston, 1993), the inherent difficulties of a referendum process based on the majoritarian logic when dealing with constitutional adjustments between majority and minority (Lusztig, 1994), the challenge of reconciling divergent claims among populations that showed little inclination for compromise (Russell, 2004), the large number of issues at stake in the Accord which gave many people a reason to oppose it even if as a whole it might have seemed acceptable (Blais et al., 1996), and a growing dissatisfaction with the Mulroney government and politicians in general (Johnston et al., 1993).

The most immediate consequence of the 1992 referendum was putting an end to the Canada Round, no legislature having subsequently ratified the Charlottetown Accord in keeping with the "formal" constitutional modification formulas, even in the provinces where the Yes option obtained a majority. In a wider sense, Charlottetown marked the end of three decades of constitutional talks aimed at bringing major changes to the fundamental law of the land, especially with respect to federalism. Since then, all the then unresolved constitutional demands have remained unsatisfied and the non-constitutional path basically seems to be the only one likely to produce changes to the institutions of Canadian federalism and the way they work.

7 These elements are discussed in the second part of this chapter.

8 For more details on the chain of events in the Canada Round from 1990 to 1992, see Reid (1990, 1991), Poels (1992, 1993) and Canada – Library of Parliament (2011a).

9 In Québec, the No option won (56.68% of valid ballots) over the Yes option (43.32%). 82.76% of registered voters exercised their right to vote (Québec – Directeur général des élections du Québec, 1992). Elsewhere in Canada, the No option also prevailed (54.3%) over the Yes option (45.7%). The Yes option won a majority in four provinces and one territory (Prince Edward Island, New Brunswick, Ontario, Newfoundland and Northwest Territories) while the No option prevailed in five provinces and one territory (Alberta, British Columbia, Nova Scotia, Saskatchewan and Yukon, in addition to Québec). The voter turnout in the rest of Canada was 71.8% (Canada – Elections Canada, 1992).

This article discusses the institutional changes – in the absence of constitutional reform – that have occurred in Canada since Charlottetown. After reviewing the key factors influencing the country's institutional and constitutional environment, we will examine, from a federalism perspective, the changes that have taken place since 1992. Lastly, we will see how these changes, achieved through a non-constitutional route, pose significant challenges to certain fundamental principles underlying the Canadian Constitution, such as federalism, the rule of law, and the protection of minorities (Canada – Supreme Court of Canada, 1998).

2. Canadian context

The failure of Charlottetown and the institutional changes Canada has experienced since then are part of a unique historical, social, legal and institutional environment. Some key factors have fashioned the evolution of the country in a particularly marked manner throughout its history. Among these factors are the multinational and asymmetric character of Canada, a complex constitutional amending process and the lack of formalism and framework in intergovernmental relations.

2.1 An asymmetric multinational federation

Since the British conquest at the expense of France in 1760, Canada has had to accommodate the cohabitation of numerous Aboriginal peoples scattered throughout its territory as well as two major linguistic communities: one English-speaking and the other French-speaking, each being present over the whole territory but concentrated in certain parts of the country. Today, nine out of ten Canadian provinces are now inhabited by an English-speaking majority, while Québec has the only French-speaking majority in North America.[10] Indeed, since the end of the French Regime, Québec, where most of the population of New France settled, has developed its own sense of national identity. Over the centuries, this identity has evolved from a nationalism based on Québec's French roots and the Catholic religion to a territorial nationalism based mainly on a common and official language, French, and a

10 According to Canada's most recent 5-year census, conducted in 2006, 81.8% of Québec's population listed French as the "language most often spoken at home", 10.6% listed English and 7.6% another language. In the rest of Canada, English is the "language most often spoken at home" by 84.2% of the population, French by 2.5% and other languages by 13.2% (Canada – Statistics Canada, 2006; data quoted from Québec – Secrétariat à la politique linguistique, 2011).

mixed culture benefiting from the contributions of Aboriginal nations living in its territory, a historical English-speaking community and many cultural communities from the four corners of the world. Another key element of the Québec identity is its civil law system, as opposed to the common law found in the other provinces (Pelletier, 2010). The populations of the "rest of Canada" have a similar sense of national identity, but based on the federation rather than a particular province[11], due in large part to the fact that they share a common language and legal tradition.

As a result of the coexistence of these two European languages, legal traditions and national groups, with one of them concentrated in a single federated entity, the Canadian federation is a unique combination of multinational federalism and territorial federalism. Though this combination has managed to come into being, its ability to adapt to new challenges brought on by the passage of time, particularly with respect to institutional and constitutional evolution, is faced with some major difficulties.

The Canadian federation we know today was created by the *British North America Act, 1867*[12]. This Act united New Brunswick, Nova Scotia and what was then called the "Province of Canada" into a new federation, the Dominion of Canada. Upper and Lower Canada, which had been forced to merge by the *Union Act, 1840*[13] to form the Province of Canada, were once again separated into two provinces in 1867: Ontario and Québec. Canada was thus the product of a simultaneous movement of integration and decentralisation that accommodated the two visions of its genesis which continue to coexist today. From the Québec perspective, the federation is viewed as a pact between the "two founding peoples", English Canadians and French Canadians, allowing them to recover the autonomous political institutions they had lost in 1840. In contrast, from the perspective of most English Canadians, 1867 is viewed rather as the birth of a brand new nation based on a common pooling of resources.

In practical terms, 1867 was the product of a complex compromise among political leaders representing the different regions and national groups involved, with the aim of achieving a delicate balance between their respective

---

11 For example, according to a survey conducted by Léger Marketing in 2010 for the Association for Canadian Studies, 58% of Québec respondents described themselves as being "from Québec only" (19%) or "from Québec first, but also from Canada" (39%), while 26% consider themselves "from Canada only" (7%) or "from Canada first, but also from Québec" (19%). In Canada as a whole, 60% said they are "from Canada only" (32%) or "from Canada first, but also from [your province]" (28%) and 19% said they are "from [your province] only" (5%) or "from [your province] first, but also from Canada" (14%). In Ontario and British Columbia, the combined percentage of respondents defining themselves as "from Canada only" or "from Canada first, but also from [your province]" was 75% and 72%, respectively (Jedwab, 2010b: 12).

12 30-31 Vict., c. 3 (U.K.). Since the 1982 repatriation of the Constitution, this Act of the British Parliament is now called the *Constitution Act, 1867*.

13 4 Vict., c. 35 (U.K.).

aspirations and interests, all within the context of a bi-national and intercolonial dialogue. Subsequent constitutional amendments, formally adopted by London, also resulted from compromises between federal and provincial government leaders. In this regard, the constitutional reform of 1982 marked the beginning of a break from this intergovernmental dialogue, the process becoming thereafter increasingly participatory and majoritarian. On one hand, under the amending formula adopted following the framework of this reform, the federal parliament and provincial legislatures were formally invested with constituent powers. On the other hand, citizen participation in the constitutional reform process has become increasingly important both at the front end of the process, with the multiplication of public consultations on constitutional positions taken by governments, and afterwards, with the advent of the referendum as an instrument of approval – or disapproval – of proposed reforms. We can trace the beginnings of this citizen involvement to 1981, when the federal government tried to legitimise through public consultations its plan to circumvent the provinces by "unilaterally" asking London to amend the Constitution.

2.2 A complex formal constitutional amending process

Notwithstanding its social make up, any substantial change to a federal country's constitution usually involves a complex constitutional amending formula that is intended to protect the interests of the parties involved. In Canada, until 1982 only the British Parliament had the power to amend the Canadian Constitution. This situation may be explained by the fact that at the time the Dominion of Canada formally acquired independence through the British Parliament's adoption of the *Statute of Westminster 1931*[14], Ottawa and the provinces had not been able to agree on a new domestic amending formula (Russell, 2004). Nevertheless, from 1867 to 1982 some amendments were made to the Canadian Constitution, including several dealing with federalism and the division of powers. At first, it was mainly the Great Depression of the 1930s and the advent of the welfare state in Western societies following the Second World War that brought about a desire, especially in English Canada, to revise the distribution of responsibilities between the two orders of government. Under the division of powers agreed upon in 1867, social issues were assigned to the provinces, even though in the 19th century, characterised by the classic liberal model, such issues were handled mainly by the private sector and religious communities. However, in light of their growing importance and the resulting financial implications, many felt that it was time for Ottawa to take charge of social policies. Hence, at the request of the federal government and the provinces, the Constitution was amended three times by London, in 1940, 1951 and 1964, to transfer to Ottawa responsibilities per-

14 22-23 Geo. V, c. 4 (U.K.)

taining to employment insurance and old age pensions. However, the burdensome nature of the process and the reluctance of some provinces, particularly Québec, to consent to jurisdictional transfers in favour of Ottawa limited recourse to this approach (Adam, 2008b).

The entrenchment of a domestic amending formula in 1982 did not make it any easier to change the basic law. Officially, the various amending formulas, defined in Part V (sections 38 to 49) of the *Constitution Act, 1982*, are such that almost all changes affecting federalism require not only the consent of the federal parliament but also that of all the provincial legislative assemblies, or at least of seven provinces representing at least 50% of Canada's total population.[15]

In addition, a certain number of statutes and constitutional conventions established during the last quarter century have complicated this process even further, such as: the adoption by the federal parliament of the *Act respecting constitutional amendments (regional veto)*[16], under which the federal government may not ratify a constitutional amendment without the support of Canada's five regions[17]; the addition of new players in constitutional discussions, in particular the Aboriginal peoples, whose very involvement is itself subject to certain constitutional guarantees; several provinces have also adopted statutes requiring them to hold a referendum in their territory before they can consent to any constitutional amendment; and finally, in the aftermath of the Charlottetown referendum, several constitutional experts argue that there is now a constitutional convention whereby any significant constitutional amendment must

---

15 There are five constitutional amending formulas in the Constitution Act, 1982:
- The "general" formula (s. 38), whereby an amendment must be authorised by resolutions of the House of Commons, the Senate and the legislative assemblies of at least two-thirds of the provinces that have, in the aggregate, at least fifty percent of the population of all the provinces;
- The "unanimous consent" formula (s. 41) which, as its title indicates, requires consent by resolutions of the House of Commons, the Senate and the legislative assembly of each province;
- The "selective unanimity" formula (s. 43) which, in the case of an amendment that applies to one or more, but not all, provinces, requires authorisation by resolutions of the House of Commons, the Senate and the legislative assembly of each province to which the amendment applies;
- The "unilateral federal" formula (s.44) which, subject to certain sections, allows the federal parliament to make laws amending provisions related to the executive government of Canada or the Senate and House of Commons;
- The "provincial unilateral" formula (s. 45) which, subject to certain sections, allows the legislature of each province to make laws amending the constitution of the province.
- It is worth noting that under the "general", "unanimous consent" and "selective unanimity" formulas, the Senate has only a suspending veto.

16 S.C. 1996, c. 1. This statute is also known as the Regional Veto Act.

17 Three of these regions correspond to the three largest provinces (Québec, Ontario and British Columbia), the other two being composed of the three Prairie provinces and the four Maritime provinces. In the latter cases, consent is required by a majority of provinces representing the majority of the population in the region concerned.

first be approved by referendum. All these factors make it much more difficult to substantially modify the Canadian Constitution than a literal reading of the constitutional amending formula might lead one to believe (Taillon, 2007). One can understand how, under these circumstances, any changes deemed necessary with respect to the federal system's institutions and practices almost always have to be realised outside of the constitutional framework.

2.3 Intergovernmental relations: increasingly important but lacking formalism or framework

Whereas the formal constitutional amendment process in Canada is characteristically rigid, the same cannot be said for intergovernmental relations in the broader sense. Born out of negotiations between the colonial political leaders of the time, the Canadian federation could have provided for coordinating mechanisms formalising this type of dialogue. However, the relatively exhaustive division of jurisdictions adopted in 1867 between orders of government, following the classic dualist model, was such that the authors of the Constitution attached little importance to governance issues relating to the federal system as a whole such as intergovernmental relations, intergovernmental agreements and provincial input in federal institutions.[18] An informal system of federative governance has nonetheless managed to emerge, based on bilateral and multilateral relations among governments, i.e. "executive federalism" (Adam et al., forthcoming). However, the combination of dualist federalism and parliamentary sovereignty is such that in Canadian constitutional law there are no formal rules to sustain intergovernmental relations: courts are reluctant to intervene in what they regard as the political arena, and intergovernmental agreements are seen as informal, political accords rather than binding legal instruments (Poirier, 2008).

In fact, up to the mid 20th century, intergovernmental conferences were quite rare and sporadic and essentially only dealt with constitutional issues and fiscal transfers. In contrast, the gradual emergence of the welfare state combined with a resurgence of constitutional discussions after 1960 led to an acceleration and transformation of this dialogue, with meetings and intergovernmental agreements becoming more and more frequent and dealing increasingly with the development and funding of public policies, most of the time in areas formally under the exclusive jurisdiction of the provinces. These exchanges, in which the federal government had always been the dominant figure, led to a restructuration of the division of roles and responsibilities be-

18 Although originally the Senate was intended to "represent the regions", in reality the Upper House has never fulfilled this role: Senators are unilaterally appointed by the federal government. With regard to the Supreme Court, it was created by a general Act of Parliament and its members are also appointed unilaterally by the federal government.

tween Ottawa and the provinces, toward an "integrated" federal model more typical of European federations (Adam et al., forthcoming). However, this evolution, expressed through a multitude of intergovernmental agreements, has occurred outside of the Constitution, without institutional support or legal guarantees, with little transparency and subject to the vagaries of political and fiscal power relationships among the partners.[19]

As a result of this restructuring, the federal government ended up playing a central role in the advent of the welfare state. This was essentially done by granting conditional federal subsidies in areas of provincial jurisdiction, which individual provinces found difficult to refuse without running the risk of penalising their citizens in relation to the others. This method of intervention was justified by the concept of a "federal spending power" that would not be limited by the division of powers (Poirier, 2004). Although this power is not written in the Constitution and has never been formally recognised by the courts, it has profoundly transformed Canadian federalism (Adam, 2008b). Québec, in particular, has refused to recognise such "unlimited" power and has always sought to limit federal spending. From Québec's point of view, a transformation of Canadian federalism as profound as that which underlies the notion of unlimited federal spending power is inconceivable without a formal amendment to the text of the Constitution. The other provinces, however, seem less bothered by such gaps between actual practice and written constitutional law. The coexistence in Canada of civil law, based on a codified legal system, in Québec, and common law, based on precedents and case law in the other provinces and the territories, could in part explain several divergences of views between Québec and the rest of the country on the role and importance of the written constitution (Pelletier, 2010).

3. Institutional evolution after the failed constitutional reforms of the 1980's and 1990's in Canada

3.1 An enduring constitutional impasse

As seen above, the Canada Round that led to the Charlottetown Accord was a direct result of the failure of the Meech Lake Accord, which was aiming to "re-integrate" Québec into the Canadian constitutional family following its exclusion in 1982. Hence, to a very large extent, the Charlottetown Accord repre-

19 Some elements of the Meech Lake and Charlottetown Accords, such as the statutory holding of annual conferences of first ministers, the protection of intergovernmental agreements against unilateral changes and the possibility of entrenching some of them in the Constitution, were aimed specifically at correcting this situation.

sented a second attempt at "reparation" in this regard. From this perspective, the inclusion of so many items not related to Québec's claims must be seen mainly as part of a strategy aimed at avoiding the pitfalls perceived in Meech by counterbalancing and putting into perspective the concessions made to Québec. To be sure, the other reforms contemplated in the Charlottetown Accord responded to many authentic and legitimate requests for change, but they represented the "cars" rather than the "engine" of the Canada Round "train". In the rest of Canada, as the public consultations held immediately following the Meech failure clearly revealed, the population would definitely have preferred to set the Constitution aside so they could get on with "real problems" (Russell, 2004). In reality, the chief petitioner for constitutional changes was Québec, and without it there would probably not have been a Canada Round.

In fact, one could generalise by stating, along with numerous authors and observers of the Canadian political scene, that the whole constitutional saga Canada has experienced starting in the 1960s, with its multiple rounds, is intimately linked to the search for a solution to the Québec issue (Meekison, 1994). The 20th century forced a redefinition of the relationship between Québec and the rest of Canada, first with the advent of the welfare state, which led to the centralisation of Canadian federalism, then with the rise of Québec nationalism, expressed through a vigorous advocacy of Québec as a distinct and autonomous society. From this perspective, it is worth looking at the reform of the Canadian Constitution in 1982 and more particularly the adoption of the *Canadian Charter of Rights and Freedoms*, which would be applied uniformly throughout the country. For the architect of this reform, Pierre Elliott Trudeau, himself a Quebecer with a French-speaking father and English-speaking mother, the changes it brought were designed to rebuild Canada's national identity on the foundations of identical individual rights for all and institutional bilingualism, while diminishing the importance of biculturalism and federalism, which he considered sources of tension (Adam, 2007).

The adoption of the 1982 reform, the only major reform Canada has successfully brought to fruition since the federation was created in 1867, could be achieved only at the price of isolating the Government and the National Assembly of Québec. However, though this episode exacerbated the tensions between Québec and the rest of Canada, it did not bring an end to the dialogue and the search for a mutually acceptable constitutional solution. It was the rejection of the Charlottetown Accord that now, almost twenty years later, seems to have definitively produced such a rupture.

The immediate repercussion of the Canada Round failure was the 1995 referendum on Québec sovereignty which essentially ended in a draw between the sovereignty option and that of keeping Québec within Canada.[20]

20 50.58% of voters supported the No (to Québec achieving sovereignty) option while 49.42% supported the Yes option. The voters turnout was 93.52% (Québec – Directeur des élections du Québec, 1995).

Since then, this significant support for the sovereignist cause has generally been fluctuating between 40 and 50% (CROP, 2011; Léger Marketing, 2009).

The Québec Liberal Party, currently in power, remains federalist but continues to make certain constitutional reforms a prerequisite condition for "Québec's adherence to the Canadian Constitution" (Québec Liberal Party, 2001). However, for the moment at least, the prevailing strategy consists in not formally attempting to reopen the constitutional file as the "fruit" is not considered "ripe" yet. In Canada, particularly outside Québec, the trauma of Charlottetown has produced a dread of constitutional reform in political circles and in the population; indeed the Constitution itself has become a taboo subject. On the one hand, many believe that when it comes to major reforms, the Constitution has become unchangeable. On the other hand, in light of what occurred in the 1980s and 1990s (Cloutier et al., 1992), there are substantial fears concerning the repercussions that could arise from the failure of a future constitutional round aimed at reintegrating Québec into the Canadian constitutional family (Pelletier, 2008). For some authors, only a real and major crisis, not just a perceived one, could lead to the reopening of the constitutional file (Russell, 2004).

3.2 Incremental institutional changes

Despite this impasse, one would be remiss in concluding that the Constitution has since been set in stone. As it had done before, since 1992 Canada has continued to evolve and adapt its federal institutions to the demands of the day. In fact, this kind of incremental change, which is typical of the British tradition, is practically written into Canada's genetic code. This is how many of the issues which were brought up in the Charlottetown Accord have since been revisited through mainly four techniques: unilateral federal measures, administrative intergovernmental agreements, constitutional case law by the courts, and finally, limited bilateral constitutional changes negotiated between governments.

Briefly, the Charlottetown Accord entailed a number of important proposed amendments to the Canadian Constitution, including:

- A constitutional interpretative clause: recognition of Québec as a distinct society in the context of a "Canada clause," which outlined a number of Canada's "fundamental characteristics," such as the commitment to a federal and parliamentary democracy, to the rule of law, to the rights of Aboriginal peoples to "promote their own language, culture, and traditions," to the presence of "minority official language communities" throughout the country,[21] as well as to multiculturalism, the respect of

21 The English-speaking community within Québec and the French-speaking and Acadian communities in other provinces and territories.

individual and collective rights and freedoms, gender equality, and equality between provinces.

- An economic and social union: a commitment on the part of federal and provincial governments to the preservation and development of the Canadian social and economic union;
- The Senate: a transformation of the Upper House into an elected senate (either through universal suffrage or through appointment by the provinces), based on equal representation from the provinces (6 seats per province and one per territory), with the rule of "double majority" to be applied on language lines for certain votes;
- The House of Commons: increase in the number of seats in the House of Commons from 295 to 337 (to the benefit of Ontario, Québec, British Columbia and Alberta), with a concurrent guarantee that Québec's representation in the Lower House never fall below 25% of the floor;
- The Supreme Court: the provision, to be written into the Constitution, for 3 of the 9 seats on the Supreme Court to be reserved for Québec judges, and for the appointment of Court Justices to be made according to lists of candidates provided by provincial and territorial governments;
- Aboriginal peoples: the recognition of Aboriginal peoples' inherent right to self-government, with the anticipated establishment of a third order of government;
- Federal spending power: the limitation of federal spending in areas of exclusive provincial jurisdiction, by providing for "just compensation" for provincial governments that decide to opt out of any new cost-shared program should they instead undertake a program or initiative that is compatible with "national objectives";
- Division of powers: clarification of the constitutional responsibilities of each order of government by recognising exclusive provincial jurisdiction in matters of workforce training, forestry, mining, tourism, leisure, housing, municipal and urban affairs and regional and cultural development, and exclusive federal jurisdiction in matters of national cultural institutions and employment insurance;
- Intergovernmental agreements: safeguards against any unilateral change to intergovernmental agreements, with the possibility of having such agreements as they relate to immigration and workforce training become part of the Constitution (Canada – Government of Canada, 1992a);
- Amending formula: each province would be granted veto power regarding any change to federal institutions (i.e. the Senate and the House of Commons) and full financial compensation for provinces that choose to preserve their autonomy in the event of a transfer of constitutional responsibilities in favour of the federal parliament.

3.2.1 Unilateral federal measures

In the category of unilateral federal measures taken after 1992 that echo some of the elements contained in the Charlottetown Accord, we must first point out the motion adopted by the federal parliament in 1995 recognising the distinct character of Québec society. Eleven years later, in 2006, a similar resolution was adopted, using the term "nation." This terminological evolution was certainly regarded in Québec as a positive development when compared to the more insipid term "distinct society" used in the Meech and Charlottetown Accords. However, although they were meant to serve as principles to guide federal action, both of these motions were essentially symbolic acts, without legal consequences. Even on a political level, their effectiveness has been called into question on more than one occasion.

Also falling under this first category of "non-constitutional" changes is the previously mentioned legislation, adopted by the federal parliament in 1996, "on regional vetoes," which sought to reflect one of Québec's demands, by prohibiting a federal minister, in certain specific cases, from proposing any resolution in view of ratifying a constitutional change in the federal parliament which would not have received the approval of the "five regions" of Canada, of which Québec is one. In doing so, this legislation indirectly attempts to alter the amending formula outlined in the Constitution.

This federal unilateral approach has also been used to bring changes to federal institutions. Hence, in the mid-2000's, the federal government adopted a formal process for selecting nominees to the Supreme Court, mainly by involving federal parliamentarians. Although provincial consultation is part of the process, compared to Charlottetown, the role of provinces is now very minor. Furthermore, it must be said that this process, which is not legally binding, was tossed aside by the federal Prime Minister at the time of the last Supreme Court appointment.

Similarly inspired by the concept of self-limitation, the federal government introduced a bill more recently which would unilaterally transform the Senate into an elected body by holding regular "consultative" elections in order to inform the Prime Minister's Senate appointments.[22] However, here again, formally, there would be no legal obligation on the Prime Minister, to appoint the elected senators, which would most certainly have required a formal constitutional amendment.

---

22 Bill C-43: *Senate Appointment Consultations Act* (introduced in the House of Commons on 13 December 2006, 39th Parliament, 1st session), Bill C-20: *Senate Appointment Consultations Act* (introduced in the House of Commons on 13 November 2007, 39th Parliament, 2nd session); Bill S-8: *Senatorial Selection Act* (introduced in the Senate on 27 April 2010, 40th Parliament, 3rd session); and finally, following the last federal election where the Conservative government sponsoring the reform finally obtained a parliamentary majority: Bill C-7: *Senate Reform Act* (introduced in the House of Commons on 21 June 2011, 41st Parliament, 1st session).

Lastly, the federal government also introduced a bill which seeks to add seats in the House of Commons for provinces where there is greater population growth.

Québec is opposed to the two above federal parliamentary reforms which, among other things, do not carry with them the benefits that had been secured in the Charlottetown negotiations: namely the option of having provincially appointed senators and its 25% guaranteed representation in the House of Commons.

3.2.2 Administrative intergovernmental agreements

In the category of administrative intergovernmental agreements that echoed the Charlottetown Accord, we may first point to the important Agreement on Internal Trade (AIT). This agreement was signed shortly after Charlottetown by all jurisdictions in Canada with the goal of limiting non-tariff trade barriers in a manner similar to international trade agreements. Likewise, one can also point to agreements on workforce training between Ottawa and the various provinces, which sought to delegate to provinces certain responsibilities and budgets that were included in the federal *Employment Insurance Act*[23]. The Social Union Framework Agreement, which was signed in 1999 without Québec's assent, could be considered similarly, insofar as its goal was to restrict federal expenditures in areas of exclusive provincial jurisdiction on the premise of the "federal spending power." In 2004, another important multilateral agreement was signed regarding health services (an area of provincial jurisdiction), this time including Québec. It featured a reference to the notion of asymmetrical federalism and incorporated a covenant signed by Québec and Ottawa giving more flexibility to Québec in its use of federal funds.

3.2.3 Constitutional case law

With regard to constitutional case law, Aboriginal issues are where the Charlottetown Accord's intentions have been most strongly felt. This is how the 1982 recognition of "the existing Aboriginal and treaty rights,"[24] which were however not defined in the Constitution, has been given teeth by the Courts. As a result, Aboriginal communities now have increased power to negotiate with governments, thereby facilitating a certain amount of territorial autonomy. By contrast, the Courts have remained very timid to enforce the division of powers between provinces and the federal government, allowing for concurrent action almost everywhere, which is hardly compatible with the clarification sought by Charlottetown. This difference between the proactive

23 S.C. 1996, c. 23

24 Constitution Act, 1982, s. 35

nature of the Courts with respect to Aboriginal rights, whose principal constitutional grounds are based on the 1982 reform, and their relatively timid approach to matters of federalism, whose written rules go back to 1867, may be a good illustration of the importance of formal constitutional revisions.

This being said, on matters of legal interpretation, several authors have pointed out the Supreme Court's consideration of each province's specific reality, particularly Québec's, in examining the justifications for some provincial measures that effectively restrict individual Canadian Charter rights (Hiebert, 1996; Kelly, 2004; Clarke, 2006). Some have seen in this case law the same result that the distinct society clause would have afforded in the Meech Lake and Charlottetown Accords (Dickson, 1996).

3.2.4 Asymmetrical bilaterally negotiated constitutional amendments

Lastly, and this is the final category of institutional changes that have taken place since 1992, it should be noted that the Canadian Constitution exceptionally includes the possibility of making certain changes that apply only to some provinces by requiring solely the consent of the federal parliament and the provinces concerned. However, most constitutionalists say that this functionality has only limited scope, arguing that it can only modify asymmetrical provisions already contained in the Constitution, and could not serve to introduce new ones. Nonetheless, it was via this kind of amendment, allowed by section 43 of the *Constitution Act, 1982*, that the provision regarding the equality of the French and English linguistic communities in New Brunswick was eventually enshrined in 1993, guaranteeing their equal right to distinct French and English cultural and educational institutions, which had been included in the Charlottetown Accord.[25]

3.3 Some implications to be considered

How important or adequate the various adjustments discussed above were with regard to the challenges which the Charlottetown Accord tried to address depends on one's point of view (e.g. Québec vs. rest of Canada, white vs. Aboriginal communities, etc.) and on the issue in question. However, beyond each measure's individual merits, when compared to Charlottetown, one common trait that characterises each of these adjustments is the lack of transparency that their implementation entailed. Even the Meech Lake process, disparaged though it was, comes off as a model for transparency in comparison. Hence it seems that an overly democratised formal process for constitutional change can paradoxically have the effect of rendering this method useless, and of forcing all necessary institutional evolution to happen in the

25 Constitution Act, 1982, s. 16.1.

shadows, by circuitous means. But the lack of transparency is not the only drawback of this kind of adjustments.

If we take the first category, unilateral federal measures, we notice right away that while some of them sought to address Québec's demands, they do not provide the permanence of constitutional amendments. This is obvious in the case of simple parliamentary motions with no legal effect, but it is also true of unilateral legal norms which can always be changed by simple majority rule. And yet it is the security of the Constitution that is at the core of Québec's demands, because in the context of a federal country, this security typically involves the protection of regional minorities (or "national" ones in Québec's case) against the dictates of a country-wide majority. From this perspective, resorting to the logic of simple majority rule to decide on important institutional changes at the federal order seems not only dissatisfying, but almost acting against the intended goal.

This contradiction seems all the more clear when we look at two particular unilateral federal parliamentary measures: that of the Regional Veto Act, and the current bill to reform the Senate, to which Québec is opposed, judging that such a reform requires a multilateral constitutional amendment. In fact, the origin of Québec's demand to have veto power on constitutional matters was essentially meant to safeguard Québec against a reform of central institutions, particularly the Senate that would be detrimental to its interests. Hence currently, not only does the Regional Veto Act seem ineffectual in this regard, but ironically, this Act is taken by many as an example of the extent of Parliament's autonomous power to unilaterally alter federal institutions such as the Senate (Newman, 2007).

The second category of incremental institutional changes, those which result from intergovernmental administrative agreements, has the advantage of avoiding the unilateral majoritarian premise just discussed, by instead using the premise of contractual agreements. However, the issue of permanence comes up again, due to the non-legal nature of most of the agreements in question. Indeed, while intergovernmental agreements are very common and frequent in Canada, they fall largely outside the scope of law. In fact, one of the primary functions of these agreements, according to authors on the subject, is to unofficially alter the jurisdictional responsibilities outlined by the Constitution (Poirier, 2008).

While it may seem like a flexible and convenient approach, this method is not without its problems. The Canadian Constitution was built on the principles of federal dualism and parliamentary sovereignty. Accordingly, legally speaking, unilateralism is the norm and the formal system leaves very little room for coordinated federalism. This is why intergovernmental agreements are condemned to remain informal and their actual effectiveness has been variable. The problem with the federal spending power itself is largely attributable to this method of handling federative relationships. What is more, despite the appeal of the "consensual" nature of intergovernmental agreements, in many cases we may question the imbalance of the power relationships between the signing parties and, consequently, the freedom of the consent given by some, especially where fiscal transfers from one order of government to another are involved. In other words, these agreements may often hide federal fiats under the cloak of mutual covenants.

On a more fundamental level, however, this kind of para-constitutional practice involves relativising to some degree the principle of the rule of law, which would seem harmful to the safeguard of minority interests. For example, it is not insignificant that Québec was the only province that refused to sign the Social Union Framework Agreement, whose intention was purportedly to limit the "federal spending power"; for Québec, the Framework Agreement carried a recognition and normalisation of this federal "power," which is not written anywhere in the Constitution. In this respect, one could say that the absence of any real impact of this agreement and the subsequent proliferation of federal programmes in areas of provincial jurisdiction seem to have confirmed Québec's concerns (Adam, 2008a).

The third category of incremental institutional change, that arising from constitutional case law, has for its part the advantage of seeking to reconcile law with practical realities, thereby insuring respect for the rule of law – even though what some would call the judges' "interventionism" could at some points be open to criticism. In this respect, the proliferation of legal challenges under the 1982 *Canadian Charter of Rights and Freedoms* has greatly raised the profile of the role of the judiciary, which has garnered much more public attention as a result. Taken in this context, more than one author has highlighted the Supreme Court Justices' concern for basing their decisions on the core values of Canadian society (Lajoie, 2009). The arbitration of federalism is no exception to this rule. One might add that it is also influenced by the fact that all of the judges presiding on superior courts in Canada, including of course the Supreme Court, are appointed exclusively by the federal government. This situation makes it such that the Supreme Court hardly ever overturns a federal law, its approach being rather to allow provincial and federal laws to coexist in the same areas. While this result may possibly correspond to the wishes of a majority of Canadians, it is at odds with both the vision of federalism prevailing in Québec and the text of the Constitution which confers exclusive jurisdictions to each order of government (Brouillet, 2010). Given the general rule that federal laws take precedence whenever there is a conflict, the hands-off approach of the judiciary on matters of federalism makes the constitutional safeguarding of provincial autonomy very relative. In this regard, the age itself of the provisions governing the division of powers may be an issue. The clarification of each order of government's responsibilities, as well as provincial participation in the process of selecting Supreme Court judges, which were proposed in the Charlottetown Accord, were intended as ways to partially counteract the current dynamic, but whether this would have sufficed is debatable.

The fourth and last category of incremental institutional change is in fact limited formal constitutional amendments as seen above. However, asymmetrical bilateral changes such as those allowed by section 43 of the *Constitution Act, 1982* seem to abide by very different rules than those which apply to multilateral amendments. In the case of province-specific amendments, while the federal parliament has to approve a proposed amendment, the consent of the majority of Canadians is not sought out. There is no need for national referenda, and as for public consultations, when and if they do happen, they consist mainly of a survey of opinions of civil society in the province concerned. In this respect, the province-specific formula is not without parallels to Great Britain's devolution process with Scotland and Wales. Hence, this approach is more akin to treaty making, which might perhaps be the best way to accommodate minority interests.

However, as we have already discussed, the architects of the 1982 constitutional reform, above all Mr. Trudeau, were not in favour of asymmetrical federalism; this is why they sought to limit the scope of this kind of change to pre-existing constitutional asymmetries, in order to avoid the possibility that a province, particularly Québec, could negotiate a special status with Ottawa, which might involve a new distribution of power that would differ from other provinces. This original intention notwithstanding, it is nonetheless the case that almost all of the formal amendments to the Constitution that Canada has brought to fruition since 1982 have used this formula. Faced with the current impasse in the area of constitutional reform in Canada, this kind of measure appears to be garnering renewed interest of late from a growing number of authors, some of whom suggest that such a formula could perhaps serve to finally establish in the Constitution Québec's distinct character (Woehrling, 2002; Newman, 2008; Cameron and Krikorian, 2008).

4. Conclusion

While they never managed to accomplish the constitutional reform they sought, the Meech Lake and Charlottetown Accords nonetheless profoundly transformed the constitutional reform process in Canada, at least *de facto* if not also *de jure* (Taillon, 2007). At the time the federation was created in 1867, this process was essentially an inter-colonial and binational undertaking, with the requirement of Québec's consent seen as a necessity. After that, the process became intergovernmental, with the continued concern of obtaining Québec's support, but with amendments being formally adopted by the parliament at Westminster in London. After the Patriation of the Constitution in 1982, which conferred constitution making powers on the Canadian federal parliament and provincial legislatures, Meech Lake made the amending process legislative, followed by the even more participative and referendum-bound proposals of Charlottetown. As it turned out, the growing democratisation of the amending process only created more potential ways for change to be blocked.[26]

It is usually in the very nature of a constitutional amendment process that any major changes that are to be made to the constitution be subjected to a level of approval that goes beyond that of simple majority rule, in order to safeguard minority interests against detrimental changes. This is particularly true of a federal system of government. But with the extended democratisation of constitutional processes, these safeguards can be quite paradoxical, since they also become an obstacle to weighing minority needs in the Constitution and may in some instance even lead to perpetuating historical prejudices. Of course the same safeguards can also restrain desires for formal constitutional change coming from the majority. However, in the latter case, where there is a will for change among the majority, one can be sure that incremental institutional changes will occur to bring it about anyway, by other means if necessary, as Canada's history has shown.

The foregoing paradox might be manageable in a relatively homogeneous society. It is not, however, so easy in a complex society, composed of various national groups. In light of the Charlottetown episode, one can legitimately question the usefulness and the wisdom of resorting to a highly participative constitutional process when it comes to adjusting the relationships between these groups, particularly in a majority/minority context (Lusztig, 1994). Multinational federations are rarely the product of a spontaneous democratic choice. If contemporary democratic requirements for constitutional reform had been applied at their origins, it is highly likely that not many federated states would have ever been created in the first place, Canada included. The difficulties that are encountered in the European Union's continued integration of new members is a useful illustration of this problem. When dealing with the relationships between various nations, intergovernmental and inter-national dialogue is still the most effective solution, but the overall challenge of reconciling this model with that of the democratic age remains.

26 It remains unclear what would have happened had the 26 October 1992 referendum received majority support for the accord from Canada as a whole, without gaining the majority needed in the number of provinces required by the formula. One can only assume that it would have been insufficient, or at least that's what the spokespeople for the Yes side maintained throughout the campaign.

References

Adam, Marc-Antoine (2007): The Constitution Act, 1982 and the Dilemma of Canadian Duality since 1760. In: The Supreme Court Law Review 37, (2), 261-284.

Adam, Marc-Antoine (2008a): Le fédéralisme, le pouvoir de dépenser et l'article 94 de la Loi constitutionnelle de 1867. Revue québécoise de droit constitutionnel, 1. http://www.aqdc.org/volumes/pdf/adam-federalisme_pouvoir_de_depenser.pdf [accessed: 13 April 2011]

Adam, Marc-Antoine (2008b): The Spending Power, Co-operative Federalism and Section 94. In: Queen's Law Journal 34, (1), 175-224.

Adam, Marc-Antoine (2008c): Fiscal Federalism and the Future of Canada: Can Section 94 of the Constitution Act, 1867 be an Alternative to the Spending Power?. In: Allan, J./Courchene, T./Leuprecht, Ch. (eds.): Canada: The State of the Federation 2006-2007: Transitions: Fiscal and Political Federalism in an Era of Change. Montréal-Kingston: McGill-Queen's University Press, 295-322.

Adam, Marc-Antoine/Bergeron, Josée/Bonnard, Marianne (forthcoming): Intergovernmental Relations in Canada. In: Poirier, J./ Saunders, Ch. (eds.): Intergovernmental Relations in Federal Countries. Montréal-Kingston: McGill-Queen's University Press.

Bernard, André (1992): Les revendications traditionnelles du Québec. In: Collective, Référendum, 26 octobre 1992. Les objections de 20 spécialistes aux offres fédérales, Montréal: Éditions Saint-Martin, 11-17.

Blais, André/Johnston, Richard/Gidengil, Elisabeth/Nevitte, Neil (1996): La dynamique référendaire: pourquoi les Canadiens ont-ils rejeté l'accord de Charlottetown? In: Revue Française de Science Politique 46 , (5), 817-830.

Boismenu, Gérard (1993): When More Is Too Much: Québec and the Charlottetown Accord. In: Watts, R. L./Brown, D. M. (eds.): Canada: The State of the Federation 1993. Kingston: Institute of Intergovernmental Relations, Queen's University, 45-60.

Bourassa, Robert (1995): Gouverner le Québec, Montréal: Fides.

Brouillet, Eugénie (2010): Le fédéralisme et la Cour suprême du Canada. Quelques réflexions sur le principe d'exclusivité des pouvoirs. In: Revue québécoise de droit constitutionnel, 3: 60-80. http://www.aqdc.org/volumes/pdf/Eugenie_Brouillet.pdf [accessed: 13 April 2011]

Burgess, Michael, (1993): Constitutional Reform in Canada and the 1992 Referendum. In: Parliamentary Affairs 46, (3), 363-379.

Cameron, David R./Krikorian, Jacqueline D. (2008): Recognising Québec in the Constitution of Canada: Using the Bilateral Amendment Process. In: University of Toronto Law Journal 58, (4); 389-420.

Canada – Elections Canada (1992): Référendum 92: Résultats officiels du scrutin / Referendum 92. Official Voting Results, Ottawa: Elections Canada.

Canada – Government of Canada (1992a): Consensus Report on the Constitution, Charlottetown, 28 August 1992. Ottawa: Government of Canada.

Canada – Government of Canada (1992b): Projet de texte juridique, le 9 octobre, 1992. Ottawa: Government of Canada.

Canada – Government of Canada (1991a): Citizens' Forum on Canada's Future: Report to the People and Government of Canada (Spicer Commission, chaired by Keith Spicer). Ottawa: Supply and Services Canada.

Canada – Government of Canada (1991b): Shaping Canada's Future Together. Ottawa: Supply and Services Canada.

Canada – Government of Canada: Constitution Acts, 1867 to 1982. http://lois-laws.justice.gc.ca/eng/const/ [accessed: 13 April 2011]

Canada – Library of Parliament (2011a): The Constitution since Patriation: Chronology, Ottawa: Library of Parliament. http://www2.parl.gc.ca/parlinfo/compilations/constitution/ConstitutionSincePatriation.aspx?Language=E [accessed: 13 April 2011]

Canada – Library of Parliament (2011b): Party Standings (1980 to date) in the House of Commons, Ottawa: Library of Parliament. http://www2.parl.gc.ca/parlinfo/lists/PartyStandingsHistoric.aspx?Language=E&Menu=HOC-Representation&Section=03d93c58-f843-49b3-9653-84275c23f3fb [accessed: 13 April 2011]

Canada – Parliament of Canada (2010): Bill S-8: Act respecting the selection of senators, introduced to the Senate 27 April 2010, 40th legislature, 3rd session. http://www2.parl.gc.ca/Sites/LOP/LEGISINFO/index.asp?Language=E&Session=23&query=7000&List=toc [accessed: 13 April 2011]

Canada – Parliament of Canada (2007): Bill C-20: An Act to provide for consultations with electors on their preferences for appointments to the Senate, introduced to the House of Commons 13 November 2007, 39th legislature, 2nd session. http://www2.parl.gc.ca/Sites/LOP/LEGISINFO/index.asp?Language=E&Session=15&query=5313&List=toc [accessed: 13 April 2011]

Canada – Parliament of Canada (2006): Bill C-43: An Act to provide for consultations with electors on their preferences for appointments to the Senate, introduced to the House of Commons 13 December 2006, 39th legislature, 1st session, http://www2.parl.gc.ca/Sites/LOP/LEGISINFO/index.asp?Language=E&Session=14&query=4899&List=toc [accessed: 13 April 2011]

Canada – Parliament of Canada (1996): Act respecting Constitutional Amendments, S.C. 1996, c. 1. http://laws.justice.gc.ca/PDF/Loi/C/C-36.7.pdf [accessed: 13 April 2011]

Canada – Parliament of Canada (1992a): Employment Insurance Act, S.C. 1996, c. 23. http://laws-lois.justice.gc.ca/eng/acts/E-5.6/index.html [accessed: 13 April 2011]

Canada – Parliament of Canada (1992b): Referendum Act, S.C. 1992, c. 30. http://lois.justice.gc.ca/PDF/Statute/R/R-4.7.pdf [accessed: 13 April 2011]

Canada – Statistics Canada (2006): 2006 Census. http://www12.statcan.ca/census-recensement/index-eng.cfm [accessed: 13 April 2011]

Canada – Supreme Court of Canada (1998): Reference Re Secession of Quebec, [1998] 2 S.C.R. 217.

Clarke, Jeremy A. (2006): Beyond the Democratic Dialogue, and Toward a Federalist One: Provincial Arguments and Supreme Court Responses in Charter Litigation. In: Canadian Journal of Political Science 39, (2): 293-314.

Cloutier, Édouard, Guay, Jean-Herman and Latouche, Daniel (1992): Le virage. L'évolution de l'opinion publique au Québec depuis 1960. Montréal: Québec-Amérique.

Collective (1992): Référendum, 26 octobre 1992. Les objections de 20 spécialistes aux offres fédérales. Montréal: Éditions Saint-Martin.

Cook, Curtis (ed.) (1994): Constitutional Predicament: Canada after the Referendum of 1992. Montréal-Kingston: McGill-Queen's University Press.

CROP (2011): Évolution du climat politique au Québec – février 2011, Montréal: CROP. http://www.crop.ca/fr/blog/2011/58/ [accessed: 13 April 2011]
Dickson, Brian (1996): Two modest observations on Québec. In: The Globe and Mail, 5 July, 1996: A19.
Duchesne, Pierre (2004): Jacques Parizeau. Volume 3: Le régent, 1985-1995. Montréal: Québec-Amérique.
Hiebert, Janet L. (1996): Limiting Right: The Dilemma of Judicial Review. Montréal-Kingston: McGill-Queen's University Press.
James, Patrick (1999): The Chain Store Paradox and Constitutional Politics in Canada. In: Journal of Theoretical Politics 11, (1), 5-36.
Jedwab, Jack (2010a): The Roots of Perception: How Some Canadian Founding Groups Feel About Others?. Montréal: Association for Canadian Studies. http://www.acs-aec.ca/pdf/polls/12646088233661.doc [accessed: 13 April 2011]
Jedwab, Jack (2010b): Québec Identity in 2011: Attachments, Identity and Diversity, Montréal: Association for Canadian Studies. http://www.acs-aec.ca/pdf/polls/Québec%20Identity%202011-EN.doc [accessed: 13 April 2011]
Johnston, Richard (1993): An Inverted Logroll: The Charlottetown Accord and the Referendum. In: PS: Political Science and Politics 26, (1), 43-48.
Johnston, Richard/Blais, André/Gidengil, Elisabeth/Nevitte, Neil (1996): The Challenge of Direct Democracy: The 1992 Canadian Referendum. Montréal-Kingston: McGill-Queen's University Press.
Johnston, Richard/Blais, André/Gidengil, Elisabeth/Nevitte, Neil (1993): The People and the Charlottetown Accord. In: Watts, R. L./Brown, D. M. (eds.): Canada: The State of the Federation 1993. Kingston: Institute of Intergovernmental Relations, Queen's University, 19-43.
Kelly, James (2004): Guarding the Constitution: Parliamentary and Judicial Roles under the Charter. In: Meekison, J. P./Telford, H./Lazar, H. (eds.): Canada: The State of the Federation 2002. Reconsidering the Institutions of Canadian Federalism. Montréal-Kingston: McGill-Queen's University Press, 77-110.
Laforest, Guy (1992): Robert Bourassa et la maîtrise du temps. In: Brown, D. M./Young, R. (eds.): Canada: The State of the Federation 1992. Kingston: Institute of Intergovernmental Relations, Queen's University, 53-75.
Lajoie, Andrée (2009): Réformer le processus de nomination des juges de la Cour suprême?. Kingston: Institute of Intergovernmental Relations, Queen's University, coll. SC Working Paper 2009 (04).
LeDuc, Lawrence/Pammett, Jon H. (1995): Referendum Voting: Attitudes and Behaviour in the 1992 Constitutional Referendum. In: Canadian Journal of Political Science 28, (1), 3-33.
Léger Marketing (2009): Referendum voting intentions in Québec. Montréal: Léger Marketing. http://legermarketing.com/documents/intvote/IVREFEN_quebec.pdf [accessed: 13 April 2011]
Leydet, Dominique (2004): Compromise and Public Debate in Processes of Constitutional Reform: the Canadian Case. Social Science Information 43, (2), 233-262.
Lisée, Jean-François (1994a): Le tricheur: Robert Bourassa et les Québécois, 1990-1991. Montréal: Boréal.
Lisée, Jean-François (1994b): Le naufrageur: Robert Bourassa et les Québécois, 1991-1992. Montréal: Boréal.

Lusztig, Michael (1994): Constitutional Paralysis: Why Canadian Constitutional Initiatives are Doomed to Fail. In: Canadian Journal of Political Science 27, (4), 747-771.

Marquis, Pierre (1993): Referendums in Canada: The Effect of Populist Decision-Making on Representative Democracy. Ottawa: Library of Parliament; Political and Social Affairs Division, Background Paper series, BP-328E.

McRoberts, Kenneth/Monahan, Patrick J. (eds.) (1993): The Charlottetown Accord, the Referendum, and the Future of Canada. Toronto: University of Toronto Press.

Meekison, J. Peter (1993): Let There Be Light. In: Watts, R. L./Brown, D. M. (eds.): Canada: The State of the Federation 1993. Kingston: Institute of Intergovernmental Relations, Queen's University, 61-86.

Monahan, Patrick J. (1993): The Sounds of Silence. In: McRoberts, K./Monahan, P. J. (eds.): The Charlottetown Accord, the Referendum, and the Future of Canada. Toronto: University of Toronto Press, 222-248.

Mulroney, Brian (2007): Mémoires. Montréal: Éditions de l'homme.

Newman, Warren J. (2007): Living with the Amending Procedures: Prospects for Future Constitutional Reform in Canada. In: The Supreme Court Law Review 37, (2), 383-416.

Northrup, David A./Oram, Anne E. (1994): The 1993 Canadian Election Study, Incorporating the 1992 Referendum Survey on the Charlottetown Accord: Technical Documentation. Toronto: Institute for Social Research, York University. http://www.isr.yorku.ca/download/CES/CES93/TECHDOC.PDF [accessed: 13 April 2011]

Pelletier, Benoît (2010): L'impact du bijuridisme sur le fédéralisme canadien. In: Revue générale de droit 40, 251-281.

Pelletier, Benoît (2008): Allocution à l'occasion du Congrès canadien des affaires constitutionnelles 2008. Québec, 18 January 2008. http://www.saic.gouv.qc.ca/centre_de_presse/discours/2008/dis20080118.htm [accessed: 13 April 2011]

Pelletier, Réjean (2008): Le Québec et le fédéralisme canadien. Un regard critique. Québec: Presses de l'Université Laval.

Poels, Anne (1992): Chronology of Events July 1991 – June 1992. In: Brown, D. M./Young, R. (eds.): Canada: The State of the Federation 1992. Kingston: Institute of Intergovernmental Relations, Queen's University, 247-280.

Poels, Anne (1993): Chronology of Events July 1992 – June 1993. In: Watts, R. L./Brown, D. M. (eds.): Canada: The State of the Federation 1993. Kingston: Institute of Intergovernmental Relations, Queen's University, 231-256.

Poirier, Johanne (2008): Une source paradoxale du droit constitutionnel canadien: les ententes intergouvernementales. In: Revue québécoise de droit constitutionnel, 1: http://www.aqdc.org/volumes/pdf/poirier-une_source_paradoxale.pdf [accessed: 13 April, 2011]

Poirier, Johanne (2004): Intergovernmental Agreements in Canada: At the Crossroads Between Law and Politics. In: Meekison, J. P./Telford, H./Lazar, H. (eds.): Canada: The State of the Federation 2002. Reconsidering the Institutions of Canadian Federalism. Montréal-Kingston: McGill-Queen's University Press, 425-462.

Québec – Assemblée nationale (2010): Referendum Act. R.S.Q., c. C-64.1. http://www2.publicationsduquebec.gouv.qc.ca/dynamicSearch/telecharge.php?type=2&file=/C_64_1/C64_1_A.html [accessed: April 13, 2011]

Québec – Assemblée nationale (1991): Loi sur le processus de détermination de l'avenir politique et constitutionnel du Québec, L.Q. 1991, c. 34. http://www.saic.gouv.qc.ca/publications/Positions/Partie3/Document25.pdf [accessed: 13 April 2011]

Québec – Assemblée nationale (1990): Loi instituant la Commission sur l'avenir politique et constitutionnel du Québec, L.Q. 1990, c. 34. http://www.saic.gouv.qc.ca/publications/Positions/Partie3/Document24.pdf [accessed: 13 April 2011]

Québec – Commission sur l'avenir politique et constitutionnel du Québec (1991): L'avenir politique et constitutionnel du Québec. Rapport de la Commission sur l'avenir politique et constitutionnel du Québec (Bélanger-Campeau Commission, chaired by Michel Bélanger and Jean Campeau). Québec: Secrétariat de la Commission sur l'avenir politique et constitutionnel du Québec.

Québec – Directeur général des élections du Québec (2000): Instruments of Direct Democracy in Canada and Québec. 3rd edition (updated by Julien Côté). Québec: Directeur général des élections du Québec, Electoral study series.

Québec – Directeur général des élections du Québec (1995): Rapport des résultats officiels du scrutin. Référendum du 30 octobre 1995. Québec: Directeur général des élections du Québec.

Québec – Directeur général des élections du Québec (1992): Rapport des résultats officiels du scrutin. Référendum du 26 octobre 1992. Québec: Directeur général des élections du Québec.

Québec – Directeur général des élections du Québec (1980): Rapport des résultats officiels du scrutin. Référendum du 20 mai 1980. Québec: Directeur général des élections du Québec.

Québec – Gouvernement du Québec (2001): Québec's Positions on Constitutional and Intergovernmental Issues. 3rd edition. Québec: Secrétariat aux affaires intergouvernementales canadiennes. http://www.saic.gouv.qc.ca/institutionnelles_constitutionnelles/positions_1936-2001_en.htm [accessed: 13 April 2011]

Québec Liberal Party (2001): Un projet pour le Québec: affirmation, autonomie et leadership. Rapport final du Comité spécial du Parti libéral du Québec sur l'avenir politique et constitutionnel de la société québécoise. Montréal: Québec Liberal Party.

Québec Liberal Party (1991): Un Québec libre de ses choix: Rapport du Comité constitutionnel du Parti libéral du Québec pour dépôt au 25e Congrès des membres. Montréal: Québec Liberal Party.

Québec Liberal Party (1985): Maîtriser l'avenir. Montréal: Québec Liberal Party.

Québec – Secrétariat à la politique linguistique (2011): La dynamique des langues en quelques chiffres. Québec: Secrétariat à la politique linguistique. http://www.spl.gouv.qc.ca/documentation/rapportssondagesstatistiques/dynamiquedeslangues/ [accessed: 13 April 2011]

Québec – Secrétariat aux affaires intergouvernementales canadiennes (2007): Les 25 ans de la Loi constitutionnelle de 1982, y compris la Charte canadienne des droits et libertés: Le Québec réitère sa position, Québec: Secrétariat aux affaires intergouvernementales canadiennes. http://www.saic.gouv.qc.ca/centre_de_presse/communiques/2007/saic_com20070417.html [accessed: 13 April 2011]

Reid, Darrel R. (1990): Chronology of Events July 1989 – June 1990. In: Watts, R. L./Brown, D. M. (eds.): Canada: The State of the Federation 1990. Kingston: Institute of Intergovernmental Relations, Queen's University, 233-270.

Reid, Darrel R. (1991): Chronology of Events July 1990 – June 1991. In: Brown, D. M. (ed.): Canada: The State of the Federation 1991. Kingston: Institute of Intergovernmental Relations, Queen's University, 207-240.

Reid, Darrel R./Herperger, Dwight (1989): Chronology of Events January 1988 – June 1989. In: Watts, R. L./Brown, D. M. (eds.): Canada: The State of the Federation 1989. Kingston: Institute of Intergovernmental Relations, Queen's University, 239-286.

Reid, Darrel R./Kendall, Christopher (1988): Chronology of Events 1987-1988. In: Leslie, P. M./Brown, D. M. (eds.): Canada: The State of the Federation 1987-1988. Kingston: Institute of Intergovernmental Relations, Queen's University, 197-252.

Russell, Peter H. (2004): Constitutional Odyssey: Can Canadians Become a Sovereign People? 3rd edition, Toronto: Toronto University Press.

Stein, Michael B. (1993): Tensions in the Canadian Constitutional Process: Elite Negotiations, Referendums and Interest Group Consultations, 1980-1992. In: Watts, R. L./Brown, D. M. (eds.): Canada: The State of the Federation 1993. Kingston: Institute of Intergovernmental Relations, Queen's University, 87-116.

Taillon, Patrick (2007): Les obstacles juridiques à une réforme du fédéralisme. Montréal: Institut de recherche sur le Québec.

Thorson, Stephanie/Eisenberg, Avigail (1986): Chronology of Events 1985. In: Leslie, P. M. (ed): Canada: The State of the Federation 1986. Kingston: Institute of Intergovernmental Relations, Queen's University, 197-252.

United Kingdom – Imperial Conference (1926): Inter-Imperial Relations Committee. Report, Proceedings and Memoranda [Balfour Declaration]. http://www.foundingdocs.gov.au/item.asp?sdID=95 [accessed: 13 April 2011]

United Kingdom – Judicial Committee of the Privy Council (1919): Reference re: Initiative and Referendum Act (Man.), [1919] A.C. 935.

United Kingdom – United Kingdom Parliament (1982): Canada Act 1982, 1982, c. 11 (U.K.). http://www.legislation.gov.uk/ukpga/1982/11 [accessed: 13 April 2011]

United Kingdom – United Kingdom Parliament (1931): Statute of Westminster 1931, 22-23 Geo. V, c. 4 (U.K.). http://www.legislation.gov.uk/ukpga/Geo5/22-23/4 [accessed: 13 April 2011]

United Kingdom – United Kingdom Parliament (1900): Commonwealth of Australia Constitution Act 1900, 63-64 Vict., c. 12 (U.K.). http://www.legislation.gov.uk/ukpga/Vict/63-64/12 or http://www.foundingdocs.gov.au/item.asp?sdID=82 [accessed: 13 April 2011]

Université de Sherbrooke (2010): Bilan du siècle, Sherbrooke, Université de Sherbrooke. http://bilan.usherbrooke.ca/ [accessed: 13 April 2011]

Watts, Ronald L. (1993): Overview. In: Watts, R. L./Brown, D. M. (eds.): Canada: The State of the Federation 1993. Kingston: Institute of Intergovernmental Relations, Queen's University, 3-18.

Woehrling, José (2002): Le recours à la procédure de modification de l'article 43 de la Loi constitutionnelle de 1982 pour satisfaire certaines revendications constitutionnelles du Québec. In: Thibault, P./Pelletier, B./Perret, L. (eds.): Les Mélanges Gérald-A. Beaudoin, Les défis du constitutionnalisme. Cowansville: Éditions Yvon Blais, 449-491.

Yale, François (2008): L'évolution de l'appui à la souveraineté du Québec: effets de la formulation de la question et effets de contexte. Mémoire de maîtrise. Montréal: Département de sociologie, Université de Montréal. http://hdl.handle.net/1866/2182 [accessed: 13 April 2011]

German Federalism after Two Reforms

Wolfgang Renzsch

1. Introduction

For a long time, German federalism, in particular intergovernmental relations between the federation and the *Länder* have been a recurrent topic on the academic as well as on the political agenda. Debates about federal reform started already before German unification in 1990, but continued afterwards with more intensity. Two issues have been addressed primarily: the efficiency or inefficiency of federal-*Länder* cooperation, and the fairness or unfairness of the intergovernmental fiscal relations, in particular the fiscal equalisation scheme. Hopes that German unification would open an opportunity to modernise the federal system, failed. Although some talked of a "lost chance", dealing with the challenge of German unification and modernising the federal system at the same time would probably have overburdened the problem-solving capacity of the political system. However, the Unification Treaty of 31 August 1990 stipulated in article 5 (BGBl. 1990 II, p. 889) that the legislature of the Federal Republic should revise the relations between the federal and *Länder* governments within the next two years. This provision reflected the fear of the West German *Länder* governments to lose political influence in a united Germany.

The reform of the federal system was originally divided into two steps. The *Bundestag* and the *Bundesrat* agreed to call a joint commission which was supposed to develop proposals for a reform mainly of the legislative powers of both levels of government (Batt, 1995; Klöpfer and Lang, 1996; Renzsch, 1996). The not less difficult task of amending the system of intergovernmental fiscal relations determined to integrate the new *Länder* was delegated to the ministers of finance of the *Länder* who established the commission "*Finanzreform 1995*" (Razeen and Webber, 1994; Renzsch, 1994). A reform of the allocation of legislative powers was certainly desirable; an amendment of the system of intergovernmental fiscal relations, however, was necessary since the Unification Treaty provided for financial assistance for the new east German *Länder* governments outside the constitutional framework until the end of the year 1994 (article 7 Unification Treaty; article 134 GG). Passing this task on to the *Länder* ministers of finance indicated that the federal and the *Länder* governments expected the *Länder* themselves to find a solution. Indeed, the result, later called Solidarity Pact I, reflected much more the common position of the *Länder* rather than that of the federal government.

2. Two federal reform commissions

Not long after the first Solidarity Pact had come into force a new debate on the federal order in general and on intergovernmental fiscal relations in particular started. In 1998 the *Länder* governments of Baden-Wuerttemberg, Bavaria and Hesse filed a suit at the Federal Constitutional Court requesting that the Court declared important parts of the fiscal equalisation law as unconstitutional and therefore void.[1] The "red-green"-government under chancellor *Schröder* elected in 1998 also placed the federal order on its agenda, when it announced its intention "to participate in the joint elaboration of an appropriate division of powers between the federation and *Länder*"[2].

However, the proceedings at the Federal Constitutional Court prevented any progress in political deliberations since none of the actors was willing to define a negotiation position as long as it might be overruled by the Court. After the Court had decided on 11 November 1999 the political debate concentrated on the implementation of its requests and – associated with this – a prolongation of the fiscal assistance for the East German *Länder*. Within a comparatively short period of time, the federal legislature agreed on a law defining the principles for fiscal equalisation (*Maßstäbegesetz* of 9 September 2001, BGBl. I p. 2302,) and on an amendment of the fiscal equalisation scheme by a law adjusting the Solidarity Pact (*Solidarpaktfortführungsgesetz* of 20 December 2001, BGBl. I, p 3955). These two laws are of relevance for the analysis that follows, as their rules should be terminated on 31 December 2019 (§ 15 *Maßstäbegesetz*; *Solidarpaktfortführungsgesetz* article 5 § 20).

On 16 October 2003 respectively on 17 October 2003, after more than two further years of preparations, the *Bundestag* and the *Bundesrat* decided to call a "Joint Commission for the Modernisation of the Federal Order". The resolution calling this commission also defined its tasks:

"The Commission shall develop proposals for a modernisation of the federal order of the Federal Republic of Germany in order to improve the ability of the federal and the *Länder* governments to act and to decide, to improve the allocation of powers and to increase the

1 http://www.bverfg.de/entscheidungen/fs19991111_2bvf000298.html: BVerfG, 2 BvF 2/98 of 11 November 1999.

2 Chancellor Gerhard Schröder, 10 November 1998, Deutscher Bundestag, 143th legislative period, 3rd session, p. 67 (A) (my translation).

effectiveness and efficiency of public policies. It shall present these proposals the legislative bodies of the federation" [3]

In particular, the commission was supposed to review

- the allocation of legislative powers to the federal and the *Länder* levels;
- the power and rights of co-determination of the *Länder* governments in federal legislation; and
- the intergovernmental fiscal relations (in particular the joint tasks and sharing of expenditure) between federal and *Länder* governments.

Additionally, the consequences of European integration were supposed be taken into account.

The commission held meetings from November 2003 until December 2004. To the surprise of most observers the commission finished its negotiations without a result, mainly due to a dispute on higher education which could not be settled. On 17 December 2004, in a meeting of only 26 minutes the two chairmen informed the Commission that they were not able to present a common proposal.[4]

This deadlock situation was hardly acceptable, in particular as many observers deemed short-sighted and purely political reasons as decisive for the failure. Indeed, shortly after the federal elections of 2005, the Christian Democrats and the Social Democrats settled the dispute in their negotiations on a Grand Coalition (Kluth, 2007: 54; cf. also Krings, 2007: 74ff.).

The final compromise counted five pages in the federal Law Gazette.[5] The important changes were:

- Article 23 para 6: In case the European Union acts in matters of primary and secondary education, culture or broadcasting falling under the exclusive legislative power of the *Länder*, the federal government must authorise a representative of the *Bundesrat* to represent the Federal Republic in the Council of Ministers.
- Article 72 para 2 restricted the formerly general "necessity"-clause in concurrent legislation of the federation of 1994[6] to ten matters.

3 Deutscher Bundestag/Bundesrat Öffentlichkeitsarbeit, 2005: 17 f. (my translation). Further information about the first federalism commission is based on this documentary.

4 Stenographic record, 11th session, 17 December 2004, pp. 279- 282, published ibid., attached CD Rom.

5 BGBl. I, 2006, Nr. 41, pp. 2034-2038; see also Maiwald, 2006.

6 The above mentioned amendment of article 72 para 2 GG of 1994 stipulated that the Federation may only use its powers in the area of the concurrent legislation if it was "necessary" for equal living conditions, or the protection of the legal and economic unity. Before this amendment, the Federation could apply its concurrent legislative powers when it considered the use as "appropriate". Whether or not the Federation used its concurrent powers depended on the discretion of the federal government alone.

- Article 72 para 3 – the flipside of the coin – allowed the *Länder* legislatures to deviate from federal legislation in six areas of concurrent legislation.
- Article 73 provided new exclusive legislative powers for the federation, in particular concerning the protection of German cultural heritage from being transferred to foreign countries, the fight against international terrorism, the regulation of weapons and explosives, the provision for the victims of war, and finally the use of nuclear power for peaceful purposes.
- Article 74 para 1 strengthened the legislative powers of the *Land* parliaments by transferring from the Federation to the *Länder* the right to legislate the prison regime, to regulate public demonstrations, sheltered homes, shop closing hours, public housing, amusement halls, fairs and markets.
- Article 74a and article 75: framework legislation of the Federation was abolished. Therefore the right to legislate the status and the obligations of civil servants (except career schemes, remuneration and old age pensions), hunting, protection of nature and landscapes etc. were transferred to article 74 para 1, i.e. to concurrent legislation of the federation.
- Article 84 para 1 changed the rights of the *Länder* in implementing federal laws and role of the *Bundesrat*. In cases the *Länder* administrations implement a federal law, their parliaments were entitled to deviate from federal administrative bye-laws unless the federal law rules otherwise. In those cases in which the *Länder* were allowed to deviate from federal regulation the federal law does not need the consent of the *Bundesrat*.
- In article 91a the construction of universities has been deleted from the list of joint tasks. It was replaced by a complex regulation of article 91b which allows cooperation of the federal and *Länder* governments, firstly in the cases of institutionalisation (*Einrichtungen*) and projects (*Vorhaben*) outside universities, secondly in projects of science and research in universities, and thirdly in the construction of buildings for research including large devices at universities.
- Article 93 para 2 subjected the “necessity clause” of article 72 para 2 GG under the control of the Federal Constitutional Court.
- Article 104a para 3 introduced a new clause ruling that a federal law needs the consent of the *Bundesrat* if it obliges the *Länder* to provide financial assistance, benefits in kind or comparable services to third persons.
- Article 104a para 6 settles an old dispute about the question which level of governments has to pay fines resulting from the violation of international obligations, in of the European law, by a formula of cost sharing.
- Article 104b replaced the old 104a para 4, however introduced two amendments. Firstly, federal grants for investments of the *Länder* and lo-

cal governments were restricted to areas the federal government has the power to legislate; secondly, these grants have to be designed with descending annual contributions.
- Article105 introduced the right of the *Länder* parliaments to set the rates for the tax on the purchase of real estate.
- Article 109 para 5 is strongly related to article 104a para 6 GG. It obliges both levels of government to respect the provision of article 104 Treaty Establishing the European Community (now article 126 Treaty on the Functioning of the European Union) concerning budgetary discipline.
- Article 125a, 125b, 125c, 143c regulate the transition from old to new law.

Taking into account the amount of changes of the Basic Law it is justified to speak of the most extensive reform of the constitution since 1969. However, a core issue of any federal order, the intergovernmental fiscal relations, remained untouched except a few marginal amendments and was left for the next reform.

Shortly after these constitutional amendments had been published in the Federal Law Gazette (28 August 2006), the *Bundestag* and the *Bundesrat* started a second round of federal constitutional reform. On 15 December both houses voted for the creation of a new commission which was supposed to develop proposals for a modernisation of the system of intergovernmental fiscal relations. These proposals should provide for reforms improving the conditions for economic growth and the creation of new jobs. The fiscal accountability of the federal as well as the *Länder* governments was to be strengthened. This rather general definition of the task became more precise due to an open list of issues which included:

- prevention of budgetary crises, development of criteria to limit public debts,
- handling of existing budgetary crises,
- revision of public tasks and standards
- reduction of bureaucracy and enhanced efficiency of public administrations, introduction of common IT-standards,
- improvement of an adequate distribution of revenues and a review of the fiscal equalisation scheme,
- enhancement of the accountability of all territorial authorities,
- improved cooperation of *Länder* governments and better chances to reorganise territories of the *Länder* on a voluntary basis,
- bundling of policies and their effect on intergovernmental fiscal relations (Deutscher Bundestag/Bundesrat, 2010: 18ff.).

The commission finished its work after two years of negotiations on 5 March 2009. Within less than four months the amendments of the constitution were published in the federal Law Gazette.[7]

7 Gesetz zur Änderung des Grundgesetzes of 29 July 2009, BGBl. I, 2009, pp. 2248-2250.

This second constitutional reform introduced

- article 91c allowing the federal and *Länder* governments to cooperate in matters of information technology as far as necessary,
- article 91d allowing evaluation of performance and "benchmarking" of public administrations,
- an amendment to the 2006 newly introduced article 104b allowing the federal government to provide financial assistance for the *Länder* also in cases of natural catastrophes and extraordinary emergency situations which cannot be controlled by a government,
- a revision of article 109 and a new article 109a which provided the core element of the 2009 reform, the "debt brake", and
- article 143c which provided transitory regulations.

Again, key questions of the system of intergovernmental relations were not answered. In particular, the commission did address neither the issue of tax legislation by the *Länder* nor the distribution of revenues between the federation and the *Länder* or the problems of fiscal equalisation among the *Länder*. The latter issue was left for future negotiations which have to be finalised until the end of the year 2019.

3. What has been achieved by two reforms?

These two parts of a still unfinished federal reform have not been completely implemented. Just about five, respectively two years after they have been adopted, an assessment of their effects turns out to be a rather challenging task. Certainly it is far too early to draw final conclusions. It took ten years until the constitutional reform of 1994 had significant effects on the political practice in Germany and only after the Federal Constitutional Court enforced the new provisions of article 72 para. 2, Basic Law, in 2004.[8] Such judicial action was necessary because federal legislation continued as if the delimitation of legislative powers had not been amended.

Therefore, the following paragraphs have to be limited to a few preliminary remarks on a certain aspects of the reforms. They focus on how the *Länder* have used their new powers and how governments have anticipated the "debt brake".

In fifty years from now, historians might look at the developments between 2002 and 2020 or even between 1990 and 2020 as a long process of constitutional adaptation of the "old" West German Federal Republic to the challenges of German Unification and European Integration. This process has

8 BVerfGE of 16 March 2004, 1 BvR 1778/01, and other decisions.

followed a logic determined by the Basic Law. Its general leitmotiv can be defined as strengthening the accountability of all levels of government. Even the "small" reform of 1994, in particular the new article 72 para 2 GG introduced a change of paradigm in German federalism going in this direction. The permanently increased precedence of federal legislation as well as joint decision-making were questioned and revised.

The 2006 reform followed this change of paradigm and tried to disentangle joint federal-*Länder* decision-making in legislation and to separate the jurisdictions of the federation and the *Länder*. This separation of powers was pursued not only with respect to legislative matters, but also and primarily in the area of administration. Part of this was the rule that the Federal Republic was supposed to be represented in the Council of Ministers of the EU by a member of the *Bundesrat*, i.e. by a member of a *Land* government, when issues of exclusive *Land* legislation are on the European agenda.

After the reallocation of powers, the next step aimed at the budget. The 2009 reform amended the Keynesian budgetary principles introduced in 1969 (achievement of an overall economic balance) and introduced new criteria based on article 104 of the Treaty Establishing the European Union resp. article 126 of the Treaty on the Functioning of the European Union. In principle, the budgets of the federation and the *Länder* should be balanced without debts. Exceptions have been limited to deficit spending in recession, natural disasters and emergency situations beyond government control. Governments borrowing money have to provide a repayment scheme for the debts. This regulation did not abolish the Keynesian principles of budgeting but – much more – introduces the omitted part of Keynes: In periods of economic growth debts have to be paid back, what never happened until now.

4. What effects can be measured today?

4.1 Limiting joint decision-making of Bundestag and Bundesrat

Whether the attempt to disentangle joint decision-making by the two chambers of the federal legislature was successful or not has been a matter of dispute. Marcus Höreth did not find major progress. According to his study, the effects are small, as the amendments reduce the number of federal laws requiring the consent of the *Bundesrat* by only five percent of all federal laws, which he considers as close to negligible (Höreth, 2007; 2008). Horst Risse, former secretary of the reform commissions, argued quite differently: He pointed out that hitherto more than half of all federal laws needed the consent of the *Bundesrat*. Addressing the causes he distinguishes between the specific requirements for a veto right of the *Bundesrat* (e.g. amendment of the constitution – article 79 GG – or regulations concerning the distribution of revenues – article 105, 106, 107 GG) on the one hand and the general rule of article 84 para 1 GG on the other (Risse, 2007). Thus, he implicitly although not overtly distinguished between constitutionally required consent[9], and those situations where the necessity of consent results merely from the regulations concerning administrative procedures. This provision has caused veto power of the *Bundesrat* in about 60 percent of the laws requiring its consent; the other 40 percent were caused by the special regulations of the Basic Law.

During the first year after the reform of 2006 came into force, the number of laws requiring *Bundesrat* consent because of article 84 para 1 GG dropped from 60 percent to about 25 percent. Of these 25 percent, about three quarters concern laws transforming international or European into German law. In these matters the federal legislature is not in the position to allow the *Länder* deviating administrative bye-laws. As a consequence it is next to impossible to relinquish the consent of the *Bundesrat*. However, these cases rarely cause political controversies.

It has been argued that the new clause of article 104a para 4 GG requiring consent if a federal law provides for grants and services at the expense of the *Länder* contradicts the intention of the amended article 84 para 1 GG. At a glance, that may be true. However, the *Länder* need a protection against financial burdens imposed on them by the federal government. Risse figured out that – during the period of time he looked at – about 10 percent of the consent requirements were caused by this clause (Risse, 2007: 710). According to his calculation of the new article 84 para 1 GG, the amount of consent demanding federal laws dropped to 43 percent during the first year after the reform from 57 percent in the previous legislative period. Therefore, Risse assesses the reform as effective, but not radical (709).

Any assessment of this part of the constitutional reform has to consider its purpose. It aimed at strengthening the accountability of all levels of government by limiting joint decision-making in order to allow a legitimate majority of the *Bundestag* to pursue its policies, and to protect the *Länder* against fiscal encroachments of the federation. Therefore the endeavours were concentrated on the clause of article 84 para 1 GG and left the special provision causing a *Bundesrat* veto aside, except for the amendment of article 104a para 4 GG. Among politicians, nobody had the intention to exclude the *Länder* from constitutional legislation, distribution of revenues or EU affairs.

The old article 84 para 1 GG intended to shield the *Länder* from federal encroachment on their administration. However this constitutional norm was hardly invoked for this purpose. Primarily it was used to protect the *Länder* from financial burdens imposed on them by federal legislation. Moreover, under conditions of a divided government, this rule allowed the opposition

---

9 Risse explains that the reform commission did not address those specific consent requirements. They were not considered as a problem (Risse, 2007: 708).

party at the federal level, commanding a majority in the *Bundesrat,* to compel a ruling majority of the *Bundestag* into bargaining on legislation. The new article 104a para 4 GG now improves the formerly imperfect protection.[10] In cases of a divided government the amendment will make it probably easier for a majority of the *Bundestag* to circumvent an adversarial majority of the *Bundesrat*.

Since in future it will be more difficult to use (or misuse) the *Bundesrat* as an instrument of the political opposition, we can expect that party politics will play a smaller role in this second chamber. That, however, does not mean that polic-making will become easier for the federal government. On contrary, when party politics lose importance in the *Bundesrat*, the federal government also is confronted with the problem that appealing to the party loyalty of "their" *Länder* governments will no longer work as in the past.[11] Thus, the small amendment of article 84 para 1 GG, which gives the *Länder* a right to deviate from the federal procedural bye-laws, might in the long run have more implications than we can anticipate as yet.

4.2 Use of new legislative powers by the Länder

The new legislative powers of the *Länder* concern primarily the regulation of public houses (smoking/non-smoking regulation) and shop closing time, tax rates on the trade of real estate, salaries of civil servants, sheltered homes and the prison regime. How would the *Länder* use their expanded powers? Taking into account the current practice of the *Länder*, two different approaches can be distinguished: individual law-making by which each *Land* does it "my way" (e.g. local fiscal equalisation) and coordinated *Länder* laws, negotiated on the "third level" among the land administration (e.g. police laws of the *Länder*). Also we have to distinguish between policy areas where no federal law existed before decentralisation, and areas where *Land* legislation can be based on a former federal law.

The *Länder* governments have used their new legislative powers received by the 2006 constitutional reform in at least six cases for autonomous *Land* legislation. Concerning non-smokers protection in public houses, there was no former federal law which could have given an orientation. In this case all *Länder* have meanwhile adopted varying regulations. Passed by a successful

10 The old provision of the former article 104a para 3 GG read that a federal law needed the consent of the *Bundesrat* if the *Länder* had to carry more than a quarter of the expenditure of federal law providing financial assistance to third parties; the new provision of article 104a para 4 GG requires the consent of the *Bundesrat* if a federal law constitutes *any* financial burden for the *Länder* because of financial assistance, benefits in kind or other services.

11 In summer 2011, it has been quite interesting to see that none of the prime minister of the CDU supported their party chairwoman and Chancellor Angela Merkel in debates on tax reductions.

referendum, the Bavarian law implies the strictest rules, generally prohibiting smoking in public houses, including festival halls or tents.[12] The other *Länder* provide more or less extensive exceptions from non-smoking rules: Hamburg, Lower Saxony and Saxony allow smoking in small pubs, however Hamburg and Lower Saxony only if no hot food is served.[13] Baden-Württemberg allows smoking in pavilions on fairs, festival halls or tents only.[14] Berlin allows "smokers' pubs" and smoking in separated rooms,[15] Brandenburg allows smokers' pubs too, but not in separated rooms,[16] while Bremen allows smoking in separated rooms.[17] Most *Länder* allow smoking in separated rooms, however under varying conditions. For instance Saxony Anhalt requests that guests must be able to have access without passing through the smokers' room or should not be molested when using the lavatory.[18]

Despite the fact that there had been a federal law before, the regulations of the shop closing time vary considerably among the *Länder*, too. Ten out of sixteen *Länder* allow shopping from Monday until Saturday all day and night long; four *Länder* restrict the opening hours on these days from 6 a.m. to 8 p.m. and 10 p.m. respectively. Two *Länder* require different closing hours on Saturdays, namely 8 p.m. and 10 p.m. respectively instead of midnight. Baden-Württemberg, which allows shopping on six days a week all day long, restricts the selling of alcohol to the time period from 5 a.m. to 10 p.m. Sunday regulations show slight differences only: eleven *Länder* apply the (old) federal regulation[19] permitting on four Sundays per year shops to be open. Other *Länder* are more liberal: Brandenburg allows six,[20] Berlin eight open Sundays.[21] In accordance with the old federal law, all *Länder* laws allow shopping at gas stations, airports and railway stations at any time. Officially, the shops are open for travel necessities. In reality, they have become more or less shopping malls for all kinds of goods. In particular airports provide large

---

12 *Gesetz zum Schutz der Gesundheit* (Gesundheitsschutzgesetz GSG); former law from 2007 (GVBl S. 919, BayRS 2126-3-UG) changed by a successful referendum 1 August 2010.

13 Hamburgische Passivraucherschutzgesetz (HmbGVBl. 2007, No. 28; p. 200); Niedersächsisches Gesetz zum Schutz vor den Gefahren des Passivrauchens, 12 July 2007 (Nds. GVBl. p. 337); Sächsisches Nichtraucherschutz (SächsNSG), 26 Oktober 2007 (SäGVBl 13/2007).

14 *Landesnichtraucherschutzgesetz* (LNRSchG) of 25 July 2007, (GBl. 2007, p. 337).

15 *Gesetz zum Schutz vor den Gefahren des Passivrauchens in der Öffentlichkeit (Nichtraucherschutzgesetz* – NRSG), 16 November 2007 (GVBl. p. 578).

16 *Gesetz zum Schutz vor den Gefahren des Passivrauchens in der Öffentlichkeit* (Brandenburgisches Nichtrauchendenschutzgesetz – Bbg NiRSchG), 18 December 2007 (GVBl.I/07, p. 346).

17 *Bremischen Nichtraucherschutzgesetz* (BremNiSchG), 12 December 2007 (Brem.GBl. p. 515).

18 *Gesetz zur Wahrung des Nichtraucherschutzes im Land Sachsen Anhalt* (Nichtraucherschutzgesetz), 19 December 2007 (GVBl. LSA 2007, p. 464).

19 *Gesetz über den Ladenschluss* (LadSchlG), 18 November 1956 (BGBl. I p. 875).

20 *Brandenburgisches Ladenöffnungsgesetz* (BbgLöG), 27 November 2006 (GVBl.I/06, [Nr. 15], p. 158)

21 *Berliner Ladenöffnungsgesetz* (BerlLadÖffG), 16 November 2006 (GVBL, p. 1045).

malls which are frequented by all kinds of customers not only travellers. Regulations for holiday resorts, and for places (and occasions) of special tourist interests have introduced further exceptions from constraints on Sundays.

Compared to the federal law on shop closing time of 2003[22], the Land legislations (or in Bavaria simply a bye-law[23]) have led to a liberalisation of the former regulation. In particular, the new *Land* laws pay respect to local particularities and interest. For instance, the mainly catholic *Länder* Bavaria[24] and Saarland[25] only allow Sunday shopping after "the main Sunday church services have taken place". Berlin was interested in long shopping hours, also on Sundays, because the city government hoped for tourists and shoppers from neighbouring regions. The Brandenburg government saw itself in a competitive situation and followed the path taken by Berlin. Between Schleswig-Holstein[26] and Mecklenburg Pomerania[27] similar effects occurred concerning special regulations for the seaside resorts at the Baltic coast. Unexpectedly, the Federal Constitutional Court intervened and stopped too liberal regulations. It held to be unconstitutional the rules on the Berlin Sunday shopping hours. With reference to article 139 of the Constitution of the Weimar Republic (which remained constitutional law according to article 140 GG), the court prevented the Land to allow shop opening on consecutive Sundays in order to protect the Sunday as a day of leisure and recreation.[28]

In contrast, the different tax rates on the trade of real estate introduced by the *Länder* are hardly more than a variation of the federal law. This law had set a tax rate of 3.5% of the price.[29] The *Länder* are now entitled to change this rate. The revenues achieved by the rates above (also below) the federal rate will not be taken into account in the fiscal equalisation scheme. Therefore, higher rates provide "real money" for the coffers of the *Länder*. So far, eight *Länder* have used their right to raise this tax. They apply rates of 4% (Lower Saxony), 4.5% (Berlin, Bremen, Hamburg, Saarland, Saxony-Anhalt) or 5% (Brandenburg, Schleswig-Holstein).[30] Other *Länder* will probably fol-

22 *Gesetz über den Ladenschluss* of 2 June 2003 (BGBl. I, p. 744).
23 *Ladenschlussverordnung* (LSchlV) of 21 May 2003 (GVBl, p. 340, BayRS 8050-20-1-A)
24 § 2 *Ladenschlussverordnung*.
25 § 8 Abs. 1 *Gesetz Nr. 1606 zur Regelung der Ladenöffnungszeiten* (*Ladenöffnungsgesetz* – LÖG Saarland) of 15 November 2006 (Amtsblatt 2006, p. 1974).
26 § 9 *Gesetz über die Ladenöffnungszeiten* (*Ladenöffnungszeitengesetz* – LÖffZG) of 29 November 2006 (GVOBL. 2006, p. 243).
27 §10 *Gesetz über die Ladenöffnungszeiten für das Land Mecklenburg-Vorpommern* (Ladenöffnungsgesetz – LöffG M-V) of 18 June 2007 (GVOBl. M-V 2007, p. 226).
28 BVerfG; 1 BvR 636/02 of 9 June 2004; 1 BvR 2857/07 und 1 BvR 2858/07 of 1 December 2009; Süddeutsche Zeitung, 2 December 2009: „Bloßes Umsatzinteresse reicht nicht", and Heribert Prantl, „Der Sonntag ist heilig".
29 *Grunderwerbsteuergesetz* (GrEStG) of 8 December 2010 BGBl. I, p. 1768).
30 See for example: *Gesetz über die Festsetzung der Hebesätze für die Realsteuern für 2007 bis 2011 und des Steuersatzes für die Grunderwerbsteuer* (Gesetz- und Verordnungsblatt

low. With the exception of Hamburg, all those *Länder* which increased the taxes rank among the poor ones in Germany. This observation supports the assumption that tax competition drives the not-so-good-off *Länder* to raise their tax rates for stabilising their budgets.

The federalism reform of 2006 also introduced "competitive elements" regarding the salaries for civil servants. Even though the salaries of *Land* civil servants were fixed before 2006 by federal law, [31] competition in this field had already existed to a certain extend. The structure of staff positions in public administration varied from *Land* to *Land*, and so did career prospects. On the other hand, in 2010, most of the *Länder* followed the decision of the federal government to increase payments, despite their new powers. The government of Baden-Württemberg, facing Land elections, and the government of Bavaria conceded higher increases for their civil servants.[32] Most of the poor *Länder* have reduced or cancelled the annual remuneration ("Christmas bonus") which, however, the *Länder* governments could determine even before the federal reforms were adopted.

The *Land* legislation on homes is still not finished as yet. It addresses the regulations of nursing homes for elderly and handicapped people who need constant care. Here again we observe a variety of approaches. Two *Länder*, Hessen and Thuringia, have not yet come up with their own legislation and thus continue to follow the regulations of the still existing federal law.[33] The other *Länder* all went their own way as even the titles of the laws (or the drafts) indicate: Home Law (Baden-Württemberg)[34], Habitation- and Participation Law (North Rhine-Westphalia)[35], Nursing- and Quality of Habitation Law (Bavaria)[36], Law concerning the Habitation-, Care- and Nursing Quality for the Elderly as well as for Persons in Need of Care and Handicapped Adults (Saarland)[37], Self-Determination Improvement Law (Schleswig-

---

Nr. 43/2006, 30 Decenber 2006, p. 1172 (Berlin); *Gesetz über die Festsetzung des Steuersatzes bei der Grunderwerbsteuer*, 16 December 2008 (HmbGVBl. 2008, p. 433 (Hamburg); *Gesetz über die Festsetzung des Steuersatzes für die Grunderwerbsteuer des Landes Sachsen-Anhalt*, 17 February 2010 (GVBl. LSA 2010, p. 69).

31 *Bundesbesoldungsgesetz* (BBesG) of 27 June 1957 (BGBl. I, p. 993).

32 *Landesbesoldungsgesetz Baden-Württemberg* (LBesGBW) of 9 November 2010 (GBl. 2010, p. 793, 826); *Bayerisches Besoldungsgesetz* (BayBesG) of 30 August 2001 (GVBl S. 410, p. 764).

33 *Wohn- und Betreuungsvertragsgesetz* of 29 July 2009 (BGBl. I, p. 2319).

34 *Heimgesetz für Baden-Württemberg (Landesheimgesetz* – LHeimG) of 10 June 2008 (GBl. 2008, p.169).

35 *Gesetz über das Wohnen mit Assistenz und Pflege in Einrichtungen (Wohn- und Teilhabegesetz)* of 18 November 2008, GVBl. 2008, p. 738.

36 *Gesetz zur Regelung der Pflege-, Betreuungs- und Wohnqualität im Alter und bei Behinderung (Pflege- und Wohnqualitätsgesetz* – PfleWoqG) of 8 July 2008 (GVBl 2008, p. 346).

37 *Saarländisches Gesetz zur Sicherung der Wohn-, Betreuungs- und Pflegequalität für ältere Menschen sowie pflegebedürftige und behinderte Volljährige (Landesheimgesetz Saarland* – LHeimGS) of 6 May 2009 (Amtsblatt 2009, p. 906).

Holstein)[38], Law for the Safeguarding of the Rights of Persons in Need for Care and Nursing in Supporting Dwelling Forms (Bremen)[39] and several others; – the smaller the Land, the longer the title of the law, and the more difficult to translate.

One of the most interesting cases is the *Land* legislation on prison regimes, in particular those for juvenile offenders. In 2006, the Federal Constitutional Court requested a law regulating the penal system for juveniles. The lack of a legal regulation in this field did not comply with the Basic Law since any encroachment on the basic rights of a citizen needs a firm legal basis.[40] After the 2006 federalism reform, this task had to be fulfilled by the *Länder*, not by the federal government. Therefore, similar to the laws concerning non-smokers' protection, the *Länder* had to pass their own laws without being able to more or less copy an existing federal law. However, this case is a good example for an unintended effect of separation of powers between the federal and the *Land* level. It reveals how decentralisation might cause new entanglements and joint decisions, although now "horizontally, among the Länder governments, instead of vertically, between levels" (Benz, 2007).

The *Länder* pursued different ways to fill the legal lacuna. Thirteen of them adopted laws for the detention of juvenile delinquents, three – Bavaria, Hamburg and Lower Saxony – did not create separate laws but integrated the special rules for adolescents in the general laws regulating the penal system. Ten out of the mentioned thirteen *Länder* agreed on a common regulation for adolescents. Bavaria, Hamburg, Lower Saxony and Baden-Wurttemberg passed new penal laws regulating the imprisonment of juveniles and adults. The remaining Länder continued to apply the still existing federal law for adults (Dünkel, Geng and Morgenstern, 2010).

The difficulties for autonomous *Land* legislation arise from two circumstances which actually restrict discretion of the *Länder* parliaments. Firstly, the legal proceedings as well as the organisation of penal courts are still regulated by federal law limiting *Land* powers. Secondly, the detention of convicts can be a cross-border issue, especially for the smaller *Länder*. Here, three aspects have to be taken into account: Firstly, prison inmates should serve their sentence close to their home in order to promote social integration after their discharge from prison independent of where the crime had been committed or where the convict had been sentenced. Secondly, not all *Länder* provide all kinds of prisons, like, e.g., for women or high security delin-

---

38 *Gesetz zur Stärkung von Selbstbestimmung und Schutz von Menschen mit Pflegebedarf oder Behinderung (Selbstbestimmungsstärkungsgesetz* – SbStG) Pflegegesetzbuch Schleswig-Holstein – Zweites Buch of 17 July 2009 (GVOBl. Schl.-H., p. 402).

39 *Gesetz zur Sicherstellung der Rechte von Menschen mit Unterstützungs-, Pflege- und Betreuungsbedarf in unterstützenden Wohnformen (Bremisches Wohn- und Betreuungsgesetz* – BremWoBeG) of 5 October 2010 (Brem. GBl., p. 509).

40 BVerfG, 2 BvR 1673/04 and 2 BvR 2402/04, Decision of 31 May 2006.

quents. Thirdly, not all prisoners comply with the prison rules. When prisoners show deviant behaviour or get involved in forbidden activities – for instance drug trafficking – they have to be taken out of their "networks" and be transferred to other prisons for security reasons. These requirements provide problems for small *Länder* maintaining only one or two prisons on average.[41]

Furthermore, some *Länder* cooperate in implementation of the penal system. The government of Saxony-Anhalt, for instance, transfers female convicts to Saxony.[42] Berlin is constructing a new prison in Brandenburg, on the soil of an entirely different *Land.* Currently, Berlin transfers inmates to prisons in Brandenburg because the Berlin prisons are overcrowded while those in Brandenburg offer empty places (see Potsdamer Nachrichten, 22 January 2010).

Therefore, the issue of regulating the prison system is not only a question of the political philosophy regarding whether a Land puts more emphasis on the deterrence of would-be-criminals or on social reintegration of the convicts after leaving jail. It is also a question of which law applies for which person. If somebody has been sentenced in one *Land* and has to serve his or her sentence involuntarily in another *Land*, it has to be decided which law would apply. In case the law of "*Land* x" provided more rights than that of "*Land* y" – for instance, allows for more visits or provides for better social support –, a prison inmate may request the rights he or she would have at their place of residence or at their place of conviction. According to experts, these questions remain completely open and nobody knows yet how the courts will decide. These uncertainties of cross-border issues due to diverging *Land* law (instead of a uniform federal law) particularly induce the smaller *Länder* to coordinate their legislation. Experts still disagree whether or not coordinated Land legislations provide better solutions compared to federal legislation.

To sum up, the legislative activities of the *Länder* in the areas of decentralised powers prove that they have used their new competences in a rather pragmatic way. The particular, mostly economic or financial interests of a Land play a more important role than ideologies or party interests. Concerning non-smokers protection, legislatures tried to balance concerns of smokers and non-smokers alike, independent on which parties have a majority. Concerning shop closing times, *Länder* with a predominating Catholic population have been more restrictive when Sundays were concerned. Besides that, the tourist industries and their interests have influenced the *Land* legislation on

41 Information provided here is based to a large extend on oral communication with the civil servant in charge of prisons in the Ministry of Justice in Saxony-Anhalt.

42 For instance Saxony-Anhalt does not have a prison for female inmates. The Land government has made an arrangement with Saxony that female convicts serve their sentence in Saxony. Also the Land does not have provisions for high security inmates. They are confined at other places.

this matter. Variations in tax policies and remuneration of civil servants reflect the financial situation of the *Länder*. As a consequence, the new *Land* laws in general did not reveal radical changes or partisan politics but aim at incremental adaptations to local circumstances.

4.3 The debt brake

The debt brake introduced in 2009 will show its full effects for the federal level in 2016 and for the *Länder* level in 2020 (article 143d para 1 GG). However, governments of both levels have already anticipated the rules by now. The federal government aims at a balanced budget in 2014, some *Länder* intend to get along without debts in 2012. A few of them had avoided new deficits even before the financial crisis of 2008/09 occurred, but could not compensate the decline of tax revenues during the crisis by regular budgetary measures. Also, three *Länder* – Rhineland-Palatinate, Schleswig-Holstein and Hesse – meanwhile introduced a debt brake in their *Land* constitutions.[43] In principle, these *Länder* have adopted the federal regulation. Others will follow.

The political objective to balance the budgets without credits has gained a hitherto unknown importance. On the one hand governments limit expenditure more than in former times. On the other hand, consolidating public budgets has become an issue of public political discourse. But it was the debt brake of the Basic Law and – probably even more – the global financial crisis of 2008/09 and the Euro crisis of 2010/11, that have changed the public attitudes.

These changed attitudes, presumably more than legal grounds, caused the Constitutional Court of North Rhine-Westphalia to apply a stricter interpretation of article 82 2nd sentence, Constitution of North Rhine-Westphalia, which allows credits up to the sum of public investments unless the economic balance is disturbed. For the first time in the history of the Federal Republic a court declared a budget unconstitutional. In its judgment of 15 March 2011[44], the court argued that it did not recognise any economic imbalance but, on the contrary, rising revenues. Therefore, it rendered the budget as not complying with the constitutional provisions.

This decision of the Constitutional Court of North Rhine-Westphalia as well as the decisions of the Federal Constitutional Court on the Berlin shop closing hours, mentioned above, and those based on article 72 para 2 GG (1994) indicate that the courts tend to more restrictive applications of constitutional provisions. The argument, that political interpretation of undetermined legal concepts has priority against legal consideration may not any longer be accepted as had been the case before. Whether that will become

43 Constitution of Rhineland-Palatinate, article 117; Constitution of Schleswig-Holstein, article 53, Constitution of Hesse, article 141.

44 VerfGH 20/10, www.vgh.nrw.de/presse/2011/p110315.htm.

questionable "judicial activism" or a proper limitation of a rather too liberal handling of constitutional rules remains to be seen.

5. Conclusion

Certainly, it is not difficult to argue that the reforms of German federalism did not meet the ambitious aims and that a "better" solution could have been possible in one or another issues. However, that would immediately provoke a dispute about what is a better solution. In political practice, "second best" solutions based on a broad consensus might be preferable. Moreover, if we consider the evolution of German federalism driven by a series of constitutional reform, it is fair to conclude that results achieved since German Unification are quite remarkable. The 1994 reform changed the paradigm of an ongoing process of centralising the regulation of public tasks and of increasing intergovernmental cooperation. Accountability of governments on both levels should be improved by a clearer delimitation of powers and a reduction of joint decision-making. This paradigm became the leitmotiv of the two reform commissions set up the first decade of 21st century. By an incremental disentangling of responsibilities, the *Länder* gained some of the political importance they had lost in former times. The second reform will – hopefully – force all government within the Federal Republic to reduce or abolish expenditures financed by new credits. The Euro crisis of 2010/11 has shown the risks of extensive public borrowing in a way hardly anyone expected.

However, the process of modernising the federal order has not come to an end. The reforms of 2006 and 2009 only mark first steps. The probably most difficult tasks, a review and reform of the intergovernmental fiscal relations are still on the agenda. The next steps not only have to revise the fiscal equalisation scheme, as some argue, but must include urgent problems such as the different cost effects of the implementation of federal laws by the *Länder* administrations, the inter-regional effects of migration within Germany and demographic effects causing different expenditures needs in regions, the horizontal effects of tax deductions by private investors, the regional distribution of tax revenues among the *Länder*, of tax legislation by the *Länder* governments, and several more. In July 2011, the prime ministers of Bavaria (CSU) and Baden-Württemberg (Green) have proposed a third federal reform commission, and the Federal Minister of Finance announced to give a speech about the federal view on fiscal federalism in September 2011. Probably, in 2020 the Federal Republic within the European Union (the impact of European integration on German federalism has to be excluded in this article) will in many respects be quite different compared to the old West German Federal Republic of 1969 or even of 1990.

References

Batt, Helge-Lothar (1995): Die Grundgesetzreform nach der deutschen Einheit, Opladen: Leske & Budrich.

Benz, Arthur (2007): Föderalismusreform in der „Entflechtungsfalle". In: Europäisches Zentrum für Föderalismusforschung (ed.): Jahrbuch des Föderalismus, Vol. 8. Baden-Baden: Nomos Verlagsgesellschaft, 180-190.

Deutscher Bundestag/Bundesrat (eds.) (2010): Die gemeinsame Kommission von Bundestag und Bundesrat zur Modernisierung der Bund-Länder-Finanzbeziehungen. Die Beratungen und ihre Ergebnisse. Berlin: Bundestag.

Deutscher Bundestag/Bundesrat Öffentlichkeitsarbeit (eds.) (2005): Dokumentation der Kommission von Bundestag und Bundesrat zur Modernisierung der bundesstaatlichen Ordnung (Zur Sache 12/2005). Berlin: Bundesrat.

Dünckel, Frieder/Geng, Bernd/Morgenstern, Christine (2010): Rechtstatsächliche Analysen, aktuelle Entwicklungen und Problemlagen des Strafvollzugs in Deutschland. Bundeszentrale für politische Bildung. http://www.bpb.de/files/5P6XI7.pdf [accessed: 6 November 2011]

Höreth, Marcus (2007): Zur Zustimmungsbedürftigkeit von Bundesgesetzen: Eine kritische Bilanz nach einem Jahr Föderalismusreform I. In: Zeitschrift für Parlamentsfragen 38, (4), 712-733.

Höreth, Marcus (2008): A Successful Failure? The Contested Implications of Germany's Federal Reforms. In: German Politics 17, (4), 408-423.

Klöpfer, Michael/Lang, Matthias (1996): Verfassungsänderung statt Verfassungsreform. Zur Arbeit der Gemeinsamen Verfassungsreformkommission. Berlin: BWV Berliner-Wissenschaft (2nd ed).

Kluth, Winfried (2007): Einführung. In: Kluth, W. (ed.): Föderalismusreformgesetz. Einführung und Kommentierung. Baden-Baden: Nomos Verlagsgesellschaft, 54-60.

Krings, Günter (2007): Die Beratungen der Föderalismuskommission. In: Kluth, W. (ed.): Föderalismusreformgesetz. Einführung und Kommentierung. Baden-Baden: Nomos Verlagsgesellschaft, 61-80.

Maiwald, Christian (ed.) (2006): Grundgesetz. Text Föderalismusreform mit Begleitgesetz und Einführung. Heidelberg: C.F. Müller.

Razeen, Sally/Webber, Douglas 1994: The German Solidarity Pact: A Case Study in the Politics of the United Germany. In: German Politics 3, (1), 18-46.

Renzsch, Wolfgang (1994): Föderative Problembewältigung: Zur Einbeziehung der neuen Länder in einem gesamtdeutschen Finanzausgleich ab 1995. In: Zeitschrift für Parlamentsfragen 25, (1), 116-13.

Renzsch, Wolfgang (1996): "Mit blauem Auge" – "auf Grund gesetzt." Über den Zusammenhang von Staatsmodernisierung und Grundgesetzreform nach der deutschen Einheit. In: Gotthard Breit (ed.): Die Bedeutung des Grundgesetzes für die politische Bildung (uni studien politik), Schwalbach: Wochenschau Verlag, 7-27.

Risse, Horst (2006): Zur Entwicklung der Zustimmungsbedürftigkeit von Bundesgesetzen nach der Föderalismusreform 2006. In: Zeitschrift für Parlamentsfragen 38, 707-712.

7. Conclusion

Federalism and Constitutional Change: Lessons from Comparisons

Arthur Benz and Felix Knüpling

1. Introduction

As mentioned in the introduction and as illustrated by the contributions to this volume, processes of constitutional change can vary widely from one federal or decentralised country to another. Nevertheless, variety does not prevent us from drawing conclusions or learning lessons, as long as we apply qualitative rather than quantitative methods of comparison.

In this concluding chapter we discuss constitutional reforms in federal and decentralising countries from such a comparative perspective in order to identify structures, processes and strategies which have proven to be indispensable for successful constitutional amendment. Thereby, we seek to enable public officials, scholars, and students to learn from the constitutional reform experiences of other federal democracies. Based on a typology of modes of constitutional change and constitutional negotiations and a systematic identification of relevant conditions affecting results, we summarise some practical suggestions how future reforms could be designed.

However, we emphasise that we do not intend to design a blueprint for reform. Rather it is our aim to shed light on some important conditions which turned out as decisive in our comparative research. Designs of a reform have to be adjusted to particular political systems and circumstances, but in doing so, responsible policy-makers should take into account some general lessons that can be learned from international comparison.

2. Patterns of constitutional change

In order to systematise patterns of constitutional change, we follow the distinction between reform and evolution (e.g. Behnke and Benz, 2008) or "explicit" and "implicit" change (Voigt, 1999). Change results from both processes, which are closely linked and can combine into either sequences or simultaneous development. We start by giving account of the patterns of reform before we delineate different patterns of constitutional evolution.

2.1 Varieties of constitutional reform

In a nutshell, reform processes can be characterised by three sub-processes. They start by initiatives of actors defining the basic agenda, continue with negotiations on an amendment proposal and end with a final decision of the institution that has the power to amend the constitution.

2.1.1 Initiative and agenda-setting

As the case studies in this volume reveal, governments mostly initiate constitutional reforms, even if other actors may have the formal power to do so (Kaltenborn, in this volume). By putting a constitutional amendment on the agenda, a government may respond to public debates or demands from political parties, experts or interest organisations. As a rule, however, it is governments and leaders of parties in parliament who set out the process of constitutional amendment and define the program of a reform.

Considering the initiative, it does make a difference whether processes of change are induced from the central level or from the regional level or whether central and regional governments jointly decide on the agenda. Reforms seem to be more successful if representatives from both levels cooperate as early as possible and define a common agenda. However, as it happened in Austria and Germany, such an agenda can include too many issues, if governments cannot agree on what is feasible and merely aggregate a "shopping list" of goals and issues. Such a list may pave the way for package deals in negotiations, but it also can end in process overloaded with details. In this regard, the Swiss reform is revealing. Its success was certainly due to a clear and coherent agenda which provided guidelines for negotiations. Moreover, a clear commitment of governments to amend the constitution, especially by the central or federal government, seems to be an essential requirement. This is a necessary, but not a sufficient condition for success of a reform.

Pressure from the regional level can induce the central government to take the lead and initiate a reform, as was particularly the case in Canada, Germany and the UK. Where this pressure stems from regionalist parties of regional governments claiming to represent distinct nations, reform processes right from the beginning tend towards asymmetric change. Canada, Spain, but also the UK, are cases in point.

2.1.2 Constitutional negotiations

When the initiative has been taken and the agenda set the scope and direction of a reform has been framed, the substance of constitutional reforms is determined in negotiation over draft bills. During negotiations, new issues can be put onto the agenda and others can be excluded. Nevertheless, actors initiating a reform have significant power to define which issues are addressed and which are excluded. Yet at the end, they need the agreement of participants in negotiation processes, while those involved in ratification are limited to voting yes or no. For this reason constitutional negotiations are highly relevant in a reform. Here, conflicts on the nature of a federal system and its multilevel structure and on the redistribution of power and resources among governments have to be dealt with.

As the contributions to this volume reveal, patterns for constitutional negotiations vary to a considerable degree, not only between countries but more often than not also between different reforms in a country. Rules for constitutional amendment rarely define who should participate in negotiations, how the process is organised and how agreements are settled. Instead, the organisation of government in general, political cultures and conventions or strategies of governments influence how negotiations are organised and which outcomes result from particular patterns. These different conditions have to be taken into account when evaluating constitutional negotiations in a comparative perspective. They explain different patterns of negotiations observable in the case studies

The distinct features of constitutional negotiations relevant for success or failure of a reform are set out below:

First, the *inclusion or exclusion of representatives* participating in negotiations is of crucial importance. The literature usually lists participants as members of committees or constitutional conventions or assemblies (Elster, 1995; McWhinney, 1981: 27-36). The case studies presented above lead us to add two more types: commissions and conferences. These four basic types can be characterised as follows:

- *Committees* are established either by parliaments or by the executives. In the first instance, they include members selected by parties in parliament, usually in proportionality to the number of their seats; in the second case, the task of elaborating a constitutional reform is delegated to civil servants and experts from central and regional governments. Parliamentary committees negotiate on constitutional amendments in the ordinary process of legislation, which may, as in France, constitute the main arena of a reform. Executive committees are established in order to de-politicise negotiations. They prepare proposals for amendments and thus define the agenda for legislation, before political parties or governments formulate their positions.
- *Commissions* include members from parliament and government. In Germany this type of organising constitutional negotiations reflected the structure of the legislature, while in Belgium it reflected the strong role of political parties in parliament and government. In either case, a com-

mission includes leading politicians who guarantee that proposals will pass formal legislation, provided that no referendum is required. Commissions are usually de facto mirrors of the lines of conflicts in the legislature, and their members anticipate potential vetoes from crucial actors or factions.

- *Conferences* are meetings of members of governments. Thus this category stands for an intergovernmental mode of negotiations that we often find in federal systems. It can be observed in Canada, even if the Charlottetown Accord resulted from a more complex process than earlier attempts to constitutional amendment the country saw. In Switzerland, intergovernmental conferences guided and controlled the work of a committee of experts.
- *Conventions* constitute more inclusive negotiations. In addition to representatives of parliaments and governments from the different levels, civil society organisations are invited to participate. While usually recommended for constitution-making, conventions are rare when it comes to a constitutional amendment. Austria and Scotland used this form. In both cases, the reform aimed at a comprehensive change of the territorial organisation. Conventions not only extend the number of actors with different interests involved in negotiations, they also raise expectations as to the scope and impact of a reform.

Table 1: Varieties of constitutional negotiation bodies

<table>
<tr><th></th><th>Parliaments</th><th>Governments</th><th>Civil Society</th></tr>
<tr><td>Committee</td><td>Canada, France</td><td>Italy. Switzerland</td><td></td></tr>
<tr><td>Commission</td><td colspan="2">Belgium, Germany</td><td></td></tr>
<tr><td>Conference</td><td></td><td>Canada, Switzerland</td><td></td></tr>
<tr><td>Convention</td><td colspan="3">Austria, Scotland</td></tr>
</table>

The type of organisation selected for preparing proposed amendments influences the mode of negotiation. According to theories of negotiations, we can distinguish between distributive bargaining, integrative bargaining and arguing (Benz, 2007). In distributive bargaining, actors pursue their individual interests, stick to their negotiation positions and try to achieve their claims as best as possible. Typically, these negotiations end up with package deals allowing each side to win in one issue area by exchanging concessions on others. Integrative bargaining is defined by similar behaviour of actors but here they are willing to make mutual concessions on an issue in order to come to a compromise. If actors negotiate in the arguing mode, they aim at a consensus on a joint decision and provide reasons why their claims are in the general interest of all participants.

In reforms to the multilevel organisation of a country, we can expect governments and parties tending to redistributive bargaining, whereas experts from the executive or from the academic sector and representatives of civil society organisation are more likely to search for compromises or negotiate in the arguing mode. This would mean that commissions and conferences tend towards distributive bargaining and committees and conventions support integrative bargaining or arguing. However, such a conclusion cannot be based on empirical evidence, as the contributions to this volume show.

The case studies reveal another significant feature of constitutional negotiation. Very seldom do negotiations take place only in plenary meetings of the different types. Instead, they are *differentiated in various dimensions* in order to manage the complexity of issues. As a consequence, different modes of negotiation emerge in the specific arenas, and they all, although to a varying degree, influence the outcome.

The following lines of differentiation seem to be particularly important:

Along *sectoral* lines, arenas of constitutional negotiations are regularly divided into sub-committees. They are set up to work on specific matters and to elaborate final formulations of amended constitutional rules. Sub-committees regularly aim at compromises, if they do not operate in the arguing mode.

Considering *membership*, negotiations can be differentiated into arenas with different types of actors. In Canada we find parliamentary committees as well as conferences of ministers and premiers convening in different contexts. In a similar way, negotiations were divided in Switzerland, where executive committees interacted with intergovernmental conferences. This separation of particular groups of actors allows for different modes of negotiation to emerge. In contrast, if a plurality of actors come together in commissions or conventions, party political orientations or interests of governments are likely to prevail in processes of distributive bargaining.

Moreover, the *territorial* structures of a state can be reflected in constitutional negotiations. Actors can form coalitions of central/federal or of regional representatives. In Germany, for instance, the *Länder* governments coordinated their positions in the negotiations on a modernisation of the federal systems in separate meetings before the commission met in plenary. Processes of negotiations can be also organised both at the central/federal level and at the regional level, as described by Nadia Verrelli for Canada. Moreover, regional interests can be included in symmetric or asymmetric ways. The second alternative can be found in the UK, where distinct processes of constitutional change were organised for Scotland, Wales and Northern Ireland (see Mitchell, in this volume). A territorial structure of negotiations can reinforce distributive bargaining, but at the same time it reduces the complexity of conflicts making them better manageable in package deals (see e.g. Hofmann, in this volume).

Differentiation of negotiations can imply *a hierarchical or a heterarchical* structure. In a hierarchical order, different groups work for a committee, conference, commission or convention where final decisions are made in plenary sessions. They contribute to the elaboration of an amendment proposal according to specified tasks and with clearly defined discretionary power. In a heterarchical structure, different sub-organisations work independently on their own agendas, with often overlapping responsibilities or memberships. In the arena where final amendment proposals are negotiated, the results are coordinated and used as input into discussions. Arguably, the second structure is more open to at least partial arguing processes than the first one. Heterarchical arrangements of negotiations can overcome the constraints of distributive bargaining, as is exemplified in the Canadian Charlottetown process (Verelli, in this volume, also: Stein, 1997).

A further aspect distinguishing patterns of constitutional negotiations has to do with the role of *experts*. They are not discussed in this volume at length, but obviously in all major reforms in federal or federalising systems experts have been included. They can be member of committees, commissions or conventions, but usually not of intergovernmental conferences. More often than not, they participate in hearings or provide expertise on particular issues. Finally, experts may be invited to evaluate the reform process and its results. Experts can come from the academic sector, from departments of central or regional governments, or from private interest organisations. Sometimes, as in Italy, experienced members of parliament, government or courts are commissioned to provide expertise (see Bassanini, in this volume).

The impact of experts is difficult to assess. In some cases, e.g. in Germany's first reform commission, academics played a prominent role in negotiations, but finally it turned out that they had a more symbolic than an effective function. In other cases, like in Austria, they were drawn into party political conflicts. In Switzerland and Canada, university professors closely cooperated with governments or members of parliament, and sometimes were even employed by government for a certain period. In many countries, academics have been regularly included in informal relations to individual representatives in negotiation bodies. As the case studies indicate, experts are more influential if they can informally but continuously communicate with participants in negotiations. Moreover, they are better able to contribute in sub-organisations than in official negotiation arenas where they compete with politicians for attention of media. However, to expect that independent experts can turn distributive bargaining in arguing processes is not very realistic and overestimates their power.

Regarding structures of constitutional negotiations, political *leadership* is obviously important. Nevertheless, it is rare to find heads of governments who engage in constitutional reforms in federal systems. Pierre Trudeau, who in the early 1980s fought for the "patriation" of the Canadian constitution, and Tony Blair, who started with an ambitious reform agenda including devolution of the United Kingdom, were exceptions. In constitutional negotiations, ministers or leading members of political parties chair the meetings and moderate processes. They play an important role in managing political conflicts, especially in final stages of the process. In earlier stages, they initiate, organise and coordinate the work of different groups. As can be concluded from several case studies, chairpersons in constitutional negotiations need both political skills and management capacities in form of an effective secretariat. Their effective power largely depends on a combination of neutrality and competence in constitutional law, or, to put it in another way, of procedural and substantial legitimacy.

Beyond the differentiation of structures, patterns of constitutional negotiations can also be distinguished according to *particular features of processes*. Three deserve mentioning:

- First, negotiating bodies can meet in *public or private*. Commissions and in particular conventions are usually open to the public, whereas committees and conferences most often hold closed sessions. The pros and cons of these alternatives have been discussed in the literature (e.g. Elster, 1993). In reality, we often find combinations of both, which can be achieved due to the differentiation of structures. More often than not, negotiations are launched by public sessions and continue with private meetings, either according to formal rules or due to the decreasing attention of media and citizens. The NFA Process in Switzerland revealed a different and apparently successful pattern. Here, the process was increasingly opened to the public with the consequence that debates became more specific and interest groups or citizens could respond to amendment proposals. However, the effect of public negotiations depends on the context. Where territorial reforms deal with problems of regional nationalism, they certainly attract more attention in the media and among citizens than in mono-nation states. In this case it seems to be necessary to open processes to the public in the very early stage of a reform, be it in form of a convention (as in Scotland) or parliamentary committees consulting with citizens (as in Canada).
- Second, processes have different temporal structures. Negotiations organised in various arenas can proceed simultaneously or sequentially. Usually we find a sequence of plenary meetings, followed by work in sub-committees, and final discussion and decision in the plenary. In some cases, negotiations at different levels take place at the same time, with the result that the process remains open for new ideas. Apart from this formal organisation of processes, the temporal order of substantial decisions seems of particular relevance. In many reform processes, negotiations aim at a package deal including controversial proposals; for this reason decisions are left open until everything is settled. While this

method allows for making deals, it risks overloading negotiations with the full complexity of a reform project, with a high risk of a deadlock at the end. Therefore, a reform which takes place in several steps, as described by Anton Hofmann for Germany, has some advantages. However, splitting up negotiations on the re-allocation of powers and negotiations on financial issues allows participants to postpone controversial matters to a later stage, with the consequence that a constitutional reform ends as an unfinished project. The Swiss experience with a sequential organisation of the reform is instructive. Here, the principles of the reform were negotiated and decided in a first stage, with further process concentrated on the implementation of these principles. As Dieter Freiburghaus and Gerald Wettstein explain, this sequencing not only reduced complexity of a comprehensive reform, it also facilitated redistributive decisions, which in the first stage were made in the "veil of ignorance" about winners and losers and in the second stage were guided by accepted principles of distributive justice.

- Third, negotiations are often supplemented by consultation with interest organisations or citizens. While negotiations aim at an agreement, consultations are about the gathering of ideas and opinions or about convincing citizens. In Canada, the Charlottetown process provides an instructive example of various ways to consult with citizens or associations. Here, the government organised conferences and invited citizens to issue opinions either via mail or via phone calls. These consultations should inform actors in constitutional negotiations about concerns and the will of the people. In Switzerland, civil society organisations are regularly heard in well established procedures and can issue recommendations or a critique of a draft amendment bill. Obviously, consultation on an elaborated draft has more effect than the early and rather unstructured consultations in the Canadian case. They also give interests groups a stronger voice than informal discussions organised by associations like in the first federalism reform in Germany, or like internet-based communication with citizens. Regardless of the particular form of consultation, such procedures often remain futile due to the limited interest of citizens in state reform. Moreover, as a number of studies has revealed (Kincaid and Cole, 2011), citizens and their representatives in associations often issue ambivalent opinions on territorial structures of a political system. While demanding decentralisation in general, they often argue for centralisation when it comes to powers relevant for their particular interests, or the other way around.

As Keith Banting and Richard Simeon once wrote, "constitution-making is a continuation of politics by other means; it involves not a radical break but an extension and often an intensification of normal processes" (Banting and Simeon, 1985: 17). In constitutional change, this often implies that negotiations hardly differ from usual patterns of politics and policy-making. As a consequence, distributive bargaining between parties or actors in intergovernmental relations prevails, and more often than not, these actors are more interested in their day-to-day affairs than in constitutional rules. In federal and regionalised states, such patterns of negotiations are prone to end in the "joint-decision trap" (Scharpf, 1988) which at best allows agreements on marginal changes of the existing constitution. Integrative bargaining and arguing on constitutional principles and norms have a better chance to evolve if multilevel constitutional negotiations clearly differ from politics as usual.

At first glance, constitutional conventions seem to provide a best form to separate constitutional and normal politics. But as the Austrian example proves, this is not necessary the case. A convention can either be exploited by parties as an arena for playing their political games, or it can turn into a venue for more or less academic discussions which are ignored by those holding power in the legislative arena.

Strategies other than establishing a convention have proved to be more effective in this regard. In general, highly differentiated patterns of negotiations are less threatened to be drawn into usual politicking, while they also provide feedback from constitutional negotiations into political processes. Again Switzerland and Canada provide cases in point, to a certain degree also Germany and the UK. Contrasting examples of less differentiated constitutional negotiations are presented in particular in the reports on Belgium, France, Italy and Austria. These are exactly the countries where federal reforms or decentralisation failed, had limited effects or turned out as not appropriate to stabilise the federal or federalising system.

2.1.3 Ratification

The fate of a constitutional reform is decided during the formal procedure, when proposals elaborated in constitutional negotiations are to be ratified and passed as a law amending the constitution. The term ratification indicates that negotiated results rarely are modified during processes of formal legislation. It goes without saying that parliaments can still revise any draft bill on a constitutional amendment. But usually these modifications concern merely limited aspects. When amendment bills have to pass by referendum, the people can only accept it or reject it. Thus those holding the right to decide on constitutional amendment de facto can apply veto-power, but not the power to shape the substantial results.

This power in ratification processes is assigned by formal amendment rules defined in existing constitutions. Rules may determine who has the right to initiate a reform and they may protect particular elements of a constitution from being changed, but their main content establishes the basic provisions of the ratification process. While discussions in practice often focus on the distinction between ratification by parliaments and ratification by referendum, Markus Kaltenborn and Carlos Closa shed light on the varieties of amendment rules in different countries. Interestingly, we cannot identify a particular pattern of amendment rules in federal systems. When unitary states change their territorial organisation, decentralise powers or revise the relations between central and regional or local governments, they regularly give governments or citizens in lower level jurisdictions a right to decide, either in consultative or binding referenda. In federal systems, representatives of regions usually have veto rights in second chambers, whereas regional parliaments or citizens in regions have a say only in some states. Thus reforms concerning the multilevel structure of a state are amended according to particular rules, but this applies to federal and to unitary states; and only some federal states (e.g. Canada) established particular rules for federal constitutional reform.

As Carlos Closa shows in his comparative study, amendment rules matter, but we cannot conclude that particular rules have particular effects. Neither the length or stability of formal constitutions nor the frequency of amendments can be explained by differences in these rules. Certainly, we should not underrate their effect on the legitimacy of constitutional change. However, even under this perspective there is the need to ponder the extension of the right to decide with the effectiveness of ratification, which seems to be influenced by different conditions. Moreover, legitimacy also depends on the structure and proceedings in constitutional negotiations.

Thus while the direct impact of different amendment rules often are not as important as is usually assumed, they can have indirect impacts by affecting constitutional negotiations, as is explained by Jörg Kemmerzell and Bettina Petersohn. Actors elaborating the drafts of a constitutional reform have to anticipate potential hurdles in ratification, in particular the opinions of those veto-players who threaten to reject a proposal. Anticipating a veto is easier when national parliaments and second chambers ratify the amendments, because representatives of these institutions regularly participate in negotiations and speak for their party or institution. It is much more difficult to predict the responses of regional parliaments, let alone those of citizens in a referendum. If they have veto rights in constitutional legislation, the prospect for success or failure of reforms clearly depends on how regional parliaments and civil society associations are included in constitutional negotiation or consultation. Moreover, public debates on reform proposals seem to be essential in order to convince politicians and citizens. In these debates, proponents of a reform are in a better position if they can explain that results of constitutional negotiations are based on reasons rather than on a compromise or a package deal brokered in partisan political or intergovernmental distributive bargaining.

2.2 Constitutional evolution

Federalism and multilevel governance constitute dynamic structures (Benz, 1985; Hooghe and Marks, 2001). Reforms may change the formal constitution, but this does not rule out that the real constitution evolves accordingly or in a different direction. Both modes of change complement each other and are linked in different ways (Behnke and Benz, 2009; Héritier, 2007). What needs to be emphasized is that successful reforms of constitutions need not continue with an implementation of the amended rules or with multilevel governance in accordance to reform goals. Reforms can prove ineffective and powerful actors who feel they have lost can try to obstruct the application of new constitutional rules. On the other hand, failed ratification of amendment bills need not end in a blockade but can induce "implicit" change (Voigt, 1999: 145-176) guided by agreements on normative frameworks or on perceived problems elaborated during constitutional negotiations.

The effects of constitutional reforms usually take time to develop. Constitutions have constraining and enabling effects on governance and policymaking, but they never determine outcomes. Furthermore, the effective constitution consists not only of written rules but also of a constitutional culture. For both reasons, practice needs to be adjusted to new rules, in particular in federal systems. In a multilevel order, a changed distribution of powers between levels of government does not materialize before it is applied in new legislation. Budgets of central and regional governments have to be adjusted in order to fulfil new tasks and to meet the new financial requirements. New institutions or decision procedures have to be complemented by informal rules during ongoing practice. Routines of intergovernmental relations have to be changed. More often than not, new problems emerge during these processes and new conflicts can arise, which may trigger disputes about the interpretation or application of constitutional amendments.

For example, reforms aiming at a "watertight" separation of powers can prevent necessary coordination of policies between levels required to cope with interdependent tasks. For this reason, the federal government in Germany had to circumvent the constraints of a new rule prohibiting intergovernmental cooperation in education policy and child care when it wanted to support *Länder* and local governments in these policy fields. Also, the distribution of resources often turns out to be insufficient after powers have been decentralised, as a number of cases studies in this volume illustrate. Intergovernmental relations tend to continue according to standard operating procedures set in stone during a longer history.

That intended results of a political decision differ from the real impact has been recognised in policy science for a long time. What has not been appropriately considered is that failed decisions can have impacts, as well. Given the dynamics of federal systems or multilevel government, constitutional evolution after a failed reform deserves particular attention. Two such types of evolution need to be distinguished here. First, evolution can gain new momentum by a negotiated agreement on a reform concept even if it is voted down in ratification. Second, it can also be driven by the need to cope with the consequences of an imminent refusal to accept or implement constitutional change.

Canadian federalism after the failed Charlottetown referendum represents the first type. As Marc Antoine-Adam and Martin Fournier show, the deadlock caused by this outcome could have ended in the secession of Quebec. However, after this alternative had been voted down by a narrow majority of Quebeckers, federal and provincial governments realised the pressure to change the federal constitution by "non-constitutional means". The principles and proposals formulated in the Charlottetown Accord provided guidelines for the decisions and the incrementally changing practices of governance. Adam and Fournier also clearly spell out the limits and problems of such a mode of federal change, in particular the widening discrepancy of the written and effective constitution.

Federal constitutional reform in Austria ended without any agreement on amendments. The Convention failed to draft a proposal and the ratification procedures never started. In response to this deadlock, the federal government initiated work on a consolidation of the complicated constitutional law and tried to implement reforms in public administration and the court system. Thus political pragmatism prevailed while the Convention became a "negative reminiscence" (as Christoph Konrath put it) to justify this approach to federal change.

In view of the risks of federal constitutional reforms, pragmatic ways of shaping constitutional evolution seem of utmost relevance. Moreover, "the strategic options are increased by a combination of these modes of change" (Behnke and Benz, 2009: 235), that is, by a long-term strategy of constitutional policy-making use of the interdependence of reform and evolution. On the one hand, "implicit constitutional change" can be advanced by "adaptation through experimentation" (Bednar, 2011) which later can be transferred into constitutional amendment. On the other hand, constitutional negotiations can pave the way for incremental change by constitutional or non-constitutional legislation, if ratification of an ambitious reform fails. However, such a strategy would require an organisation of negotiations supporting arguing, the creation of legitimacy for reform ideas or proposals by public consultation, and a long-term perspective of federal constitutional policy.

3. Conditions influencing constitutional change

The variety of patterns of constitutional change in federal and federalising systems can be explained by the different conditions influencing reform processes and evolution. As Richard Simeon recently explained, "constitutional processes – the issues that are likely to arise, the discourses in which the debate is conducted, the institutions and processes in which they are discussed and the process of ratification – are all deeply influenced by particular national contexts" (Simeon, 2009: 248). Simeon also pointed out the relevance of different starting conditions. In addition, events in the national or international contexts may impact on federal change. Finally, several case studies collected in this volume show that constitutional reforms have their own history. Later reforms sometimes built on earlier reforms which had continuing effects on agendas, substance and outcomes on ensuing constitutional debates.

In the national context, Simeon pointed out historical legacies, society and democracy and the broader political system (Simeon, 2009: 249). All three conditions can be observed as relevant in the cases dealt with in this volume. Here are some illustrating examples:

The history of a country influences constitutional change. Theories of institutional change call attention to path-dependency which is clearly visible in constitutions concerning the multilevel organisation of government (e.g. Obinger et al., 2005; Pierson, 1995). Decisions taken during times when a multilevel order of government evolved became entrenched in institutions that provided a power base for particular interests. Some years ago, Gerhard Lehmbruch has used this theory to explain the rather stable constitution of German federalism (Lehmbruch, 2002).

The story of French decentralisation told by Patrick Le Lidec illustrates this aspect, too. Here, the way the Senate is elected gives representatives of small communes a veto power against the creation of more efficient decentralised structures. Other reports also show the particular complexity of constitutions resulting from their history. The Austrian constitution may be an extreme case of intransigence of constitutional law, but other federal constitutional reforms, too, are made difficult by the legacies of history and the increase of interdependent rules. History also results in combinations of sometimes incompatible, sometimes reinforcing structures that are difficult to change without a complete overhaul of the political system. The Canadian Senate in a decentralising federalism, the German *Bundesrat* in a parliamentary democracy made up of competitive parties, or asymmetric regional autonomy in Spain, Italy and the UK are only the most obvious examples.

As Keith Banting and Richard Simeon already demonstrated (Banting and Simeon, 1985), societal conditions must be considered when comparing federal constitutional reforms. In multinational countries, the basic challenge is to meet the demands of regionally concentrated "distinct societies." Here, citizens and regional parties mobilise against the power of the centre, press for constitutional reforms and regularly demand fundamental changes to the political system. As a consequence, the level of conflict, the attention of the public and the intensity of discussions is higher than in homogeneous nation states. Here, reforms are framed as politics of identity, and distributive conflicts between governments are eclipsed by value conflicts within society. Thus, even if constitutional issues are similar in mono- and multinational states, the role of parties, associations and citizens in reform processes and in constitutional change differs significantly.

The broader political system sets important conditions for constitutional change. While we should not overestimate the distinction between unitary and federal states since it increasingly becomes blurred in what scholars label hybrid states (Loughlin, 2009), the type of the democratic system matters. Consensus democracies imply different patterns of policy-making and a different culture of managing conflicts than majority democracies (Lijphart, 1999). Both chapters on the Swiss case stress that the long experience of consensual policy-making has contributed to successful negotiations on a reform of the federal system. The contrasting case is Belgium, also a small country with a tradition of a consensus democracy, where, after the process of federalisation by means of constitutional policy had come to a halt in the 1990s, the confrontation between the regional parties prevented a consensus on a reform the state necessary to hold the federal system together.

In majority democracies, party competition can be moderated, but never restrained by political leadership of heads of government. In France, decentralisation resulted from reform projects of presidents who defined the political agenda, but could not manage conflicts on details of the multilevel organisation of the state. In Canada, the UK and Italy, prime ministers played a similar role in a democracy characterised by party competition, majority rule and a strong executive in the parliamentary democracy.

Beyond these enduring conditions, the chances for a reform to succeed very much depend on favourable circumstances. Such situations could be elections bringing about a change in parliamentary majorities, massive protests of groups in society, the success of regionalist parties, or changes in the international environment (such as the significant steps in European integration we saw in the 1990s). These conditions can create, if not a "constitutional moment" (Ackerman, 1991), that is, a transformative situation which gives rise to a new paradigm of governance and federalism, then at least a "window of opportunity" (Kingdon, 1995), a situation favourable for a major change in institutions and policies.

However, experience tells us that dramatic changes or revolutions usually cause more stability than change. German unification caused high expectations for a reform of the state, in particular the federal system, but the constitutional negotiations in a structure not unlike the one evaluated by Anton Hofmann as rather effective ended with minimal constitutional amendments, which Charlie Jeffery rightly characterised a "non-reform of the federal system" (Jeffery, 1995). Likewise, governments struggling with a severe economic crisis can hardly manage to carry out a comprehensive constitutional reform and may reduce changes to rules like a law restricting government indebtedness or modify powers to raise revenues. However, the perception of an incremental economic decline can mobilise political support for a reform.

Finally, previous reform attempts constitute a frame of reference for later reforms. Failed reforms can create a negative consensus on what should be avoided in future. A good example is the intergovernmental process ending with the Meech Lake Accord in Canada; and the Austrian Convention seems to play a similar role in current debates. Failed reforms which ended after intense negotiations can also later be used as a pool of ideas and suggestions. Successful reforms can produce leftovers for later constitutional policy, or they can set a framework to be filled in by later reforms, as can be observed in the history of federalisation in Belgium or, in a different manner, in Spain. But they may also, as reported by Franco Bassanini, provoke efforts by later governments to restore previous constitutional rules.

These and probably other particular conditions in individual countries have to be taken into consideration when comparing constitutional change, when explaining success or failure and when trying to draw lessons from experience. They should make scholars careful when formulating general statements about causes and effects of particular patterns. Those interested in practical lessons should avoid a simple transfer of ideas or supposed "best practices". Nevertheless, as argued above, variety does not prevent us from drawing conclusions or learning lessons. Comparative studies are the most important basis for policy learning. For this reason, we summarise some tentative conclusions for future constitutional policy in federal or federalising states in the final section.

4. What can be learnt for future constitutional policy?

A first conclusion which can be derived for constitutional reform in federal or multilevel system is that attention should be more focused on an appropriate organisation of negotiations rather than on ratification rules. While these rules certainly are important, they have to be regarded as given since any changes of them require constitutional amendments. Moreover, formal amendment rules never guarantee success of a reform. In contrast, negotiations not only can be shaped unilaterally by majorities in parliament or governments, or at least by agreements among federal and regional governments; they can also be decisive for the substance of amendments.

Considering this premise, the following lessons can be drawn from comparing cases and studies included in this volume:

A prerequisite for the success of constitutional reform processes is a political consensus among decision-makers on all orders of government that a reform is necessary. This does not rule out that divergent visions of what a reform should look like can form the basis of a negotiation process. But there needs to be some sort of pressure – be it induced by external events or domestic factors – that motivates policy makers to embark on an often lengthy and hazardous process of constitutional bargaining.

In order to open the way to opportunities for arguing about constitutional norms and in order to avoid distributive bargaining as far as possible, constitutional policy has to be set apart from normal policy-making and politics. To achieve this end, there is no need to organise a convention. What is essential is the definition of a particular arena for constitutional negotiations, the inclusion of actors beyond those dominating intergovernmental and party politics, and to unburden the agenda from issues of normal politics and from party politics as much as possible.

As explained above, the differentiation of constitutional negotiations has advantages, if it allows different participants to participate in a heterarchical structure. A plurality of negotiation arenas can open discussions to new perspectives, it also can stimulate productive competition for new ideas and thus generate innovation. However, such a differentiated structure requires a coordinating committee and effective leadership.

Political leadership is extremely important for the success of constitutional negotiations, as is the timing. If there is no political majority in favour within the various orders of government, a reform is unlikely to happen.

Participation of representatives from civil society can support negotiations in the arguing mode. However, federal constitutions are complicated matters and negotiators need expertise. Therefore, consultation rather than negotiations with citizens appears more appropriate. While early hearings in the reform process can stimulate open discussion in public but can fade out without substantive input, consultation held late in the process on negotiated proposals can give citizens the feeling that decisions are already made. For this reason, consultations at different stages of constitutional policy seem to be most effective and can increase legitimacy of constitutional negotiations.

Experts are important, and experience in the different countries reveals a variety of roles they can play. Participation in a political commission or convention is likely to confuse the roles of experts and of politicians. Big public hearings also do not really allow experts to support constitutional reforms. Informal communication between participants in constitutional negotiations and experts, whatever the particular form may be, is preferable.

Constitutional negotiations should not only be differentiated into particular arenas, they also should be organised in a sequence. The Swiss NFA-process provides a convincing model. Here, a first round of negotiations focused on principles and concepts for a reform. Due to this framing of the constitutional problem, all participants had to argue on basic norms and general interests regardless of their particular distributive interests. In the second round, concepts and principles fixed after the first sequence served as guidelines and frames of reference for negotiations. They constituted a "shadow of reasons" which could not be ignored in bargaining processes. For constitutional negotiations on the territorial or multilevel organisation of a state, such a manner of sequencing has significant advantages.

Effective constitutional negotiations do not guarantee that the reform proposal will pass ratification. Independent on the quality of the proposal, different factors can negatively influence politics in the legislative arena or a referendum process. Therefore, the peril of failure can never be ruled out. For this reasons, constitutional negotiations should aim at producing analyses and arguments rather than simply an amendment proposal. Negotiators should understand their role as participants in a constitutional debate which continues beyond the particular reform process.

Constitutional change never ends with the success or failure of a reform project. No reform process can solve all problems at the same time. Furthermore, constitutions evolve beyond formal amendments. For these reasons, constitutional change in federal or multilevel systems should be regarded as a never-ending task. Because this task should not be left to constitutional courts and should be fulfilled in the political process of democratic politics, continuing constitutional negotiation has to be embedded in the institutional framework of a federal system.

References

Ackerman, Bruce (1991): We the People: Foundations. Cambridge, London: The Belknap Press of Harvard University Press.

Banting, Keith G./Simeon, Richard (1985): The Politics of Constitutional Change. In Banting, K. G./Simeon, R. (eds.): Redesigning the State: The Politics of Constitutional Change. Toronto: University of Toronto Press, 1-29.

Bednar, Jenna (2011): Nudging Federalism toward Productive Experimentation. In: Regional and Federal Studies 21, (4), 499-517.

Behnke, Nathalie/Benz, Arthur (2009): The Politics of Constitutional Change between Reform and Evolution. In: Publius: The Journal of Federalism 39, (2), 213-240.

Benz, Arthur (1985): Föderalismus als dynamisches System: Zentralisierung und Dezentralisierung im föderativen Staat. Opladen: Westdeutscher Verlag.

Benz, Arthur (2007): Verhandlungen. In Benz, A./Lütz, S./Schimank, U./Simonis, G. (eds.): Handbuch Governance. Theoretische Grundlagen und empirische Anwendungsfelder. Wiesbaden: VS Verlag für Sozialwissenschaften, 106-118.

Benz, Arthur (2011): Escaping Joint-Decision Traps: National and Supranational Experiences Compared. In: Falkner, G. (ed.): The EU's Decision Traps: Comparing Policies. Oxford: Oxford University Press, 199-216.

Benz, Arthur/Colino, César (2011): Constitutional Change in Federations – A Framework for Analysis. In: Regional and Federal Studies 21, (4), 377-402.

Elster, Jon (1995): Forces and Mechanisms in the Constitution-Making Process. In: Duke Law Journal 45, (2), 364-396.

Héritier, Adrienne (2007): Explaining Institutional Change in Europe. Oxford: Oxford University Press.

Hooghe, Liesbet/Marks, Gary (2001): Multi-level Governance and European Integration. Lanham, MD: Rowman & Littlefield Publishers.

Jeffery, Charlie (1995): The Non-Reform of the German Federal System after Unification. In: West European Politics 18, (2), 252-272.

Kincaid, John/Cole, Richard L. (2011): Citizen Attitudes Toward Issues of Federalism in Canada, Mexico, and the United States. In: Publius: The Journal of Federalism 41, (1), 53-75.

Kingdon, John W. (1995): Agendas, Alternatives, and Public Policies. New York: Harper Collins College Publ., (2nd ed.).

Lehmbruch, Gerhard (2002): Der unitarische Bundesstaat in Deutschland: Pfadabhängigkeit und Wandel. In: Benz, A./Lehmbruch, G. (eds.): Föderalismus. Analysen in entwicklungsgeschichtlicher und vergleichender Perspektive. Wiesbaden: Westdeutscher Verlag, 53-110.

Lijphart, Arend (1999): Patterns of Democracy: Government Forms and Performance in Thirty-six Countries. New Haven: Yale University Press.

Loughlin, John (2009): The 'Hybrid' State: Reconfiguring Territorial Governance in Western Europe. In: Perspectives on European Politics and Society 10, (1), 49-66.

McWhinney, Edward (1981): Constitution-making: Principles, Process, Practice. Toronto: University of Toronto Press.

Obinger, Herbert/Leibfried, Stephan/Castles, Francis G. (2005): Federalism and Welfare State. New World and European Experiences. Cambridge: Cambridge University Press.

Pierson, Paul (1995): Fragmented Welfare States: Federal Institutions and the Development of Social Policy. In: Governance 8, (4), 449-478.

Scharpf, Fritz W. (1988): The Joint Decision Trap: Lessons from German Federalism and European Integration. In: Public Administration 66, (3), 239-278.

Simeon, Richard (2009): Constitutional Design and Change in Federal Systems: Issues and Questions. In: Publius: The Journal of Federalism 39, (2), 241-261.

Stein, Michael (1997): Improving the Process of Constitutional Reform in Canada: Lessons from the Meech Lake and Charlottetown Constitutional Rounds. In: Canadian Journal of Political Science 30, (2), 307-338.

Voigt, Stefan (1999): Explaining Constitutional Change: A Positive Economics Approach. Cheltenham: Edward Elgar.

Editors and Authors

Editors

Arthur Benz, Professor for Political Science at the Technische Universität Darmstadt/Germany

Felix Knüpling, Head of Programs and Partnerships at the Forum of Federations, Ottawa/Canada.

Authors

Adam, Marc-Antoine, Director, Ministère du Conseil executive, Gouvernement du Québec/Canada.

Bassanini, Franco, Professor, President of ASTRID, former Minister of the Civil Service and Regional Affairs, former Senator and Deputy in the Italian Parliament, Rome/Italy.

Bußjäger, Peter, Univ.-Doz., Director of the Institute for Federalism in Innsbruck/Austria.

Closa, *Carlos,* Professor, Institute for Public Goods and Policies of the Spanish National Research Council, former Deputy Director at the Centre for Political and Constitutional Studies in Madrid/Spain.

Colino, César, Associate Professor at the Universidad Nacional de Educación a Distancia Madrid/Spain.

Fournier, Martin, Intergovernmental Relations Advisor, Secrétariat aux affaires intergouvernementales canadienne, Québec/Canada.

Freiburghaus, Dieter, Professor em. for Public Policy and Europe at the Institute for Public Administration (IDHEAP) in Lausanne/Switzerland.

Hofmann, Anton, Ministerialdirigent, Bayerische Staatskanzlei, Munich/Germany.

Kaltenborn, Markus, Professor for Public Law and Director of the Institute of Development Research and Development Politics of the Ruhr-Universität Bochum/Germany.

Kemmerzell, Jörg, Senior Researcher, Institute of Political Science at the Technische Universität Darmstadt/Germany.

Kincaid, John, Robert B. and Helen S. Meyner Professor of Government and Public Service and Director of the Meyner Center for the Study of State and Local Government at Lafayette College, Easton, Pennsylvania/USA.

Konrath, Christoph, Scientific Service of the Austrian Parliament (Nationalrat), Vienna/Austria.

Le Lidec, Patrick, Senior Research Fellow at the National Center for Scientific Research based at the Center for European Studies of Sciences-Po Paris/France.

Mitchell, James, Professor at the University of Strathclyde in Glasgow/United Kingdom.

Olmeda, José A., Professor, former Deputy Director of the Instituto Universitario General Gutiérrez Mellado in the Universidad Nacional de Educación a Distanzia, Madrid/Spain.

Petersohn, Bettina, Researcher, Institute of Political Science at the Technische Universität Darmstadt/Germany.

Renzsch, Wolfgang, Professor at the Institute for Political Science, University of Magdeburg/Germany.

Schmitt, Gerd, Secretary-General of the Bundesrat, Berlin/ Germany.

Schwall-Düren, Angelica, Minister for Federal Affairs, Europe and Media of North Rhine-Westphalia, Düsseldorf/Germany.

Sinardet, Dave, Associate Professor at the Free University of Brussels, Senior Research Fellow of the Research Foundation – Flanders (FWO) Professor at the Facultés Universitaires Saint-Louis in Brussels/Belgium.

Verrelli, Nadia, Assistant Professor of Political Science at Algoma University, Research Associate at the Institute for Intergovernmental Relations, Queen's University, Kingston/Canada.

Wettstein, Gérard, Senior Consultant, mundi consulting ag, Bern, Switzerland, former head of the Project „Neugestaltung des Finanzausgleichs und der Aufgabenteilung zwischen Bund und Kantonen (NFA)“, Federal Department of Finance, Bern/Switzerland.

Index